THE OFFICE OF LIEUTENANT-GOVERNOR

CANADIAN GOVERNMENT SERIES

R. MacG. Dawson, *Editor*

THE OFFICE OF
LIEUTENANT-GOVERNOR

A STUDY IN CANADIAN GOVERNMENT

AND POLITICS

BY

JOHN T. SAYWELL

Assistant Professor of History
University of Toronto

TORONTO

UNIVERSITY OF TORONTO PRESS

1957

SCHOLARLY REPRINT SERIES

ISBN 0-8020-7041-8

ISBN 978-1-4875-8242-5 (paper)

LC 58-568

FOR MY PARENTS

FOREWORD

SEVERAL years ago John Saywell dropped into my office to discuss a research project he had begun on the provincial Lieutenant-Governor. I remember that I was not very encouraging, for to me the obstacles were extremely formidable. He was entering the almost neglected field of provincial government and was proposing a topic which carried him, not into one province only, but into them all. Extensive research had been made of only two provincial governments; would it not be better if he waited a while longer before attempting the wide synthesis which he proposed? This book is his quite adequate answer. I am delighted that he chose to ignore my advice, for he has done a masterly job. It has been a very substantial piece of careful research, which has involved a thorough scrutiny of the newspapers, the political biographies, the official correspondence, the private papers of the great and not so great, and other sources which looked promising.

Many people with orderly minds tend to see in the office and functions of the Lieutenant-Governor simply a copy in essentials of what they profess to find at Westminster and Ottawa. The truth is that no very exact parallel between the two major governments can be drawn, and when the Lieutenant-Governor is brought into the comparison, the points in which he resembles the sovereign and the Governor-General are found to be almost as misleading as they are enlightening. Great developments in all three positions have occurred in the last seventy-five years, and the Lieutenant-Governorship has perhaps altered the least. It is this office and its history which form the subject of this book. The study by its very nature must be one primarily of precedents; and Dr. Saywell has unearthed an impressive number to augment the few which have hitherto been common knowledge. The result throws a great deal of light on a controversial office which in recent years has tended quite wrongly to be regarded as negligible. The Canadian Government Series has already brought out two volumes dealing with provincial governments, and there are others in prospect: this cross-section of the formal executive is an attempt to ascertain what characteristics and practices may be said to be common to that office in all the provinces. It is a new departure in comparative Canadian government and one which might well be continued in other provincial fields as well.

R. MacGregor Dawson

PREFACE

ALMOST a decade ago Dr. Walter N. Sage suggested a constitutional crisis in British Columbia as a manageable subject for an undergraduate essay. Since then, as I followed the interests aroused by that assignment, my debt to scholars and critics rapidly mounted. To the late Gilbert Tucker, scholar and critic, counsellor and friend, I am indebted beyond repayment or description. Helen Cam, late of Harvard, brought to constitutional history a vitality that made the documents leap into life. David Owen, also of Harvard, combined freedom with the stimulus and encouragement the graduate student so often needs. Frank Underhill read the entire manuscript in an early undigested and almost unintelligible form.

The superbly competent staffs of the public archives across Canada made research a delight. In particular I would like to thank the staffs of the Public Archives of Canada and the provincial archives of Ontario, Hartwell Bowsfield, Manitoba's one man archives, Lewis Thomas and John Archer of the Saskatchewan archives and library, and Willard Ireland and his staff in Victoria. Without their assistance this work would have been impossible.

To those who have had the same experience it is enough to state that Eugene Forsey read the entire manuscript: inaccuracies were corrected, omissions noted, hasty generalizations challenged. In the prostrating heat of a Toronto summer Donald Creighton laboured over the manuscript, doing his best to raise the standard of the prose and the level of intelligibility. Moving through the rich sources of Canadian history with Blair Neatby was invaluable, for he was an incessant finder of facts and a constant stimulus.

Extensive research across Canada was made possible by liberal grants from the Social Science Research Council, Washington, the Canadian Social Science Research Council, the Humanities Research Council, the Committee to administer the Rockefeller Grant at the University of Toronto, and Harvard University.

Above all others is the debt I owe to my wife.

July 1957   JOHN T. SAYWELL

CONTENTS

NOTE ON ABBREVIATIONS

The following abbreviations have been used in the footnotes:

C.S.P.   *Canadian Sessional Papers*
CO   Records of the Colonial Office
G   G Series, Governor-General's Records
GGO   Office of the Governor-General, Ottawa
LLNB Legislative Library, Fredericton, New Brunswick
PABC Provincial Archives of British Columbia, Victoria
PAC   Public Archives of Canada, Ottawa
PAM   Provincial Archives of Manitoba, Winnipeg
PANS Provincial Archives of Nova Scotia, Halifax
PAO   Ontario Department of Public Records and Archives, Toronto
PAS   Provincial Archives of Saskatchewan, Regina and Saskatoon

THE OFFICE OF LIEUTENANT-GOVERNOR

CHAPTER ONE

THE NATURE OF THE OFFICE

THE OFFICE of Lieutenant-Governor combines the monarchical and federal principles in the government of the Canadian provinces. As the chief executive officer in the province the Lieutenant-Governor in his office if not in his person is the representative of the Crown and by statute, custom, and legal decisions exercises many of the monarchical powers essential to the practical and theoretical working of constitutional monarchy, parliamentary government, or cabinet government, whichever term—or combination of terms—one chooses to use. At the same time he is a federal officer charged with some specific and many unspecified tasks on behalf of the central government. The office is unique: the federal system in the United States has never offered any parallel; the Governors of the Australian states are not officials of the Commonwealth government; while the Governors of the Indian states show some striking resemblances, they appear in that remarkable document the Indian Constitution as having real statutory power; and the Canadian Governor-General, who at one time held an analogous position, represents the Queen rather than the British government and is appointed in fact by the government of Canada.

In one sense the office was created by the British North America Act of 1867, the statute that called Canada into being and provided its federal constitution. Federation was the political and economic response of the British North American colonies to the mid-nineteenth century challenges of industrialism and nationalism. Some consciousness of national destiny there undoubtedly was in Canada in the 1860's, but above all only nation-building could forestall complete economic collapse and political annexation. An age that worshipped steam and steel had little use for the venerated trinity of wood, wind, and water on which the colonial economies had been based. Free trade had jeopardized, if not destroyed, the British markets and a greater internal trade seemed essential. Railway and canal building had outrun public financing in all the colonies and only joint efforts on a broader basis offered an alternative to certain failure and inevitable bankruptcy. At the same time only *national* defence appeared to promise a secure safeguard against a belligerent nationalism and an imported Fenianism

3

in the United States, particularly at a moment when everything suggested that an economy-conscious Parliament at Westminster would soon recall the imperial legions. Nor did the tragic disruption to the south blind Canadians to the fact that their neighbours had moved quickly from tidewater to the plains and threatened soon to bridge the gap to the Pacific settlements. Unless decisive action was taken at once the probability was that this constant progression would soon leave the British colonies isolated on an alien continent. The immediate dynamics issued from a more local source, however, from Canada where the political deadlock threatened to become paralytic. Partial remedies were tried and found wanting; and in the end only a radical change effected a cure. "Events stronger than advocacy, events stronger than men," said D'Arcy McGee, "led to the inception of Confederation."

By its very name a federal state is a compromise, the issue of a contest between separatism and absorption, of a struggle between centrifugal and centripetal forces. In Canada the decision fell easily to the federal government for the circumstances of the day demanded a highly centralized state. The provinces were granted only legislative tasks of a minor and local nature (or so it then seemed), and the Dominion was endowed with the residue, with all the powers and duties presumably necessary for the "peace, order, and good government" of a nation that was to stretch from sea to sea. Federal paramountcy was supposedly assured by the assumption of the powers of reservation and disallowance previously exercised by the imperial authority, a provision supported by those who desired a strong central government for its own sake as well as by those whose chief concern was the protection of minority rights.

As the nature of Canadian federalism suggests and as Sir John A. Macdonald so often observed, the quasi-federal structure of the Third Empire served in part as the model from which the Canadian system was constructed. Both in principle and in structure "the constitution which emerged in 1867 is remarkable as much for its continuity with the past as for its introduction of federal forms."[1] And the office of Lieutenant-Governor is an interesting example of old and new since it involved the adaptation of an old institution for purposes in part new. Although it was suggested at Quebec in 1864 that the Lieutenant-Governor should remain an imperial appointee, the general opinion was clearly that he should become a Dominion official—appointed, paid, and liable to dismissal, by the central government. The power

---

[1]F. R. Scott, "Centralization and Decentralization in Canadian Federalism," *Canadian Bar Review*, XXIX (Dec., 1951), 1095.

to reserve provincial bills was to be exercised by him on instructions from the federal authorities. The connection between the new provinces and the imperial government was severed; the Governor-General alone was the channel of imperial communications; and the Lieutenant-Governor was distinctly subordinate to him. In reaching these decisions the Fathers were not unmindful of the fact—indeed how could they be in 1864-5?—that the colonial Governor played an extremely important rôle as the guardian of imperial interests and the proponent of imperial policies. The centralists who gathered at Quebec decided that his power and influence were henceforth to be used in the interests of the federal government.

The nature and extent of the Governor's power and influence are difficult to determine, particularly at a time when political and constitutional forces were rapidly altering his position. Only twenty years before Confederation the principle of responsible government had been conceded by the Colonial Office; the Second Empire had found the solution denied to the First, and almost overnight was transformed into the Third. Obviously the position of the Governor was profoundly altered by the transition from representative to responsible government. Yet in his classic advocacy of responsible government Lord Durham stated that he "would not impair a single prerogative of the Crown" and suggested rather that "the interests of the people of these Colonies require the protection of prerogatives, which have not hitherto been exercised."[2] Robert Baldwin similarly observed that the introduction of new forms "involves no sacrifice of any branch of the Royal Prerogative—It involves no diminution of the paramount Authority. . . ."[3] Lord Elgin, a responsible and reliable witness, concluded that "there is more room for the exercise of influence on the part of the Governor under my system than under any that was before devised. . . ."[4]

The Governor it is true could no longer exercise an unfettered discretion in selecting his advisers. His earlier freedom, however, has been commonly exaggerated. Governors came and went in the North American colonies, but the irresponsible Executive Council, whether affiliated with the Family Compact or the Château Clique, the wealthy landowners of Prince Edward Island or the Halifax and St. John

[2]Sir C. P. Lucas, ed., *Lord Durham's Report on the Affairs of British North America* (Oxford, 1912), II, 278.
[3]Sir A. G. Doughty, ed., "The Durham Papers," *Report of the Public Archives* (Ottawa, 1923), 333, Baldwin to Glenelg, July 13, 1836.
[4]W. P. M. Kennedy, ed., *Statutes, Treaties and Documents of the Canadian Constitution, 1713-1729* (2d ed.; London, 1930), 514, Elgin to Bruce, Sept., 1852.

oligarchy, remained undisturbed. "He may flutter and struggle in the net as some well-meaning Governors have done," lamented Joseph Howe, "but he must at last resign himself to his fate; and like a snared bird be content with the narrow limits assigned him by his keepers." Doubtless "the keepers" had changed; but the Legislative Assembly, before its domination by an intense political party, was assuredly a more amenable body than those ruling aristocracies whose self-interest alone spurred them on and with whom no Governor "was able to contend on anything like equal terms. . . ."[5]

The new motto of the British North American Governors was to be impartiality not impotence. It must be made apparent to all, wrote Grey in the memorable dispatch granting responsible government, "that any transfer which may take place of political power from the hands of one party in the province to those of another is the result not of an act of yours but of the wishes of the people themselves. . . ." While supported by a majority in the legislature the Executive Council was to be given "all fair and proper support" yet nothing was to be done that could "possibly be supposed to imply the slightest personal objection to their opponents." Refusal to act on advice was an extreme step, which should be taken with "the greatest possible discretion," for it might force the government's resignation.[6] Elgin realized that he must often consent to measures that did not "exactly square" with his "preconceived notion," but only "so long as they do not contravene the fundamental principles of morality" and only if he were convinced that they were "in accordance with the general sentiments of the Community." Neither blind obedience to the dictates of the Council nor a bellicose assertion of power by the Governor was desired. The influence of the impartial Governor was to be extensive and penetrating; it was to be "an influence of suasion, sympathy, and moderation, which softens the temper while it elevates the aims of local politics."[7]

Elgin knew that he was charting a new and treacherous course and that

. . . until that middle term which shall reconcile the faithful discharge of his responsibility to the Imperial Govt and the Province with the maintenance of the quasi monarchical relation in which he now stands towards the community over which he presides, be discovered and agreed upon—he must be content to tread along a path which is somewhat narrow and slippery, and to find that incessant watchfulness and some dexterity are requisite to prevent him from falling, on the one side, into the *néant* of

[5]J. A. Chisholm, ed., *The Speeches and Public Letters of Joseph Howe* (Halifax, 1909), I, 230, Howe to Russell, Sept. 18, 1839.
[6]Kennedy, *Statutes*, 494, Grey to Harvey, Nov. 3, 1846.
[7]*Ibid.*, 514, Elgin to Bruce, Sept., 1852.

mock-sovereignty, or on the other, into the dirt and confusion of local factions.[8]

Sir Edmund Head also emphasized the difficulties inherent in the Governor's dual capacity, and Herman Merivale observed that "it is the difficulty of reconciling this double obligation which produces most of the temporary differences & *hitches* in colonial government as at present organized in the N. Am. provinces."[9] Elgin concluded his last official dispatch from Canada with the remark that "the maintenance of the position and due influence of the Governor is one of the most critical problems that have to be solved in the adaptation of Parliamentary Government to the Colonial system," but he remained convinced that it would be "by the frank acceptance of the conditions of the Parliamentary system" rather than by an attempt "to stretch to the utmost the constitutional principles in his favour" that this influence could be "most surely extended and confirmed."[10]

The strict empiricism of the Colonial Office made impossible any definition of principles for the new order. Rather than attempt an elaborate explanation—a difficult task perhaps for the Englishman of 1846—statesmen were content to point out that the desired revolution could be effected by consistently following the principles of the British constitution. If these did not seem applicable the Governor's only guide was to be his "own careful judgement and a careful consideration of the circumstances. . . ."[11] The imperial government realized that the new-found power would often be abused and misused, but "trusted that the errors of a free government would cure themselves. . . ." In any case it was much better to give the colonial ministers considerable freedom than to have them constantly rescued and stopped short by "authoritative intervention of the Crown or of the Governor."[12]

During the fast moving drama of the next twenty years—between responsible government and Confederation—the Governors played important parts, sometimes fully exposed on an open stage and sometimes faintly concealed in the wings. Politically the colonies were immature and amid the confusion of factions and the conflict of personalities, while the boundary between local and imperial interests was indistinct, the Governor's personal influence was frequently

[8]Sir A. G. Doughty, ed., *The Elgin-Grey Papers 1846–1852* (Ottawa, 1937), I, 58, Elgin to Grey, July 13, 1847.
[9]D. G. G. Kerr, *Sir Edmund Head: A Scholarly Governor* (Toronto, 1954), 82.
[10]Theodore Walrond, ed., *Letters and Journals of James, Eighth Earl of Elgin* (London, 1872), 127.
[11]Kennedy, *Statutes*, 496, Grey to Harvey, Nov. 3, 1846.
[12]Alpheus Todd, *Parliamentary Government in the British Colonies* (Boston, 1880), 433, Newcastle to Bowen, March 26, 1862.

decisive and his prerogative power occasionally exercised. As might be expected both power and influence were more clearly marked when imperial interests were involved. Little wonder that the Fathers of Confederation, determined as they were to create a highly centralized state, desired to have the provincial Lieutenant-Governors acting on behalf of the Dominion government. The passage of the British North America Act caused no sharp break with the past and raised few immediate problems; but the old uncertainties remained. That "middle term" which would reconcile the Lieutenant-Governor's position as a federal officer with the maintenance of that "quasi monarchical relation" with his advisers was still indefinite; that "narrow and slippery" path between "mock-sovereignty" and the "dirt and confusion of local factions" was not yet clearly marked out. Would the Lieutenant-Governor be as useful to the Dominion as he had been to the imperial government? Or would there be any need for this type of federal influence in the provinces? Could the Lieutenant-Governor remain impartial in the charged political atmosphere and amid the intense party conflicts in Canada and its provinces? Or would he become the very partial instrument of the party in power in Ottawa and thus in time negate the influence hitherto possessed by the colonial Governor? These were the questions to which only the future could supply the answers.

The change in appointment did create an unprecedented situation that troubled lawyers and statesmen for many years. The Lieutenant-Governor was appointed by the Governor-General and although his Commission therefore, being under the Great Seal of Canada, ran in the Queen's name, he was not appointed directly by her. According to the British North America Act the Queen was expressly declared to be part of the central government, while the provincial governments were to consist of the Lieutenant-Governor and one or two chambers; the Governor-General was to assent to legislation in the Queen's name, while the Lieutenant-Governor was to assent in the name of the Governor-General.[13] On the other hand, however, the Lieutenant-

[13]Regardless of the clear wording of the Act, in no province has the Lieutenant-Governor ever assented in the name of the Governor-General. Ontario and Quebec used the Queen's name from the very beginning. Blake observed that it was improper to do so in assenting to or enacting provincial legislation, and although Sandfield Macdonald amended the Act respecting the statutes to provide for assent in the name of the Governor-General the provincial act has not been followed. (Toronto *Globe*, Feb. 5, 1868; *Statutes of Ontario*, 1867–8, c. 1.) Until 1894 the Lieutenant-Governors of the three Maritime Provinces gave their personal assent, but in that year New Brunswick and Prince Edward Island adopted the Ontario practice. This was undoubtedly a result of the Maritime Bank decision in 1892, and coincided with new appointments in each province. Of the ten provinces Nova

Governor possessed a Great Seal, the instrument of sovereign authority; he made appointments and summoned the legislature in the Queen's name; and in so far as the summoning, proroguing, and dissolving of the legislature were concerned, he was authorized by the Queen, in the Governor-General's Commission, to exercise "all powers lawfully belonging to Us." Unquestionably the architects of the new structure believed that the Governor-General alone would remain the direct representative of the Queen. But those practical statesmen, so used to the daily working of government, overlooked the fact that what was in practice an exercise of legislative or administrative authority was in theory an exercise of prerogative powers by the Crown or its representative.

Did the provincial Lieutenant-Governor, because of the nature of his appointment, lose these prerogative powers? Did what seemed at best a once-removed representation of the Queen mean that he possessed only those prerogatives expressly conferred upon him? Always anxious to maintain or extend their power the federal authorities replied in the affirmative; the provinces not unnaturally in the negative. The Colonial Office sided with the federal government on the ground that the Lieutenant-Governor was not a direct representative of the Queen and therefore did not possess any unspecified prerogative powers. It should have been clear, however, that unless executive and legislative power were co-extensive the whole division of legislative power within the federation would be jeopardized.

Actually the subject had arisen during the drafting of the British North America Act although its implications were not then seen. The Quebec Resolutions provided that the prerogative of pardon "which belongs of right to the Crown, shall be administered by the Lieutenant-Governor of each Province in Council" subject to instructions from the

Scotia alone adheres to what is technically the more correct of the two procedures. Ontario and Quebec also decided in 1867 to enact legislation in the Queen's name. Until 1950 all the Maritime Provinces avoided that practice and enacted legislation in the name of the Lieutenant-Governor (Governor in the case of Nova Scotia) and the assembly. In 1950 the New Brunswick Interpretation Act (14 Geo. VI, c. 140) provided that the enacting authority was henceforth to be "Her Majesty, by and with the advice and consent. . . ." The three other Maritime Provinces have not followed suit; Nova Scotia expressly re-affirmed its practice in 1954. (*Statutes of Nova Scotia*, 1954, 2 Elizabeth II, c. 2.) In both these matters the western provinces have adopted the Ontario practice. Strangely enough the Dominion government has never made any strong objection. The Minister of Justice, Télesphore Fournier, observed in 1875 that the Ontario practices were improper and then let the matter rest. (See W. E. Hodgins, comp., *Correspondence, Reports of the Minister of Justice, and Orders in Council upon the Subject of Dominion and Provincial Legislation 1867–1895* (Ottawa, 1896), 117, 120; and J. McL. Hendry, *Memorandum on the Office of Lieutenant-Governor of a Province: Its Constitutional Character and Functions* (Ottawa, 1955), 8.)

federal government.[14] Viscount Monck, then Governor-General, disapproved of the resolution because it gave "the *highest* exercise of the Royal Prerogative to the charge of officials, not even appointed by Her Majesty" and warned Macdonald that he could not recommend the clause to the British government.[15] The Colonial Secretary reached the same conclusion independently: "With respect to the exercise of the Prerogative of pardon," wrote Edward Cardwell emphatically, "it appears to Her Majesty's Government that this duty belongs to the Representative of the Sovereign—and could not with propriety be devolved upon the Lieutenant-Governors. . . ."[16] When the act was being drafted in London two years later, the Canadians "pressed very strongly all the arguments in favour of conferring the power on the Lieutenant-Governors" and had, thought Macdonald, "the best of the argument."[17] Lord Carnarvon was not convinced however and insisted that the power could be exercised only by "Her Majesty's Representative holding Her Majesty's direct authority for the exercise. . . ."[18]

Soon aware that this opinion could be turned to the advantage of the central government, Macdonald willingly cited it as the infallible ruling when the same question arose shortly after Confederation.[19] The Colonial Office, now supported by the opinion of the Law Officers, refused to alter its decision.[20] Many cases of disputed legislative and administrative authority in Canada centred on the question of the location and degree of representation, for it was apparent almost at once that escheats, the appointment of Queen's Counsel, and a variety of other matters depended in theory upon the exercise of the royal prerogative. If the Lieutenant-Governor did not represent the Crown sufficiently to possess these prerogatives then the powers would be exercisable only by the central government through the Governor-General. In other words the legal position of the Lieutenant-Governor was inextricably related to the respective legislative and administrative jurisdictions of the central and local governments. Consequently the legal position of the Lieutenant-Governor was often argued in the courts, and Canadian judges were obviously bewildered and frustrated

[14]Sir Joseph Pope, ed., *Confederation: Being a Series of Hitherto Unpublished Documents Bearing on the British North America Act* (Toronto, 1895), 48 (hereafter referred to as *Confederation Documents*).
[15]PAC, Macdonald Papers, 74, Monck to Macdonald, n.d. (about Oct. 31, 1864).
[16]*Ibid.*, 50, Cardwell to Monck, Dec. 3, 1864.
[17]Sir Joseph Pope, *Memoirs of the Right Honourable Sir John Alexander Macdonald* (Rev. ed.; Toronto, 1930), 291.
[18]PAC, Orders in Council, 1868, no. 175A, Report of the Minister of Justice, Dec. 31, 1868, approved Dec. 24, 1868.
[19]*Ibid.*   [20]*C.S.P.*, 1869, no. 16, Granville to Young, Feb. 24, 1869.

by the contradiction between what might be termed status and function. Their opinions on the whole, however, were in line with the following decision rendered by the presiding judge of the Quebec Superior Court in 1875:

Je l'ai dit: ces droits appartiennent au souverain. Or, sous notre constitution, la souveraineté est à Ottawa. Il n'y a que là que Sa Majesté soit directement représentée. . . .

Les Lieutenants-Gouverneurs dans chaque Province agissent quelquefois pour et au nom de sa Majesté, dans le cas, où *par voie d'exception,* *l'Acte de l'Amérique Britannique du Nord* leur en confère le pouvoir. Mais le Gouverneur-Général est, seul, le représentant direct de sa Majesté dans et pour toute la Puissance, et à lui seul, comme tel, est conféré l'exercise des prérogatives royales, dans les limites fixées par la constitution. . . .[21]

Even the opinion of the British and Canadian Law Officers that the provincial legislature could confer the power of appointment of Queen's Counsel on the Lieutenant-Governor was denied by the Supreme Court of Canada on a majority ruling:

. . . the British North America Act has not invested the Legislatures of the Provinces with any control over the appointment of Queen's Counsel, and as Her Majesty forms no part of the Provincial Legislature as she does of the Dominion Parliament, no Act of any such Local Legislature can in any manner impair or affect her prerogative right to appoint Queen's Counsel in Canada directly or through her Representative the Governor General, or vest such prerogative right in the Lieutenant Governors of the Provinces. . . .[22]

Meanwhile the Liberal Premier of Ontario had emerged as a determined opponent of the centralist theory of federation. Oliver Mowat, whom Sir Wilfrid Laurier eulogized as "the most correct interpreter of our constitution that Canada has produced,"[23] was a Grit of the school of George Brown. Unlike Edward Blake, who assisted him in his legal struggle, Mowat showed few signs of any national consciousness; to Upper Canada he belonged and for Upper Canada he

[21]*Church v. Blake* (1875), 1 Q.L.R. 180–1. The decision was reversed in the Court of Queen's Bench on the grounds that the question of prerogative did not apply. An *obiter dictum* was added, however, stating that the Lieutenant-Governor only represented the Queen in the particular aspects mentioned in the British North America Act; and "dans ses actes particuliers il est aussi bien le représentant du Souverain que l'est le Gouverneur-Général dans les siennes." (*A.G. Quebec v.* *A.G. Canada* (1876), 2 Q.L.R., 242.) For a listing of the relevant cases and lengthy extracts from them, see Canada, Department of Justice, *Memorandum on the* *Office of Lieutenant-Governor of a Province: Its Constitutional Character and* *Functions* (Ottawa, 1938); and for a rather better treatment of the subject, Hendry, *Memorandum on the Office of Lieutenant-Governor.*
[22]*Lenoir v. Ritchie* (1879), 3 S.C.R. 575–6.
[23]Canada, House of Commons, *Debates,* 1903, 1575.

laboured; his end was a greater provincialism, his means essentially legal. A greater provincialism meant greater political power of course, and it is one of the tragedies of Canadian history that both Mowat and Macdonald (and their successors) irresponsibly used political institutions in the struggle for political power. Mowat saw that the legislative power of the provinces, as well as their status within the federation, was in part (or could be in part) dependent upon the legal power and status of the Lieutenant-Governor; and thus for two decades he sought to have his conception of the latter's position accepted. In a lengthy dispatch to Ottawa over the signature of the Lieutenant-Governor he outlined his argument.

The position of my Government is, that the Lieutenant-Governor is entitled *virtute officii*, and without express statutory enactment, to exercise all prerogatives incident to Executive authority in matters over which the Provincial Legislatures have jurisdiction; as the Governor-General is entitled *virtute officii* and without any statutory enactment, to exercise all prerogatives incident to Executive authority in matters within the jurisdiction of the Federal Parliament; that a Lieutenant-Governor has the administration of the Royal Prerogatives as far as they are capable of being exercised in relation to the Government of the Province, as the Governor-General has the administration of them as far as they are capable of being exercised in relation to the Government assigned to the Dominion.

The B.N.A. Act does not expressly define all the powers either of the Governor-General or of the Lieutenant-Governor. It is presumed that as a matter of law the Crown might delegate to either of these Officers any of the powers of the Crown for which express provision is not made by the B.N.A. Act, or by authorized Dominion or Provincial legislation. But in the absence of any such express delegation or legislation, my Government insist that the Governor-General and Lieutenant-Governors have respectively under their Commissions, all powers incident to their respective offices, all powers necessary and proper for the administration of their respective governments, all powers usually given to or exercised by Colonial Governors.[24]

Macdonald and his colleagues were not the most sympathetic readers however, and Mowat had a much better reception at the Inter-provincial Conference of 1887 where the following resolution was unanimously adopted:

That it was the intention of the British North America Act, and of the Provinces which were thereby confederated, that in respect of all matters as to which the Provincial Legislatures have authority, the Lieutenant-Governor of every Province, as the Representative of the Sovereign in

[24]*Ontario Sessional Papers*, 1888, no. 37, Robinson to the Secretary of State, Jan. 22, 1886. Mowat's position was accepted verbatim in the Ontario Appeal Court. (*A.G. Can.* v. *A.G. Ont.* (1891), O.A.R. 38.

Provincial affairs, should have the same Executive authority as other Governors and Lieutenant-Governors of British Colonies and Provinces; that the Act has practically been so construed and acted upon in all the Provinces ever since Confederation; that it is of essential importance to the Provinces that this right should be maintained, and should be placed beyond doubt or question; that there being no express provision in the Act declaring such right and the right being in consequence occasionally denied and resisted, the Act should be amended by declaring its true construction to be according to the intention and practice as herein mentioned.[25]

When explaining the resolution later in the Ontario Legislative Assembly Mowat insisted that only an imperial statute could alter the erroneous and impossible situation created by the politicians, Law Officers, and judges.[26] There proved to be a much simpler solution.

In one classic stroke the Judicial Committee of the Privy Council repudiated the decision of the Colonial Office, the Law Officers, and the Supreme Court of Canada.[27] Lord Watson presided at this hearing by the Judicial Committee and, as was his custom, repudiated the legal validity of the centralists' argument. The object of the British North America Act, he declared, "was neither to weld the provinces into one, nor to subordinate provincial governments to a central authority, but to create a federal government in which they should all be represented, entrusted with the exclusive administration of affairs in which they had a common interest, each province retaining its independence and autonomy. . . ." The provincial governments derived none of their authority from the government of Canada; they possessed legislative powers in every sense of the word and within their assigned sphere these powers were exclusive and supreme; and, finally, the Queen did form part of the provincial governments. On the latter point no question could have arisen, observed Watson, if the Lieutenant-

[25]*Minutes of the Interprovincial Conference Held at the City of Quebec from the 20th to the 28th October, 1887, inclusively* (Ottawa, 1951), 21. Macdonald heavily marked this resolution "XXX." See: Macdonald Papers, 330, Misc. 1889, no. 1, section 3.

[26]Toronto *Globe*, March 1, 1888.

[27]In an earlier decision given by the Supreme Court the Chief Justice and one colleague dissented. The former stated: "To say then that the Lieutenant Governors, because appointed by the Governor General, do not in any sense represent the Queen . . . is, in my opinion, a fallacy; they represent the Queen as Lieutenant Governors did before confederation, in the performance of all executive or administrative acts now left to be performed by Lieutenant Governors in the provinces in the name of the Queen; . . . While I do not think it can be for a moment contended that the Lieutenant Governors under confederation represent the crown as the Lieutenant Governors before confederation did, I think it must be conceded, that Lieutenant Governors, since confederation, do represent the crown, though doubtless in a modified manner." *Mercer* v. *A.G. Ontario* (1881), 5 S.C.R. 637, 643.

Governor had been appointed directly by the Queen. But the same end was achieved, he maintained, through appointment by the executive government of Canada, which, by section 9 of the British North America Act, was expressly declared "to continue and be vested in the Queen." There was no constitutional anomaly, Watson concluded, "in an executive officer of the Crown receiving his appointment at the hands of a governing body who have no powers and no functions except as representatives of the Crown. The act of the Governor-General in making the appointment is, within the meaning of the statute, the act of the Crown; and a Lieutenant-Governor, when appointed, is as much the representative of Her Majesty, for all purposes of provincial government as the Governor-General himself for all purposes of Dominion Government."[28] Henceforth, as was indeed necessary and perhaps inevitable, legislative and executive authority were to be co-extensive. There was only limited validity, however, in Lord Haldane's boast that "whatever obscurity may at one time have prevailed as to the position of a Lieutenant-Governor has been dispelled by the decision of this Board. . . ."[29]

The certainty and unanimity of the statesmen were in sharp contrast to the indecision of the judges. Macdonald undoubtedly spoke for the architects—at least no one questioned him on the point—when he contrasted the provincial Lieutenant-Governors with the colonial Governors whom they succeeded; the latter were appointed by the Queen and were responsible to her, while the Lieutenant-Governors "will be subordinate to the Representative of the Queen, and be responsible

---

[28]*Liquidators of the Maritime Bank* v. *Receiver-General of New Brunswick,* [1892] A.C. 437 ff.

[29]*Bonanza Creek* v. *Rex,* [1916] I A.C. 580–1. Haldane's certainty led him beyond the position taken by Watson and into what would appear to be a serious misinterpretation of section 92 (1) of the British North America Act: "The references their Lordships have already made to the character of the office of Lieutenant-Governor, and to his position as directly representing the Sovereign in the province, renders natural the exclusion of his office from the power conferred on the Provincial Legislature to amend the constitution of the Province. The analogy of the British Constitution is that on which the entire scheme is founded, and that analogy points to the impropriety, in the absence of clear and unmistakable language, of construing s. 92 as permitting the abrogation of any power which the Crown possesses through a person who directly represents it." (*In re The Initiative and Referendum Act,* [1919] A.C. 943.) Blake was much closer to the intentions and the truth when he observed that the purpose of the section was to make certain that "his office under the constitution, his constitutional position as a federal officer, is not to be affected." (Cited in Hendry, *Memorandum,* 16.) A decision of the Ontario Chancery Court in 1890 treated the matter as beyond dispute: "The intention of sec. 92, sub-sec. I of the *British North America Act,* is to keep intact the headship of the provincial Government, forming as it does, the link of federal power." (*A.G. Can.* v. *A.G. Ont.,* 20 O.R. 222.)

and report to him."[30] Some years later he stated emphatically that the Lieutenant-Governor was "the representative of the Governor-General who is the representative of the Queen."[31] Monck too was convinced that the Lieutenant-Governors "do not represent Her Majesty in any other degree than every Magistrate is the representative of the supreme power."[32] The British government was of the same mind and within eighteen months of Confederation had repealed the right of the provincial officers to be granted salutes and other marks of respect.[33] When informed that under the British North America Act the Lieutenant-Governor was to open and close the legislature in the name of the Queen the imperial authorities relented, but their concession was limited and reluctant: "I have to observe that while from the nature of their appointment they represent on ordinary occasions the Dominion Government," wrote Lord Kimberley, "there are nevertheless occasions (such as the opening or closing of a Session of the Provincial Legislature . . .) on which they should be deemed to be acting directly on behalf of Her Majesty and the first part of the National Anthem should be played in their presence."[34] Lord Dufferin lamented that the dispatch had a result opposite to that intended; many Lieutenant-Governors, he wrote, were "inclined to claim the right of representing the Crown, not through a delegation from the Governor-General, but directly."[35] "Surely this is wrong," scribbled Lord Carnarvon on the margin of Dufferin's dispatch. Sir Robert Herbert, the Permanent Undersecretary, agreed that it was.[36] Soon afterwards the Colonial Secretary undertook to define "in a more explicit manner the powers and position of the Lieutenant-Governors":

. . . However important locally their functions may be, [the Lieutenant-Governors] are a part of the Colonial Administrative staff, and are more immediately responsible to the Governor General in Council. They do not hold Commissions from the Crown, and neither in power nor privilege resemble those Governors or even Lieutenant Governors of Colonies to whom, after a special consideration of their personal fitness, the Queen, under the Great Seal and Her own hand and signet, delegates portions of Her Prerogatives and issues Her own instructions.[37]

[30]Canada, Legislative Assembly, *Parliamentary Debates on the Subject of the Confederation of the British North American Provinces* (Quebec, 1865), 42 (hereafter referred to as Canada, *Confederation Debates*, 1865).
[31]Macdonald Papers, 522, Macdonald to Morris, Feb. 18, 1873.
[32]PAC, G 17, 9, Memorandum for the Privy Council, Sept. 4, 1867.
[33]G 21, I, no. 193A, Buckingham and Chandos to Monck, Oct. 19, 1868; Macdonald Papers, 114, Army Headquarters to Doyle, Jan. 5, 1869.
[34]G 21, I, no. 193A, Kimberley to Dufferin, Nov. 7, 1872.
[35]PAC, B 119, PRO 30/6/27, Dufferin to Carnarvon, Dec. 21, 1874.
[36]*Ibid.*
[37]*C.S.P.*, 1875, no. 11, Carnarvon to Dufferin, Jan. 7, 1875.

Although Dufferin considered this definition "very satisfactory" it was of little value in a positive sense. Nor was Lord Watson's decision in 1892 accepted as the final or right word. E. F. Newcombe, Deputy Minister of Justice from 1893 to 1924, refused to accept it "as settling the question of the position of Lieutenant-Governors except for purely representative purposes";[38] even a Liberal Secretary of State, Sir Richard Scott, declared in 1906 that the implication in the decision that there was only a territorial distinction between the Lieutenant-Governor and the Governor-General had "never been countenanced by the Federal Governments";[39] and after reading all the legal rulings, Earl Grey concluded that "the Governor-General is the only direct Representative of the Crown in Canada."[40] The War Office too disregarded the decision and in 1894 again prohibited the playing of the National Anthem for the Lieutenant-Governor. The Colonial Office successfully interceded and the Governor-General was informed that "the Secretary of State for War will not object to 6 bars . . . being played at the opening and closing of the Legislature on the understanding that the concession does not extend to any other ceremonials."[41]

By this time, however, the British authorities were tiring of the endless complaints arising from disputed precedence and the endless queries regarding the honours to be granted the provincial Lieutenant-Governor, and as a matter of convenience decided to place him in the same category as those appointed by the Queen. But the ghost of Sir John Macdonald thwarted this simple solution. The Lieutenant-Governor, Sir Joseph Pope acidly declared, was not a colonial Governor at all, he was simply an official appointed by the Governor-General in Council to administer the local government of a subdivision of a colony, who possessed only delegated powers to perform minor tasks.[42] The Colonial Secretary finally decided that the Lieutenant-Governors were to be treated as colonial Governors in everything but salutes.[43] The Admiralty was authorized to fire a 15-gun salute when

[38]GGO, file 1290B, Official Memorandum re Bourverie Correspondence, 1932.
[39]Ibid.
[40]GGO, file 2450A, part 4, Grey to Murphy, March 11, 1910.
[41]G 21, no. 193A, Ripon to Aberdeen, Jan. 5, 1895.
[42]GGO, file 1290B, Memorandum for the Governor-General, Jan. 19, 1904. "Speaking with great deference," wrote Pope, "I may say that I do not for a moment believe that it was the intention of the framers of such despatches in the early days of Confederation to regard the Lieutenant-Governor of a Province of Canada as a Lieutenant-Governor of a colony. To treat them as such would, in my opinion, be detrimental to the prestige both of the Dominion of Canada and the office of its Governor-General." Pope's remarks were forwarded to the Colonial Secretary over the signature of the Governor-General. (Ibid., Minto to Lyttelton, May 5, 1904.)
[43]GGO, file 2450A, part 2, Lyttelton to Minto, June 3, 1904.

the provincial legislature was opened and closed "on the ground that the Lieutenant-Governor *may then be* looked upon as a Representative of the Sovereign" but it was pointed out that a "Salute in such cases would be regarded not so much as a personal honour to the Lieutenant Governor as a ceremonial observance emphasizing the importance of the event."[44]

This remained the official ruling for over a quarter of a century. In 1932 the United Kingdom government secured the consent of the government of Canada to end the distinction between the provincial Lieutenant-Governors and Governors directly representing the Crown.[45] The Undersecretary of State informed the Lieutenant-Governors that "in the past salutes were accorded to the Canadian Lieutenant-Governors at ports as a matter of courtesy only. Only Lieutenant-Governors holding Commissions *direct from the King* were entitled to Salutes under the Regulations. Hereafter Lieutenant-Governors of the Canadian Provinces will be entitled to a similar honour as of right."[46] It should be noted that this was a result of administrative convenience; it did not represent any recognition of changed status nor did it grant any new status.

Although slightly elevated by protocol the Lieutenant-Governor has fallen in the table of precedence. In 1867 he was given rank immediately after the Governor-General and the senior officer commanding the British military forces. Twelve years later the Macdonald administration recommended that members of the federal cabinet should rank above the Lieutenant-Governor, but the Colonial Office refused to sanction the change.[47] The same request was made by Macdonald in 1886, by Sir Mackenzie Bowell in 1896, and by Laurier in 1905 and 1911, for "it had long been felt anomalous that Advisers of the Crown, whose prestige and influence are co-extensive with the Dominion, should take rank after Lieutenant-Governors of Provinces—their own nominees—whose term of office is virtually dependent upon their good pleasure."[48] Nothing was done until 1939, however, when during the visit of King George VI the Mackenzie King government decided that at all federal functions the federal cabinet ministers would take precedence over the Lieutenant-Governors. Later a new table of precedence was drawn up. On all occasions the Prime Minister takes

[44]G 21, I, no. 193A, Lyttelton to Grey, Feb. 1, 1905.
[45]See GGO, file 2450A, part 2.
[46]PAM, Lieutenant-Governors' Correspondence, Undersecretary of State to Lieutenant-Governor, April 13, 1932.
[47]PAC, Orders in Council, approved May 26, 1879; G 12, Landsdowne to Granville, April 16, 1886.
[48]G 21, I, no. 193A, Memorandum by Pope, Jan. 31, 1911.

precedence over the Lieutenant-Governor and at Dominion functions the members of the cabinet do as well. This revision, it might be added, has not been universally well received. In 1927 the federal government agreed to let the Lieutenant-Governors retain their title "Honourable" for life, but there has been a consistent refusal since the early 1880's to grant any precedence to retired Lieutenant-Governors.

Until the turn of the century the federal government opposed any increase in the dignity of the office, even though the Lieutenant-Governor was a Dominion officer. The thrifty Mackenzie, who probably spoke for the Grits, argued that "the style in which these Governorships were commenced was, in my opinion, a great mistake. They should have been plain, simple positions like those of the Judges, without any pretence to State show, or expectation of lavish entertainment, political or social." The Liberal Prime Minister felt so strongly on the matter that he wondered whether "some bold step should not be taken by the Provincial Governments to terminate the absurd show of Regal splendour, so entirely out of keeping with actual circumstances."[49] Many years later Sir John Thompson declared that it was "a matter somewhat of federal concern that the dignity of the office should not be impaired, but not, I think of so much concern that we should be willing to bear . . . the expense of keeping up the dignity otherwise than by providing a suitable salary."[50] Pope bluntly asserted that "if we are to have ten representatives of the Crown in Canada, each one mimicing the Vice-Regal ceremonial which properly appertains to the office of Governor-General, the result cannot be but that representative Government in this country will become more or less of a farce." Recognition of the pretensions of the Lieutenant-Governors, he added, "ere long will land us in absurdity."[51]

Pope wrote when the magnification of the dignity of the office was at its height. Macdonald had never recommended Lieutenant-Governors for honours simply because of their office, but Laurier and Sir Robert Borden secured knighthoods for all their appointees in Quebec, Ontario, and Manitoba, and for Barnard in British Columbia and Lake in Saskatchewan. Other proposals pointed in the same direction: G. W. Ross, Premier of Ontario, wanted the Lieutenant-Governors to be imperial officers once again;[52] and it was agreed at the Interprovincial Conference of 1913 that the title Lieutenant-Governor was

[49]PAC, Mackenzie Papers, 5, Mackenzie to Mowat, Jan. 29, 1876.
[50]PAC, Thompson Papers, Thompson to Kirkpatrick, Oct. 22, 1894.
[51]PAC, Correspondence of the Secretary of State, 1908, no. 1882, Pope to Major Panet, Sept. 19, 1908.
[52]La Presse, July 4, 1902.

too lowly and should be changed to Governor.[53] This tendency did not survive the first war, although a change in name is still cherished in some quarters.

This brief discussion of protocol and precedence is not as unimportant as might at first sight appear, for in the public mind the Lieutenant-Governor is a social figure not really a part of the constitution at all. He is the splendid dignitary who opens the legislature amid the roar of cannons and the clash of cymbals, the resplendent functionary who entertains royalty, receives debutantes, and graciously presides at the New Year's Ball or the summer garden party. As has been remarked, popularity and a reputation for a task well done will depend more on the generosity of his table and the excellence of his wine cellar than on the careful surveillance of the machinery of government. But it should not be forgotten that "no amount of champagne, good dinners, smart aides-de-camp will atone for one administrative blunder."[54]

As a social figure the Lieutenant-Governor must, like the Governor-General, "show an interest in every form of public activity, from a charity bazaar to a university celebration; he must be accessible to all men that he may learn of them as they of him; he must visit every corner of his dominion, and become, for the time being, not only one of its citizens, but by adoption a perfervid son of each town and province."[55] His social duties are by no means clear-cut and vary from province to province and incumbent to incumbent, according to means, ability, and provincial tradition. He is generally expected to remain in the capital during the session and hold some function at its opening and closing. During the session most Lieutenant-Governors entertain members of the legislature. Long ago one Premier felt that this "might both properly and constitutionally be of great service in promoting harmonious action in that body,"[56] but now it provides only the opportunity for relaxation. As head of the provincial government and as representative of the Dominion authority the Lieutenant-Governor must act on occasion as host for both governments, and visiting dignitaries are constantly being wined and dined. Officers in the armed forces in particular seem to look upon the Lieutenant-Governor as an individual designed for their pleasure. Most Lieutenant-Governors are listed as patrons of worthwhile organizations and lend their names

[53]*Minutes of the Proceedings in Conference of the Representatives of the Provinces, October, 1913* (Ottawa, 1951), 73.
[54]Ex-Governor, "His Excellency the Governor," *National Review*, XV (1890), 623.
[55]John Buchan, *Lord Minto: A Memoir* (London, 1924), 173.
[56]PABC, Attorney General's Letter-book, McCreight to Trutch, May 10, 1872.

(and often their energy) in support of many laudable endeavours. Frequent trips throughout the province serve to bring him into the sight of, if not in contact with, a great many people, none of whom have travelled far to see him and none of whom go home particularly impressed. Political opinions publicly proclaimed are forbidden him and both in word and deed he must be ever on his guard not to give offence to any racial, religious, or sectional group.

The extent and nature of the Lieutenant-Governor's social functions depend largely upon the provincial government, for the province provides everything but his salary. The province of Quebec spends annually in excess of $175,000 on Bois de Coulonge, the residence of the Lieutenant-Governor, and a large staff of secretaries, chauffeurs, and aides. British Columbia spends over $80,000 on Government House, Victoria, with its extensive gardens, and the staff needed to maintain it. The other provinces trail far behind, some providing only an office, a corresponding secretary, and a meagre expense account.[57] From 1867 on the tendency in most of the provinces was towards increased expenditures; and in spite of recurrent criticism from progressive groups, particularly in Ontario and western Canada, it was not until the depression of the 1930's underlined the incongruity of subsidizing what was termed "social snobbery and class distinction" that the trend was reversed.

The only charge upon the federal government is the salary of the Lieutenant-Governor. This was set at $8,000 for Ontario and Quebec and $7,000 for the other provinces in 1867. But the ink was hardly dry on the first budget when requests were received from every Lieutenant-Governor for an increase in salary, and in 1872 the Macdonald government granted an increase of $2,000 across the board. From that day to this the salary has remained unchanged.[58] As the cost of living rose the salary became sadly insufficient. In 1932 Prime Minister Bennett refused to ask the Lieutenant-Governors to accept the general salary reduction among the employees of the federal government because he knew of no one of them "who at the end of his term of office has not found himself indebted to his own private means for some sum, sometimes small, sometimes large, depending upon his sense of obligation with respect to the hospitality he dispenses."[59] During the second

[57]Only Quebec, British Columbia, Nova Scotia, Newfoundland, and Manitoba maintain a Government House. Government House in British Columbia recently was destroyed by fire.
[58]When Prince Edward Island entered the federation in 1873 the Lieutenant-Governor was given a salary of $7,000. In 1948 this was increased to $8,000. (Canada, House of Commons, *Debates*, 1948, 5419.)   [59]*Ibid.*, 1932, 3001.

world war the Lieutenant-Governors of Nova Scotia and Quebec were given substantial allowances to enable them to entertain the constant flow of high-ranking servicemen.[60] Finally, in 1952 the federal government appropriated $86,000 to be expended on a sliding scale in each province according to need for "travelling and hospitality."[61] The Prime Minister justified the grant on the grounds that the Lieutenant-Governors were often asked to entertain on behalf of the federal government and that it was ridiculous to assume that this could be done with their salary.

Had Macdonald and Laurier been sitting in the house, they would have been startled to hear Prime Minister St. Laurent declare that it was becoming increasingly difficult to find men willing to take office as Lieutenant-Governor in many of the provinces because of the disparity between income and expenditure. Their problem had been to choose between a number of ambitious candidates. The difficulty of which the Prime Minister spoke in 1952 clearly shows that the nature of the office has changed. Macdonald and Laurier regarded the office as one of political and constitutional importance. To them the Lieutenant-Governor was a federal officer, not a social figure; the qualifications were political experience and some knowledge of constitutional practice and constitutional law, not an established social reputation. The appointment was one of the highest and most important made by the central government and the Lieutenant-Governors featured on the front page rather than the social page of the dailies. While this was so there was an abundance of candidates for every vacancy.

Alexander Galt observed in 1864 that the office would provide "the opportunity for rewarding merit" in Canada,[62] and until relatively modern times the office was a receipt for political services rendered. Those services were often of the highest possible order. If no Canadian Prime Minister has become a Lieutenant-Governor—although the office in Ontario was long regarded as the only suitable position to which Macdonald could retire—a list of the pre-1914 Lieutenant-Governors reads like a roll call of the near-great in Canadian political history: Belleau, Letellier, Masson, Angers, and Chapleau; Howe, Archibald, Wilmot, and Tilley; Howland, Campbell, and Mowat; Morris, Cauchon, and Aikins. Howe accepted his virtual dismissal from the federal cabinet and his appointment as Lieutenant-Governor of Nova Scotia with pleasure: "It crowns my long and trying public

---

[60]Ibid., 1944, 1633. The Lieutenant-Governor of British Columbia was a millionaire who had no need of such a grant.
[61]Ibid., 1952, 973-6; Regina Leader-Post, March 20, 1952.
[62]Macdonald Papers, 52, Galt's Sherbrooke Speech, Nov. 23, 1864.

life with the highest position open to me in my native province."[63] John Sandfield Macdonald wished to give up his position as Premier of Ontario for the office of Lieutenant-Governor in 1868, a desire incomprehensible today;[64] and Lemuel J. Tweedie resigned as Premier to become Lieutenant-Governor of New Brunswick in 1907. These men regarded the office as one of real importance, not merely a peculiar fungus with colour but little life.

This is not to deny that the office was a political pasture, but it was a pasture for those whose very active days were over, yet who still had the proven capacity to perform useful services. It was, said Macdonald, "a proper reward for a statesman who from age, ill health or other circumstances has earned retirement from political life. . . ."[65] Of its own will the federal cabinet would not appoint indispensable politicians and many aspirants were rejected because they were too young or active "to be shelved in a position of that kind."[66] Political dispensability thus ranked with political experience and political acceptability among the qualifications for the office. Neither Macdonald nor Laurier ever considered personal wealth or social graces as factors worthy of serious consideration.

Of the sixty-four Lieutenant-Governors permanently appointed between 1867 and 1911 only one, W. M. Clarke (Ontario, 1903–8), had had no political experience; of the seventy-six appointed since 1911 twenty-nine have had no political experience. The following rough figures clearly indicate the changing nature of the appointments.

Background	1867–96	1896–1911	1911–21	1921–55
Prov. leg.	84%	67%	47%	38%
Prov. cabinet	50%	47%	26%	17%
Commons	56%	42%	52%	24%
Senate	36%	25%	10%	—
Fed. cabinet	44%	17%	16%	11%

Between 1867 and 1896 the average Lieutenant-Governor had spent ten years in provincial politics, four years in the House of Commons, and two years in the federal cabinet; between 1921 and 1953 he had spent five years in provincial politics, two years in the House of Commons, and two months in the federal cabinet.[67] Nineteen Lieutenant-

[63]PAC, Howe Papers, 67, Manuscript by Syd Howe.
[64]Macdonald Papers, 341, Lindsay to Macdonald, June 2, 1868; 247, Macpherson to Macdonald, June 2, 1868.
[65]Ibid., 514, Macdonald to White, June 5, 1868.
[66]PAC, Laurier Papers, 579, Laurier to Oliver, June 28, 1909.
[67]The figures for the 1921–53 period would be much lower if Saskatchewan were excluded. Since the Liberal defeat in 1944 the federal government has appointed four former Liberal M.L.A.'s and cabinet ministers who averaged over twenty years in the assembly and almost fifteen in the cabinet.

Governors came from the Senate in the Macdonald-Laurier era, eighteen came directly from the House of Commons, and ten came from the bench. Since 1911 one has left the Senate, five the House of Commons, and four the Bench. Professor Ward has calculated that the parliaments elected between 1867 and 1891 contained an average of fifteen Lieutenant-Governors, while those elected since have contained less than four. He had indicated also that 4.4 per cent of the members of the House of Commons elected between 1867 and 1896 became Lieutenant-Governors, 3.5 per cent of those elected between 1896 and 1911, and only 1 per cent of those elected between 1911 and 1935.[68]

It is significant perhaps that the average age of the Lieutenant-Governors has increased from fifty-six years before 1911 to sixty-five years since 1911. This suggests that the federal government has ceased to be concerned whether an active and able agent guards its interests. It shows too that as the office has declined in prestige men have been unwilling to accept it until their public or private career has definitely come to an end. Many of the Lieutenant-Governors of whom mention shall be made were relatively young men: Trutch (45), Cornwall (45), Morris (46), Schultz (48), Bulyea (46), Robitaille (45), Angers (49), and Chapleau (52).

To explain every appointment would necessitate not only a short political biography of every Lieutenant-Governor but virtually a political history of modern Canada. Like all patronage the office was used in the political interests of the appointing authority, in this case the party in power in Ottawa. Sometimes the post was given to compensate certain elements for non-representation in the federal cabinet, sometimes to swing rebellious or dissatisfied racial, religious, or sectional factions into line. On occasion an appointment was made in the interests of a friendly provincial government. A number of judges have been appointed when, either because of old age or poor health, they were unable to stand the strain of sustained periods of mental or physical activity. The office was most valuable, however, as a pasturage for unwanted federal cabinet ministers. Provision had to be made for compulsorily retired ministers who could hardly remain in Parliament. Only the office of Lieutenant-Governor and the Bench carried sufficient prestige to enable a minister to accept the change without humiliation. To strengthen his cabinet Macdonald appointed Howland, Howe, Wilmot, Tilley, Aikins, McLelan, and Campbell as Lieutenant-Governors. *Grip* rightly portrayed Cauchon as the unwanted child left on Manitoba's doorstep by his frustrated mother, the Mackenzie adminis-

[68]Norman Ward, *The Canadian House of Commons: Representation* (Toronto, 1950), 144–8.

tration. Political exigencies compelled Thompson to send Chapleau to Quebec, and Abbott and Bowell to send Dewdney and Patterson to a western exile. Laurier preferred younger men to Mowat and Joly and after the gestures of 1896 made vacancies in his cabinet by sending them to Ontario and British Columbia as Lieutenant-Governors.

The nomination of the Lieutenant-Governor has always been the special prerogative of the Prime Minister. In 1896 Sir Charles Tupper sanctified by Order in Council what had hitherto been an accepted convention, and this Order has been confirmed by most succeeding administrations.[69] In practice however the appointment has been treated like all others of a similar nature and those most vitally concerned have been consulted. Although Macdonald took an active interest in all the appointments and seems to have been personally responsible for those in Ontario and the west, he appears to have accepted the advice of his colleagues as far as the other provinces were concerned. Thompson apparently believed that the provincial representatives in the cabinet had the right to be consulted, responsible as they were for the political management of the province.[70] Laurier virtually abdicated his "special prerogative" and delegated his right to select.[71] Evidence is not available for more recent times, but it is likely that Laurier's practice has been continued unless there are disagreements within the cabinet or the appointment is one that vitally affects the party as a whole.

Macdonald, his colleagues, and his successors, unquestionably considered the necessities of the provincial wing of the party, whether in power or in opposition, and at times made appointments in its interest. Yet there was never an open admission of the necessity of that consultation. Playing from weakness during the controversy over the Quebec appointment in 1876, the baffled Mackenzie brought upon himself a demand from the provincial Liberal party, then in opposition, of its right to be consulted.[72] As might be expected Laurier made an irregular practice of consultation or consideration into an accepted political convention and openly sought the advice and recommendation of the provincial party. "If there is a man who above every other has the right to advise in such matters," he declared, it was the provincial

[69]Canada, House of Commons, *Debates*, 1946, 433. See A. D. P. Heeney, "Cabinet Government in Canada: Some Recent Developments in the Machinery of the General Executive," *Canadian Journal of Economics and Political Science*, XII (Aug., 1946), 298–9.

[70]See Thompson Papers, Thompson to Scott, Feb. 11, 1893.

[71]See Laurier Papers, 92, Laurier to Warburton, Nov. 28, 1898; 402, Laurier to Templeman, March 5, 1906.

[72]Mackenzie Papers, 6, Mackenzie to Thibideau, Dec. 8, 1876.

Liberal Premier; "whilst I grant you this, I do not mean to imply that I abdicate my judgement, and if he were to offer some advice which would not be suitable, I would do as I do under all circumsances—take my own course."[73] The Liberal Premier referred to, Walter Scott of Saskatchewan, agreed with Laurier: "The appointment is one of the things wholly in the gift of the Prime Minister but, as we are a friendly Government, we may naturally expect to be taken into confidence."[74] Consultation with "friendly" governments would seem to have become a normal procedure although the federal government has repeatedly refused to admit it in theory. This consultation, however, is political, not constitutional; it is with the Premier as provincial leader of the party in power at Ottawa, and has not as a consequence been extended to provincial governments that, by the same definition, are considered unfriendly. This subject has been discussed twice in recent years.

In 1944 the recently elected C.C.F. government in Saskatchewan asked to be consulted on the next appointment. The "courtesy" of prior consultation, so Premier Douglas believed, had been shown to the preceding Liberal administrations in the province, and rightly so "in view of the fact that such a position intimately affects the life of the province." Prime Minister King emphatically repudiated the implication that a convention of consultation had been established.

Under established constitutional practice, the Government of Canada must accept full responsibility in the matter of appointment of Lieutenant-Governors. This being so, you will, I have no doubt, readily appreciate that the Dominion Government cannot share its authority. To depart from precedent in a single instance would involve corresponding variations of the long established practice in other similar cases. Because of the possible far-reaching consequences, a firmly established constitutional procedure cannot be changed without serious and important reasons.[75]

King did not deny that Premier Douglas' Liberal predecessors had been consulted; he denied only that consultation with the provincial government was either proper or necessary.

A year later another distinctly unfriendly government raised the same issue. Observing that the term of the Lieutenant-Governor of Quebec was about to expire, Premier Duplessis publicly stated that it was "customary for the federal government to consult with the provincial government" on the matter of appointments. King immediately

---

[73]Laurier Papers, 641, Laurier to Davis, Aug. 27, 1910.
[74]PAS, Scott Papers, Scott to Putnam, Oct. 27, 1910.
[75]Correspondence between Premier Douglas and Prime Minister King, 1944, through the courtesy of Premier Douglas.

replied that the British North America Act assigned the exclusive right of appointment to the federal authority. The Premier of Quebec attempted to counter this indisputable statement of fact with a constitutional argument of his own concoction.

The fact that there is a lieutenant-governor for each province is an additional proof of the complete autonomy of the provinces.

We consider that the nomination of a lieutenant-governor is comparable to that of an ambassador. As you know, an ambassador is not accredited to a government without his name having previously been submitted to the authority to which he is delegated. In our opinion, this diplomatic courtesy which is inspired by an excellent courtesy, is the one which should be applied relative to the nomination of a lieutenant-governor, and specially so since it is the province which assumes the very large proportion of the expenses occasioned by the exercise of these important functions.

It is a question here of principle and I would like to believe that the federal government will continue this tradition of courtesy and sane diplomacy which is in conformity with the spirit and letter of the federal pact.

To which King replied:

If there is any consultation with the provincial government it is simply consulted as a matter of courtesy and not of right. It was merely as a courtesy that I wrote to you. . . . To suggest that there is the slightest analogy between the office of lieutenant-governor and a diplomatic post is to suggest that the provinces are not a part of the nation, and that the government of the country should not exercise its jurisdiction in all parts of the country.

The federal government has, in fact, the same responsibility to maintain and to exercise federal jurisdiction as have the provincial governments to exercise jurisdiction within their appropriate spheres, and I am sure you are as anxious as I am myself that each government should recognize and respect the appropriate responsibilities of the other.

Premier Duplessis denied the right of the federal government "to arbitrarily make the appointment of a lieutenant-governor on its own authority, and without prior consultation with the government of the province interested," and concluded his correspondence with the hope that "the federal government will be respectful of the rights of the province, and abstain from committing an act contrary to the spirit and letter of the federal pact, as well as to the democratic prerogatives of a provincial government."[76]

Premier Douglas was aware of the difference between the law of the

[76]The correspondence is printed in the *Montreal Gazette*, Jan. 20, Feb. 3, 1945. See also E. A. Forsey, "Lieutenant-Governors are not Ambassadors," *Saturday Night*, March 20, 1948.

constitution and the political conventions surrounding it; Premier
Duplessis obviously confused the two. But in this he has not been alone.
A staff writer for the Toronto *Globe and Mail* in 1946 was horrified
to hear that Premier Drew, "like the rest of the people of Ontario,"
learned of the appointment of a new Lieutenant-Governor only when
he read of it in the press. "To those versed in constitutional practice,"
observed the writer, "the statement of the Premier indicated the Dominion Government had ignored the Ontario Government and the
traditional practice of consulting the Provincial Government before
appointing a Lieutenant-Governor."[77] Since Mr. Drew's administration was Conservative and the federal government Liberal, it might
better have been written: "to those versed in political and constitutional practices the statement of the Premier indicated that the
Dominion Government had ignored the Ontario Government, thus
maintaining the traditional practice of consulting the provincial governments only when they are controlled by the political party in power
at Ottawa."

What all this means in effect is that the appointment of the Lieutenant-Governor is a jealously guarded political preserve. Politicians
have appointed politicians for political reasons and often for political
ends. The maxim that the strength of the Crown rests upon the conviction that its neutrality is always beyond suspicion is of limited
applicability in the Canadian provinces, for it is paradoxical to speak
of impartial politicians. Logic in this instance is supported by historical
evidence, and it is fair to say that as long as the Lieutenant-Governor
was regarded as an important officer, not just something to be filed
under patronage and ignored, his neutrality was never beyond suspicion. The Governor-General too has been a political appointee, but
no matter how active his political life had been in England his prejudices were hardly applicable in Canada in spite of the deceptive
identity of the party labels. The Lieutenant-Governor, on the other
hand, has belonged to one of the parties actively engaged in the struggle
for power and he has usually practised his art and won his reward in
the very province to which he is appointed. In the province he has
political friends and political enemies, and even if he feigns amnesia
and tries to forget his past one or the other will jar his memory.[78]

Of all those who spoke on the Quebec Resolutions in the Canadian

[77]Dec. 14, 1946.
[78]This is not to suggest that their political loyalties invariably affected the
Lieutenant-Governors' actions, but rather that it was generally supposed that they
would.

Assembly Christopher Dunkin alone seriously drew attention to the almost inevitable political character of the office. The colonial Governors, he observed, were not attached to any political party in the colony and could thus profess to be neutral and would be so accepted unless their actions belied their professions.

> . . . But suppose any of our politicians . . . to be assuming this *rôle* of lieutenant-governor in any of our provinces. He has this disadvantage to begin with; he has to that moment been passing through that ordeal of abuse under which every prominent public man in this country must have suffered before attaining any distinction whatever. . . . He has been known as a politician and will be held to be favorable or unfavorable to this or that party in the province he governs. . . . how then will he be able to hold that position of equilibrium between political parties, which, if he is not to fail utterly in his *rôle* of governor, he must maintain?[79]

Admit with Galt and Macdonald that politicians had to be appointed; agree with Lord Dufferin that an impartial Canadian did not exist since "party spirit runs so high";[80] still the problem would not appear to have been completely insoluble.

The very real and very serious evils of partiality could have been in great part alleviated by the appointment of non-residents to the office in the various provinces. A Nova Scotia Conservative, for example, while being recognized as a politician, would have been less likely to offend Ontario Liberals than an Ontario Conservative with whom they had battled for years. There would be no personal rivalry, no grudges to be settled, and no coterie of friends around Government House to give it the air of a party convention. George Brown of the *Globe* suggested such a course, but his views were given scant attention in Ottawa.[81] The first appointments established the precedent and since 1867 only residents have been appointed as Lieutenant-Governors in the eastern provinces. To the western provinces both Macdonald and Laurier sent eastern Canadians, but the appointment of Joly to British Columbia in 1900 and Patterson to Manitoba in 1895 caused such wide-spread criticism in the two provinces that the practice has not been repeated.

Secondly, the federal government could have assumed an obligation to appoint men of moderate views and actions. Although Macdonald and Mackenzie, Laurier and Borden, agreed that men with what

[79]Canada, *Confederation Debates*, 1865, 503–4.
[80]C. W. de Kiewiet and F. H. Underhill, eds., *Dufferin-Carnarvon Correspondence 1874–1878* (Toronto, 1955), 7, Dufferin to Carnarvon, March 13, 1874.
[81]Toronto *Globe*, June 11, 1868.

Macdonald termed *"animus revertendi"* should not be appointed, they failed to live up to their laudable professions. The federal ministers occasionally refused to make an appointment on the grounds of excessive partiality, but this was always an excuse, never the real reason. Laurier, for example, informed F. C. Wade, an aspirant for the office in British Columbia, that it would not be proper "to call to the Lieutenant-Governorship one who had just been in such violent conflict with the Prime Minister of the Province"; yet he appointed T. W. Paterson who had been in even more violent conflict with the Premier of British Columbia only a few months before his appointment.[82] Borden described the rumoured appointment of Wade as "absurd, monstrous, and ridiculous,"[83] yet when in power he appointed Sir James Aikins, leader of the Conservative opposition in Manitoba, as Lieutenant-Governor of that province less than a year after Aikins had stormed the province denouncing the Liberal Premier and the previous Lieutenant-Governor. And a year earlier he had sanctioned the appointment of the most determined opponent of the Liberal government in Saskatchewan as Lieutenant-Governor of that province. King was no better, and in 1925 appointed a defeated Liberal minister in Nova Scotia over the government that had caused his defeat a few months before.

As in all societies where place is often a matter of bread and butter, the political game in Canada has been fast and vicious and played with a minimum of rules. Thus no one expected the Lieutenant-Governor to be impartial. The Liberals fully expected William Howland to be "the tool to a Tory administration as Lieutenant-Governor of Ontario,"[84] and the "impression was very general," that he might call on the Conservatives rather than Mowat when the Blake administration resigned in October 1872.[85] Eight years later, when it was rumoured that Macdonald was to become the next Lieutenant-Governor of Ontario, some Liberals believed that nothing "would appeal to Sir John A. more than the probability of his being able to break up the Reform majority in Ontario: if he became Lieutenant-Governor our Premier would require all his majority to pull him through the next three years.[86] The appointment of that arch-intriguer Israel Tarte was advocated on the grounds that "from the pinnacle of

[82]Laurier Papers, 603, Laurier to Wade, Dec. 13, 1909.
[83]Canada, House of Commons, *Debates*, 1909, 531.
[84]Toronto *Globe*, June 11, 1868.
[85]PAO, Blake Papers, Mackenzie to Blake, Oct. 14, 1872.
[86]PAO, Clarke Papers, Watson to Clarke, March 10, 1880.

that high position he would be as useful to the faithful in political matters as the Pope is in religious."[87] It is not surprising then that in the years following Confederation any action by the provincial Lieutenant-Governors, regardless of the nature or justice of the motives, was denounced as political intrigue. The consequences of this state of opinion on the Lieutenant-Governor's position as a representative of the Crown and as a federal officer have been from the very beginning of the utmost importance.

[87]Laurier Papers, 59, Ward to Laurier, Dec. 24, 1897.

CHAPTER TWO

THE LIEUTENANT-GOVERNOR AND HIS MINISTERS

THE RETENTION of cabinet government in each of the British North American colonies after 1867 meant that the provincial Lieutenant-Governor remained "the image, in little, of a constitutional king," although on this point the British North America Act itself was silent. As Mowat later observed, "to a large extent his duties and authorities are left to be implied and inferred from his character as Lieutenant-Governor or 'Chief Executive Officer,' and from the known constitutional rights and duties, therefore, belonging to the office of Lieutenant-Governor, so far as relates to the Government and Legislature of the Province."[1] There was no need to spell out the constitutional relationship between the Lieutenant-Governor and his advisers, for after an experience of twenty years it could be assumed that the Canadians were thoroughly familiar with it. In state papers, in the House of Commons, and before the courts, it was repeatedly affirmed that the principles and conventions governing the relations between the monarch or Governor-General and his advisers were applicable to the Canadian provinces.

Constitutional monarchy, as it functions in the United Kingdom and Canada, is based essentially on the dictum that the Sovereign reigns but does not govern and that all official action is the result of formal advice tendered by ministers responsible to the legislature. The monarch's routine powers may still be summed up in Bagehot's now classic statement; "the right to be consulted, the right to encourage, the right to warn." The right to be consulted on all matters involves the right to be fully informed at all times, and, as Sir Ivor Jennings observes, the monarch has the opportunity to be the best informed individual in the United Kingdom.[2] The right to encourage and the right to warn may often take the form of very strong persuasion that

---

[1]*C.S.P.*, 1877, no. 89, 95, Report of the Attorney General of Ontario, Feb. 11, 1875. See also *C.S.P.*, 1877, no. 13, 3–9, Blake to Carnarvon, *circa* July 1, 1875. Chief Justice Howell of the Manitoba Court of Appeal stated: "The Lieutenant-Governor can dismiss his ministers and call on others, he can refuse to take the advice of his ministers and can order investigations as to their actions, and has many wide executive powers, none of which are to be found in *The B.N.A. Act*. In fact we might say that the Act is the merest skeleton vesting British law making power in Canada. . . ." (*Re Initiative and Referendum Act*, 35 W.L.R. 1016.)

[2]Sir Ivor Jennings, *Cabinet Government* (Cambridge, 1951), 318 ff.

unquestionably is taken into account by the cabinet when considering policy. It is always open to the monarch to refuse to act on the advice tendered; the ministers must in that event accept the decision, thus theoretically making it their own, or they must resign, thus leaving to the monarch the burden of finding other ministers to assume *ex post facto* responsibility for the refusal. Such actions are rare, however, and the power of the chief executive officers under responsible government is basically negative. As the sagacious Sir Edmund Head noted, "a governor's power is mainly that *nothing can be done without him*. He has only to doubt & hesitate & require further demonstration. His power of positive action *independently* must be small but so much the better for his tranquillity of mind."[3]

Although in theory the position of the Lieutenant-Governor, as far as relations with the cabinet are concerned, is roughly analogous to that of the Queen, the similarities do not often hold up in practice— eloquent testimony to the impossibility of transplanting institutions with the expectation that environment will not radically alter their growth. Today the Lieutenant-Governors of the Canadian provinces are divorced from the actual work of government. In some provinces the first the Lieutenant-Governor will hear of government policy, other than press reports and street-corner gossip, will be in the Speech from the Throne, usually given to him only a day before the legislature opens in order that he may perfect his delivery. In others the Premier might pay a short social visit every fortnight or so and in general terms brief the Lieutenant-Governor on major developments. There is no expectation of anything but complete acquiescence.

This has not always been the case. The exclusion of the Lieutenant-Governor has unquestionably been a gradual process, varying in speed from province to province and accelerated or retarded by the character of the individuals appointed and the men in power. Some Lieutenant-Governors willingly renounced their rights and abdicated their position, while others sought to maintain or restore the influence of the office. Sir John Gibson, for example, Lieutenant-Governor of Ontario from 1908 to 1911, asked Laurier if he ever went to "Government House to consult the Governor-General," if he discussed "important measures with him before introducing them," and if he kept him "informed as to the state of public business?" Said Gibson:

My recollection is that Sir Oliver and the Premiers who followed him were pretty particular about such matters as indeed they always are in the old country; but whatever may have been the practice in my immediate pre-

[3]D. G. G. Kerr, *Sir Edmund Head: A Scholarly Governor* (Toronto, 1954), 37.

decessors time after the Ross Government went out, nothing is ever discussed with *me*. I have now and again sent for the Premier to talk over some matters that from the public press I know are coming on but Whitney has never yet come down to Government House to see me on public business.[4]

Gibson was a Liberal and had been a prominent member of the Ross government whose defeat by Sir James Whitney had ended the long Liberal reign in Ontario. Moreover, Gibson was a federal officer and the relations betwen the Whitney and Laurier administrations were not of the best. Still, Gibson's complaint would probably have been seconded by most of his colleagues in office across Canada. On the same day as he wrote Laurier he sent the following letter to the Premier:

As the end of the Session draws nigh I begin to fear that you may be forced or at all events induced to introduce legislation that ought to be very seriously and maturely considered—You are a believer in British Constitutional methods and practice, and yet I wonder if there ever was a Premier in modern days in the Mother Country who so seldom consulted the Representative of the Crown.

I know that your predecessors kept the Lieutenant-Governor constantly informed of what was going on in the House and no step was ever taken *in matters outside of purely routine business* without being first submitted to and approved by him.

I am writing this Privately but under a very strong feeling of anxiety that so long as the Crown is represented by me there should not be a lapse from British Constitutional Customs and practice which though in many cases apparently formal only is really important.[5]

The Lieutenant-Governor's pressure was not in all probability very effective.

The difficulty is that there is no sure method by which the Lieutenant-Governor can uphold or enforce his rights unless he wishes to exercise (or threaten to exercise) the extreme sanction of dismissal. Obviously much depends upon his own ability and character and the personality of his leading ministers; but unless there is a general acceptance of the view that the Lieutenant-Governor holds a high and important and real position he may be regarded as nothing more than a nuisance. Of Sir Charles Fitzpatrick, one of the more experienced and able Lieutenant-Governors appointed since 1914, M. Robert Rumilly writes:

Son goût du faste n'implique aucune intention de se limiter à des fonctions d'apparat. Lieutenant-gouverneur, sir Charles pretend non seulement

4PAC, Laurier Papers, 669, Gibson to Laurier, March 4, 1911.
5PAO, Whitney Papers, Gibson to Whitney, March 4, 1911.

régner, mais, dans une certaine mesure, gouverner. Autoritaire sous des dehors aimables, il exige les dossiers, demande des explication à *ses* ministres, retard la signature des arrêtés en conseil. Le premier ministre tout puissant, et foncièrement timide, recule devant l'éclat qui ne pourrait être que foudroyant. Il rage en silence. Gouin oppose une résistance passive, accumule des griefs dans le fond de son coeur fermé, cache un dossier contre Fitzpatrick dans une armoire secrète, et ne se laisse aller qu'une fois à rager tout haut devant un de ses secrétaires: "Il me fera mourir!"[6]

Sir James Aikins, another forceful, capable, and experienced Lieutenant-Governor, "developed, as his term of office increased, rather a high idea of his powers and it is no secret that his ministers had a good deal of trouble with him during his last two or three years of office."[7] Aikins' "high idea" was actually little more than "the right to be consulted, the right to encourage, the right to warn," yet by the 1920's to accept these conventions was, according to J. W. Dafoe, to *humour* the Lieutenant-Governor.[8] Bagehot's trilogy of rights appears to be no longer accepted in Canada; the Lieutenant-Governor has now a right to little more than what Professor Beck terms "a superficial acquaintance" with the work of government.[9]

It would be impossible to follow with any precision the transformation of the office since 1867. All that can be done profitably is to enumerate some of the factors that might have caused it. To suggest that the passage of ninety years is not in itself of the utmost significance would be ridiculous, but it must be remembered that an officer who in 1867 probably had more influence and power than Queen Victoria has today much less than her great-great granddaughter.

The change from colony to province had significant if not immediately apparent consequences. While the Colonial Office was not by nature meddlesome it had never quite adjusted itself to the new era of responsible government, and thus was prepared to uphold and at times encourage independent action by the Governor. It was always emphatic that his position be respected and maintained. Nor were the Governors—most of them slightly contemptuous of colonial politics and politicians—likely to accept political exclusion easily. After 1867, however, it was the colonials themselves—some of whom had partici-

[6]Robert Rumilly, *Histoire de la Province de Québec* (Montreal, 1940–1955), 24, 48–9, 95. The appointment of Fitzpatrick was not well received in Quebec because he was English-speaking. But he did become something of a nuisance. For example he apparently "dug up some old statute about provision for a private chaplain and installed one." (PAC, Dafoe Papers, M 74, Stevenson to Dafoe, Nov. 3, 1922.)
[7]Dafoe Papers, M 75, Dafoe to Colquhoun, Aug. 6, 1929.
[8]*Ibid.*
[9]J. M. Beck, *The Government of Nova Scotia* (Toronto, 1957), 179.

pated in the struggle for responsible government—who established the standards of political action and the pattern of constitutional development, who were the Lieutenant-Governors or who instructed the Lieutenant-Governors. More specifically it was the Canadians who gave direction in constitutional matters and Canadian practices that were frequently followed, for the government of United Canada became in effect the government of the new Dominion. And although the forms of responsible government had been granted to the colonies about the same time, political forces in Canada had led to a more rapid constitutional development.

At Confederation, for example, the Lieutenant-Governors of the Maritime Provinces regularly attended meetings of the Executive Council, a practice that had virtually ceased for all practical purposes in Canada in the 1850's. Long before Confederation, of course, the bulk of work was done in cabinet, or more technically in Committee of the Executive Council. But even the occasional assembling of the full Council, with the Lieutenant-Governor in the chair, could not but enhance his authority and influence. It is impossible to discover what weight the Lieutenant-Governors had in Council or how long they continued to attend and preside, for the records provide merely a summary of conclusions and the theory of attendance was maintained long after attendance had in fact ceased. From outside evidence it is quite clear that Sir Hastings Doyle frequently discussed matters of policy with his ministers in Council and that the meetings were often the scene of stormy controversies, and it is likely that the Lieutenant-Governors of New Brunswick and Prince Edward Island took an equally active part in Council meetings.

Judging from the records of Council in Nova Scotia it would appear that the Lieutenant-Governor attended until February 1876, but the scholar who knows most about it has stated emphatically that no one attended after January 17, 1873.[10] In Prince Edward Island the Lieutenant-Governor attended, periodically at least, until 1887, and when he was not present the complete minutes of the meeting were sent to him for his approval.[11] The Council records in New Brunswick suggest that the Lieutenant-Governor either attended Council personally—an unlikely possibility—or was deemed to be in attendance and later approved the complete record of the meeting until 1896-7,

[10]Provincial Secretary's Office, Halifax, *State Books*; Beck, *Government of Nova Scotia*, 291. The Lieutenant-Governor of Nova Scotia still receives and approves the complete record of the meeting. (*Ibid.*, 332.)
[11]Frank MacKinnon, *The Government of Prince Edward Island* (Toronto, 1951), 183. The Lieutenant-Governor still approves the record.

at which time single Orders in Council were for the first time drawn up and submitted for his approval.[12] In Manitoba and British Columbia, as shall be seen in the next chapter, the first Lieutenant-Governors shared in the work of both Council and cabinet for some years after the two provinces entered the federation. There is no reason to doubt that in all the provinces the influence of the Canadian practice accelerated the transition from a real to a theoretical presence at Executive Council meetings.

The colonial Governor was not only the representative of the Queen but also was the representative of the Colonial Office; and as the guardian of United Kingdom and imperial interests and as the proponent of imperial policies he was expected to use both his influence and his prerogatives. This responsibility to a higher authority lingered for some time after Confederation and the provincial Lieutenant-Governors were regarded as the special guardians of the rights of the Dominion government and the national interest in the province. Such a position necessitated constant preoccupation with the work of government; a close supervision of provincial affairs was expected by the central government and the laggards were frequently reprimanded. During the Ontario-Manitoba boundary dispute, for example, Macdonald felt that Sir Alexander Campbell, then Lieutenant-Governor of Ontario, was not adequately playing his part and asked him to read Bagehot. His object in so doing "was simply this—that you naturally look to your present office as a place of rest, and would like to be bored as little as possible with business. Bagehot described in his graphic and interesting style—that the duties of the Crown are real and not merely ceremonial and dwells especially on the duty of the Sovereign to warn his Ministers."[18] But the Lieutenant-Governor has long since ceased to be of any importance as a federal officer. For many years there has been no pressure on him from his political superiors to be *au courant* of the local political situation, and lacking motivation, compulsion, and the backing of the central government the Lieutenant-Governor has accepted political exclusion.

Moreover, the responsibility of the Lieutenant-Governor after 1867 was to a very different body. As the agent of the federal government he was also in a sense the agent of a political party. Thus while the Prime Minister of the United Kingdom might readily confide in the monarch (and the Canadian Prime Minister in the Governor-General) knowing, or at least trusting, that his confidence will not be betrayed, the provincial Premier will not, for he has no such assurance of political

---

[12]LLNB, *Records of the Executive Council*. The post-1880 records are in the hands of the Clerk of the Council.
[13]PAO, Campbell Papers, M 26, Macdonald to Campbell, Feb. 3, 1888.

neutrality. If they belonged to different political parties it was inevitable that the ministers would regard the Lieutenant-Governor as "a *Black Sheep* in their midst."[14] An aggressive and determined incumbent like Lieutenant-Governor Schultz of Manitoba, although a notorious partisan, could successfully insist on full information and could sometimes, using the national interest as his justification and both federal power and his prerogatives as his sanction, warn his ministers away from various actions and policies. But such a relationship based on threats and fear, inculcating suspicion and enmity, could not be lasting and in all probability did more in the long run to lessen the influence of the Lieutenant-Governor than otherwise. If, as is commonly stated, the monarch's position of influence is attributable to his supposed impartiality and independence, then the converse is perhaps equally true, and the present insignificance of the Lieutenant-Governor, his merely "superficial acquaintance" with the work of government, is due in great part to his real or imagined political partisanship.

The decline in stature of the office is also the result of the marked change in the type of appointments. (It is equally true of course that the appointments reflect the changing conception of the importance of the office in the minds of the federal ministers.) Macdonald's assertion that the Lieutenant-Governors were seldom recruited from the front rank of Canadian statesmen needs some qualification, for until the turn of the century—or even until the beginning of the long Liberal reign in 1921—the office was usually filled by prominent and capable, often outstanding, politicians and/or statesmen: Archibald and Howe, Wilmot and Tilley, Campbell and Mowat, Morris and Cauchon, Chapleau and Fitzpatrick, to mention the most memorable. Accustomed to a position of great influence and power such men as these were hardly willing to become "rubber stamps," to use a phrase common today. Moreover, the provincial Premier and his colleagues, usually having much less ability and experience than the Lieutenant-Governor, were often prepared to profit from any assistance he might be able to give them. If both were of the same party the Lieutenant-Governor on occasion became virtually a member (a shadowy member perhaps) of the cabinet; and if he were not, yet seemed to be thinking of the best interests of the province, what harm could there be in accepting the unsolicited help of the opposition?

Until 1911 at least the relationship between the Lieutenant-Governor and the Premier in Quebec was always close, except during the four short periods when the two were of different parties, and the

14Macdonald Papers, 114, Doyle to Macdonald, Feb. 26, 1869.

Lieutenant-Governor's position as an elder of the party enabled him to wield a significant influence.[15] In Nova Scotia, Doyle continually rode herd on his ministers, Adams G. Archibald served almost as the legal adviser to his governments, and his successor, M. H. Richey, was the image of Bagehot's sovereign. The Lieutenant-Governors of New Brunswick tended to overshadow the provincial Premiers during the fifteen years of unstable non-party government after 1867. But when Andrew Blair finally showed signs of forming a stable administration, Sir Leonard Tilley, one of the nation's most accomplished statesmen, gave without stint of his vast experience and accumulated political wisdom. A succession of experienced and respected easterners —Archibald, Morris, and Aikins—gave the office in Manitoba considerable prestige. Even the mediocre appointees of the federal government in British Columbia were incomparably more able as a rule than the Premiers thrown up by provincial politics, and exercised substantial influence as a consequence.

Sir Henri Joly's career was exceptional perhaps, but it does illustrate the relations that may often have existed in many of the provinces. Joly went to British Columbia as Lieutenant-Governor in 1900 after having served twenty-four years in the Quebec legislature and one year as Premier of Quebec, eleven years in the House of Commons and four years in Laurier's administration. For the first three years of his term Joly attempted to secure some stabilization of provincial politics, although his efforts met with little success. In 1903, following his dismissal of the Prior government, Joly called on Richard McBride to form a cabinet, persuaded him to adopt party lines, and thereafter pursued a policy of benevolent paternalism. McBride was extremely able, yet handicapped by youth and inexperience. Rarely absent from his office in the legislative buildings, the Lieutenant-Governor assisted his Premier in every possible way; their correspondence is full of sound and disinterested advice on every subject. Joly was pleased with what he termed "our new departure" and informed his son that "they have the means to do well for the Province. May God help them to do honestly and fearlessly their duty. I do my best to encourage them and do feel more hopeful for the future than I have ever felt since I came here."[16] When he left office in 1906 Joly was able to sum up his position as being that of an "adviser to my advisers."[17]

---

[15]Events in three of the four periods are of unusual interest and are discussed later: on the first occasion a government was dismissed; on the second a dissolution was refused; and on the third a government was dismissed.

[16]PABC, Joly Papers, Joly to Edmund Joly, Dec. 14, 1903 and Jan. 17, 1904.

[17]*Ibid.*, March 22, 1906. See also PABC, McBride Papers, 1903–6, *passim.*

Such a statement today is an echo from an age long past. During the last half century as the provincial governments have increased in power and stature the ability of those making a career of provincial politics has risen markedly. The same period has witnessed a striking change in the type of men appointed to the office of Lieutenant-Governor. Very often the Lieutenant-Governor has had little political experience, his knowledge of constitutional practice and law has usually been limited, and realizing his ignorance of matters political, constitutional, and legal he has willingly abdicated his functions to a Premier who can boast of greater experience and probably greater ability.

Other causal factors could be enumerated, but in the end the conclusion seems inescapable that the Lieutenant-Governor has become *le roi fainéant* because the Canadian people generally have so willed it, if such loose terminology be permitted. The constitutional history of the nation (as it happened and to a greater degree as it has been written) has to a large extent centred on the growth of Dominion autonomy and the removal of the fetters on Canadian self-government imposed by the imperial government. The Governor-General, of course, was often the instrument through which this control or supervision could be exercised. But he was also the representative of the Crown, the embodiment of monarchical principles in the Canadian governmental system. The twofold nature of the Governor-General's position has escaped its many critics in times past, and in arguing for the removal of imperial control they have also tended to argue (consciously or unconsciously, wisely or ignorantly) for the abolition or diminution of all powers and rights possessed by the Governor-General. The position of the Lieutenant-Governor has undoubtedly been greatly affected by the argument and the apparent consequences of its success.

If the Canadian constitutional atmosphere is dominated by a liberalism hostile to supposedly arbitrary power, the social and psychological is dominated by factors equally unhealthy for the Crown's representative. As Sir Harold Nicolson observed, "the balance between the rights of the Sovereign and the rights of Ministers, rests upon congenital experience, acquired tradition, instinctive feeling, frequent personal contact and unreserved mutual confidence."[18] In Canada and its provinces these factors are seldom or never present; our national experience has worked in a different milieu and thus towards a different conclusion. Moreover, while the sense of attachment to the Queen and the throne, to the British connection and the Commonwealth partnership, is cer-

[18]Sir Harold Nicolson, *King George V—His Life and Reign* (London, 1952), 475.

tainly deep-seated, it is not reflected in or even extended to the officers who fulfil the monarchical functions and embody the monarchical principles and traditions in the governmental system, nor indeed has it much rational relation to the workings of the political and constitutional machinery at all.

Having said this one must immediately admit a paradox, for while the Lieutenant-Governor does not occupy an important position in the constitutional structure, while his rights have been generally overlooked and his counsel only on occasion given more than perfunctory consideration, the instances of discretionary action are many. To account for this is not particularly difficult. As Gibbon Wakefield once remarked, although the Governor is less than a King the people over whom he reigns are less than a nation. And the contrasts between the United Kingdom and a Canadian province are great indeed. On one hand, an electorate of many millions and a parliament of six hundred; strong, stable, and well-organized political parties based on usually observable and meaningful economic and social factors and with recognized leaders; a cabinet of mature and experienced politicians, most of whom believe that political ethics ought to exist; and finally a tradition of political service firmly embedded in some sections of the population at least. On the other, an electorate of a few hundred thousand— sometimes less—and a legislature of from thirty to one hundred; often weak, ephemeral, and poorly disciplined political parties frequently little more than personal factions and usually indistinguishable on any valid grounds; cabinets composed of inexperienced politicians, weakened by personal feuds and petty ambitions; and no tradition of state service or ethical principles in politics. Goldwin Smith neatly, if a little unfairly, summarized the contrast:

> We have not here, as you have in England, a class of men able and willing to serve the country for itself. . . . There is no independent gentry. Politics become a trade. Nor is there any basis of principles for the parties, which are more factions wrestling for power with their villainous "machines." The parliamentary system of Great Britain has been extended to the Colonies without the things necessary to make its working rational and pure.[19]

Such sharp contrasts and harsh judgments have much less validity today than when Smith wrote, but for the bulk of the period under study in-fighting was the hallmark of provincial politics. To this day the purely physical distinctions remain. As a result provincial Lieutenant-Governors have been more frequently faced with difficult con-

[19]Arnold Haultain, ed., *A Selection from Goldwin Smith's Correspondence* (Toronto, n.d.), 444, Smith to Lord Mount Stephen, Aug. 6, 1905.

stitutional problems than their greater prototypes in the United Kingdom and in Ottawa. This must always be kept in mind when considering the exercise of discretionary or reserve powers; unprecedented actions are not necessarily unconstitutional, they may simply be the result of unprecedented circumstances.

The Colonial Office had realized that in an immature and amoral political society the responsibility for the maintenance of effective and honest government was very real, and the colonial Governors were "imperatively bound to withold the Queen's authority from all or any one of these manifestly unlawful proceedings by which one political party, or one member of the body politic, is occasionally tempted to endeavour to establish its preponderance over another."[20] As A. B. Keith noted, "with ministries new to responsibility, with an imperfectly formed and not completely effective public opinion, it was felt that some security for the observance of true principles of responsible government was necessary, and this was found in the Governor, who was held even in matters of purely internal interest to be under the obligation of securing the observance of constitutional government."[21] This concept of personal responsibility was accepted in the colonies without question and lingered in the Canadian provinces for some time after Confederation.

The "watchdog" or "guardian" theory is readily understandable and justifiable. Unless the ministry's majority in the legislature is slender and shaky, as it was in the House of Commons in 1873, it need fear little, for Parliament to this day has retained a little of its mediaeval character as an "occasion." It is essentially an arena where grievances can be aired and government policy subjected to a superficial examination, and it is ill-suited to act as a court of inquiry into the details of administration. The cabinet releases only the information it wishes and well-disciplined back-benchers can be depended upon to thwart by sheer weight of numbers any attempt by the opposition to push questions to embarrassing conclusions. Fully aware of the impotence of both legislature and electorate when a party is firmly entrenched, and having no high regard for (or trust in) the politicians in office, intelligent opinion—partial as it may often be—has frequently turned to the chief executive as the last check.

The Lieutenant-Governor faces one great danger in prohibiting what he considers to be an illegal or unconstitutional act by his govern-

[20]Alpheus Todd, *Parliamentary Government in the British Colonies* (Boston, 1880), 104.
[21]A. B. Keith, "Ministerial Responsibility in the Dominions," *Journal of Comparative Legislation*, XVII (1917), 228.

ment. His action may provoke a crisis, perhaps the resignation of the cabinet, and be made the issue of a political contest. He cannot appeal personally to the electorate on the constitutional question, explaining and supporting his decision, but must depend on the opposition, if it is willing, to support him. By this very fact, however, the matter takes on a political tone and the original constitutional motivation is lost to sight in a fog of partisan discussion. Finding such prospects unpleasant many Lieutenant-Governors have probably resisted what may have been a strong urge to intervene.[22]

Perhaps the most frequent appeal to the Lieutenant-Governor has followed a general election when the government appeared to be defeated but did not immediately resign. Given the two-party system election results are generally decisive, but the same is not true if several parties are in the field or if party allegiances are loosely regarded. Common sense and good practice alike suggest that when the result is in doubt the government should meet the legislature as soon as possible in order to test its strength. On occasion however—and this is particularly true of the provinces where party lines were from time to time virtually non-existent—the cabinet, having lost its majority, may deliberately refuse to meet the legislature in the hope that time, chance, and the judicious use of patronage will have a salutary effect. In any case few administrations leave office soon enough to please the successful and naturally acquisitive opposition, and an appeal to the Lieutenant-Governor to accelerate the transfer of power is often made as a matter of course. These almost routine requests need not detain us. Several cases of considerable interest might profitably be discussed, for although by no means typical they do illustrate the type of circumstance that has arisen and may arise in the future.

It was clear to all after the October 1886 general election in Quebec that the Conservative government led by J. J. Ross had lost its majority, but it was not clear whether Honoré Mercier, the Liberal leader, had won a majority, for there were several small groups acting independently of both parties. The Conservatives hoped that given sufficient time they could secure the support of some independents. They feared, however, that the Lieutenant-Governor, L. F. R. Masson —a Conservative and a former member of Macdonald's administra-

---

[22]The recorded instances of discretionary action unquestionably constitute only a fraction of those that occurred, for unless the issue was contested or prolonged it would not have become a matter of record, nor would the press receive any intimation of it. A gentle suggestion in the office or the club might often have been sufficient. Tales of intervention or near-intervention abound in every provincial capital.

tion—might force the resignation of the Ross government or insist on an early meeting of the legislature. This was the course demanded by the Liberal press, and as one leading Conservative wrote, although Masson was not "a timid man," it was feared that "his over-sensitiveness might lead him into error, through a sense of duty."[23] To his Quebec colleagues who sought his advice Macdonald replied that the precedents established by Disraeli in 1880 and Gladstone in 1886 were unfortunate and that the "only proper and constitutional course" was for Ross to remain in office until the legislature met.[24] Reluctantly and after much hesitation Macdonald consented to write directly to the Lieutenant-Governor. He observed that no party had a clear majority and that Ross was "still around with all the powers of your Constitutional adviser" and had "clearly the right to meet the Legislature and submit to its decisions."[25] Masson was fully aware of the political manœuvres afoot and was determined to be rigidly impartial.

I agree with you that the ministry have come out of the election in a minority; if there could have been any doubt during the first days after the elections, there can be none at present; some of the parties whose goodwill they might have expected to enlist having of late decidedly pronounced against them. I am not however so sure that the regular opposition are also in a minority; I would rather be inclined to think they are—irrespective of *their party*—in a small majority of one. . . .

I also agree with you that Parliament is the tribunal which should decide who has the majority of the two contending parties and that as a general rule a ministry should be allowed to receive the verdict of Parliament if they so wish it, and I have neither by act or word exercised a pressure to the contrary. I do not think however that a ministry, aware that they are in a minority, would be acting in the best interests of the people—to say nothing of their party—if they do not, as soon as they have come to that knowledge, take means to have Parliament called at as early a day as the public service will permit. On this point I may without impunity tell *you* that my Government and myself have felt alike and a reasonable time for calling Parliament mentioned.[26]

---

[23]Macdonald Papers, 205, Chapleau to Macdonald, Oct. 21, 1886. Langevin thought of going to Quebec to see the Lieutenant-Governor but Chapleau warned Macdonald that Langevin's presence at Quebec "might itself influence Masson adversely. There is a man who could (and would at your request) advise him in a friendly manner. It is Baby. . . . Nobody would suspect his presence at Spencer Wood; he is intimate with Masson as in the old time [that is, before Masson became increasingly identified with Castor and *nationaliste* sentiments]. I have asked Dansereau to write on the question to help Masson. He has done it in *La Presse* (*La Minerve* would have been suspected, and *Le Monde* is too large for such études)." See *La Presse*, Oct. 16 ff, 1886.

[24]PAC, Caron Papers, file 10263, Macdonald to Caron, Nov. 3, 1886.

[25]Macdonald Papers, 527, Macdonald to Masson, Dec. 8, 1886. See further chap. iv.

[26]Macdonald Papers, 119, Masson to Macdonald, Dec. 9, 1886.

The issue then was settled: Masson would take no positive action
(unless his government had already agreed on the date of the session
under duress!), nor would he permit the prostitution of the constitution for political ends; the legislature would decide, but it would decide
soon. The legislature assembled in January 1887 when, in spite of
frantic last minute efforts to escape the inevitable, the government was
defeated and Mercier came into office.

The circumstances in British Columbia in 1882–3 were much more
complicated because of the general political immaturity and instability
in the province. In June 1882 Premier Walkem resigned and the
Lieutenant-Governor, C. F. Cornwall, asked Robert Beaven to form
a government and later granted him a dissolution. Although party
lines did not exist in the province it was quite clear after the July
elections that Beaven had not secured a majority. Soon afterwards a
majority of the members-elect declared in an open letter to William
Smythe, apparently their chosen leader, that the administration had
not their confidence and should therefore resign. The letter was obviously for the information of the Lieutenant-Governor. Beaven
blandly retorted that he would meet the legislature in the spring of
1883 and continued in his official duties as if he had just received an
overwhelming endorsation. Following the defeat of a government
candidate in a crucial by-election fifteen of the twenty-five members-
elect formally petitioned the Lieutenant-Governor for an immediate
session. Two weeks later an Order in Council summoned the Legislative Assembly for January 25, 1883. When the assembly met the
Beaven administration was censured for refusing to meet the legislature
following its obvious defeat and resigned. Premier Smythe later stated
in the legislature that the Lieutenant-Governor had forced Beaven to
issue the Order in Council.[27]

Little can be said in support of the attempt of the opposition in
Saskatchewan to force the government's resignation in 1929. The
Liberals had lost their majority in the June 6 elections, yet with
twenty-eight seats they were still the largest party, the Conservatives
having twenty-four and the Progressives and Independents ten. Under
the circumstances the government had every right to remain in office
and meet the legislature. The opposing parties nonetheless attempted
to force its resignation by advising the Lieutenant-Governor, H. M.
Newlands, that the Conservative leader had been elected as leader of
the "co-operating groups," the implication being that he and not the

[27]Victoria Daily Colonist, Dec. 5, 1882 and Jan. 27, 1883; and the Victoria
newspapers generally from July 1882 to Jan., 1883.

Liberal Premier now possessed the confidence of the newly elected legislature.[28] The Conservative press then tried to bully Newlands, a Liberal, who, it was suggested, would never let the government remain in office after such emphatic proof that it no longer possessed a majority. If he did so he "would raise the question of what Lieutenant-Governors are for."[29] The Premier declared that he planned to remain in office until the assembly met, but in reply to the opposition leader's statement that no appointments made in the interval would be honoured promised that only routine business would be transacted. Within two weeks the Conservative press throughout western Canada was demanding the dismissal of the government and had in fact commenced a bitter personal attack on the Lieutenant-Governor:

. . . . But that His Honor, the Lieutenant-Governor should be a party to this defiance of the popular will is a matter for comment and straight speaking.
    The Gardiner Machine government was voted out on June 6. The present Newlands-Gardiner-Cameron coalition has no standing either in law or ethics. . . . They must tell His Honor, if need be that if he desires to take part in party politics he must vacate Government House and seek a nomination or a position in the staff of the machine.[30]

The government wisely called an early session and resigned after being defeated on the election of the Speaker and on a deliberate vote of confidence.[31]

Appeals were made to the Lieutenant-Governor on different occasions. The Ontario opposition repeatedly asked the Lieutenant-Governor to compel the harassed Ross ministry to have a by-election that it had put off for eighteen months.[32] In Prince Edward Island the Lieutenant-Governor was criticized for permitting the government to postpone for five months the return of writs from a by-election on which its fate depended.[33] When a cabinet crisis suddenly forced Premier Parent of Quebec to cancel the meeting of the Quebec legislature shortly before it was to open in 1905, the opposition asked the Lieutenant-Governor to compel him to meet the legislature. Only after consulting the highly respected Speaker of the Assembly did the Lieutenant-Governor agree to Parent's request.[34]

The warning that appointments made by the supposedly defeated

[28]Saskatchewan, Legislative Assembly, *Sessional Papers*, 1929–30, 59–60.
[29]*Regina Daily Star*, June 13, 1929.
[30]*Ibid.*
[31]Saskatchewan, Legislative Assembly, *Sessional Papers*, 1929–30, passim.
[32]*Canadian Annual Review*, 1903, 150 ff.
[33]*Ibid.*, 1911, 537 ff.
[34]Rumilly, *Histoire*, XI, 200 ff. *See also* the Quebec press, Feb.–March 1905.

administration in Saskatchewan in 1929 would not be honoured by its successor raises the question of the powers and rights of a retiring government. After every election when the government appears to have been defeated the opposition press diligently watches governmental action and is quick to see in every minor appointment a virtual inundation of the public offices with political appointees. Frequently both the Premier and the Lieutenant-Governor are publicly warned that these appointments will not be honoured if a change of government occurs, and it is suggested as a rule that the Lieutenant-Governor restrict the activities of his advisers. Unquestionably, if there are good reasons for supposing that the government will not remain in office, the cabinet has not the power that it possessed before the election, and in all probability the Lieutenant-Governor has injected a note of moderation into the petulant political discussions and plans that inevitably follow defeat.

As the Lieutenant-Governors are federal officers and frequently look to the federal government for advice and instructions, Dominion precedents are significant. After the resignation of the government had been decided upon but not formally submitted in November 1873 the Macdonald cabinet rushed through a large number of appointments, from tax collectors to Lieutenant-Governors. Mackenzie later recommended that many of these appointments be revoked:

The rule in Canada has been that Ministers against whom a motion of Want of Confidence is pending have exercised no authority except such as is incident to the routine of their respective offices; similarly, and for the same reasons, they do not conduct any Parliamentary work until such a motion is disposed of.

While this Committee does not dispute that the right to make appointments necessarily remains in the hands of every Administration . . . yet it is evident that such a power is liable to be abused by an improper exercise of it, and that no Ministry can with propriety exercise the ordinary authority to create new offices and make appointments to such offices, when their existence as Ministers is imperilled. . . .[35]

Dufferin replied that every administration had the right to make appointments until it left office and that every minister, in cleaning up the work of his department, had the right to fill vacancies and fulfil pledges. He agreed however that the right "should be used with moderation and discretion," and convinced that some of the appointments were unwarranted he agreed to their revocation.[36] Lord Aberdeen on the

[35]PAC, Orders in Council, approved Nov. 13, 1873.
[36]*Ibid.*, statement appended to the Order by Dufferin. It is interesting to note that Mackenzie had originally declared that many of the appointments were to be

contrary refused to sanction some of the recommendations made by Sir Charles Tupper after his defeat in June 1896, partly on the grounds that they could not be revoked. For some reason most commentators agree with Tupper that the Governor-General's action was a "fatal mistake";[37] but it should be remembered that Laurier was shown the correspondence and accepted full responsibility,[38] that the Colonial Secretary endorsed Aberdeen's action without reservation,[39] and that Tupper himself later wished to withdraw some of his recommendations from the official record and keep the constitutional issue a secret.[40]

The Aberdeen-Tupper crisis served almost at once as a precedent in British Columbia, when Lieutenant-Governor McInnes concluded that his government had not been sustained by the electorate in 1898. McInnes at once informed the Premier that his activities must henceforth be restricted to matters of routine administration, obviously expecting that like Tupper his Premier would resign. But when Premier Turner remained in office (apparently knowing less of the 1896 crisis than the Lieutenant-Governor!), he was rudely dismissed.

Although McInnes' motives were different, as shall be seen, he was not the first Lieutenant-Governor to circumscribe the activities of an administration whose position seemed endangered by an election. In Nova Scotia Archibald refused to approve appointments following the elections of 1878 and 1882 when it was obvious that the government had been defeated.[41] The government of New Brunswick willingly accepted the Lieutenant-Governor's refusal to sanction its recommendations following its defeat in 1908.[42] A perfectly credible press report suggests that Masson did not on all occasions follow the advice tendered by the Ross government after the October 1886 election.[43] Five years later Lieutenant-Governor Angers insisted that Mercier limit the government to routine activities during the investigation of alleged misappropriations by a Royal Commission.[44] After the Conservative defeat of 1897 in Quebec Lieutenant-Governor

cancelled, but in the end, probably because of Dufferin's attitude, he took a more moderate stand. (See, for example, Mackenzie's correspondence with A. G. Jones in the *Report . . . of the Public Archives of Nova Scotia*, 1952, 33–6.)

[37]*C.S.P.*, 1896 (2), no. 70, 7, Memorandum from the Prime Minister to the Governor-General, July 6, 1896.

[38]PAC, G 12, 85, Aberdeen to Chamberlain, July 24, 1896.

[39]G 3, 30, Chamberlain to Aberdeen, Aug. 10, 1896.

[40]G 12, 85, Aberdeen to Chamberlain, July 24, 1896.

[41]PAC, Thompson Papers, Archibald to Thompson, July 4, 1882; *Halifax Morning Herald*, Sept. 19, 1878; *Halifax Morning Chronicle*, July 7, 1882.

[42]*St. John Daily Telegraph*, March 21, 1908.

[43]*Montreal Herald*, Jan. 29, 1887.

[44]See chap. v.

Chapleau informed Laurier that the Castors were not taking their defeat gracefully and, like Tupper the year before, had recommended three appointments to the upper house. But Chapleau, for personal and political as well as constitutional reasons one suspects, firmly refused to make the appointments: "je reste froidement constitutionnel, et . . . les journaux à scandale n'auront pas de plaisir à mes dépens."[45] In more recent years other Lieutenant-Governors have refused to permit large payments of money, even though called for by statute, between the date of defeat and resignation. Unquestionably the powers and rights of a defeated government are not equal to those possessed by one that still possesses in full measure the confidence of the electorate and the legislature, and it is clearly the duty of the Lieutenant-Governor to make sure that the ministry acts with moderation.

The same may be said for wholesale dismissals of political opponents by a government assuming office. If the retiring administration has made an unfair use of its power it is natural that the succeeding administration will do the same. Dufferin in 1873, Lorne in 1878, and Aberdeen in 1896 permitted their governments to cancel some appointments and dismiss some officials, but they demanded in each instance that just cause be shown. In the provinces the politicians appear to have been allowed generally to play fast and loose with the constitution, perhaps because patronage was often all there was to struggle over. There is evidence now and again, however, which suggests that some Lieutenant-Governors did restrain their advisers, and it is likely that such action was not uncommon. The federal government has never encouraged its officers in this respect but has on the contrary tried to keep them clear of crises over what were doubtless considered to be minor matters.[46]

Firmly entrenched governments have often a tendency to ride rough-shod over the opposition, to treat all criticism as specious, and to use

[45]Laurier Papers, 45, Chapleau to Laurier, May 15, 1897.
[46]See for example Macdonald Papers, 516, Macdonald to Doyle, Feb. 15, 1870; PANS, Lieutenant-Governors' Correspondence, Memorandum for Council, Dec. 14, 1867; ibid., Doyle to Moody, Jan. 23, 1869. In 1911 the Lieutenant-Governor of Prince Edward Island momentarily refused to accept recommendations for dismissal that he felt were unfair, unwise, and perhaps illegal, and sought the advice of the Governor-General. The reply of the Borden cabinet is interesting: "It is his right to examine the reports of his Council submitted for his approval; to call for full information and, if necessary, explanations in regard to all matters treated of therein. He can constitutionally refer back to his Ministers for reconsideration any recommendations made to him. Should, however, they adhere to their original position, it is the duty of the Lieutenant-Governor to follow the decided and sustained advice of his responsible advisers, unless he is prepared to assume the responsibility of demanding their resignation and of calling to his counsels a new administration." (GGO, file 2450A, part 8, Report of a Committee of the Privy Council, approved Dec. 20, 1911.)

their majorities to kill any request for an inquiry into the details of policy or administration. Such things as a bad press may force the government to permit an investigation, although if the individuals and the terms of reference are unscrupulously dictated by the administration, as they probably will be if possible, the results can usually be foretold. The extent to which political power can be used to prevent, or worse still to prejudice legitimate inquiry is a question that Canadians may some time have to answer; at present as in the past the power of the majority seems virtually limitless. No other course being open, the opposition has at times formally appealed to the Lieutenant-Governor over the head of the cabinet. As a rule these requests must be ignored, that is, passed on to the Premier for his consideration, or the Lieutenant-Governor would soon become little more than the plaything of the opposition. On occasion, however, the charges may appear to be sufficiently serious and well-founded to justify pressure from above. On two occasions a Lieutenant-Governor has actually forced his government to accept a Royal Commission. In Quebec A. R. Angers selected the personnel and dictated the terms of reference; since he used the report of the Commission as the basis for the dismissal of the Mercier administration the incident will be discussed in another connection.[47] The second instance calls for detailed examination here.

As soon as the 1915 session of the Manitoba legislature opened, the Conservative government led by Sir Rodmond Roblin, which had been returned in 1914 with a substantial majority, was charged with the illegal misappropriation of the public funds granted for the construction of the legislative buildings. Roblin finally agreed to an examination of the charges by the Public Accounts Committee, a majority of which was Conservative, but only after the opposition had bluntly refused to accept his denial. As might have been expected the majority report absolutely cleared the administration, while the minority report emphatically declared that almost one million dollars had been fraudulently overpaid, that key witnesses had been kept away from the Committee, and that crucial documents were apparently missing. These assertions were formally repeated in the assembly and a Royal Commission was demanded.

Following the government's wooden refusal to appoint a Royal Commission the opposition included their charges in a petition to the Lieutenant-Governor, D. C. Cameron, a Liberal appointed by Laurier in 1911 on the advice of the local Liberals. Cameron had been following the controversy for some time:

[47]See chap. v.

The suspicion that something might be wrong in connection with the contract for the Capital building first came to my mind in September, 1914, on reading newspaper reports of the statement by the Minister of Public Works, Honorable Dr. Montague, during the Special War Session of the Legislature, that the original contract price would be greatly exceeded. I was particularly struck by his statement that the cost of foundations would exceed the estimate by $700,000.00.

From that time I took an increased interest in the progress of the work, but nothing developed until the Session of the Legislature which opened on February 9, 1915. The reading of newspaper reports of evidence before the Public Accounts Committee from day to day strengthened my suspicion that there was something wrong and this was still further strengthened by the fact that the efforts of the Opposition Members of the Public Accounts Committee were led and directed by Mr. A. B. Hudson, who represents possibly the most important constituency in Manitoba, Winnipeg South, and whose standing in his profession was such that I felt I had to recognize the gravity of the alleged irregularities, which it was plain to me he was making every effort to have proven. My alarm was still further aroused by the speech made by Mr. Hudson in the Legislature on March 30th, 1915, in which he charged that there had been total overpayments of some $827,200 to Thomas Kelly & Sons, Contractors, and in connection with which he moved for an investigation by Royal Commission.

On March 31st, 1915, I noted that speeches in the Legislature by Government supporters indicated that it was the intention to refuse a Royal Commission. On the evening of March 31st, 1915, Mr. T. C. Norris, Leader of the Opposition, came personally to Government House and presented a petition signed by the twenty-one members of the Opposition.[48]

On the morning of April 1 Roblin "of his own motion" consulted the Lieutenant-Governor for the first time since the crisis began.[49] According to Cameron the Premier readily agreed to his suggestion that a Royal Commission be appointed, although from the press one gathers that there were several meetings between the two men punctuated by hurried meetings of the cabinet.[50] On the afternoon of the same day Roblin announced that there would be an investigation by a Royal Commission and the legislature was prorogued. It was widely suspected that Roblin had been forced to choose between the Commission and a dissolution, but his biographer states that the choice was between the Commission and dismissal.[51] Although Conservative newspapers defiantly declared that the government had nothing to hide, the following telegram to Robert Rogers, Borden's Minister of Public

[48]PAC, Hudson Papers, Statement of the Lieutenant-Governor.
[49]Ibid.
[50]Canadian Annual Review, 1915, 619–25.
[51]H. R. Ross, Thirty-five Years in the Limelight; Sir Rodmond Roblin and His Times (Winnipeg, 1936), 167.

Works and the Conservative "boss" in the west, suggests otherwise. Roblin and Rogers had everything to hide:

> Governor Cameron in collusion with Grits here. Has under his authority directed Government to appoint Royal Commission to enquire into Kelly contracts. Important that he should accept Government's nominees for the Commission. There is danger that he may refuse. If he should, it will precipitate crisis. Your interest in Dominion Election at stake. Better protect your position and see that Cameron follow advice of Government. He is broke as you know. I think this very important and should be attended to at once.[52]

Rogers replied that he was "acting strongly in the matter": "Governor has absolutely no right to take matters into his own hands. His plain duty is to follow the advice of his advisers."[53] So Roblin and the Conservatives would have liked to believe; the Lieutenant-Governor, however, saw his "plain duty" in a different light.

Roblin next saw Cameron on April 6 and asked to delay the appointment of the Royal Commission until he returned from an essential trip to eastern Canada, supposedly to see his ailing father but doubtless to see Rogers and other leading Conservatives. During the conversation the Premier mentioned Alexander Haggart, a Conservative appointee to the Manitoba Court of Appeal, as a possibility for the Commission, and apparently took the Lieutenant-Governor's silence for consent. On the day following Cameron officially informed the Premier that work on the building should be stopped at once, that Chief Justice Mathers and Justices Galt and Macdonald should be the members of a Commission to be appointed at once, and that the Commission should be given the widest possible terms of reference.[54] Roblin immediately went to Government House and after "a long interview" the Lieutenant-Governor agreed to postpone the appointment of the Commission until Roblin returned from the east.[55] After his return Roblin made every effort to place his own nominees on the Commission, but Cameron felt that those he had named "would be more acceptable to the people of the Province."[56] The Lieutenant-Governor also refused

---

[52]Dafoe Papers, M 123, Simpson to Rogers, April 1, 1915.
[53]*Ibid.*, Rogers to Simpson, April 1, 1915.
[54]PAM, Roblin Papers, Cameron to Roblin, April 7, 1915.
[55]Dafoe Papers, M 123, Roblin to Rogers, April 7, 1915.
[56]Roblin Papers, Cameron to Roblin, April 16, 1915. Cameron did allow the government to appoint Sir Hugh John Macdonald in the place of Galt: ". . . I remain of the opinion that under the circumstances it is for me to decide. . . . In my letter of the 7th inst. I named the three gentlemen qualified, as I think, in every way. . . . The Chief Justice should, in any case, be one, but as offered to you, I would have no objections to appointing Sir Hugh John Macdonald in place of either of the two latter." (*Ibid.*, April 19, 1915.)

to sanction the terms of reference formally advised in an Order in Council and insisted that "its terms should be wide enough to authorize the fullest enquiry as to whether there has or has not been a misuse of public moneys, and if there has been to clearly fix the responsibility."[57] Cameron had in fact withdrawn his confidence. Unable to accept the legal advice of his Attorney General he sought that of Chief Justice Howell, informing the latter that he no longer trusted his ministers.

Once the Royal Commission was appointed the game was up. If Roblin had not always been aware of what had transpired he had become familiar with the irregularities during the month of April. It was obvious that large sums had been fraudulently spent, that money had come back mysteriously into the party's campaign fund from the "extras," and that the Conservative party organizer had been in the midst of it all. Moreover, key witnesses had been hastily sent away, government employees could not be found, and important records had been secreted or destroyed.[58] Roblin realized that his political career had been ruined, and fearing dismissal as soon as the Royal Commission reported, he elected to resign. A new government was formed by T. C. Norris, the Liberal leader, and the legislature was dissolved.

The Lieutenant-Governor's actions were constantly and vigorously discussed during the election campaign that followed. Sir James Aikins, elected as Conservative leader following Roblin's resignation, asserted time and time again that he had no "quarrel" with the Lieutenant-Governor and tried to steer clear of the constitutional issue that others were attempting to create. A brilliant jurist and an able parliamentarian, Aikins doubtless realized that the party could gain nothing by denouncing Cameron's action; the Lieutenant-Governor had done nothing wrong; he had insisted only that the accused be brought to trial. At the same time, however, Aikins had spent two days with Cameron in April in a futile attempt to convince him that the Lieutenant-Governor was simply a "rubber stamp." This was common knowledge and the Liberal press would let neither Aikins nor the electorate forget it. Many of Aikins' supporters showed less wisdom and

[57]*Ibid.*, April 19, 1915.
[58]Manitoba, Legislative Assembly, *Sessional Papers*, 1916, No. 17 contains the report of the Royal Commission. See also: *ibid.*, 1916, No. 18, 964 ff. Roblin and Rogers overlooked nothing in their attempt to escape the embroglio. On April 30 Roblin wired Rogers as follows: "Close friends say very desirable that [X] son of the Commission now with Strathcona Horse be given a commission, say lieutenant. See General . . . and explain situation so he will understand and act promptly. Am sure he will do this for me." (Dafoe Papers, M123.)

following Rogers' lead engaged in a bitter attack on the Lieutenant-Governor, whom they denounced as "the intriguer," "the conspirator," "the plotter," and the "machine politician." The Liberals gladly supported Cameron and begged the electors to do the same. The election was an overwhelming Liberal success: the party won thirty-nine of the forty-six seats, most of them by very large majorities; the two members of the Roblin administration who chose to run were defeated; and Aikins himself was defeated by 600 votes in a constituency in which he was popular and respected and which he had represented in the House of Commons. As soon as the results were known large crowds gathered outside Government House. Cameron acknowledged the tribute:

I thank you for your cheers and music of course . . . but not being in public life, I have nothing to say about the stirring events that have taken place today, except that I think the electors have sent out an answer that if there has been any wrong-doing in the province it was not with the consent or will of the people.

I have heard to some extent the result of the polling today, and whatever part I have taken the people have vindicated to the fullest extent. I claim no credit for what I have done, for any man who would not act as I did would not be worthy to represent the King. It has given great satisfaction to me, and I am sure to those within sound of my voice that the people have risen, and that they have said plainly that men in public life must be honest. In this province there has been a great departure from this course, and we have a right to be satisfied with the result today.[59]

Cameron may have been wrong on Reciprocity in 1911, but all that could be forgotten now.

As in Anglo-Saxon criminal law, an eye for an eye and a life for a life was the operative principle in western politics until relatively recent times. With the aid of the Lieutenant-Governor the Liberals had displaced the Conservatives in Manitoba, and it was only right that the balance should be restored in Saskatchewan where a Liberal government led by Walter Scott had been in office since 1905. How better to bring about this reversal than by a *coup d'état* modelled on that in Manitoba? When Lieutenant-Governor Brown's term expired in October 1915 Rogers selected, and Borden appointed, R. S. Lake as his successor. Although Lake was not at home in rough and tumble politics (and could thus never rise to the top in the west), he was an important, popular, and respected Conservative who had both in the west and in Ottawa shown himself to be a vigorous and determined

[59]*Manitoba Free Press*, Aug. 7, 1915. On the campaign see the Winnipeg press from May 12 to Aug. 6, 1915.

opponent of the provincial government in Saskatchewan. From the date of his appointment rumours had circulated that his mission was to rid Saskatchewan of Scott. The Premier and his colleagues had little reason to doubt the rumours, for Rogers "had practically conveyed a threat personally to Mr. Calder [Minister of Railways in Scott's cabinet] to effect that unless Mr. Calder succeeded in putting a stop to the investigations in Manitoba there should be reprisals against the Government of Saskatchewan."[60]

No sooner had the session of 1916 opened than the Conservative opposition charged the government with grave scandals in the highway department and in the administration of the liquor laws, charges that involved members of the cabinet indirectly and members of the assembly and Liberal party organizers directly. The Premier immediately informed the Lieutenant-Governor of the accusations and admitted that at first glance it seemed likely that some members of the assembly and the civil service were guilty as charged.[61] Any definite accusation of a member of the cabinet, added Scott, would be investigated by a Royal Commission, otherwise examination of the charges would be made by committees of the legislature. During the interview Scott observed that leading members of the opposition had taunted him with a dissolution "sooner than you think" and that there was a widespread belief that Lake was expected to imitate Cameron's tactics. Of course Scott "had replied to every single person who had mentioned such rumours to him" that the Lieutenant-Governor was "the very last man in Canada to do anything or to sanction the doing of anything which was not strictly regular, constitutional and proper." On the whole Scott was satisfied with his first interview: "As to the First Estate of the Realm —rigidly correct—no friction at all—I faced it with the utmost frankness and can detect no adverse sign."[62]

While Scott was thus congratulating himself the Lieutenant-Gov-

[60]PAS, Scott Papers, Royal Commission on the Bradshaw Charges. This is a record of a number of interviews between Scott and Lake from Feb. 19 to Feb. 25, 1916. Scott carefully summarized each discussion and Lake later approved the summary as accurate. The following account is from this source unless otherwise indicated.

[61]A similar course had been followed by the Premier of Ontario when the famous Gamey scandals were revealed. With the Conservative press demanding dismissal, Ross agreed to a Royal Commission. The government was ridden with corruption and the Lieutenant-Governor was bombarded from all sides: one individual suggested that he "suspend the government and appoint a commission of Judges to take charge of the affairs of Ontario until this question is settled." (PAO, Lieutenant-Governors' Correspondence, O'Neill to Clarke, May 12, 1903.) On this episode see Canadian Annual Review, 1903, 128 ff; Ontario press, March 10 to June 4, 1903.

[62]Scott Papers, Scott to Brown, Feb. 21, 1916.

ernor was reading a petition given to him by the opposition leaders, which, like that in Manitoba, recited the charges and prayed for the appointment of a Royal Commission. Early the next morning Lake summoned Scott to Government House, handed him the petition, and declared that in his opinion the circumstances "required the immediate appointment of a Royal Commission which should investigate all of the charges. . . ." In view of Scott's emphatic refusal to accept this suggestion the Lieutenant-Governor "intimated his intention to consult Chief Justice Haultain and observed that it was exceedingly embarrassing at such a time to be unfamiliar with constitutional law and practice. . . ." Scott did not object formally to this intimation, but following a discussion with his colleagues he informed the Lieutenant-Governor that the Attorney General was his legal adviser and that any appeal to an outside authority was tantamount to an admission of loss of confidence. The implication of course was that the government would have to resign. Unwilling to face that eventuality the Lieutenant-Governor decided not to see Haultain and, after further consideration, agreed that there was no need for a Royal Commission.

Although several Royal Commissions were appointed later to investigate some of the charges, the victory at this time lay definitely with the government. Lake was clearly insecure, unfamiliar with convention and law, and embarrassed by his past political associations. It seems clear that the Conservative strategy had been well planned and that Rogers was prepared to exercise whatever influence and pressure he could from Ottawa. But Lake does not appear to have been a party to it, and during the last recorded interview he asked Scott "whether there was any possibility of Mr. Rogers at Ottawa doing anything further to cause a complication of matters." Scott replied "that he could scarcely be surprised at any action which Mr. Rogers under the circumstances might take." Even if Scott were not, the Attorney General was apparently prepared to resign on the grounds of lack of confidence. John S. Ewart, with whom Scott was in contact and who was to be employed as a constitutional expert for the government if a crisis materialized, was much less inclined to make an issue of Lake's proposed action: "a green representative," Ewart felt, "is entitled to a certain latitude as regards practices and usages."[63]

The dispute did serve to alter the relations between the Lieutenant-Governor and the Premier in Saskatchewan. Early in the discussions Lake said that although he was unfamiliar with the "practices and usages" of the office, he had expected to be in closer touch with the

[63]Ibid., Scott to Calder, Feb. 29, 1916.

Premier and the work of government generally. Scott admitted that he had "fallen into inexcusably careless ways" as a result of his political and personal intimacy with Lake's Liberal predecessors. Scott retired in October 1916, but his successor, William Martin, was extremely careful on all occasions to keep the Lieutenant-Governor informed, explaining all matters that came up by letter or in conversation, until Lake finally had to suggest that it was unnecessary "to come up and see me on these occasions unless it is a matter of unusual importance."[64] It is difficult to tell how long this closer relationship lasted. It does not exist today.

Further west the Conservative government in British Columbia, heavily laden with accumulated charges of corruption, was tottering to an inglorious fall. Almost every day during the spring session of 1916 new evidence was brought to light: "sluggers" had been imported from Seattle to vote in by-elections; the Premier's law firm was closely associated with a number of government enterprises; and, finally, very large excess payments had been made to British Columbia's white elephant, the Pacific Great Eastern Railway. While admitting that excess payments had been made to the P.G.E., Premier Bowser stated that they had been made legally and for good reasons and refused to consider even a committee of investigation. The opposition leader petitioned the Lieutenant-Governor, in the now traditional manner, repeating the charges, swearing that they could be proved, and asking for an inquiry.[65] The Lieutenant-Governor, E. G. Prior, who as Premier had been dismissed from office in 1903, sent the petition without comment to Bowser, who rightly declared that it was intended "to prejudice Your Honour's mind in respect of the good faith and integrity of Your Honour's constitutional advisers."[66] Prior may well have realized that there was little point in exerting any pressure on his ministers, for an election was approaching and the defeat of the government was universally regarded as inevitable. A Select Committee later found the charges concerning the P.G.E. to be substantially correct.

Lieutenant-Governor Cameron was taken to task by the Conservative press for consulting Chief Justice Howell, a man of known Liberal sympathies. Scott and his Attorney General had likewise strongly opposed Lake's proposed communication with Chief Justice Haultain, long the leader of the Saskatchewan Conservative party. Cameron admitted that he had lost confidence in his legal adviser, and Scott observed that Lake's action would prove that he had also. Lake was

[64]PAS, Martin Papers, Lake to Martin, Dec. 11, 1918.
[65]PABC, Premiers' Papers, Inward 1916, Brewster to Prior, May 26, 1916, enc. in Prior to Bowser, May 29, 1916.
[66]Ibid., Official Letterbook, Bowser to Prior, Aug. 3, 1916.

apparently troubled by this constitutional refinement and seemed to feel that he had every right to seek advice on matters of law. Undoubtedly he felt that his ministers' advice would be a mixture of law and politics and under the circumstances could not be taken as the last or only word. One's sympathies are almost completely with the Lieutenant-Governor; the Attorney General of a province is a politician first and a law officer second, and any advice that he tenders will as a rule be governed by that order of precedence. One exception comes at once to mind. In 1937, against the wishes of the Premier and the party caucus, the Attorney General of Alberta advised the Lieutenant-Governor that certain bills were beyond the power of the province to pass. The advice was unquestionable, but the Attorney General was forced to resign for having acted in the strictest sense as the Lieutenant-Governor's legal adviser.[67]

It is well known that Queen Victoria and George V, either personally or through their secretaries, sought legal and constitutional advice from individuals outside the cabinet, "Her Majesty's irresponsible advisers" as Lord Palmerston once described them. Since impartiality can be assumed in the United Kingdom such practices have not been condemned. But in Canada no one expected or believed in the possibility of political impartiality; small men refused to believe that any man was great enough, be he Governor-General, Lieutenant-Governor, or judge, to overcome even momentarily his political prejudices. To seek outside advice then was to seek the advice of enemies; the advice given by Haultain, in Scott's mind, would be that given not by the Chief Justice but by a life-long Conservative. (This explains too the struggle over the composition of the Royal Commission in Manitoba.) The practice, however, was probably not infrequent: Lieutenant-Governor Schultz often consulted the Chief Justice concerning bills passed by the provincial legislature before he gave his assent;[68] the Lieutenant-Governor of Alberta consulted the Chief Justice before reserving three bills in 1937;[69] and the Lieutenant-Governor of British Columbia asked the advice of the Chief Justice in 1882. In the case last mentioned the request for advice was refused on the grounds that at all times on all matters the advisers of the Lieutenant-Governor must be responsible to the legislature and "the Judges cannot be such advisers."[70]

More often the Lieutenant-Governor has sought advice from his

[67]See chap. VIII, 215–16.
[68]For example Macdonald Papers, 264, Schultz to Macdonald, March 24 and March 31, 1890.
[69]See chap. VIII, 217.
[70]PABC, Misc. MSS Collection, Memorandum for Lieutenant-Governor Cornwall from M. B. Begbie, Chief Justice, March 3, 1882.

friends, particularly his trusted political friends from pre-office days and usually from the one who secured his appointment, whether it be the Prime Minister or another member of the federal cabinet. As a Dominion officer, of course, he has every right to seek instructions from the federal government on matters affecting its rights and interests. But a line must be drawn between matters of Dominion and provincial concern, and that line, as Elgin observed, "is somewhat narrow and slippery." Moreover, the advice tendered by federal ministers has also been as a rule based on political rather than constitutional or legal considerations. Only one Lieutenant-Governor seems to have applied for a strictly legal ruling from the law officers in Ottawa, or in other words from the officials of the Department of Justice. Had this proved to be an acceptable course the problem of "irresponsible advisers" might have been solved for the Lieutenant-Governor as it had been for the colonial Governor by the reference of questionable matters of law to the Law Officers of the Crown in the United Kingdom. Unfortunately politics again intervened.

Following the 1925 electoral victory the new Conservative government of Nova Scotia introduced a bill to abolish the almost exclusively Liberal Legislative Council. The assembly readily passed the measure, but the council unceremoniously rejected it. Anticipating this the government had prepared an Order in Council providing for the appointment of enough new members to the council to secure passage of the bill in the upper chamber. The same procedure had been discussed many times in the past and there was considerable doubt whether the government had the power to appoint an unlimited number of councillors. The Deputy Attorney General prepared a lengthy brief for the government and the Lieutenant-Governor in 1925 in which, after examining all the evidence, he concluded that the legal right did reside with the administration. The Lieutenant-Governor personally concurred, but in view of the long and chequered history of the issue concluded that greater certainty would be desirable. Consequently he sought a legal ruling from the Department of Justice. He was advised that since the matter admitted of some doubt the best solution would be a reference to the courts. This in time was done and the Judicial Committee of the Privy Council eventually upheld the view of the provincial government.

There is no indication that the Premier of Nova Scotia opposed the reference to the Department of Justice. The decision, however, was reached in confidence between the Lieutenant-Governor and his ministers, and although the reference was widely suspected neither party chose to make it public. But Prime Minister King foolishly and improperly wired the details to the provincial Liberal leader who immediately brought the matter to the attention of the assembly. The Premier refused to comment on the discussions with the Lieutenant-Governor or the appeal to the law officers. "If the Prime Minister of Canada is so lacking in appreciation of constitutional procedure as to disclose confidential communications passing between the Lieutenant-Governor and the chief law officers of the Crown at Ottawa," he declared, "this does not afford any reasons for my departing from the correct practice." King's indiscretion was of a nature to discourage other Lieutenant-Governors or provincial governments from making a similar appeal to what conceivably could be an independent and impartial legal authority. It was, as Dr. Eugene Forsey has said, "a shocking and inexcusable breach of constitutional propriety" and could not be justified on any grounds.[71]

The easiest and safest course for a Lieutenant-Governor is to obey the contemporary Canadian dictum that the representative of the Crown is a rubber stamp. Excluded from the work of government, regarded as a nuisance if he dares to question and probably as an old tired man if he dares to warn, the Lieutenant-Governor has ceased to be "the image, in little, of a constitutional king." The physical image he may be, but the substantive image he is not. The Lieutenant-Governor seems to be a new species: to some akin to a goldfish and to others not unlike a fungus. Yet to adhere rigidly to the oft-repeated pronouncement that the Lieutenant-Governor is a rubber stamp is to follow neither the course wisdom suggests nor the course the constitution permits.

[71]E. A. Forsey, "Constitutional Annus Mirabilis," *Public Affairs*, XIV (autumn 1951), 45; Norman Mackenzie, "Constitutional Questions in Nova Scotia." *Journal of Comparative Legislation*, II (1929), 87–95; *Halifax Morning Chronicle*, March 10, 16, 17, 1926; *Halifax Evening Mail*, March 11, 1926.

CHAPTER THREE

THE INAUGURATION OF RESPONSIBLE GOVERNMENT IN MANITOBA AND BRITISH COLUMBIA

Two PROVINCES entered the Canadian federation before they had achieved responsible government. Manitoba did not have even representative institutions in 1870, while British Columbia had enjoyed partially representative government for only a few years before its entry in 1871. Yet from the moment of creation both were to possess a constitution identical in principle to those in the eastern provinces. To the first Lieutenant-Governors in Manitoba and British Columbia fell the task of inaugurating the new régime, and until the constitutions were established in practice, as well as on paper, the position of the Lieutenant-Governor was unique, paramount, and crucial. On him, it would be little exaggeration to say, depended in great part the success of the venture in nation building.

Against its better judgment the federal government had created the province of Manitoba in order to satisfy the inhabitants of Red River, who, after successfully resisting the first, almost farcical, attempt to assert Canadian control of the newly purchased Northwest Territories, had demanded the creation of a province "with all the rights and privileges common to the different Provinces of the Dominion." Faced with this determined ultimatum the Macdonald government drafted and passed the Manitoba Act in 1870. To a small province carved from the vast Canadian west was given responsible government and full provincial status within the federation. It was in many ways a magnificent concession indeed, even to a people in arms, for there was every likelihood of failure—complete and absolute. The birth was at least a decade premature: society was primitive, ingrown, and stagnant; ten of the twelve thousand inhabitants were half-breeds, offspring of the unions—demanded and blessed by the fur trade—of the winterers and the voyageurs with Indian women; political experience was seldom to be found, little government being necessary for the simple life of the parish, the fur trade, and the buffalo hunt.

Above all the province was bitterly divided by those forces that had called it into being. The aftermath of 1869–70 was a generation of racial, religious, and linguistic conflict; a "corrosive fog" of bitterness, suspicion, and hatred lingered over Manitoba for decades, blinding all but the most tolerant and impartial. Canada too had been divided: Quebec understood (or thought she did) and sympathized with the fears and aspirations of the *métis*; what the Canadian party lacked in Manitoba it compensated for by calling into play the fierce passions and prejudices of staunchly Anglo-Saxon and Protestant Ontario. This division in eastern Canada prevented the federal government from taking the one step that might have assured the successful establishment of self-government in Manitoba. Legally at least, an amnesty would have cleared the slate and, more important, would have calmed the fears of the *métis*. Without it the bulk of the population, the late "rebels," remained for many years insecure and afraid.

After William McDougall's tragic blunder the federal cabinet was aware how important it was to select a capable person to fill the office of Lieutenant-Governor. Fortunately perhaps, Macdonald was seriously ill in the spring of 1870 and the appointment lay in the hands of Sir George Cartier, leader of the French-speaking wing of the Conservative party. A number of likely prospects were considered, but were for various reasons rejected. Before any decision had been made the debate began on the Manitoba Act. In the House of Commons on May 7, 1870, Adams G. Archibald made a speech notable for its breadth, its tolerance, and its justness. "Is it any wonder," he asked, "that a community so secluded from all the rest of the world, uninformed of all that is transpiring around them, should be subject to great, to unreasonable alarms, when suddenly the barrier is burst . . . ?" Archibald repeatedly emphasized the serious and difficult task it would be to re-establish law and order. "But the readiest mode of doing so," he declared, "is, at the same time, to show these people that their fears are unfounded, that their rights shall be guaranteed, their property held sacred, and that they shall be secured in all the privileges and advantages which belong to them, as Britons and as freemen."[1]

A few days later Cartier asked Archibald to go to Fort Garry as the first Lieutenant-Governor of the nation's first new province. Archibald had no desire to remain in politics, although he had every prospect of a great future. Actually he looked rather to the Bench, but since no position was then available, he somewhat reluctantly agreed to go to Manitoba. A gifted lawyer, a politician of considerable experience, a gentleman universally recognized for his calm and sound judgment, Archibald was in every respect an excellent choice. He had

[1]Canada, House of Commons, *Debates*, 1870, 1425 ff.

previously been suggested for the same office in Nova Scotia, New Brunswick, and Ontario—for Ontario by no less a person than George Brown in the *Globe*. Moreover, the party owed a good deal to Archibald, but with the two titans, Howe and Tupper, in or about the cabinet, there was little for him in Ottawa. As far as Cartier was concerned these qualifications were secondary. The important fact was that while not infected by the narrow racial and religious prejudices of either Ontario or Quebec Archibald had shown a good deal of sympathy for the *métis*. In Manitoba the knowledge that Cartier had selected his close friend had an immediate salutary effect: "On a au moins en notre faveur le Gouverneur qui, il n'y a pas a en douter est parfaitement bien dispose," wrote Joseph Dubuc to Louis Riel.[2] "My profoundest respects to Mr. Archibald," wrote Riel, "we much desire his coming."[3]

Manitoba had been given a constitution. It was the Lieutenant-Governor's task to deliver safely this premature provincial government, to spank breath into a lifeless frame. The dry, matter of fact words in his instructions gave no indication of the immensity and complexity of the undertaking; they did not reveal that on his arrival in the province he would be the government of Manitoba. Following "the Constitutional principles and precedents which obtain in the older Provinces," Archibald was to appoint "some suitable persons" to the Executive Council, choose the Legislative Councillors, divide the province into electoral districts, hold an election, and summon the legislature.[4] Simple and straightforward as the instructions might have seemed, their fulfilment demanded statesmanship of the highest calibre. Fundamentally the basic problem was this: self-government was impossible without the participation of the *métis*, but the one act —a general amnesty—that could have assured their whole-hearted co-operation had been side-stepped if not openly refused. As Archibald later informed the Governor-General:

. . . the part I had to play there was rather difficult. Half our people had been in rebellion. In the eyes of the law they were guilty of High Treason, yet Parliament chose not only to give these people the elective franchise but to confer Responsible Government on the country. . . . I had to conduct my administration by men who possessed the confidence of the Assembly,—I could hardly hope to engage as Minister any man who should have to proclaim it as his duty to hang the men whose votes had raised him to office. It was necessary, therefore, to choose between

2PAM, Riel Papers, folio 3R, Sept. 6, 1870.
3Canada, House of Commons, *Journals*, 1874, 37, Riel to Taché, July 24, 1870.
4*C.S.P.*, 1871, no. 20, 4–6.

two alternatives. Either to let byegones be byegones, or to administer responsible Government in a new form, that of opposing, instead of carrying out the well understood wishes of the people.[5]

Archibald not only "let byegones be byegones" but also did everything in his power to secure the amnesty that he realized was essential to reconcile the *métis* to the new order. Doubtless he and Cartier had agreed on this "short memory" policy before he left Ottawa; it was the only sane, practical, and expedient policy, the only one with any chance of success.[6]

Before taking his first cautious steps the Lieutenant-Governor carefully surveyed his ground. He found the people "in a state of much excitement" and he took great "pains in endeavouring to tranquilize them and lead them to see how important it is . . . that all leading men, irrespective of party, should come forward and give me their aid in establishing a Government that can secure the peace of the country on a solid foundation."[7] Bishop Taché and Donald A. Smith were willing assistants and were constantly consulted, while even John C. Schultz, the vociferous and vindictive leader of the Canadian party, was slightly impressed by the need for harmonious action. Archibald spent two weeks touring the province, interviewing parish leaders and meeting delegations, forming an estimate of its needs, personnel, and potentiality.

In his search for Executive Councillors the Lieutenant-Governor was hampered by the political inexperience of most of the inhabitants. Some of the Canadian party had had some experience in Ontario, but a government led by them would have served only to stimulate the *métis* once again to armed protest. The natural leaders of the French-speaking people, on the other hand, had been stigmatized by

[5]PAC, PRO, FO 5, 1427, fol. 184, Archibald to Lisgar, April 19, 1872, enc. in Lisgar to Kimberley, May 23, 1872. Archibald was more explicit in his first official dispatch to the Secretary of State for the Provinces: "There is very great uneasiness among the population. The French assert that they were promised an amnesty, and many of them declare there can be no solid peace till that promise is fulfilled. The English party, many of whom were sufferers in the late troubles, declare that it is impossible peace can prevail, till the principal actors in the late troubles are arrested and punished, and they are very uneasy lest it should be the intention of the Government to pass over all these matters and let the men from whom they have suffered go unpunished." (*C.S.P.*, 1871, no. 20, 15, Sept. 17, 1870.)

[6]It was the only policy that would secure the support of Mgr Taché, the Bishop of St. Boniface. "The astute prelate at St. Boniface becomes daily more and more master of the situation. He . . . holds the broken promise of the Canadian Government . . . *in terrorism* over Governor Archibald. He is making better use of the Amnesty than if it was declared. . . ." (PAC, Taylor Papers, M 117, Taylor to Davis, Jan. 6, 1871.) See also PAC, Macdonald Papers, 517, Macdonald to Archibald, Nov. 1, 1870.

[7]*C.S.P.*, 1871, no. 20, 10, Archibald to Howe, Sept. 10, 1870.

the uprising and would have been accepted by neither the moderates within the province nor the incensed Ontario electorate, whose representatives formed an effective pressure group in Ottawa. Within two weeks Archibald had found a route between Scylla and Charybdis:

Thinking it now time to organize a Government, and that I had become sufficiently acquainted with the people to form some idea of the material out of which this could be formed, I have chosen a man representing each section of the population here, and appointed them Members of my Executive Council. Mr. Alfred Boyd is a merchant of good standing here. He is a man of fair abilities, of considerable means, and very popular among the English half-breeds. He was chosen by the Parish of St. Andrew's (the most populous parish in the settlement), as a delegate to the Convention of last winter. While highly esteemed among the English party, he is not obnoxious to the French. I have appointed him Provincial Secretary.

Mr. Marc Amable Girard is a French Canadian from Varennes, below Montreal, who has recently moved here. He is a notary by profession, has been Mayor of Varennes, and is a gentleman of some property, and of good standing and seems to be the nominee of the French party. I have appointed him Provincial Treasurer.[8]

With the assistance of his cabinet of two, Archibald worked rapidly and decisively. Girard and Boyd were in no sense responsible ministers —there was nothing to be responsible to unless it was the commanding figure of Taché—but were simply officials appointed to assist the Lieutenant-Governor in his administration of public affairs. The administrative machinery was quickly developed as the appointments of sheriffs, coroners, constables, and census takers were hastily gazetted. In preparation for the first provincial election Archibald divided the province into twenty-four electoral districts using, on Taché's advice, the parish as the basis for division.

The political campaign began long before the foundations were laid. In a manner reminiscent of Sir Charles Metcalfe, the Lieutenant-Governor led his own party into the fray. Macdonald had told him that "much depends on the successful start of your legislative machine, and you would be quite justified in taking a personal interest in the result of the elections, so as to secure the return of a body of respectable men representing the various races and interests."[9] The issue was Archibald's policy of conciliation and toleration, which, as James

[8]Ibid., 15, Archibald to Howe, Sept. 17, 1870. There was no representative of the Canadian party. Girard and three others, Dubuc, Royal, and Clarke, went to Manitoba in the summer of 1870 at Cartier's request to provide political leadership for the métis. James Taylor declared that Taché had asked for such men. (Taylor Papers, M 117, Taylor to Davis, Jan. 6, 1871.)
[9]Macdonald Papers, 517, Macdonald to Archibald, Nov. 1, 1870.

Taylor noted, had done much to overcome the *métis'* "distrust of Canadian officialdom."[10] The Lieutenant-Governor was assured of the support of the twelve French-speaking parishes: ". . . nous devons nous rallier autour du Lieutenant-Gouverneur et appuyer sa politique sage et libérale parce qu'il est l'ami de tous les bons citoyens," declared the *métis* leaders.[11] He was supported as well by a large section of the English-speaking population, led chiefly by the "old settlers" as distinguished from the new elements from Ontario that had entered the province in the 1850's and 1860's.[12] The opposition to the Lieutenant-Governor labelled his supporters "administration candidates" and the tag was willingly accepted.[13] Archibald not unnaturally came in for considerable personal abuse from those opposed to him and his policy:

> Instead of meriting support and approval, His Excellency deserved condemnation. We are yet without responsible Government through his procrastinating weak policy. . . . The Governor has two irresponsible advisers, and even they are only figure-heads. . . . Then look at the appointments that have been made. . . . Could anything show more clearly the Governor's lack of sympathy with the loyal party?[14]

Archibald was not greatly concerned with the rantings of Schultz and the "loyal party" and confidently believed that he would be supported "by a fair majority in the local legislature."[15]

His expectations were fulfilled. Only five opposition members were elected, none of whom represented the extreme wing of the Canadian party. The Lieutenant-Governor was elated. Boyd had been opposed by a popular and respected individual who, during the fifty years he had lived in Manitoba, had built up many family connections and boasted of great influence. Yet Boyd's majority was large and Archibald took his success "as a ratification on the part of the people of the Division of the policy which Mr. Boyd represents."[16] The jubilant Riel spoke for the *métis*: ". . . lieu de McDougall, Monsieur Archibald! Au lieu de méchants, ennemis du pays, ce bon nombre d'honnêtes gens,

[10]L. B. Irwin, *Pacific Railways and Nationalism in the Canadian-American Northwest, 1845–1873* (Philadelphia, 1939), 136, Taylor to Davis, Nov. 22, 1870.
[11]*Manitoban*, Dec. 10, 1870. This paper was the government organ and Archibald on occasion wrote the lead articles. See F. A. Milligan, "The Establishment of Manitoba's First Provincial Government," *Papers Read before the Historical and Scientific Society of Manitoba*, Third Series, V (1950), 12. This article and an unpublished M.A. thesis by the same author are two excellent studies of this period in Manitoba.
[12]Milligan, "Manitoba's First Provincial Government," 12.
[13]*Ibid.*
[14]Cited in *ibid.*, 14.
[15]Macdonald Papers, 187, Archibald to Macdonald, Dec. 11, 1870.
[16]PAC, Correspondence of the Secretary of State for the Provinces, 1871, no. 579, Archibald to Howe, Dec. 31, 1870.

nos amis."[17] The "loyal party," composed largely of the volunteers who had come out with Colonel Garnet Wolseley in 1870, was less pleased, and according to one report, ran wild in the streets and released prisoners in the jail causing "indescribable tumult." Exaggerated though the account may be it does give some idea of the milieu in which Archibald had to work:

The officer in command, Lt. Colonel Jarvis, obtaining a hearing with great difficulty—the men taunting him that their object in enlisting had been revenge, and not the pacific policy of Governor Archibald. . . . I cannot resist the conclusion that the Lieutenant-Governor and his secretaries are virtually prisoners. I am informed that the Ontario troops —many of them Orange men—are secretly plotting the expulsion of Governor Archibald. . . . I am forced to consider the possibility of anarchy and civil war within the next thirty days. . . .[18]

After the excitement of the election had abated Archibald was left free to concentrate on the formation of a permanent Executive Council. He had no intention of giving up his position as party leader and *de facto* Premier, not at least while it was his policy and his reputation that were at stake. Each of the new members of the cabinet —H. J. H. Clarke, Thomas Howard, and James McKay—was appointed individually, and although Clarke became Attorney General and government leader in the assembly he was not the Premier. Archibald made this very clear in a letter to Macdonald:

My object has been to pick out the best four men I could find in the Assembly and add one who will be in the Legislative Council when formed. . . . The three Councillors were duly appointed. . . . Before appointing them I discussed with them individually the policy which I had pursued and intended to pursue, so as to see that they were prepared to give it a hearty support. This they have promised to do.
I called them together on the 14th and handed them a memo of the work that was to be done before calling the Assembly together. . . . In fact I gave the Council a memo of 32 Bills which would be absolutely necessary to form the sketch of a Provincial Constitution, and have set them to work to get their hands in. I intend our laws to be simple and plain—to suit the country as it is, and to leave them to develop with the country.[19]

The Lieutenant-Governor of necessity was acting in the best Tudor tradition. To the seven-man Legislative Council Archibald appointed seven of his supporters; it was a closed shop.

The first session began in March 1871 with the Lieutenant-Governor

[17]Riel Papers, Riel to Taché, Jan. 8, 1871.
[18]Taylor Papers, M 117, Taylor to Davis, Feb. 21, 1871.
[19]Macdonald Papers, 187, Archibald to Macdonald, Jan. 16, 1871.

very firmly in the saddle. The Minutes of the Executive Council reveal that it was he who "submits," "states," and "suggests." He established his private secretary on the floor of the assembly, as it was impossible to attend himself. On occasion, however, the Attorney General sought to escape this close supervision, but his attempts were in vain: "Mr. C. succeeded in getting the Bill through the Lower House where its provisions were not understood, before I was aware of its contents, but when I found out what was going on, I had the Bill arrested in Council, and drafted another to be substituted for it as an amendment, which was adopted, and which I insisted on Clarke's agreeing to when it came back."[20] On the whole Archibald was satisfied with the first session, although "a pretty firm hand with friends and foes" had been necessary. Macdonald too was content with the work of his proconsul and congratulated him on the body of legislation passed.

Yet already there were faint rumblings of discontent in Ontario where the protests and complaints of the Canadian party in Manitoba were being constantly received. From the beginning Macdonald denied any responsibility for the course pursued by Archibald.

With respect to any course taken by Governor Archibald, all I can say is that it is not from any instructions from Canada [he informed an irate Ontario supporter]. In selecting him, the Government thought they were getting an unexceptionable man. A thorough stranger to the party politics of the NorWest, a native New Brunswicker [sic] and a Presbyterian, he had no prejudices of race in favour of any of the contending parties at Manitoba, and his undoubted Protestantism was the best security against yielding to Catholic pressure. . . . If the original intention of keeping it a Crown Colony to be governed by instructions from Ottawa, had been carried out, we would of course have been responsible for his action there; but the granting of responsible Government entitles him to "paddle his own Canoe," without reference to us.[21]

In Manitoba the Cartier-Archibald-Taché policy of conciliation had so far proved successful. The first tentative beginnings in self-government had been made without mishap. While congratulations flew between Winnipeg and Ottawa, however, events moved swiftly to a crisis in the Canadian west and Archibald's policy was soon to be submitted to a conclusive test. There had been for some time rumours of a Fenian attack on Manitoba led by W. B. O'Donoghue, ex-

20*Ibid.*, Archibald to Cartier, May 26, 1871. A year later Archibald wrote that "public considerations" alone made him tolerate the Attorney General: "His indiscretions which amount almost to madness, his utter disregard of Law and his arrogance combine to make a compound of which I trust there are not many examples in the Dominion". (*Ibid.*, Archibald to Macdonald, Feb. 24, 1872.)
21*Ibid.*, 518, Macdonald to Brown, Feb. 9, 1871.

associate of Riel in the provisional government.[22] Late in September 1871 a group of Fenians assembled near Pembina on the American side of the border and prepared to invade the new province. The invasion was predicated on the discontent assumed to prevail among the *métis* and any hope of success was dependent upon their support. As Archibald realized only too well, "the leader of the raid had been a member of the Provisional Government; the other members of that Government were in the Province, outlawed for their offences, abused by one press and thrown over by the other, and yet exercising a large influence among the population of their own race and creed. Under these circumstances the chances were that the French would join the enemy. I had a tough battle to fight." For two weeks before the raid materialized the Lieutenant-Governor "laboured unremittingly with the French clergy and with the representatives of the French parishes in the Assembly," pointing out "the advantages in one line, the danger and ruin in the other."[23] The advantages to be gained by loyal and decisive action were, of course, that such conduct would materially assist the granting of an amnesty. On October 4, 1871, Archibald issued a proclamation summoning all citizens to bear arms in defence of the province. Three days later Riel informed the Lieutenant-Governor that he could count on the support of the *métis*: "Votre excellence a pu se convaincre que sans avoir été enthousiastes nous avons été dévoués."[24] On the following day a large body of armed and mounted *métis* assembled on the river bank opposite Fort Garry where Archibald reviewed them, thanked them for their loyal support, and shook hands with several of the leaders, among whom was Riel. Meanwhile, unknown to those in Manitoba, the crisis had passed; what might have become a serious attack became, through the promptness of American border forces, a farcical venture.

The incident convinced Archibald of the soundness and success of his policy. In a letter to Macdonald he emphasized the seriousness of the situation and insisted that the Prime Minister "must judge of these things from my standpoint, not yours." "With you it is a question of popularity—of newspaper criticism—with me it is one of life or death, and I never felt more convinced that I was right, than during the last

[22]As early as September 12, 1871, Archibald had advised Ottawa of the rumours and had pointed out that he had insufficient men to guard the arms and ammunition, not to mention his obligation to defend half a continent. (*Ibid.*, 187, Archibald to Macdonald.)
[23]Canada, House of Commons, *Journals*, 1874, 140, Memorandum by Archibald, Nov., 1871. See also PAC, CO 42/700, Lisgar to Kimberley, Nov. 8, 1871, and enclosures.
[24]Riel Papers, Riel to Archibald, Oct. 7, 1871.

week, when for a while the action of the French halfbreeds seemed trembling in the balance."[25] This could hardly comfort Macdonald, to whom political popularity was synonymous with life and serious newspaper criticism with death; and in eastern Canada, where the execution of Thomas Scott had been neither forgiven nor forgotten, the handshake had caused a storm of protest. The federal cabinet first sailed with the winds that blew in strongly from Ontario. Howe, the Secretary of State for the Provinces and an old acquaintance of Archibald's, was nominated to reprimand the Lieutenant-Governor, in part perhaps as a defensive manœuvre. Howe first observed that Archibald's conciliatory policy had been regarded as an unduly pro-French policy in Ontario where it had caused considerable uneasiness, while the handshake had confirmed every suspicion and had unquestionably alienated many of the government's supporters. Perhaps the Lieutenant-Governor had been deceived. When the danger first arose "all the English and Loyal people turn out," but for several days Riel "maintains his position of armed neutrality, ready to fall upon the rear of the Canadians. . . ." Only when informed by scouts that the attack had been squelched did the *métis* leaders gallantly give their support.

All this would have been funny enough, and we should have had a hearty laugh throughout the Dominion had the "Army of observation" been left "alone in their glory." Had they come to you a coldly civil answer would have been all they deserved. But that you should go to them, overlook their strange conduct, and shake hands with Riel at their head, has excited a feeling of astonishment and regret everywhere, except perhaps in the Province of Quebec. . . .

The newspapers of course have been busy with this strange event. I am not bound to notice what appears in them, and of course do not, but on the floor of Parliament it will be different. We must meet the question there, and I should not be much surprised if an angry debate is followed by a very large desertion of our Ontario supporters. At the elections which must come off in June next, this handshaking will cost some seats in that region or I am much mistaken.

I write thus frankly that you may clearly apprehend the gravity of the subject. . . .[26]

Macdonald asked the Dominion Land Agent in Manitoba to secure the inside story of Riel's conversion and double-game. The facts, he believed, would put an end to the troublesome pressure from Quebec for an amnesty.

The facts clearly vindicate Archibald and his policy. As early as

[25]Macdonald Papers, 187, Archibald to Macdonald, Oct. 7, 1871.
[26]PAC, Howe Papers, 9, Howe to Archibald, Nov. 4, 1871.

July 1870 Cartier had impressed Taché with the need for the *métis* to be the most loyal of all, and the Bishop had unquestionably passed this on to Riel.[27] When rumours of the proposed raid first circulated in Manitoba Riel had assured Taché that the *métis* would have nothing to do with the Fenians. As the crisis developed the *métis* leaders met frequently and, although they were dissatisfied with Canadian policy in Manitoba and although they realized that O'Donoghue "avait besoin d'eux pour le succès de la déclaration de l'indépendance du pays," the consensus of opinion was that the government should be supported.[28] There were some who preferred strict neutrality, but in the end the influence of Riel, backed as it was by that of the clergy, carried the day and the decision was made to answer the Lieutenant-Governor's proclamation. Had Archibald followed a different policy over the previous year the decision might well have been otherwise, and Manitoba might once again have had to be taken at the point of a sword.

But the facts were not known in Ottawa. The cabinet knew only that Archibald had taken the hand of Riel and that Ontario was up in arms. For six weeks or more this question was paramount at Ottawa. Macdonald was told that the government could be saved only by the recall of the Lieutenant-Governor. A vote of censure on Archibald, if not on the Macdonald administration, was considered inevitable. By the end of November the cabinet had stiffened and had decided to support Archibald, if only because there seemed to be no possible alternative. "Of course the whole thing is fastened upon us here," wrote the Prime Minister, "and at present it is useless to attempt to argue that the responsibility does not rest upon us. We can only hope that the influence of time and the rise of other subjects for public discussion may remove this cause of political disquiet from the public mind."[29] Yet not for a moment was Archibald permitted to forget that his action threatened the very existence of the Conservative administration. After lengthy talks with Tupper, Macdonald repeated that the cabinet would "fight the battle à outrance but both Tupper and I think that you ought not to be taken unawares."[30] The Lieutenant-

[27]Canada, House of Commons, *Journals*, 1874, 39–9 and 46, Cartier to Taché, July 5, Nov. 2, 1870.
[28]Riel kept a record of these meetings and two drafts can be found in the Riel Papers. One draft has been translated and edited by A. H. de Trémaudan, "Louis Riel and the Fenian Raid of 1871," *Canadian Historical Review*, IV (June 1923), 132–44.
[29]Macdonald Papers, 519, Macdonald to Archibald, Nov. 31, 1871.
[30]*Ibid.*, Dec. 12, 1871. This probably means that if a vote of censure were passed on the Lieutenant-Governor, as was fully expected, the government would be forced to dismiss him.

Governor made few further attempts to justify his action and his policy, realizing perhaps that the time was not ripe for sober analysis. On the contrary he accepted full responsibility for all that had happened and sent a blank resignation to Ottawa. "You must not allow any act of mine to weaken your Government by diminishing your hold on any class of your supporters," he wrote, so "use my resignation when and as you please. . . . I could bear reproach from the enemies of the Government, but the knowledge that their feelings are shared by many of your friends, paralyzes my usefulness here."[31]

In Manitoba the still impotent "loyal party" attempted to make political capital out of Archibald's embarrassment; its members rabidly denounced the Lieutenant-Governor and demanded the immediate dissolution of the legislature. Archibald kept Macdonald fully informed and the latter, who only a year before had written that the Lieutenant-Governor "should in fact be a paternal despot," now suggested that he "play the game of a Constitutional Governor—le Roi fainéant." Point out, said the Prime Minister, "that in your character as a Constitutional Governor it is your bounden duty to see that the Constitution so conferred is carried out in spirit and in letter— that the whole theory of the Constitution is, that the people speak by their representatives in Parliament, and that you are bound to take the advice of the Ministry which has the confidence of that Parliament."[32] Such a specious argument would indeed have been found amusing in Manitoba where Archibald was regarded as the real, not the formal, head of the government.

The Lieutenant-Governor refused outright the demand for a dissolution, but in his own interests he called an early session of the legislature. In the Speech from the Throne, admittedly written to elicit "criticism and elicit an unmistakable reply," Archibald stated: "Your loyal response, irrespectively of race and creed, to the call made upon you to rally round the flag of the Empire, is a convincing proof of the soundness of the policy which, notwithstanding the troubles of the past, has aimed to treat you all as one people, interested in a common country, and sharers of a common destiny. . . ."[33] Both houses unanimously agreed. With this approval behind him Archibald proceeded to deliver the severest lecture ever given to the federal government by a Lieutenant-Governor. Unless responsible government were to be withdrawn the people of Manitoba must be allowed to govern themselves, or "if they are to be responsible to the people of other

[31]Macdonald Papers, 187, Archibald to Macdonald, Dec. 31, 1871.
[32]Ibid., 519, Macdonald to Archibald, Dec. 12, 1871; ibid., 517, Macdonald to Archibald, Nov. 1, 1870.
[33]Manitoba, Legislative Assembly, Journals, 1872, 7.

provinces the members should be elected there." Perhaps, suggested Archibald, the federal government should erect gallows not hustings.

> You allow the electors to choose members, you allow the members to make and unmake ministries, but electors and members are to exercise their functions with ropes around their necks. Was there ever before a responsible Ministry resting on a House of whose constituents more than half were liable to be hanged. . . .
> If then you cannot punish without recalling constitutional Government, what use is there in keeping up the pretence of calling these people outlaws. In my view you have to choose between revoking responsible Government, and admitting that you cannot go back to inflict punishment for offences in which half the population were implicated, committed before responsible Government was conceded.

He was convinced that the policy of letting "byegones by byegones" was the only one possible, but if the federal government thought otherwise there was nothing to prevent it from completely repudiating him. "I am quite content to await the time when a healthier public opinion will take the place of the feverish excitement lately prevailing in some parts of the Dominion. Meanwhile, let a different experiment be tried. At the end of a year of such a *régime*, it will be seen whether as proud a chronicle can be given of peace and progress as the one we have just recorded."[34]

While his resignation rested in Macdonald's pocket, Archibald herded his government through a trying but successful second session. He continued to take an active part in the work of the Executive Council, although there are now indications that much of the business was being done in informal cabinet meetings. He continued too to supervise government policy and legislation in the assembly and again had trouble with the Attorney General whom he once threatened to dismiss.[35] Government through factions, among which power constantly oscillated, necessitated frequent reorganizations, and the Lieutenant-Governor continued to act independently, even to the extent of bringing into the cabinet a bitter personal enemy of the government leader in the assembly.[36] Unquestionably it was essential that the Lieutenant-Governor continue to act as Premier and party whip for it was his policy on which the government had been elected and only his personal influence held the cabinet together. In the ab-

[34]Canada, House of Commons, *Journals*, 1874, 153, Archibald to Howe, Jan. 20, 1872.
[35]Macdonald Papers, 187, Archibald to Macdonald, Feb. 24, 1872.
[36]PAM, Minutes of the Executive Council, March 14, 1872.

sence of political parties there was really no alternative government —only the anarchy of faction.[37] Meanwhile Macdonald had craftily drawn the dragon's teeth by announcing just before the House of Commons met that Archibald's resignation had been received. The subsequent very tame and ineffective opposition inquiry was easily handled. Macdonald made no attempt to escape responsibility for the Lieutenant-Governor's action, although he did make it clear that Archibald had acted throughout on his own discretion, and denied that the federal officer had been forced to "withdraw."[38] Time, Macdonald's favourite political weapon, had served him well again. In June 1872 Archibald was asked to remain in office, if only for a short time, and he agreed.[39] Gilbert McMicken, the Dominion Land Agent in Manitoba, who had previously described him as "weak and timid," now strongly urged that he be asked to remain and finish his term.[40] But Archibald was determined to have his resignation accepted; being burned in effigy, affixed to his figure "a cross with brutal allusions to Archbishop Taché and the Catholic Church," had ceased to be a source of amusement.[41] He stayed in Manitoba long enough to supervise the federal elections, performing notable services in that connection, and then left—even before an Administrator had been appointed. Opinions differed in the province and in the rest of Canada, but the Secretary of State for the Colonies, who might be regarded as an impartial observer, noted with regret that Archibald had resigned; he "appears to me to have administered the Government with success in circumstances of peculiar difficulty," wrote Lord Kimberley.[42]

If the new system of responsible government had not been introduced with all its refinements, Archibald had at least made an excellent beginning. Basic to the satisfactory functioning of democratic government is the whole-hearted co-operation of the people governed. The Lieutenant-Governor's conciliatory policy had swung the bulk of the population behind his administration, or into constitutional opposition, and once this had been done the success of the Manitoba experiment was virtually assured. Sporadic violence by the extremists served only

[37]Political parties did not appear for six or seven years, and then they tended to represent racial and religious groups, the very eventuality that Archibald wanted to avoid.
[38]Canada, House of Commons, *Debates*, 1872, 37 ff.
[39]Macdonald Papers, Archibald to Macdonald, July 3, 1872.
[40]*Ibid.*, 246, McMicken to Macdonald, July 12, 1872. "I am quite confident of this, you will never get one to succeed him who would more honestly and warmly serve *you.* . . ."
[41]Taylor Papers, M 117, Taylor to Hales, April 22, 1872.
[42]PAC, G 3, 5, Kimberley to Lisgar, June 12, 1872.

to accelerate the process of adaptation. Both the late leaders and the chief sufferers in the insurrection, although still influential, had been to some extent neutralized. There was no longer the imperative necessity to handle the *métis* with kid gloves, and the Lieutenant-Governor could soon assume the supposedly impartial attitude towards all factions that had seemed doomed to failure while the half-breeds remained aloof, unco-operative, and suspicious. During Archibald's régime new leaders had arisen in the parishes or had immigrated from Canada, often unconnected with the past and anxious only for the future. New issues had arisen as well, practical issues, and the events of 1869–70 were no longer the sole basis for political action. Under Archibald's tutelage the province had matured and gained in wisdom, although it would be dangerous to exaggerate the extent of such gains. "It must be borne in mind that virtually the Governor is the Government," wrote McMicken late in 1872. "A more unfit machine for governmental work than the present local 'cabinet' cannot be imagined and it is no less deplorable than that there is no material in the country by which a new one could be called into existence or a satisfactory reconstruction hoped for. The times and circumstances are peculiar and require a man as Governor peculiarly fitted for them."[43]

Alexander Morris was in many ways admirably fitted for the office of Lieutenant-Governor in Manitoba. Long interested in the west, a politician of considerable experience, a lawyer of some stature, and an individual without extreme racial or religious phobias, even though he came from Upper Canada, he seemed to satisfy even the most severe requirements. As Chief Justice of Manitoba for a short time he had been able to study the province and its government at first hand before becoming its second Lieutenant-Governor. He realized that the amnesty question was the biggest obstacle to political stability and decided that the time had come for frankness. A general amnesty, he declared soon after his appointment, had been neither promised nor granted, and (taking a leaf from Lord Sydenham's book) he advised the inhabitants of Manitoba to turn their attention to immediate and practical objects rather than concern themselves with problems beyond their power to solve. This forthright statement, whether true or not, at least cleared the air; if it offended the *métis* it reconciled the "loyal party." Archibald himself had advised Morris that a firmer hand would be possible with the *métis*, for "there is not the same occasion now, as then, for bated breath."[44]

[43]Macdonald Papers, 246, McMicken to Macdonald, Nov. 8, 1872.
[44]PAM, Morris Papers, Archibald to Morris, Dec. 17, 1872.

In spite of his apparent reluctance to play the part of Premier and party whip vacated by Archibald, Morris was forced by circumstances to carry on in his predecessor's wake for over a year. For his lack of inclination to be a monarch who governed as well as reigned there are several explanations. Temperamentally and physically he was ill-suited for such a task; "his sensitive and nervous temperament unfit him and in short he cannot and should not be required to bear the strain of such responsibility," said a close friend when Morris was suggested for the office.[45] In addition Morris was unquestionably infected by the liberal tradition in Upper Canada that had been founded on opposition to irresponsible government.[46] Finally, he realized that many difficult situations could be avoided if he were the constitutional figure-head and threw the onus of responsibility on his ministers who in time must begin to govern as well as reign. The inevitable end of such a policy was explained by Joseph Royal, editor of Le Métis and star ascendant in the provincial cabinet.

. . . M. Morris se retrancha dans l'irresponsabilité de sa charge, et ne cessa d'indiquer ses ministres comme les seuls possédant l'initiative et la responsabilité. . . .
Dès ce moment il fut facile de prévoir ce qui allait arriver. N'ayant plus personne à sa tête, pour le diriger et le contrôler, le Cabinet devait, en peu de temps, prendre la caractère d'un simple Comité de la Chambre ou les ambitions personnelles, les dissidences et la guerre même ne tardèrent pas à se declarer, si on juge par les echos du dehors. Sous M. Archibald, pareille chose était impossible, car cet homme énergique acceptait franche-ment la responsabilité épineuse de premier ministre de son propre Cabinet, et il agissait comme tel. Sous M. Morris, le premier ministre disparut, et il ne resta plus que l'image froide et impassable de l'autorité royale, le Lieutenant-Gouverneur.
Parfaitement indépendants les uns des autres dans l'administration de leurs départements respectifs, les ministres agirent chacun à sa guise. . . . Cela n'aurait duré deux semaines en Canada; cela dura deux ans à Manitoba. . . .[47]

The movement for responsible government did not come exclusively from above. Even in Archibald's time members of the Executive Council met informally in cabinet and made decisions that were kept from the Lieutenant-Governor. His control of his councillors in the assembly had not been absolute, and it was more his influence with the métis leaders and the clergy that had kept the administration party together. The pressure from below, however, was inspired not by a quest for the

[45]Macdonald Papers, 246, McMicken to Macdonald, Oct. 13, 1872.
[46]See L. H. Thomas, The Struggle for Responsible Government in the North-West Territories 1870–1897 (Toronto, 1956), 62 ff.
[47]Le Métis, Aug. 1, 1874.

vindication of a principle but rather by individual ambition. Morris may have forced the issue, or precipitated it, by his partial abdication of responsbility, but even before this had become apparent Clarke, the Attorney General, had instigated a crisis in council, the object of which was to have himself recognized as Premier. Although it was not then apparent, it would seem in retrospect that Archibald's system had begun to collapse before his retirement. Not only was the factional balance, which had been so precariously effected, being slowly yet inevitably destroyed, but there were also competing individuals within each faction aspiring for the glory and gold of office. While acting as Administrator, Morris had been forced to speak sharply to his cabinet and Macdonald had warned him that "although you have got responsible government nominally, nevertheless, you must be, for the want of one, a paternal despot for some time to come."[48]

Like Archibald, Lieutenant-Governor Morris was forced to shepherd his government through the session of the legislature. Various measures proposed by his council he refused to sanction, others he re-drafted and approved, while many he simply drew up and handed to his ministers. The rôle he was forced to play, the difficulties he faced, and the results he obtained are colourfully described in two letters to Macdonald, then observing the experiment from a safe distance. Three days after the session began McMicken reported:

> Morris is keeping well and up to his work managing the animals composing his Ministry in a way truly wonderful and with a tact and power which his most intimate friends could not have attributed to him the possession of. He has played off Royal against Clarke, Clarke against Royal, McKay against them all, keeping them like Barnum's hobby family. . . . Himself so far yielding no vantage point but in every step fortifying his position for a time coming when he will by force of circumstances be above the necessity of playing the lion tamer or neutralizing the poison fluid in the fangs so often charged for a fatal spring. How he got his Ministers to agree to such measures as are announced by his Speech is really a wonder and for which he deserves the greatest credit. The violent parties are struck dumb—no sore point has been left untouched by the healing measures and so far all betokens well. . . .[49]

Morris added detail if not colour:

> The speech has demoralized the opposition in and out of the house and pleased the people. It taxed all my skill to keep my team together. The split in the French is now so decided and Clarke is leader in the house of the (loyal) natural party and Royal of the other party.
> Clarke wanted to be premier and was backed by the other three. Royal

[48]Macdonald Papers, 522, Macdonald to Morris, Dec. 9, 1872.
[49]Ibid., 246, McMicken to Macdonald, Feb. 8, 1872.

saw in it an opportunity to go out and break up the Government. There is now no premier. Royal consulted the bishop . . . and notified me of his intentions.

I did not choose to have a break and sent for Clarke and told him I could not change the understanding on which the Government was formed but would do so if a change of Government took place, and he must be content with being the recognized leader of the Government in the House. He yielded and behaved well as he has done ever since I came here. So I told Council how I had arranged it, and all went on as before.[50]

Thus Morris had committed himself to a constitutional change as soon as possible. He welcomed the prospect of being relieved of "the constant *test* of keeping the Government together, whose personal feuds and antagonisms are so great that I am weary of constantly whipping them into line."[51]

For over a year the situation remained unchanged. Morris was often away from the capital and deeply immersed in other official business, for he was also Lieutenant-Governor of the Northwest Territories. Members of the cabinet felt less and less the firm supervision that Archibald had wielded and that Morris had for a short while maintained. Crisis followed crisis, yet none was sufficient to force a wholesale reconstruction. Left to themselves the ministers intrigued against each other, secretly and openly, in the press as in the parishes, the latent feuds always near the breaking point. By the spring of 1874 the end was imminent. Royal, the political leader of the *métis* and the engineer of the crisis, briefed Riel:

. . . la Législature se réunit le 2 juillet, et il est très probable que le ministère sera défait. Tout le monde est aujourd'hui d'accord que le manque de responsabilité ministérielle est une des causes de nos maux depuis 14 à 15 mois. Le système inauguré par M. Archibald était sage, je crois, et a produit sous lui d'assez bons résultats: malheureusement, M. Morris n'a pas voulu ou n'a pas pu le comprendre; de là bien des choses regrettables que vous connaissiez aussi bien que moi.[52]

When the legislature met on July 3, 1874, the administration was defeated at once on a vote of confidence.[53] Royal immediately sent a letter of resignation to the Lieutenant-Governor, in which he stated that "ayant été appelé au Conseil par l'Hon. M. Archibald, votre prédécesseur, c'est entre les mains de Votre Excellence que je crois de voir placer ma résignation."[54] Clarke, the government leader in the

[50]*Ibid.*, 252, Morris to Macdonald, Feb. 7, 1873.
[51]Morris Papers, Morris to Campbell, Oct. 22, 1873.
[52]Riel Papers, folio 3–L, Royal to Riel, June 18, 1874.
[53]Manitoba, Legislative Assembly, *Journals*, 1874, 30.
[54]Morris Papers, Royal to Morris, July 3, 1874.

assembly, declared that he would not resign in the face of a vote concocted in the back room of a tavern and sprung by surprise, but would proceed with the business of the session. Morris refused to permit such an action, however, and Clarke resigned.[55] "The position was very embarrassing," wrote Morris, "as I practically had *not the power of dissolution.*"[56] A new redistribution bill had proven to be completely unsatisfactory, a measure for the abolition of the Legislative Council was on the agenda, and there were no Voters' Lists. The *Free Press Weekly* of July 11 succinctly summed up the Lieutenant-Governor's dilemma: "Public sentiment he must have been aware demanded just such legislation as that promised by the defeated Government, and it therefore became necessary to construct from the Opposition a Government that would adopt and carry out the avowed policy of those they were supplanting."

Morris realized that the normal practice, when there was no recognized leader of the opposition, was to call on the mover of the resolution of want of confidence, but by such a course, he informed Prime Minister Mackenzie, he could not have achieved his ends. For on one point he was determined: he was going to abandon Archibald's paternal system and find a Premier, not a council. After consulting the Speaker of the assembly and other leading figures, Morris asked M. A. Girard to form a new administration. Morris met his new council on July 8 when he made it clear that Girard was Premier and that the others belonged to the cabinet as a result of his advice. "I am glad that responsible government in its perfect form is at length in force in the north west," he wrote at once to the Prime Minister.[57] In an official communication to the Secretary of State, Morris was more explicit: "I would call your attention to the fact that in forming the Government I did so through the intervention of a premier thus introducing responsible Government in its modern type into the Province. The previous ministry was selected personally by my predecessor and none of its members were recognized as first minister."[58]

Thus, four years after Manitoba had been admitted as a province within the federal system and had been endowed with full powers of responsible self-government in keeping with that status, the constitutional transformation had been effected. The responsibility for maintaining effective government, which Archibald had necessarily and

---

[55]*Ibid.*, Clarke to Morris, July 4, 1874.
[56]*Ibid.*, Morris to Mackenzie, July 10, 1874.
[57]Morris Papers, Morris to Mackenzie, July 10, 1874.
[58]PAM, Lieutenant-Governor's Dispatch Book, Morris to the Secretary of State, July 13, 1874.

willingly assumed, was at last thrown upon a Premier responsible to the legislature. Nonetheless, political forces do not always change as quickly as constitutional forms; and in the absence of party lines, in an intense political atmosphere where personal feuds and petty ambitions were the rule rather than the exception, with society relatively immature and standards of political conduct relatively low, and with English and French elements competing for ascendancy or security, the position of the Lieutenant-Governor was to remain for many years influential and his opinion or action often decisive.[59]

Meanwhile a similar transition had been effected in British Columbia in less time and with much less trouble. British Columbia was in every way better fitted for its new status than Manitoba had been. Although provincial society was neither mature nor cohesive there were no racial or religious antagonisms to obstruct the natural working of representative institutions. Partially representative government had existed for some time in the Crown Colony and, peopled as it was from Great Britain, Canada, and the United States, there was to be found a reasonable amount of political experience. An administrative machine that had extended its sway over the whole colony, although

[59]Although he had given up his position as Premier and head of the cabinet Morris continued to attend council meetings. Since the end of Archibald's term more and more work had been done in cabinet, council meetings were less frequent, and the intervention of the Lieutenant-Governor less apparent. From the beginning of 1874 there are increasing signs that Morris may not always have been in attendance, and one notes the use of the phrase "by and with the advice of the Executive Council." After the selection of a Premier the council had a head, and although the forms were retained it is quite apparent that the Lieutenant-Governor was not always present. On many occasions, however, it is obvious from the council records that he did attend: to make cabinet changes, to discuss matters affecting the Dominion government, Indian policy, and other general subjects. That a close relationship continued to exist is suggested by the fact that in May 1876 the Lieutenant-Governor's secretary was made Clerk of the Executive Council. Using the Executive Council records in the Lieutenant-Governor's papers Milligan states that his attendance was last recorded on May 31, 1876. The official records of the council, however, show that the form was retained long after that date. In November 1877 when Alexander Begg became Clerk of the Council he neglected to enter the Lieutenant-Governor as present, but "His Honour" was carefully entered by another hand. It is quite obvious, however, that Morris had ceased to attend under normal circumstances, and it is quite likely that the absence of council records in his official papers roughly dates the final withdrawal. In November 1877 he informed Macdonald that Cauchon, his successor, would not cause the local government much trouble, particularly because "I broke up some time ago, the paternal system of Government, and the Council now meet by themselves. I have had all sorts of people scolding me about representation, but I have adhered to my policy." (Macdonald Papers, 252, Morris to Macdonald, Nov. 22, 1877; see also Milligan, "The Lieutenant-Governorship in Manitoba 1870–1882," unpublished M.A. thesis, University of Manitoba, 1948, 189; PAM, Lieutenant-Governor's Papers; Executive Council Office, Winnipeg, Executive Council records.) Later Governors attended on occasion. Schultz frequently called council meetings in his office or in the chamber, but these were never entered in the formal register of council meetings.

spasmodically perhaps on the outskirts, was operating continuously if not smoothly. The colonial Governor was still the most powerful figure in the colony but the basis was there for responsible self-government. For some years in fact the familiar demands for responsible government had been heard in British Columbia, and Governor Musgrave informed the Colonial Secretary that "the most prominent agitators for confederation" were "a small knot of Canadians who hope that it may be possible to make fuller representative institutions and Responsible Government part of the new arrangements." While commending confederation, Musgrave condemned responsible government on the grounds that it was "inapplicable to a Community so small and so constituted as this—a sparse population scattered over a vast area."[60] Provincial status inevitably meant responsible government, however, and diligent official that he was Musgrave passed an act in the spring of 1871 that provided for a fully representative Legislative Assembly and an Executive Council selected from among its members. This did not necessarily mean that responsible government would be introduced as soon as British Columbia entered the federation; indeed, provincial status was achieved on July 20, 1871, but it was some time before the new form of government was established in practice.

When the time came to select the first Lieutenant-Governor, Macdonald and his colleagues were seriously hampered by their ignorance of British Columbia and British Columbians. As an intimate knowledge of the province was considered to be essential only a resident of the province could be appointed, for no one in eastern Canada knew anything at all of the west coast. When in Ottawa negotiating the terms of union, Joseph Trutch had shown himself to be a zealous and knowledgeable advocate of the transcontinental railway, and in a number of ways had impressed Macdonald and Cartier. As Chief Commissioner of Lands and Works in the colonial government and as government surveyor for a number of years Trutch had an unsurpassed acquaintance with the province and its people and had demonstrated a capacity for administration. Trutch reluctantly accepted the appointment. Macdonald foresaw no complications in British Columbia: "He will have an easier time than you have had," he informed Archibald, "but his task will not be nearly so interesting."[61]

Trutch's appointment was only moderately well received in British

[60]PABC, Lieutenant-Governor's Dispatch Book, Musgrave to Granville, Oct. 3, 1869.
[61]Macdonald Papers, 519, Macdonald to Archibald, July 12, 1871.

Columbia. The Lieutenant-Governor was placed in the difficult position of having to initiate a system of government that, as councillor and negotiator, he had strenuously opposed. Macdonald had assured the British Columbians that Trutch was "fully prepared to administer Public Affairs under the principles of Responsible Government."[62] But his assurances did not stop the grumbling and on his arrival in Victoria from Ottawa, where he had been long closeted with Macdonald and Cartier, the Lieutenant-Governor took the first opportunity to outline his proposed course and to calm unnecessary fears. After referring to his earlier opposition to responsible government he publicly stated that "having now undertaken to carry that system into operation in our Province it is not only a matter of duty but a point of honor for me to strive to the utmost to ensure its successful working." He pointed out, however, that an immediate change was inexpedient.

I regret that under the peculiar transition state in which we now are I do not see the practicability of immediately forming a responsible ministry. In the first place because there are no constitutional representatives from whom such a ministry can be selected, and also because it would be a presumption in me, as I think, to anticipate the votes of the people of British Columbia by naming any one individual as possessing their confidence beyond others.

I propose therefore, as I am now advised, and unless a necessity not now foreseen should occur, not to make any selection until the election which will take place at the earliest practicable date, and in the meantime to take mainly on myself the responsibility of carrying on the necessary current business of the country, trusting that my action whilst so doing will be favorably accepted.[63]

Disappointed politicians, already grasping for the spoils of office, complained a little, even though Trutch made it clear that few appointments would be made until a responsible ministry had been formed. But his was a logical course: "I quite approve," wrote Macdonald, "it puts your position in a proper light and beyond mistake."[64]

There were no political parties deserving of the name in British Columbia—there were to be none for over a quarter of a century—and Trutch faced a thorny problem in choosing men to assist him until the elections. He avoided the charge of partiality (or hoped he had) by appointing two members of the old colonial council to temporary positions in his first Executive Council. A lawyer was essential and Trutch succeeded in persuading John Foster McCreight to take office

[62]*Ibid.*, Macdonald to Helmcken, July 17, 1871.
[63]*Victoria British Colonist*, Aug. 16, 1871.
[64]Macdonald Papers, 519, Macdonald to Trutch, Sept. 12, 1871.

as Attorney General, a man who he believed commanded "the respect and confidence of the community to a greater extent than any other members of the profession—although he has hitherto consistently abstained from politics. . . ."[65] In making the appointments the Lieutenant-Governor repeatedly stressed that they were only "for the time being and until the elections, which will be held at the earliest possible period, admit of more permanent arrangements being made."[66]

Premier as well as Lieutenant-Governor, Trutch set his ministers to work preparing for the elections, establishing electoral divisions and appointing returning officers. Other extraneous matters consumed his time and energy as well: a number of Indian tribes were upset, not knowing exactly what the change implied for them; the San Juan Island controversy had blossomed once again; the British government seemed determined to move the last naval vessel from Esquimalt and Trutch was equally determined to prevent this; and to complicate matters still further the province was bankrupt. While the Lieutenant-Governor dealt with these problems all other eyes were focused on the forthcoming elections. "I think I can manage to get some decent men to take a hand in the government," said Trutch, "although most of our representatives will be *queer kittle cattle* I fear."[67] He apparently took no active part in the elections—there was nothing like Archibald's "administration candidates" in any case—although in view of Amor de Cosmos' election cry that it was "no treason, no public wrong to ignore the nominees of Governor Trutch" it is probable that he used his personal influence in McCreight's interest.[68] Much to the Lieutenant-Governor's satisfaction McCreight's standing at the head of the poll in Victoria, by far the most important constituency, meant that he could logically be asked to form the first permanent administration, and on his recommendation Trutch appointed two other members of the Legislative Assembly to the Executive Council. The Lieutenant-Governor may have had a share in the formation of the cabinet, but McCreight was recognized as Premier and the choice of ministers as his responsibility.[69]

Trutch's satisfaction with the first provincial administration was not shared by the editors of the two Victoria papers, both members of the legislature who desired a place in the sun. These men, de Cosmos of the *Standard* and John Robson of the *British Colonist*, were prob-

[65]*Ibid.*, 278, Trutch to Macdonald, Aug. 22, 1871.
[66]PABC, Lieutenant-Governor's Letterbook, Trutch to Good, Aug. 17, 1871.
[67]Macdonald Papers, 278, Trutch to Macdonald, Oct. 9, 1871.
[68]*Victoria Daily Standard*, Nov. 21, 1871.
[69]PABC, Crease Papers, Crease to Frank, Nov. 13, 1871.

ably the two strongest political figures in the province; both had been instrumental in securing federation and both had long advocated responsible government. The three cabinet ministers, on the contrary, had little political experience, all three (and the Lieutenant-Governor) had opposed responsible government, and two of them had even spoken strongly against federation. In many ways the cabinet was weak and vulnerable, and there was some truth in Robson's petulant assertion that "the present Ministers will be cob-webs for the next House to sweep away."[70]

Lieutenant-Governor Trutch continued to guide the ship of state until the assembly met in February 1872. The Minutes of the Executive Council reveal his presence at every meeting. Less formally he shared with McCreight and his colleagues the preparation of a legislative programme for the session. All the while Trutch was uneasy as to his own position and finally sought Macdonald's advice.

I wish you would also if you please give me a hint as to how far my speech in opening the House is supposed to express my own opinions or to be simply an expression of the policy of my responsible Ministers, as I confess I am somewhat puzzled on this point—of course I know how this would be in the House of Parliament at home—or at Ottawa but are we under the same understanding here?[71]

In an apologetic letter six weeks later he explained that "I am so inexperienced as indeed are all in this Province in the practice of Responsible Government . . . that I step as carefully and as guardedly as I can—and while teaching others I feel constantly my own extreme need of instruction on the subject. . . ."[72]

Macdonald replied that if a responsible ministry had been formed before the legislature assembled the speech should be on advice. "This is the Constitutional doctrine," he rightly observed, although "at the same time from your position you can exercise a legitimate influence in pressing upon them the various topics that should be mentioned or avoided."[73] After the elections and the formation of the McCreight administration Macdonald congratulated the Lieutenant-Governor on what appeared to be a notable achievement. With the Victoria papers before him, however, he naturally had some doubts as to the stability and permanence of the new government, and, afraid perhaps that Trutch might be inclined to play an over-zealous role, took an early opportunity to deliver another lecture on responsible government.

[70]*Victoria British Colonist*, Nov. 15, 1871.
[71]Macdonald Papers, 278, Trutch to Macdonald, Oct. 9, 1871.
[72]*Ibid.*, Nov. 21, 1871.
[73]*Ibid.*, 519, Macdonald to Trutch, Oct. 27, 1871.

"When your Legislature meets," wrote the Prime Minister, "you will ascertain whether they have the confidence of the people or not, and you will gracefully accept any Ministry that may be indicated by a vote of that august body." If the government were defeated Trutch was instructed to send for the leader of the opposition or if there were none for the "mover of the Resolution which amounts to a vote of want of Confidence. . . ." "Give him Carte Blanche as to the individuals composing his Council and accept with perfect equanimity his nomination. The responsibility is his and not yours, and it will be for the Legislature to approve or reject the new Government."[74] Macdonald had obviously no desire to be embarrassed by the actions of another Lieutenant-Governor; nor did he want to have the Lieutenant-Governor, a Dominion officer, closely involved in the struggle for political power that was bound to take place.

Ably and persistently aided by the Lieutenant-Governor the cabinet drafted a legislative programme that pleased even the factious opposition, and Trutch's Speech—for in the end it was his—was described as "an able State Paper . . . bold and liberal . . . loyal and statesmanlike."[75] Trutch took all the credit that was due him. "I have done all I could to place My Ministry fairly before the House and before the country," he boasted, "and unless they make any compromising mistakes there is every reason to expect that they will continue to be supported as they now are by at least two thirds of the Members."[76] Once the session began Trutch seems to have considered that his essential task was almost completed. At council meetings, which he attended as a matter of course, few political matters were discussed and the Lieutenant-Governor seldom interfered in domestic political affairs. All the work of local government was done in cabinet.

Although ineffectively and unimaginatively led in the assembly, the McCreight administration struggled through the session. In the absence of party divisions or even factional discipline the government depended on a fluctuating support. Some bills, obviously cabinet measures, were introduced as private members' bills, and in this way was avoided the stigma attached to the defeat of the government. Generally fortunate enough to secure good majorities, McCreight refused to accept an adverse vote as a sign of lack of confidence. Robson and de Cosmos vigorously attacked this system in their papers and the Premier was finally forced to declare that any interference with the estimates would be tantamount to a want of confidence resolution. The assembly heeled

[74]Ibid., Dec. 18, 1871.   [75]Victoria British Colonist, Feb. 17, 1872.
[76]Macdonald Papers, 278, Trutch to Macdonald, Feb. 20, 1872.

and passed the budget unscathed. The session was as successful as could have been expected and Macdonald hastened to congratulate his officer: ". . . the Province of British Columbia may now be considered as fairly launched, with a responsible crew on board; so that hereafter the duties of Lieutenant-Governor will be rather of a sinecurist character."[77]

Judge Crease wrote early in May 1872 that "Trutch still runs the mill . . . it's a one man government still (in disguise)," but there is little evidence to suggest that Trutch dominated the cabinet.[78] No doubt his influence and advice were often important and were often sought. Formal council meetings were held at which he presided, but only routine matters or subjects peculiarly within his competence as a federal officer—defence, Indian affairs, relations with the Dominion government—were discussed. Nevertheless, it was generally believed in the province that he was still the power behind the throne, so to speak, and Robson attempted to raise the cry of irresponsible government that he had heard in Upper Canada as a young boy. "The Premier has been dancing attendance on his 'master,' as if he were a mere lacky. There is not a Minister who, even if he had an opinion of his own (an extremely problematical proposition), would dare to express it. And this is called Responsible Government."[79] Trutch informed Macdonald of the attacks being made upon him and pointed out how unfair and inaccurate they were:

And I may further tell you that although during the initiation of this new system of government in this Province and up till the end of the Session of the Assembly I took of necessity a more direct part in the management of public affairs than under ordinary circumstances belongs to a Lieutenant-Governor—during the past six months I have kept carefully aloof from the discussions and confidences of the Ministry in their political or party matters being well aware that it is not expedient that I should be or be supposed to be—a partizan in such matters within the Province.[80]

[77]Ibid., 520, Macdonald to Trutch, April 16, 1872.
[78]Crease Papers, Crease to Langevin, May 1, 1872.
[79]Victoria British Colonist, Nov. 10, 1872.
[80]Macdonald Papers, 278, Trutch to Macdonald, Oct. 24, 1872. As soon as he appointed a responsible government Trutch began his withdrawal. Council regulations commenced in November 1871 and completed in December clearly contemplated the work of government being done in cabinet or committee and forwarded as minutes or orders for the Lieutenant-Governor's approval. From the spring of 1872 on, meetings of the Executive Council were held with decreasing frequency. Within a year they had fallen to about three a month and in 1874 only eighteen meetings are recorded in the council minutes. At many of these meetings the Lieutenant-Governor appears only to have given his formal assent to a batch of orders, while often it is merely recorded that the Lieutenant-Governor had given his assent to orders since the last meeting. At others, however, he appears to have read and discussed dispatches from Ottawa concerning the railway dispute and

The Lieutenant-Governor was in fact becoming bored. His office he found "less interesting as its duties are less responsible and give less occupation. . . . It presents no inducements for the exercise of mental energy." It was "an honourable leise [sic] becoming and acceptable" to one of advanced years, but "tedious and irksome to one at my time of life—of naturally active mind, and habituated for years past to such exciting business avocations as are characteristic of all new countries. . . ."[81]

The Legislative Assembly assembled for its second session on December 17, 1872, and the *British Colonist* of that morning made its final bitter attack on the McCreight administration. "The Ministers are the appointees of an appointed Governor. They are not the legitimate offspring of the new constitution. They are the results of accidents,—peradventure the offspring of personal prejudice." Behind this attack was a Robson–de Cosmos alliance to defeat the government, a design of which McCreight and Trutch were fully aware. Rather than avoid a crisis the Premier deliberately inserted a statement in the throne speech in order to call forth a resolution of non-confidence. Defeated by one vote, the Premier resigned. There was no recognized leader of the opposition, nor did the mover of the resolution seem a likely prospect for office. The Lieutenant-Governor sent at once for de Cosmos who consented to form a new administration. The selection was as wise as any that could have been made, although it was doubtful whether he could retain a majority in the assembly. As Trutch wrote:

There will be a grand fight throughout the Session I expect as the House is divided into three nearly equal sections, McCreight's, De Cosmos' and Robson's the latter having (to his infinite disappointment) not been in-

other matters. On one occasion his presence is attested by the summary of a conversation that took place. Only eight meetings were held in 1875: at three Trutch tabled and discussed correspondence concerning the Pacific railway; at another the Speech from the Throne received his approval; at a fifth he urged the government to protest the removal of a Royal Navy vessel from Esquimalt; once he wished to discuss with the Attorney General the difference between Lieutenant-Governor and Lieutenant-Governor in Council, showing perhaps some concern for constitutional and legal forms; and on one occasion he wished to discuss with council the validity of orders sent to him over the signature of the Provincial Secretary. Trutch continued to attend occasional council meetings until he left office. His successor, A. N. Richards, appears not to have assented to orders in a formal Executive Council, and if he ever had occasion to discuss matters with his ministers apparently did it informally. The records of the Executive Council become simply a register of orders and reports of the Committee of the Executive Council. It might be noted that because of his support of the Mackenzie administration on the railway dispute Richards was virtually boycotted by his governments. (See in PABC the following sources: Minutes of the Executive Council, State Books, Lieutenant-Governor's Correspondence, Register of Executive Council Reports, Provincial Secretary's Correspondence, Miscellaneous Executive Papers.)

[81]Macdonald Papers, 278, Trutch to Macdonald, Nov. 25, 1872.

cluded by De Cosmos in his Cabinet. Whether De Cosmos' Ministry will stand depends on McCreight as Robson's friends will oppose bitterly. I fancy McCreight will in general help De Cosmos—although on some questions he must with his friends vote against him—and if the Robson wing of the House join McCreight on any of these points as I think they will try to do De Cosmos will be in a minority. . . . My great object, [concluded the Lieutenant-Governor] will be to maintain the strictest impartiality.[82]

This incident may be taken as the final step, the convincing proof, that the transition to responsible government had been made. The Lieutenant-Governor willingly accepted the defeat of the government he had appointed to office and of a Premier of whom he thought a good deal; he accepted as Premier one who had been a political opponent for many years and who had recently vigorously attacked him in the press; and this at a time when it would have been an easy matter indeed to assist McCreight in a reconstruction of the government—an easier matter actually than the formation of a new administration. What is significant in this period of transition is not that the Lieutenant-Governor exercised considerable political influence for eighteen months on the outside, but that he ceased to be politically effective so soon. In the absence of organized political parties, with the political scene dominated by personal feuds and factional rivalries, in a society where few men would refuse office under any circumstances, it would have been relatively easy for a Lieutenant-Governor of Trutch's ability to play a key rôle for a much longer period. Many Lieutenant-Governors in the history of the office have attempted to do so in much less auspicious circumstances.

[82]*Ibid.*, Dec. 31, 1872.

CHAPTER FOUR

THE SELECTION OF A PROVINCIAL PREMIER

THE ONLY discretionary power of the Crown seldom to be questioned is that of personally selecting the first minister. The Lieutenant-Governor's foremost responsibility is to see that the government of the province is carried on, and upon the demise of one administration he must immediately seek a successor. Theoretically his discretion is unlimited but in practice the selection of a Premier is usually automatic. The individual chosen must be able to form a ministry that will be supported in the legislature; this principle alone narrowly restricts his choice and generally presents him with one man to whom he must look. Situations do arise, however, where the simple and well-known precedents and conventions do not apply: where there is no majority party, or where it is leaderless; where an alliance of groups has forced the retirement of the government but is itself without cohesion, direction, or a recognized leader; where a Premier resigns or dies and leaves a disputed succession. Such cases are common wherever cabinet government exists, with the result that the discretionary power of the Crown is more than a fiction. This is particularly true in the Canadian provinces, for the recognized conventions, which grew up in a relatively stable two-party system, are more frequently inapplicable. Political parties have been immature and unstable, sometimes extremely shadowy organizations and occasionally non-existent. Party discipline has been weak and ineffective and a profusion of personal splinter groups has often been the rule rather than the exception. Third and fourth parties have periodically mushroomed overnight, upsetting the traditional two-party structure and creating unusual and difficult political and constitutional problems.

If only two parties are in the field the Lieutenant-Governor's task raises no problems. On the defeat of the government, whether in the legislature or in an election, the leader of the opposition must be asked to form an administration. No Lieutenant-Governor has overlooked the recognized opposition leader; Chapleau, to whom it was once suggested, rightly declared that "ce serait se moquer les traditions representatives."[1] If the party is leaderless at the moment of victory

[1] PAC, Tarte Papers, 13, Chapleau to Tarte, May 17, 1897; see also PAC, Laurier Papers, 45, Chapleau to Laurier, May 15, 1897.

88

the hierarchy or the members-elect usually meet at once to elect a leader. Until this has been done the Lieutenant-Governor is wise to take no action and to ask the retiring administration to remain in office. There is nothing to be gained by a premature attempt to anticipate the selection.

Rather than wait for the members-elect of the anti-Confederation party in Nova Scotia to select a leader after their smashing victory in September 1867, Sir Hastings Doyle sought the advice of Joseph Howe, the dean of the party but not the leader of the provincial wing. Howe advised the Lieutenant-Governor to ask R. A. McHeffy, a member of the Legislative Council, to form a government. Doyle followed this advice and McHeffy undertook to form a ministry. The latter soon discovered that the party was not prepared to accept him as leader, however, and following "a 'Caucus' of Members and Supporters of the Government" William Annand informed Doyle that he was to be the Premier and presented the Lieutenant-Governor with the names of his colleagues in the cabinet.[2] There was some criticism of Doyle's action and the retiring Premier asked permission to inform the legislature that he had not been responsible for the selection of McHeffy.[3] Fifteen years later, following the defeat of the Conservatives, Lieutenant-Governor Archibald asked Albert Gayton, the only Liberal with previous cabinet experience, to form an administration. Gayton accepted the responsibility but finding that he could not secure sufficient support within the party informed the Lieutenant-Governor that W. T. Pipes had been elected as party leader and suggested that he be called.[4]

The most difficult problem arises when the two-party system has broken down and no party is returned with a clear majority. Frequently under such circumstances the government chooses to test its strength in the legislature. But if it resigns without doing so convention suggests that the Lieutenant-Governor must call upon the leader of the largest opposition party. If the person so selected declines to form a ministry or is unable to do so the Lieutenant-Governor may then exercise wide discretionary powers. This in part explains the action of Lieutenant-Governor McInnes of British Columbia in 1898. The leaders of both opposition factions had publicly refused to work under the other. Accepting their public statements as valid and without asking either to form an administration, McInnes chose Robert Beaven, an old political

---

[2]PAC, G 21, file 24B, Doyle to Monck, Feb. 13, 1868; PAC, Howe Papers, 4, Doyle to Howe, Oct. 1, 1867; *ibid.*, 9, Howe to Doyle, Oct. 5, 1867.

[3]PANS, Lieutenant-Governor's Correspondence, Blanchard to Doyle, Feb. 6, 1868; Nova Scotia, Legislative Assembly, *Debates*, 1868, 28, 55, 56.

[4]Halifax press, July 18–Aug. 3, 1882; PAC, Macdonald Papers, 117, Richey to Macdonald, Aug. 2, 1884.

warhorse who for some years had not been able to win a seat in the legislature, in the hope that the two groups could combine under his leadership.[5]

The convention that the Lieutenant-Governor is bound to look first to the leader of the largest party has been questioned. The Conservative government led by Sir William Hearst was overwhelmingly defeated in the Ontario election of 1919. But with forty-five United Farmers, twenty-nine Liberals, twenty-five Conservatives, and eleven Labour it was quite evident that no party had a majority. To further complicate matters the United Farmers had no leader. The Lieutenant-Governor, Sir John Hendrie, foolishly thought aloud.

Now we have two parties without leaders and two with leaders neither of which can form a government that would have a majority support in the House. We have two class parties, represented and elected to represent certain classes in the community. It is entirely different to former situations where, with two parties, the one in power was defeated and the defeated Prime Minister advising the Lieutenant-Governor to ask the Leader of the other party to form a Cabinet. . . . Under the circumstances it is my opinion that I could call any man in the House or out of it, who could obtain the support of a majority in the House, and ask him to form a government.[6]

Even after time for reflection a writer in the *Canadian Annual Review* agreed that the Lieutenant-Governor could "constitutionally call any leader who showed a reasonable chance of forming a coalition or upon whom he was advised to call by the outgoing Prime Minister."[7] The Liberal leader, H. H. Dewart, developed his own constitutional conventions to suit the need of the moment: the Lieutenant-Governor had no discretion whatsoever; before the election there had been two parties in the legislature, the Liberal and the Conservative; one had been defeated and the other *ipso facto* must have won. The "natural course" was for the Lieutenant-Governor to call upon the "successful leader" of the Liberal party to form a government. "It will be time enough to consider the calling-in of an outsider when it appears that it will be impossible for the groups to get together which joined in the common cause of establishing popular government."[8] This alliance, of

[5]See chap. v.
[6]Toronto *Globe*, Oct. 23, 1919.   [7]1919, 666.
[8]Toronto *Globe*, Oct. 22, 1919. Dewart's claim was of course the lament of one who had seen almost certain victory snatched from his grasp by the sudden rise of a third party. In British Columbia the C.C.F. had battered away at the coalition government for years. Just as they had the ministry reeling the Social Credit party emerged and, as a result of the government's weakness, won the election of 1952 by one seat, and that after a tantalizing recount which if it had gone to the C.C.F. would have made it the largest party. Although it was never officially supported by any individual or party, there was a "feeling in the air" that the C.C.F. deserved office.

course, was to be under the "successful leader" of the Liberal party. While all three statements were wrong, Dewart's was absurd. His success was indeed of an unusual variety, for not only had he failed to profit by the Conservative collapse but his party had actually lost one seat.

Spokesmen for the United Farmers alone recognized the proper course to be followed by the Lieutenant-Governor; since they were the largest party and had been promised the support of the Labour group, thus having a guaranteed majority, the Lieutenant-Governor was bound to wait until they had selected a leader and then to ask him to form a government. And this was in fact what Hendrie did after his momentary and perhaps regretted aberration in constitutional speculation. Even without the promise of Labour support the U.F.O. leader, when chosen, was clearly entitled to attempt to form an administration.

Lieutenant-Governor McInnes faced a much more difficult problem following the defeat of the Martin government in the 1900 elections in British Columbia. There were no provincial party lines and owing to the disintegration of such groups as had existed there was no outstanding figure among the opposition members-elect. McInnes eventually selected James Dunsmuir, a man of means but without political experience or an organized following, because he "believed that that gentleman represented the policy which the people had declared for, and that he was in a better position than any other member to harmonize the contending factions of the opposition."[9] McInnes' freedom of choice was practically unlimited. There was no guarantee that Dunsmuir would be able to command a majority in the Legislative Assembly.

A defeat in the legislature usually indicates that an organized opposition exists ready and willing to assume the responsibility of governing. In the event of such a defeat the Lieutenant-Governor merely calls upon the recognized leader of the opposition to form a new government. It may be, however, that no such individual exists. Trutch had pointed this out to Macdonald and had received the following advice:

If your present Ministry is defeated you will of course send for the person who acts as leader of the Opposition. If there be no organized Opposition with a leader, but only a number of individuals dissatisfied with the existing Ministry, and each acting on his own hook, I think your course will be to assume that the mover of the Resolution which amounts to a vote of want of Confidence, is the man to be sent for, if his Resolution carries.[10]

Macdonald's advice was probably the best and only advice that could

[9]C.S.P., 1900, no. 174, McInnes to the Governor-General, June 14, 1900; Vancouver World, June 26, 1900. See chap. v for the necessary background.
[10]Macdonald Papers, 519, Macdonald to Trutch, Dec. 18, 1871.

have been given under the circumstances, and it was undoubtedly based on the assumption that the most powerful figure among the opposition would have led the attack on the government and thus have introduced the motion of non-confidence. Trutch did not follow Macdonald's advice in 1872, however, for the latter assumption was unjustified. He selected the most able man from the opposition benches rather than the vigorous but unstable member who had introduced the resolution of censure. Four years later he selected a man who had neither introduced the want of confidence motion nor spoken at any length on it.[11] Lieutenant-Governor Cornwall asked William Smythe to form a government in 1883 not because he had introduced the vote of censure on the Beaven administration but because most of the opposition members seemed to look to him as their leader. Of McInnes' selection of Joseph Martin in February 1900 Sir Richard Cartwright wrote: "His selection of Martin in the first place and his passing over the recognized leader of the opposition is at variance with all consti-tutional usage and is a monstrous precedent."[12] The Ontario Grit was talking nonsense: although Martin had not introduced the motion on which the C. A. Semlin government was defeated, he was unques-tionably the man who had secured the defeat; and since there was no "recognized leader of the opposition" the choice of Martin was as logical as that of anyone else.[13] Three years later the leading Liberal in opposition led the attack on the E. G. Prior government, but the Lieutenant-Governor asked Richard McBride, a Conservative, to form a government after the dismissal of Prior, presumably believing that he was the strongest figure among the opposition.

In New Brunswick where, as in British Columbia, party lines did not exist for many years after Confederation, two precedents supported Macdonald's dictum. An independent member was able to have his candidate elected Speaker in 1871 and it was to him that the Lieu-tenant-Governor turned when, later in the session, the government resigned.[14] In 1883 Andrew Blair persuaded the assembly to pass a resolution of non-confidence and when the ministry resigned Blair was asked to form a new administration.

When the Lieutenant-Governor of Ontario spoke in 1919 of the

[11]In 1876 Trutch picked A. C. Elliot to form a government. Elliot had recently emerged as one of the most able opponents of the government and had won an important victory in Victoria, the most important constituency in the province.
[12]Laurier Papers, 150, Cartwright to Laurier, April 7, 1900.
[13]See chap. v, 136.
[14]New Brunswick, Legislative Assembly, Journals, 1871, 11; LLNB, Lieutenant-Governor's Correspondence, Wilmot to the Secretary of State for the Provinces, Feb. 22, 1871.

retiring Premier "advising" as to his successor he was voicing what appears to be a unique, but apparently commonly accepted, Canadian variation of established constitutional conventions. In all probability if it is not clear who should be summoned the Lieutenant-Governor will seek the opinion of the defeated minister, but "if there is one firmly established point in British constitutional practice, it is that a retiring Prime Minister has no right even to offer advice as to his successor, let alone have it accepted."[15] Hearst realized this in 1919, even if Hendrie did not, and informed Sir John Willison that "he could not offer advice to the Lieutenant-Governor unless he were asked to do so."[16] Hearst however was an exception and Lieutenant-Governor Hendrie's statement could be buttressed by three score more—by politicians, by journalists, by academics, and by Lieutenant-Governors—in a similar vein.

At times this novel doctrine has been pushed even further. It has been said that if a Premier cannot with a clear conscience recommend a successor he must stay in office or dissolve. Mackenzie King's declaration in 1926 that he "could not assume the responsibility of advising" Lord Byng to send for Mr. Meighen is well known.[17] But King has not been alone. Following the Liberal defeat in Saskatchewan in 1929 the Attorney General, in an attempt to explain why the government had not resigned, stated that "we could not recommend a successor. It was impossible honestly to recommend under the circumstances that the Lieutenant-Governor should call on Dr. Anderson to form a government." "It is only the duty of the Government to resign and recommend a successor," he continued, "provided the Government is entirely satisfied that the successor it recommends can carry on the affairs of the province in the legislature."[18] The followers of Mr. George Drew in Ontario once supported this doctrine. Since Premier Drew was not prepared to assume the responsibility of advising the Lieutenant-Governor to call to his councils a Socialist cabinet led by Mr. Jolliffe, he asked for a dissolution following his defeat in the legislature in 1945.[19] It should hardly be necessary to point out that the responsibility for finding a successor rests on the Lieutenant-Governor and the responsibility for forming a new administration that can secure

[15]E. A. Forsey, "Mr. King and Parliamentary Government," *Canadian Journal of Economics and Political Science*, XVII (Nov., 1951), 451.
[16]A. H. U. Colquhoun, *Press, Politics and People; the Life and Letters of Sir John Willison* (Toronto, 1935), 280, Willison to Byng, Sept. 2, 1921.
[17]Forsey, *loc. cit.*
[18]Saskatchewan, Legislative Assembly, *Sessional Papers*, 1929–30, 13, 19.
[19]E. A. Forsey, "Constitutional Issues in Ontario," *Canadian Forum*, May, 1945; Toronto press, March 22, 1945 ff.; see also chap. VI, 152.

the confidence of the legislature rests on the individual selected. The defeated Premier, by the very fact of his defeat, has lost the right to advise.

On the other hand if the Premier resigns while still retaining the confidence of the legislature, whether for personal or party reasons, common sense suggests that his advice would be asked and probably followed. It is true of course, as Macdonald declared when asked for advice on the point, that "the Crown may or may not ask the retiring Premier whom he should send for and when the advice is given he may or may not follow it." The Prime Minister realized that it was the "usual practice" to allow a retiring but undefeated Premier to suggest his successor, but he was careful to add that the Lieutenant-Governor was "in no way bound to accept his suggestion." With the Premier's retirement "the Government or rather the Ministry was ipso facto dissolved, and you were free as Lieutenant-Governor to send for whom you pleased. The absolute uncontrolled right to choose a Premier is according to Bagehot and other late constitutional writers the only *personal* prerogative remaining in the Sovereign."[20] Although the succession has sometimes been unexpected and caused some criticism—such as that of Mowat in Ontario, Murray in Nova Scotia, and Prior in British Columbia—the Lieutenant-Governors have accepted the suggestion of retiring Premiers without recorded opposition.[21]

The incident in Nova Scotia that occasioned the above advice from Macdonald is of interest in this connection. Early in July 1884 the Premier, W. T. Pipes, informed Lieutenant-Governor Richey that he planned to resign soon and asked him whether he would be able to nominate his successor. Richey refused to commit himself until Pipes had actually resigned, but with the resignation in his hands he permitted the Premier to suggest that W. S. Fielding be asked to succeed him:

Having regard to the position held by you as leader of the Administration your resignation would appear by constitutional usage to involve its dissolution but inasmuch as this resignation as I understand you has taken place simply for personal reasons and the government led by you received throughout the late session the support of the legislature and I am entitled to regard it as continuing to enjoy the confidence of the country I shall be pleased to receive from you any suggestion you may be willing to make as to the gentleman to whom my confidence might advantageously be given. . . .[22]

20Macdonald Papers, 526, Macdonald to Richey, July 29.
21It was feared that the Lieutenant-Governor would not follow Blake's advice to call on Mowat. See chap. i, 29.
22PANS, Lieutenant-Governor's Correspondence, Richey to Pipes, July 15, 1884.

Richey must have known that there were serious rifts within the party, for when he asked Fielding to form a government he emphasized his satisfaction with the composition of the cabinet as it then stood and stated that he expected nothing more than a minor reorganization.[23] It was soon apparent that Pipes' recommendation was not supported by his ex-colleagues. Several of them so informed the Lieutenant-Governor and asked him to hear them before allowing Fielding to go any further, while two openly threatened to resign. Having selected Fielding, however, Richey felt bound to support him until he declared his inability to form an administration. In time the difficulties were smoothed over and Fielding began his long reign as Premier of Nova Scotia. The Lieutenant-Governor had unwittingly been the instrument of a Pipes-Fielding plan to confont the cabinet and perhaps the party with a *fait accompli*. He was in no way at fault, however, and in fact received Macdonald's congratulations for the "ability" with which he exercised his "*Sovereign* functions."[24]

Usually under similar circumstances a leader is selected by the party in convention or caucus before the Premier resigns. If this is not done the Premier-designate would be well advised to consult members of the cabinet before consenting to take office. J. A. Calder wisely refused to accept the responsibility of forming a cabinet in 1916 until he had consulted his colleagues, although the retiring Premier, Walter Scott, had recommended his selection. He discovered that W. M. Martin was the favoured candidate and so informed the Lieutenant-Governor who then called on Mr. Martin.[25] The latter, after having served as Premier for six years, refused to suggest a successor when asked but called instead a meeting of the caucus and informed the Lieutenant-Governor that Charles Dunning had been elected.[26] Dunning in turn refused to give any advice when in 1926 he received a summons from Ottawa, but after a meeting of the caucus informed the Lieutenant-Governor that James Gardiner had been chosen to succeed him.[27] The same procedure was followed in Alberta after the resignation of J. E. Brownlee in July 1934. In this case, however, the Lieutenant-Governor refused to accept R. G. Reid, the choice of the caucus, until he had proved his ability to form a cabinet.[28]

A Premier who has been forced to resign because of pressure from

[23]Macdonald Papers, 117, Richey to Macdonald, Aug. 2, 1884. ". . . but without mentioning my wishes further or tramelling him with my stipulations left him free to negotiate."
[24]Macdonald Papers, 526, Macdonald to Richey, Aug. 18, 1884.
[25]Regina press, Oct. 16–20, 1916.   [26]*Ibid.*, April 4–5, 1922.
[27]*Ibid.*, Feb. 22–6, 1926.   [28]Edmonton press, June 30–July 10, 1934.

within the party, though the party itself controls the legislature, is in a different position from one who retires of his own free will. His recommendation may be sought and followed, but like a defeated Premier he has no right to expect either. Such situations are generally the result of serious divisions within the party and the selection of a successor may present difficulties which even the party cannot overcome. The Lieutenant-Governor may then exercise his personal discretion unaided or he may seek the advice of those politicians whose judgment he respects above all others or he may be compelled to accept the advice of his political superiors. The province of Quebec offers the most fruitful area of study in this connection for the many divisions of opinion within provincial political parties have often led to changes in the balance of power and consequent reconstructions and changes in leadership.

In 1873 leading Conservatives agreed that the Chauveau administration could not remain in office. Sir Hector Langevin forced the Premier to resign, persuaded Gidéon Ouimet to succeed him, and made sure that the Lieutenant-Governor would ask Ouimet to form a government.[29] Eighteen months later, with the administration hopelessly tainted by the Tanneries Scandal, it was agreed that Ouimet also had to go. It was essential that the party remove the stigma of corruption and with that purpose in mind the unspotted Charles Boucher de Boucherville was selected by a Conservative Lieutenant-Governor. Robert Rumilly states that the latter did not ask the advice of Ouimet, although it is clear that the Premier knew that de Boucherville would be asked.[30] Lieutenant-Governor Caron may have acted independently, but it is more likely that he consulted leading federal Conservatives. A decade later the problem of succession was complicated by the existence of two candidates, each supported by a faction within the Conservative party. Premier Mousseau's resignation was demanded by several groups, one of which had persuaded J. J. Ross to take his place. Before Mousseau resigned, however, the Quebec City faction persuaded A. R. Angers, a judge, to accept office if asked, and although it was realized that Lieutenant-Governor Robitaille, following the suggestion of L. F. R. Masson, would ask Ross, it was felt that this summons need not be final. On January 22, 1884, Caron who seemed to be the leader of the pro-Angers group was informed that "Angers ready to

[29]Macdonald Papers, 245, Chauveau to Macdonald, Jan. 8, Feb. 25, 1873; *ibid.*, 552, Macdonald to Cartier, Feb. 17, 1873; *ibid.*, 226, Ouimet to Macdonald, Oct. 12, 1880.
[30]Robert Rumilly, *Histoire de la Province de Québec* (Montreal, 1940–55), I, 321; Macdonald Papers, 346, Ouimet to Macdonald, Aug. 12, 1874.

form cabinet as premier if properly asked. Friends expect that sufficient pressure will be brought upon Ross and Lieutenant-Governor. Come down properly authorized by Sir John to this effect otherwise trip useless."[31] Another informant wired: "Ross must recommend him and Ottawa must make Governor call him."[32] Caron contacted Macdonald, but before anything further could be done Ross had accepted office.

As Lieutenant-Governor, Masson himself faced a troublesome, if not difficult, succession problem two years later. After the Quebec election of 1886 the Conservatives realized that the Ross administration had lost its majority and that only by means of a radical reconstruction could the party avoid an almost inevitable defeat in the legislature.[33] For the second time Angers was selected for it was believed that he could rally the Castors and the nationalist Conservatives. Ross was to resign and advise Masson to call on Angers. The Premier had lost his majority; Angers was not in the cabinet or in the legislature. Would Masson accept this advice? Macdonald informed Caron, who had sought advice on the constitutional point, that if Ross resigned before the house met the Lieutenant-Governor would not be bound to call on the Liberal leader, Mercier. (This was indeed true, but Macdonald's *obiter dictum* that even if the government were defeated in the legislature Mercier would not have to be summoned was unrealistic as well as fallacious.[34]) Heartened by the Prime Minister's advice, Caron informed his friends in Quebec that "arrangements should be concluded with the Lieutenant-Governor."[35] Masson was not an easy man to convince and eventually Macdonald was asked to use his powers of persuasion. Reluctantly he wrote:

I need not tell you that in my opinion the best interests of the Dominion would be prejudiced by that discreditable person M. Mercier forming a Government. I feel sure that you as an individual agree with me and that as Governor you would do what you properly and constitutionally could to prevent such a calamity falling on Quebec. Now I understand but not from Ross that he would like from the bad state of his health to leave office, if some reputable man of his party were sent for to form a new administration.

This would seem to be a nice thing for you to do, if as I hear the

[31]PAC, Caron Papers, 3, Charlevoix and Belleau to Caron, Jan. 22, 1884.
[32]*Ibid.*, n.sig. and n.d.   [33]See chap. ii, 42 ff.
[34]Caron Papers, file 10263, Macdonald to Caron, Nov. 3, 1886.
[35]*Ibid.*, Caron to Landry, Nov. 27, 1886. Angers realized that Masson might prove to be an obstacle. "All this of course," he wrote Macdonald, "is provided the Lieutenant-Governor makes no difficulty to a dissolution if necessary, and it is difficult to ascertain his opinion. . . ." (Macdonald Papers, 119, Angers to Macdonald, Nov. 3, 1886.)

consequence would be the formation of a *Bleu* Ministry with a majority.

Should Ross resign Mercier has no claim to the succession. The matter rests with you and I should trust that you would save the Country from untold disasters by accepting Ross's advice as to his Successor.

I can assure you that I feel greatly the responsibility of writing to you— but we are both lovers of our Country and should not hesitate *to act* and *to speak* when we think that its best interests are involved.[36]

Masson had been hopefully yet accurately described in the Liberal press as "as honorable and high-minded a gentleman as ever lived," "not a statue or a mummy," a man in whom the people have the "greatest confidence," and a man of "unspotted reputation." And on this occasion he lived up to his press. Although it was written in "the same friendly spirit" as was Macdonald's his answer was cold comfort for the Conservatives. With pretended naïveté Masson replied that Ross appeared to be in excellent health; in any case, he added, there were "grave doubts whether any man in his party could do better than him. . . ." The Lieutenant-Governor's position was an unenviable one, he lamented, but he assured Macdonald that he planned "to steer a straight and constitutional course feeling keenly the responsibility which rests upon me, knowing in advance the obloquy which will be heaped upon me whatever I do, but trusting that you will approve my conduct on the whole and be convinced that I have done only what I believed right."[37]

As the fateful day approached when the Ross government would be tried and found wanting in the legislature every effort was made to ascertain precisely what the Lieutenant-Governor was planning to do (or was prepared to accept). Masson permitted his views to reach the party through his son-in-law.

Voici quel serait le raisonnement du Lieutenant-Gouverneur: Il n'est pas sûr que Ross ait la majorité. Il y a doute. Que la chambre se prononce et si Ross, même sur la question de l'Orateur, prouve qu'il a la majorité, alors, de suite il acceptera son avis et appellera pour lui succéder l'homme qu'il soit, que le premier designera. Mais actuellement dans le doute serieux où il se prouve, s'il accepte la resignation de Ross, pour raison de mauvaise santé, il ne peut pas appeler d'autre que son premier lieutenant i.e. Taillon. . . . En agir autrement, demander comme premier un homme en dehors de la chambre, ou même un homme en dehors l'administration actuelle serait de la part du lieutenant-Gouverneur se servir de sa position —dans un temps où il est douteux que son premier ministre ait la confiance de la deputation—pour favoriser unconstitutionellement un parti aux dépens de l'autre.[38]

[36]*Ibid.*, 527, Macdonald to Masson, Dec. 8, 1886.
[37]Macdonald Papers, 119, Masson to Macdonald, Dec. 9, 1886.
[38]PAC, Landry Papers, Landry to Angers, Dec. 23, 1886.

Nothing really could be clearer or more just. Despite his desire to help the party and his lack of sympathy for Mercier (although he was *rielliste à Ottawa*), Masson was not prepared to give free rein to a defeated Premier. Whether under Ross or Taillon the administration would face the house. A majority would enable the Premier to speak in a much different voice. But a majority there could not be unless the immediate prospects of Angers' succession attracted the Conservative *nationalistes*.[39] There was no solution. A few days before the legislature assembled Ross did resign and Taillon undertook to form an administration that would meet the house. Defeat was inevitable and when it occurred the Lieutenant-Governor sent at once for Mercier.[40]

Lieutenant-Governor Jetté faced a very different succession problem in 1905. Despite the success of his snap dissolution in 1904 Premier Parent was forced to retire in the face of an insurgent movement led by Lomer Gouin, a young member of his cabinet. Had he been asked, Parent would have advised Jetté to call on Adelard Turgeon, also a member of his government, and Turgeon might have been successful. But Gouin was determined to become Premier. For two months the political scene in Quebec was confused and complicated by "the general mix-up of Federal and provincial politicians, and personal undercurrents within the party."[41] Laurier had previously admitted that "en raison de circonstances incontrôlables" he would of necessity concern himself with the problem of leadership and take upon himself the responsibility for a decision, although during the crisis he feigned neutrality.[42] Jetté attempted to find some settlement that would bring an end to the internecine strife. In the end he asked Gouin to form a government, his fears supposedly being first calmed by Gouin's solemn promise that he would not pursue an anti-clerical policy.[43] The part taken by Jetté, Laurier, and other federal Liberals is not clear; but it is evident that the Lieutenant-Governor was an important and perhaps crucial figure throughout the lengthy crisis.

[39]Even then a majority was unlikely. Had Masson permitted the proposal to be carried out he could never have granted Angers a completely unwarranted dissolution had the new Premier been immediately defeated. This was part of the scheme, however. Landry suggested that a confidential declaration be obtained from the *nationalistes*—"uniquement destinée au Lieutenant-Gouverneur"—showing their support for Angers. (*Ibid.*)

[40]Rumilly, *Histoire*, V, 211 ff.; Charles Langelier, *Souvenirs Politiques* (2 vols.; Quebec, 1909–12), I, 257–8. The *Montreal Herald* of January 29, 1887 reported that Taillon did not inform Masson of his defeat, but that the Lieutenant-Governor sent for the Clerk of the House, found out what had happened, and told Taillon that he must resign. Although the journal was not very reliable the story is credible for Taillon was desperately attempting to reconstruct and stay in power.

[41]*Canadian Annual Review*, 1905, 310.

[42]Laurier Papers, 311, Laurier to Langlois, April 1, 1904; 350, Laurier to Langlois, Jan. 11, 1905.   [43]Rumilly, *Histoire*, XI, 200 ff.

The sudden death of the Premier likewise burdens the Lieutenant-Governor with the responsibility of personally selecting a successor. If illness has been prolonged there will of course be an acting Premier to whom the Lieutenant-Governor can first look, although it is open to question whether convention decrees that he must be asked to form a new administration.[44] The acting Premier was asked to form a government in British Columbia on two occasions, 1887 and 1889, and in Prince Edward Island in 1933; in each instance he succeeded without difficulty. Following the death of Premier Macdonald of Nova Scotia in 1954 the Lieutenant-Governor, after talking with members of the cabinet, asked Harold Connolly, the acting Premier, to take over. It was agreed, however, that his ministry would be temporary and that he would remain Premier only until a full-dress party convention selected a new leader. Premier Connolly was not endorsed by the convention and a new government was eventually formed.

Before his death in 1914 Sir James Whitney, Premier of Ontario, made out a political will, to be opened and executed by the members of his cabinet. In his will he listed four possible successors in order of merit and eligibility: J. J. Foy, a Roman Catholic who he realized would not accept; Frank Cochrane, a member of Borden's cabinet who was not expected to come back to provincial politics: W. H. H. Hearst and I. B. Lucas, both of whom had equal claims although the former's geographical position better qualified him.[45] The Lieutenant-Governor asked Dr. R. A. Pyne, the acting Premier, to form a new government, but Pyne refused on the grounds that he was too old and possessed no legal experience. When asked to suggest the name of one of his colleagues Pyne mentioned Hearst, as the will strongly suggested, and the Lieutenant-Governor acted on this suggestion.[46] Premier Marchand of Quebec left no will before his death in 1900, but he had clearly designated F. L. Béique as his successor. After his death, however, his wishes were completely disregarded. A large majority of the members of the assembly signed a round-robin in favour of J. E. Robidoux and the party generally seemed to endorse him. But Robidoux's known *rouge* background, and his association with Mercier was bound to cause some alarm among the ecclesiastical hierarchy, an event that Laurier and the federal Liberals viewed with alarm. Lieu-

[44]Lord Aberdeen contemplated overlooking Bowell in 1894 on the grounds that he had been acting Prime Minister during Thompson's temporary absence only. Lord Ripon felt that Bowell should at least be consulted. PAC, Lady Aberdeen's Journal, Dec. 12, 1894.
[45]PAC, Hearst Papers, Miscellaneous, dated May 17, 1914.
[46]*Ibid.*, Pyne to Hearst, Sept. 13, 1918.

tenant-Governor Jetté, "un ami des évêques," would only have summoned him with the greatest reluctance. A third and safe candidate
appeared in the person of S. N. Parent, and, probably on the advice
of Laurier, the Lieutenant-Governor, "a l'étonnement général," asked
Parent to form a new administration.[47]

If the legislature is in session when the Premier dies the members
can meet quickly and elect a successor, as they did in Prince Edward
Island in 1908 and 1936, and in British Columbia in 1918. For the
Lieutenant-Governor to assume that one man stands out above all
others and to ask him to form an administration may prove to be a
waste of time. Lieutenant-Governor Nelson felt that Charles Pooley
was such a man and asked him to form a government in British
Columbia following the death of John Robson in 1892. Pooley accepted the task but soon found out that his colleagues did not agree
with the Lieutenant-Governor and he was thus forced to inform Nelson
that J. H. Turner would be a more acceptable Premier.[48] Three years
earlier Nelson had asked Robson, the acting Premier, to assume office
on the death of A. E. B. Davie. Robson refused to accept the task
before consulting his colleagues, even though he was clearly the logical
successor.[49] Nelson should have realized in 1892 that with a cabinet
composed solely of ambitious individuals and united by little more than
a desire to stay in office the selection of a Premier was at best a ticklish
business.

Because of divisions within the majority party and the absence of
real leadership, two Lieutenant-Governors have been given the opportunity to exercise an unusual amount of discretion in the selection of
a Premier. In the spring of 1896 Premier Taillon of Quebec and several
of his colleagues entered the federal cabinet in a last desperate attempt
to salvage the Conservative party. The Lieutenant-Governor, J. A.
Chapleau, was then on vacation, and at no time sought the recommendation of Taillon. The provincial party was divided and leaderless;
pitted against each other were the Castors, led by T. C. Casgrain, and
the moderate Conservatives, of which element Chapleau himself was
really the leader. Before the Lieutenant-Governor's return Casgrain
had started a movement "pour se faire boomer et se faire recommander
par Taillon,"[50] and it is likely that if asked the ex-Premier would have

[47]Laurier Papers, 311, Langlois to Laurier, March 30, 1904; Rumilly, *Histoire*,
IX, 243 ff.; P. A. Choquette, *Un Demi-siecle de Vie Politique* (Montreal, 1936),
162.
[48]*Victoria Times*, July 2, 1892.
[49]*Victoria Colonist*, Aug. 4, 1889.
[50]PAC, Lemieux Papers, 12, Dansereau to Chapleau, May 1, 1896.

suggested Casgrain. But Chapleau had spent a lifetime fighting the Castors, had seen his life's work ruined by their intransigence, and was unquestionably determined to avoid the succession of another ultra-montane government if it was at all possible.[51] First he talked with Thomas Chapais, a Castor and an intimate friend of Casgrain. The Lieutenant-Governor observed that the party was badly divided and suggested that Casgrain, although a logical candidate, was impossible because his brother-in-law, Angers, was the leading Quebec minister in Ottawa: "Le peuple crierait au pact famille."[52] Chapleau then suggested G. A. Nantel (knowing the Castors would never agree) but Chapais assured him that the remnants of Taillon's administration would not accept him. It was then agreed that E. J. Flynn, a moderate like Nantel but less odious to the Castors, would be an acceptable compromise. Undoubtedly Chapleau had Flynn in mind all the time, only like a shrewd dealer in used books he set his original price very high. A moderate cabinet was formed; Chapleau had scored his last victory but one over those he had fought for a quarter of a century.

The Lieutenant-Governor of Alberta, George Bulyea, played a less independent but more active part during a crisis within the provincial Liberal party and government in 1910. After an overwhelming victory in the election of 1909, Alexander Rutherford's government was threatened by the disaffection of a body of its supporters led by a former member of the cabinet. The pretext for the revolt was the government's agreement with the Alberta and Great Waterways Railway Company, which was as Bulyea realized "an insane proposition."[53] A vote of censure was almost a certainty and the Lieutenant-Governor believed that "following Gouin's precedent in Quebec" he would have to call on the insurgent leader.[54] Such an event would split the party in two, and not relishing the prospect the Lieutenant-Governor, one of the foremost Liberals in the Territories before 1905, taxed his energies in an attempt to get the Premier and the rebel, W. H. Cushing, to compromise.

All his efforts were in vain and with the threat of complete disintegration daily increasing, Bulyea turned to the federal Liberals. He informed Laurier that "chaos reigns" and asked him to see if Peter

[51]On Chapleau see H. Blair Neatby and John T. Saywell, "Chapleau and the Conservative Party in Quebec," *Canadian Historical Review*, XXXVII (March 1956), 1–22.
[52]Rumilly, *Histoire*, VIII, 48.
[53]PAS, Scott Papers, Bulyea to Scott, Feb. 17, 1910. On the political background see Lewis Thomas, "The Liberal Party in Alberta," *Canadian Historical Review*, XXVIII (Dec. 1947), 411–27.
[54]Scott Papers, Bulyea to Scott, Feb. 17, 1910.

Talbot, a Liberal Senator from Alberta, would take over.[55] Neither side was willing to accept Talbot, however, and the wrangle continued. In the legislature the government defeated a motion of censure but was forced to accept a committee of inquiry, and pending its conclusions the assembly was adjourned. Bulyea and Senator J. H. Ross had meanwhile hit upon a solution and the Lieutenant-Governor forced it upon the tottering Rutherford cabinet. Arthur Sifton, Chief Justice of Alberta, was to resign from the bench, Rutherford was to resign as soon as the legislature reassembled, Sifton was to be summoned to form a new administration, and the legislature was to be immediately prorogued until the fall, thus giving Sifton time to heal the party wounds and organize a strong cabinet.[56] At the last moment Rutherford and his colleagues threatened to disavow their agreement. The Lieutenant-Governor was forced to move quickly, for if the assembly met and the government were defeated by the rebel group he feared that Cushing would have to be called.

Sifton was with me until about 12 and I confess I did not sleep much. However before morning I figured out a plan of campaign and had made up my mind to take matters into my own hands. I figured that the Cross crowd had kept Rutherford in ignorance of the proposition they had made to the Chief and intended to show Rutherford plainly that he was being made a tool of and if he had not resigned then the only interpretation that could be entertained was that he was tied up in some way with the A and GW and should be fired on general principles. As soon as Rutherford was over I telephoned to Sifton and asked him if he was prepared to step in if I created a vacancy and if he was I would guarantee a vacancy before three [the hour the Assembly was to meet]. He said he was so I was prepared for war. However this was not necessary. Shortly after I heard from Sifton Marshall wired me that a delegation was to wait on Rutherford and tell him to get out and this was carried out and the sponge was thrown up at 11.[57]

When the assembly met, the Lieutenant-Governor, after having so closely avoided dismissing his government, informed it that Rutherford had resigned and that Sifton had agreed to form government. Before any protest could be made the assembly was prorogued.[58]

Lieutenant-Governor Bulyea, completely justifying the confidence that had been placed in him in 1905, had indeed played an extraordinary part. As one writer commented, whether Sifton "should have been called when there was an Opposition leader with two regular

[55]Laurier Papers, 618, Bulyea to Laurier, March 9, 1910.
[56]Ibid., 631, Bulyea to Laurier, May 17, 1910; PAS, Scott Papers, Ross to Scott, March 27, 1910.
[57]Ibid., Bulyea to Scott, May 26, 1910.
[58]Alberta, Legislative Assembly, Journals, 1910, 89.

followers, and an insurgent Liberal leader with 13 followers; whether the Lieutenant-Governor should have waited until a division in the House had decided the problem . . . were the questions of the hour."[59] Bulyea was quite aware of the "questions of the hour" both as Lieutenant-Governor and as a Liberal. He knew too that the report of the committee, although inconclusive, would result in the government's defeat and that the subsequent accession of Cushing would irreparably split the party. The consequences were too disturbing to contemplate and Bulyea was prepared to adopt extreme measures to avoid them. As he informed Laurier, "I am afraid that I had to do a few things that a Lieutenant-Governor is not supposed to do but I think I was justified by the results."[60] There was some criticism of his actions, yet not as much as might be expected for western Canadians were accustomed to Lieutenant-Governors in politics. Less than five years before the strategical value of the office had been clearly revealed.

In 1905 the Laurier administration succumbed to the almost irresistible demand from the Northwest Territories for provincial status and from the Territories carved two provinces, Alberta and Saskatchewan. As the machinery of responsible government had already been achieved the first Lieutenant-Governors faced no problems such as had confronted the Lieutenant-Governors of Manitoba and British Columbia many years before. But it was up to them to select the first provincial Premiers and set the wheels of the new governments in motion. A. E. Forget, the Lieutenant-Governor of the Territories, was appointed to the office in Saskatchewan, and Bulyea, then one of the most prominent territorial Liberals, was made Lieutenant-Governor of Alberta.[61] As soon as possible after September 1, 1905, these two men would be responsible for the selection of the first Premiers of the new provinces.

If Laurier's original expectation that the "government of the territories would naturally become the government of Saskatchewan" had been fulfilled, F. W. Haultain would have become the first Premier of Saskatchewan.[62] Since 1897 Haultain had been Premier of the territorial government and for a decade before that had been a member of the Advisory Council and Chairman of the Executive Committee. Although a Conservative, his government had been broadly non-

[59]*Canadian Annual Review*, 1910, 514.
[60]Laurier Papers, 634, Bulyea to Laurier, June 15, 1910.
[61]See John T. Saywell, "Federal politics and policies and the Lieutenant-Governor; Saskatchewan and Alberta, 1905," *Saskatchewan History*, VIII (autumn 1955), 82.
[62]Laurier Papers, 377, Laurier to Bulyea, July 25, 1905.

partisan and after the election of 1902 he had secured the support of twenty-four of the thirty-five members of the legislature. Haultain had inspired the autonomy movement and had led the delegation to Ottawa in the spring of 1905 to arrange the terms of union. Until this moment Laurier and the western Liberals reluctantly agreed that "following precedent" Haultain would have to be asked to form the first ministry in Saskatchewan.[63]

During the autonomy negotiations, however, it soon became apparent that Haultain and Laurier differed on the four essential points involved. On all but one Haultain unquestionably voiced the desires of westerners regardless of party, and on all Laurier was eventually forced to compromise. But Haultain refused to accept the compromises and in an open letter to the Prime Minister, universally recognized "as a gauntlet of defiance to the Federal authorities and an indication that he would do what was possible to fire the western heather against the autonomy legislation," criticized the entire settlement.[64] Moreover, he openly allied himself with the Conservative party and became their chief spokesman on western affairs; he was "in all the secrets of the enemy and helping them to the extent of his ability."[65]

Haultain's actions provided the western Liberals with a heaven-sent opportunity to oppose his selection as Premier of Saskatchewan, for they had always been in favour of the formation of two tightly-knit Liberal administrations in the west. Yet Laurier was still unwilling to approve any suggestion that Haultain be overlooked. Openly at least he subscribed as always to the argument that the federal government should not interfere in the internal affairs of the provinces (although in actual practice he was constantly meddling in Quebec). When Haultain campaigned vigorously on behalf of the Conservative candidates in two crucial Ontario by-elections in June, 1905, however, Laurier capitulated:

When in the early part of the struggle which followed the introduction of the bills, Haultain went out of his way, to openly take sides with the opposition, I am free to admit that I was keenly disappointed but even then I did not come to the conclusion that the breach was irreparable. When however he threw himself into the contests of London and North Oxford and especially when he announced his intention of carrying on provincial elections on the avowed policy of destroying the school system . . . he left us no alternative, but to accept the declaration of war.[66]

[63]*Ibid.*
[64]*Canadian Annual Review*, 1905, 57.
[65]Scott Papers, Scott to Bulyea, May 20, 1905.
[66]Laurier Papers, 377, Laurier to Bulyea, July 25, 1905.

Despite this emphatic assertion the Prime Minister still regretted "the impossibility of doing what, under ordinary circumstances, would have been the obvious thing."[67]

Thus it was decided. Lieutenant-Governors Forget and Bulyea would call the designated leaders of the provincial Liberal parties, who turned out to be Walter Scott and Alexander Rutherford, to form the first administrations. Throughout there was no question but that the Lieutenant-Governors would do as the party leaders decided; in fact both men were closely involved in the negotiations. The personal discretion of the Crown was used frankly and openly in the interests of the central government and the Liberal party. The selection of Scott instead of Haultain did not pass without criticism, however. Although Laurier stated in the House of Commons that the choice of the Premiers was the exclusive concern of the Lieutenant-Governors, few were deceived. The *Montreal Gazette* stated the general argument against the government most succinctly: "In passing Mr. Haultain over, and selecting for the premiership one of his principal political opponents, a gentleman who was not a member of the late territorial legislature, Lieutenant-Governor Forget made himself a part of the Federal Liberal machine, and sacrificed a part of his title to the respect his office should secure him, and which his record gave reason for thinking he would maintain."[68] Forget later declared that this was his only official action which "had met with severe criticism." "Despite all that had been said," however, "he felt sure, in his conscience, that he had done his duty. But whether he had made a mistake or not . . . , his mistake, if it was a mistake, was then and has since been approved by a great majority of the Province."[69]

The Scott administration won two-thirds of the seats in the first legislature and under a number of leaders remained in power until 1929. The election of 1905 was fought in great part on the autonomy settlement. While denying any subservience to Ottawa or to Laurier, Scott fully endorsed the agreement, while Haultain formed a Provincial Rights party, the programme of which centred around complete provincial autonomy, better financial terms for the new provinces, and the absolute separation of federal and provincial politics. A feature of the latter plank was his attempt to make an issue of Forget's action: did the electorate want an agent of the Liberal party and the federal government in Government House? Scott in turn readily admitted that Haultain had been the logical choice until he had declared his inten-

[67]Scott Papers, Scott to Bulyea, July 25, 1905.
[68]Sept. 5, 1905.   [69]*Regina Morning Leader*, Oct. 15, 1910.

tion of wrecking the settlement: "That the Crown acted upon Liberal advice is a charge I shall not try to refute."[70]

That the advice was not from provincial ministers but from the Laurier administration was the point emphasized by Borden when the House of Commons next met. The Prime Minister denied that he had interfered in any way. The Lieutenant-Governor had the constitutional right to select any man in Saskatchewan, he declared, and under the circumstances it would have been criminal to pick Haultain.[71] Later in the year, with incontrovertible evidence in his hands that Laurier had only gradually and reluctantly agreed to the virtual deposition of Haultain, Borden asked: "What right has the Prime Minister of Canada to do with the passing over Mr. Haultain? Is that not the business of the Lieutenant-Governor of Saskatchewan? Have we not a constitution in this country under which we are supposed to have lieutenant-governors who act independently of the federal authority? Is not the whole basis of our constitution dependent upon that principle?" Borden observed that Laurier's interference was a strange commentary on the Liberal doctrine of provincial rights, and with much less truth concluded that the Lieutenant-Governor was "not an officer of the federal government; he is the direct representative of the Crown, and any attempt to undermine the dignity and independence of such an officer is in my opinion a blow against the spirit and indeed against the letter of the constitution."[72]

Similar criticisms have been made in more recent times, by scholars as well as politicians. They are only justified in part. The Lieutenant-Governor is a federal officer, appointed by the federal government and subject to its instructions. To what extent he could exercise his discretionary powers in the interests of that government had never been determined, just as the "narrow and slippery" line between the interests of the colonial and imperial governments had never been delineated for the colonial governor. Mr. C. C. Lingard has suggested that the by-passing of Haultain was as unjustified as that of Macdonald would have been in 1867.[73] Many comments could be made on this strange assertion. Above all it should be remembered that Macdonald was the prime mover and staunchest supporter of the settlement that had brought Canada into being, while Haultain was determined to ruin the autonomy agreement of 1905. The selection of Haultain could in

[70]Cited in Canada, House of Commons, *Debates*, 1906, 111.
[71]*Ibid.*, 52.
[72]*Ibid.*, 1906–7, 26–7.
[73]C. C. Lingard, *Territorial Government in Canada—the Autonomy Question in the Old North-West Territories* (Toronto, 1946), 248–51.

some ways be compared to the selection of Joseph Howe or Antoine Dorion as Prime Minister of Canada in 1867.

Furthermore, a case can be made for the selection of Scott and Rutherford. Although the territorial government had been non-partisan, there was a general desire once provincial status had been achieved to establish the two-party system in each province. Haultain had made this inevitable by his alliance with the federal Conservatives, even if it had not been before. For all practical purposes then the territorial government had been dissolved before it formally came to an end. If a party government there was to be, it can be argued that the responsibility of the Lieutenant-Governor was to select the leader of the party which possessed the confidence of the electorate. Forget found this argument to be a convenient excuse, if not reason, for the selection of Scott. "Les Lieutenant-Gouverneurs n'ont donc, à mon avis," he wrote, "d'autres alternative, que de choisir leur premier Ministre dans celui des deux partis politiques qui, pour le moment, semble avoir la majorité."[74] The question was, of course, which party had a majority?

Judging from the affiliations with federal parties listed in the *Parliamentary Guide* the majority of the members of the territorial legislature were Liberals. But there was, so Forget felt, a surer guide: the federal election of 1904 had been contested on strict party lines —as the provincial election of 1905 would be—and seven of the ten Members of Parliament were Liberals. This "ne laisse aucune doute" the Lieutenant-Governor concluded.[75] The illogicality of gauging political power in the provinces by the vote in a federal election is immediately apparent, but in 1905 it was less open to question than perhaps on any other occasion for it was to be, after all, the policy of the federal government that was at issue and upon which the electorate would be asked to express an opinion.

The circumstances in 1905 were not unlike those in 1867 when new administrations had to be formed in each of the four original provinces. Had he been more of an historian, Laurier might have described the course then adopted to counter Conservative criticism, for in every case the political interests of the central government were taken into consideration. New Brunswick was at best lukewarm to Confederation, yet when Tilley and Charles Fisher resigned Sir Hastings Doyle formed a ministry led by A. R. Wetmore, an ardent Liberal federationist. Nova Scotia was almost unanimously opposed to the federation of the

---

[74]Laurier Papers, 374, Forget to Laurier, July 10, 1905.
[75]*Ibid.*

colonies and if the wishes of the people were to be considered Howe or one of his followers was the logical successor when Tupper resigned. But with the obvious intention of splitting the Liberal opposition in the province, Sir Fenwick Williams, undoubtedly acting in conjunction with Tupper, formed a coalition ministry led by Hiram Blanchard, a Liberal who supported federation, and P. C. Hill, a Liberal Conservative. The Lieutenant-Governor did this, despite vigorous and widespread criticism, "to insure the passing of such laws as are rendered necessary by the course of events, and *to meet the wishes of the central government.*"[76] The anti-confederates won all but one seat in the first provincial election, adequate commentary on the wisdom of his selection as far as provincial politics were concerned.

The problem in Ontario and Quebec was less difficult, for a majority of their representatives had voted for Confederation in the Canadian Assembly in 1865. Macdonald and Cartier apparently permitted Sir Narcisse Belleau to exercise his personal discretion in Quebec, and the Lieutenant-Governor asked his intimate friend Joseph Cauchon to form the first provincial ministry. A man of great experience and ability, an ardent advocate of federation, and a strong political figure, Cauchon was a logical choice. He first stated that it would be impossible, but finally agreed to form a government and take office without salary until the new machinery was in working order. His original fears were justified, however, for he was unable to secure an English-speaking colleague from the city of Montreal and thus had to relinquish his task.[77] Belleau then turned to P. J. Chauveau who was more acceptable to Cartier and Galt, the two men whose influence supposedly made a Cauchon administration impossible,[78] and for six years Chauveau governed Quebec in the interest of Cartier and the federal Conservative party.

Ontario was predominantly Liberal, while the Macdonald administration, though in name a coalition, was in fact predominantly Conservative. The clear Liberal majority in Upper Canada, given an impartial Lieutenant-Governor, would have assured a Liberal provincial government. But Macdonald wanted a coalition government in Toronto as well as in Ottawa, and selected John Sandfield Macdonald, a Liberal but an enemy of George Brown and the majority of

[76]PAC, Correspondence of the Secretary of State for the Provinces, 1867, file 6, Williams to Monck, July 4, 1867. It must have been generally realized that there was little chance of the Blanchard-Hill administration being sustained.

[77]See the Belleau-Cauchon-Dunkin correspondence published in *Le Canadien*, Jan. 3, 1868.

[78]Rumilly, *Histoire*, I, 64.

the Reform party, to "hunt in pairs" with him. The two Macdonalds agreed on the composition of a coalition ministry and the intimation that Sandfield Macdonald was to be summoned was in some manner passed on to the provisional Lieutenant-Governor, Major-General H. W. Stisted. The "nefarious influence" of the federal government and the Macdonald Conservatives was widely denounced, but *ex post facto* public opinion is usually a poor match for accomplished prerogative action.[79]

In 1867 as in 1905 the selection was determined in great part by the known policy that would be pursued by the respective candidates for the office of Premier. The same was true on several other occasions: in Quebec, 1874 and 1896; in Manitoba, 1870 and July 1874; in British Columbia, twice in 1900 and in 1903; and in Alberta in 1910. Very few Lieutenant-Governors, however, have exercised their influence beyond that point as far as the composition of the cabinet or the government's policy is concerned. Doyle felt that there should be at least one Roman Catholic in the Nova Scotia cabinet in 1867, a conclusion that any Premier was likely to reach independently.[80] Richey told Fielding in 1884 that he was satisfied with the "*personnel* of the Government as it existed" but left the new Premier free to form his own ministry.[81] There is good reason to believe that Joly and McBride agreed on the introduction of party lines before the latter formed his government in 1903. Soon afterwards Joly refused to sanction the appointment of John Houston as a member of McBride's cabinet on the grounds that Houston's rowdy conduct had convinced him that he was unfit to be a minister of the Crown. McBride did not resign (nor did he protest) and thus assumed responsibility for the refusal.[82] Other Lieutenant-Governors have questioned or criticized appointments to the cabinet, but this is the only case on record of an outright refusal that succeeded.

Good practice suggests strongly that the Lieutenant-Governor or the Sovereign should not attempt to commit the government to certain policies in advance. His task is to secure a Premier who can command

[79]Macdonald Papers, 247, Macpherson to Macdonald, July 3, 7, 1867; Toronto *Globe*, July 10–11, 1867; Sir Joseph Pope, *Memoirs of the Right Honourable Sir John Alexander Macdonald* (Toronto, 1930), 372–3.
[80]Howe Papers, 4, Doyle to Howe, Oct. 1, 1867.
[81]Macdonald Papers, 117, Richey to Macdonald, Aug. 2, 1884.
[82]PABC, McBride Papers, Houston to Joly, Oct. 23, 1903, and Joly to Houston, Oct. 24, 1903. For political reasons McBride probably encouraged his refusal. It was essential that Houston be asked, but three members of the cabinet strongly opposed his appointment and McBride himself had little personal regard for him. To overlook him completely, however, would unquestionably have forced him into opposition.

the confidence of the legislature and in whom he has confidence. This task alone may be at times extremely difficult, the course to be followed is not always clear, and the Lieutenant-Governor may have to use the best judgment that he can muster. The provincial Lieutenant-Governors have been confronted with a number of complicated succession problems and on the whole have solved them with commendable success. And as long as parliamentary and cabinet government exists in the provinces so too will the discretionary power of the Lieutenant-Governor.

CHAPTER FIVE

THE PREROGATIVE OF DISMISSAL

No ENGLISH monarch has dismissed a ministry since 1834, and even that was hardly an outright dismissal. As a result any discussion of the prerogative of dismissal in studies of English government appears somewhat academic. One seldom reads, however, that the legal power to dismiss a government is no longer possessed by the Sovereign. Leading British statesmen, from Melbourne to Asquith, agree on the point, and few constitutional authorities venture to suggest a contrary opinion. All make it clear that a sharp distinction must be drawn between "legal power" and "constitutional right," and it is when the implications of this distinction are made clear that the whole subject takes on an academic, slightly unreal, appearance. For, while admitting the "legal power" to dismiss, these scholars and statesmen cannot imagine the circumstances in which such an act could occur without grave damage to the generally understood and accepted conventions of the constitution.

In Canada this gap between what is legally possible and constitutionally permissible is much narrower, for, however wishful our thoughts, however numerous opinions to the contrary, and however alike the superficial resemblances, constitutional conventions in Canada and the United Kingdom do differ. This point has been mentioned before, and only the determination of some scholars to forget it makes its repetition essential. A. B. Keith recognized that English precedents could never be applied to Canada in any hard and fast way when he wrote that "in the Dominions the reserve power may easily be held to be more necessary, in view of the fact that parties sometimes seem to have little regard for anything save their immediate advantage, but that it should be rarely used is undoubted, and examples of its employment are rare."[1] Examples are indeed rare in Canada. No Governor-General has dismissed his government, although Lord Dufferin momentarily considered it. But five provincial administrations have been dismissed, and as the last case occurred in 1903 the question must concern others than the precedent-hunting antiquarian. The purpose

[1]A. B. Keith, *Responsible Government in the Dominions* (2d ed.; Oxford, 1928), I, 123.

of this analysis is not to justify or condemn the actions of any of the Lieutenant-Governors—we have no objective standards against which to make such judgments in any case—but to penetrate the obscurity that has surrounded these events and determine, if not evaluate, the major reasons impelling the Lieutenant-Governors to such an unusual exercise of their power.

In a rare moment of good feeling Gladstone and Disraeli agreed in 1878 that the Queen had every right to dismiss a government; and as if he had marked their words, the Lieutenant-Governor of Quebec transformed opinion into practice. On the surface at least the dismissal appears to have resulted from a vital disagreement on policy. Apparently without consulting the Lieutenant-Governor, Luc Letellier de St. Just, the government had introduced and passed two measures to which he took strong objection. Although he had frequently urged his ministers to reduce expenditure while the provincial revenue was declining and the credit of the province was heavily burdened, Letellier made only a mild remonstrance to an act providing new taxes for railway subsidies. But his opposition to another railway measure was sufficiently strong, in his mind at least, to justify dismissal.

Long before Letellier was appointed as Lieutenant-Governor the provincial government had undertaken to build a railway along the north shore of the St. Lawrence from Quebec to Ottawa, the cost of which was to be shared by the government and the municipalities along the route. The history of politics and railways in Canada is too closely connected to be conveniently separated, and the North Shore line was from the first turning of the sod a political railway. Progress was slow and, for political as well as technical reasons, the route was frequently altered. Some municipalities, not without political motives on occasion, met the dilatoriness and jobbery of the government with a refusal ot pay their share of the cost. Thus in 1878 a bill was passed designed to force payment if, after a hearing, the government decided payment was legitimately due. The substitution of executive for the more normal judicial action was understandable in view of the interminable delays usually attendant upon legal proceedings; but it was a principle to which Letellier, on his own admission, could never subscribe as the government knew from previous encounters with him. Failure to consult him suggested that the government was aware of his opposition to such a practice, and, through no fault of his own, placed him in direct conflict with the legislature. There was much to be said against the bill, and even Mackenzie, whose excessive "Gritism" made him intolerant of any discretionary powers being exercised by the

Crown, observed that the Lieutenant-Governor "could shew a good constitutional argument for reserving the Bill for the central authority."[2] For several days Letellier studied the government's explanations, which he had called for, and "after mature deliberation" concluded that he could not "accept the advice of the Premier in reference to the sanction to be given to the Railway Bill."[3] Moreover, he admitted a general lack of confidence in his advisers and dismissed the government, thus forestalling his Premier's probable willingness to accept his decision to reserve the bill.[4]

The railway bill was more than a pretext for the dismissal, but it alone does not explain Letellier's decision. Fundamentally the *coup d'état* was the result of a profound philosophical, political, and personal incompatibility between the Lieutenant-Governor and his first minister. Letellier, "an old *rouge* of long memories, steeped in animosities,"[5] had been sent from the Mackenzie cabinet to Spencer Wood to superintend the work of an ultra-Conservative government. The appointment was not well considered. Although Mackenzie assured Lord Dufferin that Letellier was "always a moderate man in expression of very decided views," neither the background nor the temperament of the new Lieutenant-Governor were of a nature to qualify him for his task.[6] Since 1850 he had been engaged in constant warfare against the Conservatives and the intensity and bitterness of his campaigns had become almost legendary in the province of Quebec. Appointed to the Senate in 1867, he had not forsaken the stump, which was, far more than any public office, his medium. His energy of late had been expended in the liberal conflict with the Roman Catholic Church, and his efforts in this connection had not endeared him to the hierarchy in either Church or State.[7]

To make matters much worse the Premier, Charles Boucher de Boucherville, was an ultramontane. There could be no common meeting ground between the veteran *rouge* and the extreme *bleu*—soon to be regarded as the leader of the Castors—who was convinced that

[2]PAC, Mackenzie Papers, 6, Mackenzie to Pelletier, March 4, 1878.
[3]*C.S.P.*, 1879, no. 19, 7, Letellier to de Boucherville, March 1, 1878.
[4]Since the Lieutenant-Governor is authorized to reserve provincial bills as a federal officer, resignation of the government does not follow. If the bill had been vetoed, thus indicating a lack of confidence, the ministry would either have had to resign or assume responsibility for it. The Attorney General later declared that "under the circumstances" the government would have been prepared to concur in reservation. (*Ibid.*, 10.)
[5]W. S. MacNutt, *Days of Lorne* (Fredericton, 1955), 20.
[6]Mackenzie Papers, 6, Mackenzie to Dufferin, n.d.
[7]Nor did Letellier cease his work along this line when appointed. See *ibid.*, Mackenzie to Letellier, June 7, 1877; Robert Rumilly, *Histoire de la Province de Québec* (Montreal, 1940–55), II, *passim.*

religion and politics, Church and State, could not be separated, and who genuinely believed that Catholic liberalism, even in Canada, was insidious and sinful. Nor could there be that man-for-man respect so often found between bitter political enemies, for de Boucherville was not even a politician, let alone a fighter. His political position was based on a tradition of seignorial eminence and leadership—a kind of North American *noblesse oblige*—and in a sense he stood aloof from the baser activities of the politicians. He had become Premier at a time when only his outstanding personal reputation for honesty and integrity was considered sufficient to remove the stigma attached to the Conservative party and government as a result of the Tannery scandals a few years before Letellier was appointed. In short, there could be no sympathy between Lieutenant-Governor and Premier, there could not even be a modicum of the mutual confidence essential to the easy working of responsible government.[8]

Had de Boucherville been less stern and inflexible a serious rupture might possibly have been avoided. It must have been at once apparent that Letellier would not be easy to get along with and that all the tact and diplomacy possessed by the cabinet would have to be marshalled to keep the ship of state off the rocks. For Letellier had rather a grandiose opinion of his position. Not only did he justly claim the right to be consulted on all matters of administration and policy, but he seemed to feel as well that his opinion, whether solicited or not, was virtually binding on the government. He later informed Dufferin that

after having studied the general state of the affairs of our Province, after having become convinced that legislative and administrative changes were becoming more and more necessary, I decided upon using with moderation, and with the greatest possible discretion, the influences attached to my position in order to obtain the realization of that which I deemed to be of the greatest advantage to the Province.

I regret to state to Your Excellency that, although M. de Boucherville did, on most occasions take my advice in good part and generally approved of it, he nevertheless almost always acted as though he had never received it. Nevertheless, far from using my authority to obstruct his action in any way, I invariably treated him with great indulgence. . . .[9]

The influences that Letellier believed were attached to his position were perhaps not as weighty as he imagined. The truth seems to be

[8]The Attorney General, also an extreme *bleu*, due to some personal slight soon after Letellier's arrival, refused to go to Spencer Wood. This has often been cited as an important factor leading to the dismissal.
[9]*C.S.P.*, 1879, no. 19, 12, Letellier to Dufferin, March 18, 1878.

that the Lieutenant-Governor was neither an acute nor a profound observer of the changing Canadian constitution. He took particular umbrage at the failure to consult him on several important measures and declared that he had been "assured on unquestionable authority that during the government of the Earl of Elgin . . . his ministers were most scrupulous in consulting him on every question that arose, whether of administration or legislation."[10] On another occasion he stated that all the powers of "Sydenham, Metcalfe, Cathcart, Elgin and Monck, and by Sir Charles Bagot and Sir Edmund Head, are . . . now wielded by the Lieutenant-Governor of Quebec."[11] Letellier had no doubts regarding the power of dismissal: "Without this, what power would he have? Why indeed have a Governor at all?"[12]

De Boucherville, who doubtless regarded Letellier as a dangerous intruder, made little attempt to placate the Lieutenant-Governor or to instruct him in constitutional history and practice. The government was "disposed, as far as possible, to pay proper deference to his views and wishes," but "as responsible Ministers we considered it to be our duty to advise His Honor not to be bound to act upon advice from him."[13] At the same time, the accusation that the Premier tended to disregard the Lieutenant-Governor contained a good deal of truth. Letellier's Conservative predecessor had been old and ill, and the practice had arisen of taking his assent for granted and considering the Lieutenant-Governor as the silent partner in the work of government. Thus in every way the two men were poles apart; grievances accumulated; there was no hope of a restoration of confidence during a friendly conversation; and when a serious issue arose the rupture was complete.

Letellier's disagreement with his government over its railway and financial policy was very real and very significant. Indeed, one finds it difficult not to endorse his point of view without reservation. Provincial finances were extremely shaky, provincial credit was heavily pledged, and the government experienced great difficulty in placing loans at any reasonable rate of interest. It was unquestionably a time for caution. Yet the government forged ahead, lavishly subsidizing railways and throwing the province deeper and deeper into debt. The truth was that rival railway interests had captured the legislature, and

---

[10]*Ibid.*, 37, Letellier to the Secretary of State, Dec. 9, 1878.
[11]Toronto *Globe*, Oct. 3, 1879.
[12]*Ibid.* He added, however, that "such a step is of the gravest possible moment, and cannot be justified unless the variance of opinion . . . has arisen on issues clearly and deeply affecting the public interest, and on which the verdict of the country is apparently certain to be given against the contention of those Ministers."
[13]*C.S.P.*, 1879, no. 19, 23, de Boucherville to Dufferin, April 2, 1878.

when Letellier suggested that the government should radically alter its railway policy de Boucherville told him that it was impossible.

He very frankly avowed that these grants, though they were for the development of the Province, had been necessitated by political considerations; that without them the support of the members whose counties were traversed by those railways would cease to be secured to the Government; that there would be no means of having a majority; that those members formed combinations—'Rings'—to control the House.[14]

Although the Premier later denied that anything so serious existed, his disclosure, undoubtedly made in a rare moment of free-speaking, was not wide of the mark. Early in the year a prominent Quebec Conservative had written as follows to Macdonald:

The Archambault matter has been arranged. Quebec interests, to a great extent, have been sacrificed to Montreal exigencies. But we felt that the paramount interest was to save the Government De Boucherville, in view of the general federal elections. There is however a stumbling block in the way of the administration. Several RR Companies are clamouring for help. Mr. De Boucherville seems to believe that it is impossible to grant it under the financial circumstances of the Province. Hence a great deal of dissatisfaction among the M.P.P. representing these different companies and a supposed combination among them, to force the hand of the government. . . . I look upon this as a serious danger unless Mr. De Boucherville can be induced to give in—I know nobody but you to exercise some influence over him. . . .[15]

Letellier's conclusion when, during the session of 1878, de Boucherville "made no attempt to escape from that deleterious influence" but "sought to favor them anew" was that the government did not possess a "constitutional majority."[16] Better to save the province than the government, he felt, and with his power-laden conception of the office of Lieutenant-Governor he found it an easy matter to dismiss the de Boucherville administration.

The Conservatives naturally believed that the Lieutenant-Governor had acted as an instrument of the Liberal party. Since 1867 the Conservatives had been firmly entrenched in Quebec, their control of the provincial government and party machine almost assured the success of the federal wing of the party, and to make matters worse the Liberals could see no hope of removing them. Like the knife of a skilled surgeon dismissal was quick and sure. Even if the Liberal government that

[14]*Ibid.*, 15, Letellier to Dufferin, March 18, 1878.
[15]PAC, Macdonald Papers, 200, Caron to Macdonald, Jan. 26, 1878. Letellier and de Boucherville actually agreed! Yet it was the Premier to whom Letellier took the strongest objection.
[16]*C.S.P.*, 1879, no. 19, 15, Letellier to Dufferin, March 18, 1878.

succeeded de Boucherville could not maintain itself in power it could give invaluable assistance to the federal party in the forthcoming federal elections. This is an attractive argument, for it is quite clear that Letellier would have taken no action detrimental to the interests of his party. It is probable that he consulted Henri Joly de Lotbinière, the Liberal leader in Quebec, before dismissing the government to make sure that he would form a government if asked. But of direct connivance in the dismissal there is no evidence. Even the most violent Quebec Conservative was forced to admit that "whatever may be my private opinion, as to the fact, I know of no direct evidence extant of any advice to the Lieutenant-Governor from Ottawa."[17] Letellier himself wrote to Mackenzie: "I thank God not to have at any time asked your advise [sic] on the dismissal of M. De Boucherville and to have acted in the same way with your colleagues."[18] Many English-speaking Liberals found it difficult to support Letellier, but confronted with a *fait accompli* tried to make the best of a difficult and embarrassing position.[19] Laurier maintained that Letellier had "upset the applecart" and "decided to take no part in the matter."[20]

It is possible that Letellier may have aspired to the role of King-Maker. A re-orientation of Quebec politics was taking place in the late 1870's, a re-orientation that culminated in the Liberal victory of 1896. The Cartier Conservative party was disintegrating due to the rise of the *programmistes*, the Castors, of which group de Boucherville was a prominent member. Many of the moderate Conservatives, *l'école de Cartier*, were restless under the leadership of the ultramontane party and had begun to look to J. A. Chapleau as their leader. These men seemed to prefer an alliance with moderate Liberals to form a centre party, isolating the extreme *rouge* on the one hand and the extreme *bleu* on the other. In 1877 the youthful Chapleau, then a member of the de Boucherville cabinet, held out an olive branch to the moderate Liberals and "a profondément scandalisé un groupe important du parti conservateur."[21] Many Liberals, apparently convinced of the futility of trying to wrest the province away from the Conservatives, were inclined to regard such a proposal with favour.

[17]Macdonald Papers, 349, Wurtele to Macdonald, April 4, 1878.
[18]William Buckingham and G. W. Ross, *The Hon. Alexander Mackenzie—His Life and Times* (Toronto, 1892), 482, Letellier to Mackenzie, April 15, 1878. See also PAC, Mackenzie Papers, 6, Mackenzie to Pelletier, March 4, 1878; P. B. Casgrain, *Letellier de Saint-Just et Son Temps* (Quebec, 1885), 267 ff.
[19]See chap. IX, 235 ff.
[20]Lucien Pacaud, *Sir Wilfrid Laurier: Lettres à Mon Père et à Ma Mère* (Arthabaska, 1935), 9, Laurier to Pacaud, March 5, 1878.
[21]Charles Langelier, *Souvenirs Politiques* (2 vols.; Quebec, 1909–12), I, 121.

As early as 1875 Mackenzie, Blake, and Galt had considered this union,[22] and Letellier may well have felt that he was in an ideal position to bring these schemes to fruition. When informed of the railway "Rings" he suggested that a coalition of moderates might prove to be a better instrument of government than the Conservative party led by de Boucherville.[23] Of course a coalition could not have taken place under an ultramontane Premier, but might have succeeded under Chapleau. Letellier intimated that his original intention, when he dismissed de Boucherville, may not have been to call on the Liberal leader but on some other member of the Conservative party. The Premier's refusal to suggest a successor, he said, left him no alternative to the selection of Joly. That he had Chapleau in mind is quite clear, for he later observed with some pride that the party had sent de Boucherville to the Senate and had elected Chapleau to take his place.[24] Such considerations as these, however, must be assigned to the realm of speculation—possible, probable, but not proved.[25]

The next dismissal occurred in Quebec thirteen years later. Much of the turbulent political history of the intervening period has been commented on elsewhere as the Lieutenant-Governor was always closely involved. Letellier was unceremoniously dismissed by the federal government. His successor in Spencer Wood refused Joly a dissolution in 1879 and the Liberal Premier resigned. Although strong in the country, the Conservatives suffered from internal dissensions, and only through successive reorganizations was the party able to maintain its hold on office. The hanging of Louis Riel not only intensified this internal decay, but also gave the Liberals a much-needed issue that proved sufficient to bring them to power in January 1887. A more dynamic, if less able, champion of provincial rights than Mowat, the Liberal Premier, Honoré Mercier, soon indicated that his frontal attack on the central government and the party in power at Ottawa was not to end with his accession to office. It was not long before the Conservatives saw in Mercier "un danger imminent, non seulement pour le parti, mais pour la Confédération même. Pour Mercier, les institutions fédérales, c'est l'ennemi, et Dieu sait la somme de préjuges, qu'il saura ammonceler pour le combattre."[26] Moreover, this new threat to the still shaky federal system coincided with the full blossoming of Mowat's legal attack and the rise of a strong and truculent provincial rights

[22]PAO, Blake Papers, Mackenzie Correspondence, 1875, *passim*.
[23]*C.S.P.*, 1879, no. 19, 15, Letellier to Dufferin, March 18, 1878.
[24]*Ibid.*, 38, Letellier to the Secretary of State, Dec. 9, 1878.
[25]For the aftermath of the dismissal see chaps. VI, IX.
[26]PAC, Caron Papers, file 12796, Ross to Caron, Oct. 16, 1888.

movement in Manitoba. Five years less one month after he had taken office Mercier was dismissed by a Conservative Lieutenant-Governor.

Mercier had been summoned to form a government by a Conservative Lieutenant-Governor, L. F. R. Masson, despite the attempt of Macdonald and some Quebec Conservatives to prevent his accession. Not long afterwards Masson resigned and "as an old friend" begged Macdonald to use great discretion in selecting his successor.

The Province has passed through a very severe crisis; the question of the relations of the Lieutenant-Governor with his ministers and parliament has since the last provincial elections been almost continuously before the public through the press of both parties now eulogizing, now threatening, now addressing the chief of the Executive, and I think I am not over-rating the importance of the decision you are going to come to, by saying that on it depends greatly the political quietness of the Province. Parties, though broken up in fragments are excited, very excited and I think this is the time more than ever when caution should be used.[27]

Masson could afford to be high-minded; Macdonald, to whom the internal organization of his cabinet and party was of more importance than political quiet in the province of Quebec, could not. He offered the post first to Langevin and then to Chapleau, both rash partisans, and on their refusal accepted the recommendation of the third Quebec faction that A. R. Angers be given the appointment.

Masson may well have questioned the wisdom of the Prime Minister. Angers had been a prominent member of the de Boucherville cabinet in 1878 and had now come to Spencer Wood at a time when Mercier, who had been a member of Joly's Liberal ministry, was just across the Champs de Bataille. (Five years later it was to be an easy matter for the Liberals to charge that Angers had been moved chiefly by the desire for revenge.)[28] There was much to be said for the appointment, however. No Conservative had forgotten the *coup d'état* of 1878, and while others had remained in active political life Angers had served on the bench for a decade.[29] Furthermore, he was not a professional partisan, but, like many ultramontanes, assumed rather a detached attitude towards politics. The Conservatives hailed his appointment with unrestrained glee, terrified as they were by the actions of Mercier, to whom, not without some justice, they had affixed the labels "César-Mercier" and "l'Autocrate de Québec." As one reported: "nos amis

---

[27]Macdonald Papers, 119, Masson to Macdonald, May 24, 1887.

[28]Israel Tarte is later reported to have stated that Angers was appointed to dismiss Mercier "on the first favourable occasion." (Langelier, *Souvenirs Politiques*, I, 281.) Tarte makes no mention of this in his own study of the crisis. (*1892—Procès Mercier* (Montreal, 1892).)

[29]The appointment was designed, it was said, to bring him back into politics!

sont dans la terreur et s'attendant à destitutions nombreuses d'un moment à l'autre—Ils n'ont d'espoir que dans la nomination d'un Lieutenant Gouverneur qui fera respecter l'esprit de la constitution et la justice. . . ."[30] Angers was such a man: principled, strong in mind and body, experienced in both politics and law.

It would be difficult to imagine amicable relations between Mercier and Angers. Like Letellier and de Boucherville, even more so perhaps, the two men provide a study in contrast: the one fiery and emotional, extremely unstable, always opportunistic, and quite willing to sacrifice political morality for political advantage; the other haughty and logical, aloof and authoritarian, and devoted like all ultramontanes to certain basic factors in private and public life. Not only must the Lieutenant-Governor have disapproved of his Premier as a man, but he also objected to much of his policy. In 1888 he objected to one measure proposed by his government, which he felt was arbitrary and unjust, but concluded that after a "judicious warning" he could do no more without exposing himself "to the recriminations of the Liberal press."[31] During the next session he expressed grave concern over the fairness of several bills, yet at the same time he refused to reserve another to which the federal government took strong objection unless specific formal instructions were sent to him from Ottawa; any other course, he declared, would place him in opposition to his government.[32] Mercier appears to have accepted his admonitions and objections with good grace, and once declared that the Lieutenant-Governor "surveille les affaires publiques avec intelligence, mais sans s'écarter jamais des règles constitutionnelles."[33]

By 1890 it was everywhere apparent that the Mercier régime was hopelessly corrupt. Laurier contemplated resigning as Liberal leader, presumably on the grounds that no Quebec Liberal could escape the stigma. "The system adopted by Mercier," he sadly informed Blake, "is in almost every respect repugnant to my convictions. But there is no choice between him and his opponents."[34] When, during the session of 1890, Mercier seemed prepared to grant a subsidy of three million dollars to the Quebec Bridge Company, at a time when provincial finances were in a critical state, the Lieutenant-Governor was ready to take a very strong stand, and, in view of the crisis that would probably follow, wished Macdonald to inform the Governor-General of all that

[30]Caron Papers, file 11693, Ross to Caron, Oct. 15, 1887.
[31]Macdonald Papers, 186, Angers to Macdonald, Sept. 13, 1888.
[32]Ibid., Jan. 28, 1889.
[33]Cited in Rumilly, Histoire, VI, 59.
[34]Blake Papers, Laurier to Blake, May 31, June 13, 1890.

was happening.[35] By January 1891 Angers was prepared for another crisis that he sensed was approaching, and warned Macdonald against dumping the soiled Langevin in Spencer Wood.

Presently, I assure you that the Lieutenant-Governorship is not a sine-cure, with an extravagant and very often unconstitutional ministry led by Mr. Mercier, fresh from the people with a majority of 25 in a house of 73. . . . Further, knowing the inner of things here as I do, I may be allowed to express the doubt whether Sir Hector has the required diplo-matic skill to get on with Mr. Mercier. I sincerely believe that a crisis might occur within two months. And what then? Such an eventuality on the eve perhaps of your general elections would divert the attention of the electorate from the real issue and you would be making the elections here not on the merit of your government, but on what might be called a new *coup d'Etat* inspired from above.[36]

Come the crisis did, but it was Angers, not Langevin, who was respon-sible for a new *coup d'état*.

Some years earlier the government of Quebec had undertaken the construction of the Baie des Chaleurs Railway, but the company formed to carry out the work had defaulted and construction had stopped. In 1890 the Mercier administration authorized the conversion of the bonds and debentures and paved the way for the formation of a new company that was to receive a large subsidy and was to assume the debts of its predecessor, payment for which was to come from the subsidy. Before surrendering his contract, however, one of the officials of the old company presented a claim for $175,000. Mercier was absent at the time and the acting Premier, Pierre Garneau, "droit comme l'épée du roi," hesitated to pay such a large sum without real authorization. He was assured by other members of the cabinet that all was in order, but before taking any action he confided in the Lieu-tenant-Governor, an old friend though on the opposite side of the political fence. He told Angers that he was uneasy about the whole matter and felt very much like resigning.[37] Angers, who trusted Gar-neau above all others in the cabinet, refused to consider his resig-nation: "being the Prime Minister accredited to me during the absence

---

[35]Macdonald Papers, 186, Angers to Macdonald, March 14, 1890.
[36]*Ibid.*, Jan. 22, 1891.
[37]Laurier shared Garneau's uneasiness. "I have just been informed that the Local Government intends to pay a certain 'party' a large sum of money for his old state claim on the North Shore Railway. I have good reason to believe that the payment of any amount, large or small, to anyone on such a claim would be a very dangerous mistake. I hope that you will warn Mercier, as the consequences would certainly be of a character detrimental to his government." (Pacaud, *Laurier,* 54, Laurier to Pacaud, April 20, 1890. The letter should be dated 1891 in all probability.)

of the Hon. Mr. Mercier, you cannot leave me without an adviser; what you have to do is to resist and to conform in all respects with the law."[38] Garneau secured verbal and written assurance from the Attorney General that the payment was legitimate and finally consented to authorize it.

As federal money was involved the matter came before the Canadian Parliament and was referred to the Senate Committee on Railways. Because of the protests made by several interested parties, and because of the interest shown by the Conservative senators from Quebec, the committee decided to make a full investigation and secured authority to send for witnesses and records. Before its work was completed, the committee, dominated by Conservatives, had probed deeply into Mercier's "system" and the picture soon emerged of a government entangled in webs of patronage, favouritism, and shady dealings. To secure a contract or an appointment, or to have a book endorsed for use in the schools, the hopeful aspirant had to work through a political intermediary who secured an adequate "rake-off." Chief among these friends of the government were Ernest Pacaud, editor of L'Electeur and the chief party organizer, Cléophas Beausoleil, Mercier's law partner, and Lomer Gouin, the Premier's son-in-law. Much of the money thus obtained went back into the party chest and was used for personal and political purposes. As far as the railway was concerned, it appeared that Pacaud, the "wire-puller of Quebec," had received $100,000 of the $175,000 paid by the government; it appeared as well that this payment was essential if the undertaking were to succeed, for Pacaud was behind it all; and it was quite clear that Pacaud had at once met several personal notes against members of the cabinet and had paid other debts connected with the recent federal elections. Pacaud and members of the cabinet refused to appear before the committee: Pacaud left hurriedly for Paris, Garneau was ill, and the others refused on the grounds that it was none of the Senate's business.[39]

The political world watched impatiently as the Senate committee heard witnesses and examined documents. The Liberals attempted to

[38]Royal Commission—Inquiry into the Baie des Chaleurs Railway Matter (Quebec, 1891), 831, Angers to Mercier, Sept. 7, 1891.
[39]Canada, Senate, Journals, 1891, Appendix 2A. Some Conservatives, among them the editor of La Minerve wished to have the ministers forced to come before the committee. As Joseph Pope realized, however (and he probably spoke for the cabinet), "it would play the devil in Lower Canada and give Mercier just the cry he wants." Angers realized this only too well and was again reassured by Pope that "the controlling influences on the Committee quite see the impolicy of forcing the recalcitrant witnesses to attend." (PAC, Landry Papers, Pope to Taché, Sept. 1, 4, 1891.)

spin out the investigation until prorogation when the committee would come to an end. But the Conservatives realized their opportunity too well to let that plan succeed.[40] As the daily revelations were published the Conservative press in Quebec became increasingly exultant and constantly urged the Lieutenant-Governor to take some action to end the provincial disgrace. The Liberal press glumly reminded the Conservatives of their attitude during the Letellier crisis. All the while the incumbent of Spencer Wood gave no outward indication of his feelings or probable action.

Angers pesait les conseils contradictoires de Tarte et de Pelletier. Il pesait surtout les faits. Raide, sans doute, partisan, si l'on veut, Angers était trop honnête homme pour recourir, sans raison grave, aux procédés violents contre Mercier. Mais il avait l'intégrité sourcilleuse; un détournement d'un sou l'eût choqué. Et l'attitude des accusés achevait de creuser, entre eux et lui, un gouffre. A Spencer-Wood Angers annula toute invitation et consigna sa porte.[41]

Behind closed doors Angers and his secretary were busy. Through Joseph Pope, Assistant Clerk of the Council, the Lieutenant-Governor received official reports of the evidence given before the committee. Through Pope also he secured copies of the documents relating to the Pacific Scandals inquiry in 1873. On August 27, 1891, Pope assured him that the report of the committee would "aid greatly in enabling one to arrive at a proper understanding of the case, being very clear and succinct."[42] Several days later Angers informed Mercier that he was writing to him on an important subject and asked him not to leave the city without leaving his address.[43] A week passed. "Le Lieutenant-gouverneur n'entretenait plus de relations avec ses ministres que par correspondence et par messagers. Les affaires furent à demi arrêtées. Les ministres et leurs amis observèrent une discrétion absolue."[44] On September 7 Angers finally sent the completed letter to Mercier. In it he reviewed the history of the Baie des Chaleurs negotiations, pointed to Garneau's reluctance to conclude the agreement with the payment of $175,000, but observed that the Attorney General had guaranteed the legality of the transaction. Consequently, "I was justified in believing, up to the time that certain revelations . . . were made, that the government would conform to the law. . . ." The disclosures before the Senate committee, he wrote, caused him "great alarm" for the sum was paid to a man to whom the government owed nothing. "There

[40]PAC, Landry Papers, Pope to Taché, Sept. 1, 1891.
[41]Rumilly, *Histoire*, VI, 246.
[42]Landry Papers, Pope to Taché, Aug. 28, 1891.
[43]*Ibid.*, Angers to Mercier, Sept. 1, 1891.   [44]Rumilly, *Histoire*, VI, 246.

would seem to exist between the government and the creditors of the Province a barrier at which tribute is levied before justice is done to claimants," said the Lieutenant-Governor with obvious reference to the "system" which had been laid bare before the committee. Under the circumstances he asked Mercier for full explanations and requested his concurrence in the appointment of a Royal Commission composed of three judges named by the Lieutenant-Governor. Meanwhile, the Premier was "to limit the action of the government to acts of urgent administration" and was not to spend a cent without the personal approval of the Lieutenant-Governor.[45]

Mercier admitted that the claim for $175,000 had been unfounded and that Pacaud had received $100,000. He insisted, however, that the government could not be held responsible, for the claim had been certified by officials of the company. The Premier preferred an investigation by a committee of the Legislative Assembly, rather than by a Royal Commission, on the grounds that it would "give better guarantee and occasion less inconvenience."[46] Angers bluntly refused to consider this suggestion, fully aware of the "guarantees" it would give, and Mercier then advised the appointment of a commission of one judge—named by the government. In so doing he observed that "my duty imposes on me the obligation of offering you my advice on this occasion, and that it is for Your Honour to make known to me the *valid reasons of recusation* which you might have against the judge or judges whom I might propose."[47] The Lieutenant-Governor was not persuaded by these strong words, and rather than hand in his resignation Mercier submitted.

Whether valid or not, Angers' reason was simply that he had lost confidence in his government. In all probability he had already decided on dismissal unless the commission was able to whitewash the administration. This unlikely prospect could hardly be considered: the Senate committee had revealed the system on which the Mercier government operated; the Conservatives had been gathering intimate information concerning the cabinet for several years and played the rôle of prosecuting attorneys before the commission with vigour;[48] and finally, two of the three members of the commission were Conservatives. Laurier informed an Ontario supporter that "the opinion seems

[45]*Royal Commission*, 1891, 822–39, Angers to Mercier, Sept. 7, 1891. Of the judges, Baby and Davidson were Conservatives, and Jetté, the President, a Liberal.
[46]*Ibid.*, 863, Mercier to Angers, Sept. 15, 1891.
[47]*Royal Commission*, 1891, 865, Mercier to Angers, Sept. 16, 1891.
[48]See Caron Papers, file 12868, Beaubien to Caron, Jan. 16, 1890; general correspondence, Fitzpatrick to Caron, Sept. 30, 1891.

to be well founded that Angers will dismiss his ministers upon the report of the commissioners, and that he is determined to find therein a pretext, if failing to find a reason for such a course."[49] The statements by several prominent Conservatives that local elections could soon be expected strongly suggested that dismissal was in the offing. Mercier was virtually helpless: "Il eut une réaction aveugle, maladroite, d'homme traqué."[50]

Although the evidence placed before the Royal Commission continued to shock even the most seasoned Canadian politicians, it gradually became apparent that only with great difficulty could the commission find against the ministers in a strictly legal sense. The Liberals took on new hope. Yet everyone knew that the ministry was guilty of scandalous conduct. Laurier realized that the report "must exonerate Mercier from blame," but added that "he must reconstruct his cabinet and open a new leaf in his book. We are trying hard a few of us, to get Joly to go in with him. Joly's accession to the cabinet would give universal satisfaction, and it would make impossible any such frauds, as Baie des Chaleurs."[51] Everyone waited for the report of the commission, no one more impatiently than the Lieutenant-Governor. It was not that Angers was anxious to see the content of the report, for all along he had been in communication with the commission, submitting evidence and commenting on statements made, and had been in daily receipt of the evidence. He was concerned rather because the government of the province had been at a stand-still for several months and, more important—as Mercier repeatedly informed him—a session of the legislature had to be held by December 30, 1891. On December 1 Angers advised the commission of these facts, repeated his determination to do nothing until the report was submitted, and asked when it would be ready. Jetté replied in a few days.[52]

Ten days later, with the report still not completed, Jetté became ill. The Lieutenant-Governor wrote at once to Judge Baby, an old political crony, and asked for a report. In his letter he observed that the legislature would either have to meet or be dissolved by December 30, "dans ce dernier cas sur l'avis de nouveaux ministres." "Je ne puis déterminer mon action sans avoir votre rapport. De là doit vous apparaître la gravité de la situation."[53] Baby and Davidson were fully aware of the gravity of the situation and decided at once to submit an interim

[49]PAO, Edgar Papers, Laurier to Edgar, Oct. 19, 1891.
[50]Rumilly, *Histoire*, VI, 259.
[51]Edgar Papers, Laurier to Edgar, Nov. 28, 1891.
[52]Landry Papers, Angers to the Royal Commission, Dec. 1, 1891; Jetté to Angers, Dec. 2, 1891.   [53]Landry Papers, Angers to Baby, Dec. 11, 1891.

report to the Lieutenant-Governor that would enable him "d'adopter telles procédés que vous croirez bons dans l'interêt de la province. . . . "[54] Two days later their preliminary conclusions were sent to the Lieutenant-Governor. As Laurier had prophesied, Mercier was aquitted of direct connivance; the payment of $175,000 was fraudulent, an "audacious exploitation of the provincial treasury"; four members of the cabinet, in addition to the Premier, were exonerated; Garneau was guilty of carelessness; and another was fully aware that Pacaud had received the money and knew for what purpose it had been spent.[55] Jetté refused to be associated with the report and asked permission to submit his personal observations, which, as everyone knew, would tend to clear the administration.[56]

Mild as it was the Baby-Davidson report convinced the Lieutenant-Governor that the Mercier administration was not fit to govern the province, or perhaps it would be more accurate to say that it buttressed a long-standing conviction. After reciting the conclusions reached by the two judges Angers informed the Premier that

Le rapport ci-haut,—l'incurie et les illégalités dont l'action du ministère est entachée,—les faits et circonstances qui ont précédé, accompagné, motivé et suivi son action,—l'emission de lettres de crédit au montant de $175,000 en violation de la loi du Trésor, sans la sanction du Lieutenant-Gouverneur et au détriment du crédit public,—la malversation et la détournement de la somme de $175,000 de sa destination législative,—le paiement qui en a été fait à Mr. Armstrong auquel il n'était rien dû par le gouvernement ni par la compagnie en argent,—le partage des $100,000 prélévées sur Mr. Armstrong et l'emploi qui en a été fait pour payer les dettes de plusieurs des ministres et subventionner plusieurs députes partisans du cabinet,—les contradictions qui existent entre la preuve et les explications ministérielles,—le silence que ces explications ont gardé sur certains faits d'une extrême gravité propres à plusieurs des ministres,— tel que le tout est prouvé et établi par l'enquêtte et le rapport ci-haut, m'imposent la conviction que le ministère n'est pas dans une situation à aviser avec sagesse, désintéressement et fidélité le représentant de la Couronne.

En face de la persistance du ministère à demeurer en office nonobstant l'incurie et les illégalités de son action et les constations de l'enquête,— il ne me reste, pour protéger la dignité de la Couronne et sauvegarder l'honneur et les intérêts de la Province en péril, que le remède constitutionnel de vous retirer ma confiance et de vous révoquer vous et vos collègues de vos fonctions d'aviseurs du représentant de la Couronne et de Membres du Conseil Exécutif.[57]

[54]Ibid., Baby to Angers, Dec. 12, 1891.
[55]See ibid., Angers to Mercier, Dec. 16, 1891; Rumilly, Histoire, VI, 260–2.
[56]Landry Papers, Jetté to Angers, Dec. 14, 1891.
[57]Ibid., Angers to Mercier, Dec. 16, 1891; Mercier to Angers, Dec. 17, 1891.

Mercier's reply was that of an enraged man, of a frustrated man whose great political power could not overcome the single will of the Lieutenant-Governor. Angers, he declared, was not "un chef d'exécutif impartial, mais un adversaire politique, sublissant l'influence extérieure de mauvais conseillers et de mauvais passions" who was so impatient to return power to his political friends that he could not even wait for the final report of the commission. The Royal Commission itself was a farce, for the dismissal had been decided upon before its appointment. And was it not odd that Angers, so long associated with the Conservative party in Quebec, should suddenly become so concerned about corruption? "Vous dites que vous me retirez votre confiance: vous vous faites illusion, car vous le savez bien: vous me l'avez toujours refusée cette confiance. Vous êtes sorti des luttes actives de la politique pour monter sur le banc ou vous êtes toujours rester partisan. Vous avez laisser le banc judiciare pour aller à Spencer Wood, et là encore, vous avez tenu, tout le temps que j'ai été votre aviseur, la conduite d'un partisan politique." But the Premier had no need of the Lieutenant-Governor's confidence for he had that of the people, and because he possessed that confidence he was going to defeat the Lieutenant-Governor and save the province: "Je vous dénonce à l'opinion publique, de qui vous relevez comme les autres, et j'éspère que le jour n'est pas éloigné où les représentants du peuple, reprenant le pouvoir dont vous les avez privé temporairement, vengeront la constitution violée par vous, qui aviez juré de la protéger." Enjoy your reward: "vous recevrez bientôt de M. Abbott votre maître, le prix de votre trahison nationale."[58] Remember all the while, however, that "votre conduite, Monsieur, dans toute cette malheureuse affaire, met en danger nos institutions politiques et porte atteinte sérieusement à l'autonomie

[58]It was declared then and has been since that Angers agreed to dismiss Mercier on the understanding that he would be called to the Senate and the Dominion cabinet. Unfortunately for the argument Angers had been asked to enter the cabinet on several occasions before the crisis. The fact that Abbott would ask him to leave Spencer Wood late in the summer of 1891 strongly suggests that there was no collusion between the two men or even a scheme being discussed within the party at that date. Angers had no sooner dismissed Mercier, however, than he received another request from Abbott to join his government. Angers refused: "I think it is impossible for me to leave Quebec at present. The elections have to be fought for a great part on my back. My leaving the cabinet to its own resources would weaken them. Mr. de Boucherville and his colleagues think so." Moreover, wrote the Lieutenant-Governor, to move so quickly to Ottawa would cast doubts as to his action and character: "the liberal press in the province has so loudly published that I was acting to get my reward from Ottawa in the shape of a portfolio in your cabinet, that it would be giving it a *semblant du raison* if the thing occurred now. We have both been pointed out as conspirators in the matter, and nothing should be done that would credit such a slander." (PAC, Angers Papers, Angers to Abbott, n.d., *circa* Jan. 3, 1892.)

de notre province: gardez en la responsabilité devant le pays et devant l'histoire." Mercier could never live up to his promise to return to power and to remove the Lieutenant-Governor, for he was never to return to public office. The country failed him. Some historians have not.

As soon as he dismissed Mercier, Angers summoned de Boucherville to form a government (the wheel had turned full circle), granted him a dissolution, and eagerly awaited the results of the election.[59] The electorate overwhelmingly rejected Mercier; only a handful of Liberals were returned and the Conservatives had a clear majority of thirty-five. The federal Liberals either refused to support Mercier, or did so without enthusiasm. No motion of censure on the Lieutenant-Governor was introduced in the House of Commons. Liberal opinion was best stated in the *Globe*:

We cannot regard the result with unmixed feelings either of regret or of satisfaction. We do not like to see even the name of Liberalism in Canada associated with defeat or dishonour. . . . The best feature of the situation is that the people of Quebec have undoubtedly acted from worthy and honourable motives. They were determined that whatever other results might follow they would make it impossible for these men to govern the province. They were tired of extravagance and corruption. . . .[60]

The Governor-General, Lord Stanley, sent a clear and impartial statement to the Colonial Secretary soon after the election.

Whether they were technically guilty or not there is no doubt that Mr. Mercier and his colleagues have been greatly discredited by the various transactions which have come to knowledge in the course of the past year in connection with the finances of Quebec. Many prominent Liberals have disassociated themselves from the late Premier and have either taken no part in the elections or have supported his Conservative opponents. The influence of the Roman Catholic Church which is especially great in the rural districts has been thrown on the side of honest government and its advice has been somewhat cynically interpreted by the electors as being adverse to Mr. Mercier and his party.

There has been a considerable attempt on the part of the latter to evade the question immediately at issue and to trade upon Franco-nationalist sympathy and it is perhaps the most significant feature of the present election that the cry that opposition to Mr. Mercier meant oppression of the French Canadian Race—has been totally disregarded notwithstanding that it was upon that cry that he came into office in 1887 after the execution of Riel.

[59]Because of the investigation, the dismissal, and the dissolution, more than one year passed between meetings of the legislature.
[60]Cited in Canada, House of Commons, *Debates*, 1892, 1750.

In the other Provinces the Liberal feeling which could otherwise have been in favour of Mr. Mercier has been neutralized by the disgust at his maladministration of the finances of his Province and by the certainty that its largely increasing debt would before long necessitate an appeal for help from Dominion funds.[61]

Angers' actions have been unfavourably compared with Dufferin's during the Pacific Scandal crisis in 1873. Dufferin realized that dismissal was within his power, but he did not feel warranted in ousting the Macdonald government on the evidence at his disposal.[62] Nor did he feel justified in removing his confidence from the ministers while retaining them in office; this, he said, "would be a novel fact in Constitutional history, and might have proved difficult of execution."[63] At one point he did exert some pressure on Macdonald to resign, but rather than force the issue he allowed him to stay in office until the Prime Minister himself realized the game was up.[64] There were several important differences between the two crises, however, that go far to explain the different courses pursued. The findings of the Senate committee were much more substantial and trustworthy than the Huntington charges and the commission's conclusions. Macdonald possessed only a slim and ill-disciplined majority in the House of Commons and there was every reason to believe that the legislature would return a true verdict; even so, Dufferin declared that "inasmuch as the decision of Parliament might itself be partially tainted by the corruption disclosed, he should hold himself free to require the resignation of his Ministers in the event of their winning by anything short of a very commanding majority."[65] Mercier, on the other hand, had a very large majority, one that could be depended upon under any circumstances to support the government. Most important of all was the personal factor: Dufferin trusted Macdonald; Angers did not trust Mercier. And then of course there were politics.

By 1903 British Columbians had almost come to accept the prerogative of dismissal as a working feature of the constitution, for during the preceding five years three governments had been dismissed. This period provides a perfect illustration of the grave danger of applying the accepted conventions of cabinet and parliamentary government as they developed in England (or even in Ontario) to politically under-developed areas. Since the creation of the province in

[61]PAC, G 12, 85, Stanley to Knutsford, March 9, 1892.
[62]Canada, House of Commons, *Journal*, 1873, 35, Dufferin to Kimberley, Aug. 15, 1873.
[63]*Ibid.*
[64]G. E. Buckle, ed., *The Letters of Queen Victoria* (2d. series; London, 1928), II, 288–9.   [65]*Ibid.*, 288.

1871, British Columbia had been governed by combinations of personal factions rather than by political parties. After the "Fight Ottawa" period ended in the late 1880's there were no real issues to divide or unite these factions. A government that could successfully refrain from offending its more important supporters was assured of long tenure, for the population of the province was small and widely scattered and the electorate was thus easily controlled by a ministry with adequate patronage at its disposal. General economic improvement in the late 1890's wrought sudden changes in the provincial economy, and a policy of drift was no longer sufficient. A flood of new money and new people rushed into the province, stimulating old industries, creating new ones, and transforming almost overnight the political, social, and economic bases of provincial life. While the province moved rapidly out of its adolescence the government failed to keep pace, but seemed instead to disintegrate in the face of new challenges and new responsibilities. A handsome majority secured in 1894 had almost disappeared by 1897; members of the cabinet had become careless and charges of corruption and inefficiency were legion; presented with opportunities never before visualized nothing characterized the government so much as its lack of initiative and imagination, its inability to move boldly and decisively. When John H. Turner, the last Premier in the Smythe dynasty established in 1882, sought a further mandate in July 1897 there were demands from all sides for a change of government. Even in eastern Canada and in England the fitness of the administration was seriously questioned.

The first reports from the constituencies revealed that the government had lost its majority, but it was soon evident that both government and opposition would have nineteen seats in the next house.[66] The members of the opposition had been unable to agree upon a leader, however, and were in fact united only in their desire to defeat the Turner ministry. Doubtless a call to office would have stimulated them to form some combination, but to all appearances the government was still the largest and strongest political group. Nonetheless, the opposition press at once demanded the resignation of the administration on the grounds that it had lost the confidence of the electorate, and in certain quarters it was suggested that the Lieutenant-Governor might be well advised to exercise his prerogative of dismissal.

Thomas Robert McInnes had been Lieutenant-Governor since

[66]Included on the government side were two members from Cassiar, a northern constituency where the elections were held several weeks later. Since most of the voters were dependent upon government patronage for their livelihood there was never any doubt as to the result there.

November 1897. McInnes had served in the House of Commons from 1878 to 1882 as a Conservative and had been appointed to the Senate in the latter year. Convinced that unrestricted reciprocity was a preferable alternative to Macdonald's national policy, McInnes switched allegiance before Laurier came to power. Through his own persistent efforts he obtained the appointment in 1897. His term of office, cut short by his dismissal in 1900, was the most eventful in the nation's history.

A few days after the election McInnes refused to approve several Orders in Council, informing the Premier that he could not "look on the result of the general elections for this province . . . as other than adverse to your administration, and an expression of want of confidence on the part of the people." Unless he could become convinced that the government had "the support of a majority of the new legislative assembly" McInnes planned to refuse to accept Turner's advice "in regard to new appointments to office, in regard to special expenditures of money not provided for in the current estimates, unless shown that an urgent necessity exists for the same in the interests of the province."[67] Turner submitted without protest, although on occasion the two men differed on the meaning of "urgent necessity." The Premier did not deny that he had lost his majority, and in fact attempted to come to an agreement with some members of the opposition.

McInnes had modelled his course on that of Lord Aberdeen who, it will be remembered, prompted the resignation of the Tupper ministry by his refusal to sanction several appointments. Turner did not choose to follow Tupper's example, however, much to the annoyance of the Lieutenant-Governor, who felt that resignation was "the only proper, as well as dignified, course for a ministry to adopt, which had thus been given to understand that it no longer enjoyed the confidence of the representative of the Crown."[68] McInnes did not want "to take any decided action" until the Cassiar election had been held, although the results there "whether favourable or otherwise" would not in his opinion "reverse the verdict of the electorate."[69] But he soon became impatient. The province was suffering from the inactivity of the government, and since he did not feel warranted in restoring his full confidence in Turner he felt compelled to seek other advisers.

For, as I would not feel justified in granting you another dissolution and appeal to the electorate, and as, after a careful study of the situation, I am

[67]C.S.P., 1899, no. 89, 11, McInnes to Turner, July 14, 1898.
[68]Ibid., 18, McInnes to Turner, Aug. 15, 1898.
[69]Ibid., 12, McInnes to Turner, Aug. 8, 1898.

convinced that you could not command a majority in the assembly, I shall not put the province to the delay or to the expense of a special session of the legislature, merely for the purpose of formally demonstrating what has already been sufficiently demonstrated to me by the general elections.[70]

Later he added that he had not been advised "wisely, disinterestedly and faithfully," admittedly quoting Angers. He took a leaf from Letellier's book too and criticized Turner for failing to consult him about the redistribution bill of the previous session.

Turner urged McInnes to recall his letter of dismissal. While denying any desire "to hold office contrary to the will of the people," the Premier claimed the right "to await the verdict at the hands of their representatives duly elected and in parliament assembled."[71] The course adopted by the Lieutenant-Governor was "fraught with grave danger," it was contrary to "the spirit of the age," and it would be "watched with increasing vigilance by a people, proud of, yet jealous of any infringement of their liberties."[72] McInnes had acted with calm deliberation, however, and had no intention of turning back. For a moment it looked as if the dangerous experiment might fail. Knowing that the opposition factions could not agree upon a common leader, McInnes asked Robert Beaven, once a prominent politician but now without seat in the legislature or personal following, to form a government in the hope that the factions would coalesce under his nominal leadership. After four fruitless days Beaven was forced to relinquish the task and McInnes turned to Charles Semlin, the leader of the opposition in the previous assembly. Realizing that the alternative was a return of the Turner government, Joseph Martin reluctantly agreed to take office under Semlin and thus united the opposition.[73]

Semlin remained in office for eighteen months, until his government in turn was dismissed. The Premier was clearly not up to the task before him; the cabinet was dominated by Martin and Carter Cotton, both of whom had brought their factions into the government camp, and obeisance to Semlin was not even a formality. In less than a year the two men were in open and violent disagreement, and in July 1899 Martin left the cabinet. Since he had been the driving force in the administration and had been responsible for the notable legislative achievement of the previous session, the defection was serious; it was,

[70]*Ibid.*, 13, McInnes to Turner, Aug. 8, 1898.
[71]*Ibid.*, 16, Turner to McInnes, Aug. 9, 1898.
[72]*Ibid.*, 22, Turner to McInnes, Aug. 26, 1898.
[73]There was no guarantee that the new government could secure a majority and McInnes considered another dissolution. Martin had recently arrived in the province after a stormy political career in Manitoba and Ottawa.

in fact, open to question whether the government could survive. Almost immediately the opposition press and spokesmen agitated for an early session, and within a few weeks it became quite apparent that the Lieutenant-Governor shared their views.

Late in August 1899 McInnes asked Semlin to consider the advisability of an early session.[74] Receiving no answer, he decided to meet with the cabinet and persuade the members to do as he wished.[75] Some members of the cabinet, meanwhile, sought to check the Lieutenant-Governor's scheme by having pressure exerted from Ottawa. Aulay Morrison, Liberal member for New Westminster, was the vehicle through which they contacted Laurier. Morrison informed the Prime Minister that

. . . Governor McInnes will force an early session of the Legislature which will tend under the existing circumstances to precipitate a General Election. . . . Apart from any constitutional objection there might be to such action on the Governor's part it is manifestly unfair of him to exercise his prerogative in such an indecent and arbitrary manner. However, leaving aside the provincial aspect of the case a general election would sadly embarrass the Liberal Party in British Columbia. . . .[76]

Morrison urged Laurier to stay the hand of the Lieutenant-Governor, and outlined the argument that might be followed:

That Governor McInnes as a supporter of the Dominion Government and one who owes something to the Liberal Party be advised to keep at least within constitutional bounds in this matter. To refrain from doing anything gratuitously in his official capacity which tends to embarrass the Government in this Province. . . . Another circumstance which I submit, should justify your communicating with him, is that in the event of a dissolution, an investigation into his conduct towards the present Government will be demanded and upon such strong grounds that I fear the effect will be disastrous to him and serve as a strong card in the Tories hands against us all over the Dominion. The Governor with his usual vanity gives the information that he is moulding your policy as regards British Columbia so that any break of his as anticipated may be attributed to our party.

Morrison's letter first came into the hands of R. W. Scott, the Secretary of State. In a note to Laurier, Scott observed that McInnes had already dismissed one government and could not "afford to dismiss a second cabinet without cause; if he does we may be pressed to recall him." "McInnes seems to have very crude notions of constitutional government," he added, "and as we appointed him I presume it is

74PAC, Laurier Papers, 123, Morrison to Laurier, Aug. 27, 1899.
75Ibid., 124, Bostock to Laurier, Sept. 8, 1899.
76Ibid., 123, Morrison to Laurier, Aug. 27, 1899.

desirable that he should be kept, if possible, from the commission of gross errors of judgement."[77] With Laurier's approval, Scott sent McInnes a hasty warning: "I presume that the members of your Government have no intention of giving Martin the opportunity he would like by calling the Legislature before the usual time of meeting, and your Ministers are the proper judges of the time to summon the Assembly. . . ."[78] McInnes admitted that he had been urging his ministers to "meet the Legislature by the end of October or appeal to the electorate," but in deference to Scott's opinion he withdrew his request. Personally, he remained convinced that the province was suffering from the existing political unrest and uncertainty.[79]

Once again McInnes had tired of his government and wished to see it defeated. Checked on one side, he turned to the other. During the next month he constantly badgered his ministers—questioning appropriations, refusing to approve recommendations, demanding explanations—and so enraged Semlin that the Premier wanted to resign, "taking the Gov's action as a want of confidence."[80] He was persuaded by his colleagues, however, "to temporize rather than play McInnes' game." The crisis that the Lieutenant-Governor had attempted to bring forth was once more prevented. After lengthy conversations with him in Ottawa, Laurier was able to report that "any intention on the part of the Governor to dismiss his ministers is altogether improbable."[81]

When the assembly met on January 4, 1900, it was apparent that the government no longer possessed a working majority. For several weeks one member, likely to vote with the opposition, was absent, and even so the government was repeatedly sustained by the casting vote of the Speaker. As one observer remarked, only "if the session is a short one and no very prominent question arises" would the government last through the session.[82] The return of the absent member coincided with the introduction of a redistribution bill, the first important measure of the session, and the government was defeated. Semlin informed the Lieutenant-Governor of his defeat, which he had accepted as a general vote of non-confidence, and requested time to consider his position. In the three days of grace given to him, Semlin succeeded in coming to an agreement with three members of the

[77]Ibid., Scott to Laurier, Aug. 30, 1899.
[78]C.S.P., 1900, no. 174, 1, Scott to McInnes, Aug. 30, 1899.
[79]Ibid., 2, McInnes to Scott, Sept. 12, 1899.
[80]Laurier Papers, 128, McKechnie to Templeman, Oct. 23, 1899, enc. in Templeman to Laurier, Oct. 24, 1899.
[81]Ibid., Laurier to Templeman, Nov. 3, 1899.
[82]PAC, Sifton Papers, Bodwell to Sifton, Jan. 5, 1900.

Turner cabinet whereby they agreed to support him in return for two seats in the cabinet and some change in policy.[83] Semlin then assured McInnes that he would be able to command a majority in the assembly, although he could not (or was unwilling to) name the members who had agreed to enter the coalition. As the projected union of forces had not been consummated Semlin asked for further delay.[84]

A few hours later McInnes dismissed the Semlin government. In a lengthy letter, which he had obviously been preparing for some time, he cited all the grievances that had arisen during the previous year. He complained in particular that Semlin's assurances in August 1899, when McInnes had attempted to make him meet the legislature or dissolve, that he possessed the confidence of the assembly and the people "were not well founded": ". . . notwithstanding the confidence you expressed to me . . . you have not been able to pass a single measure, and I believe it to be now sufficiently demonstrated that the interests of the province have suffered, and are suffering, in consequence of the weak and unstable Government."[85] Meanwhile, Laurier had been informed that the Lieutenant-Governor was "only too eager" to dismiss Semlin and that in all probability he would call on Martin. "There should be no stone left unturned," wrote his informant, "to avert such a calamity."[86] Scott immediately wired McInnes to give Semlin more time to reconstruct, rather than force a dissolution or a change of government.[87] But the deed had been done.

As Morrison forecast, the Lieutenant-Governor asked Martin to form a government, Martin being, in his opinion, the man "best able to meet the necessities of the situation, create decisive issues, and establish final order, and something like usual political conditions out of the chaos of factions into which provincial parties have been rent."[88] Before the assembly could be prorogued Martin's selection had been repudiated by a vote of twenty-eight to one. Only with great difficulty

[83]PABC, Premier's Letterbook, Martin to Mills, March 19, 1900; Press, Feb. 23-8, 1900.
[84]There can be no doubt that Semlin did come to some agreement with the Turner faction and that this would have given him a majority in the assembly. By a vote of 22:15 the assembly endorsed Semlin's resolution: "That this House, being fully alive to the great loss, inconvenience and expense to the country of any interruption of the business of the House at the present time, begs hereby to express its regret that His Honor has seen fit to dismiss his advisers as in the present crisis they have efficient control of the House." The opposition leaders with whom he was arranging the coalition supported him. (British Columbia, Legislative Assembly, *Journals*, 1900, 78.)
[85]*C.S.P.*, 1900, no. 174, 9-12, McInnes to Semlin, Feb. 27, 1900.
[86]Laurier Papers, 142, Morrison to Laurier, Feb. 27, 1900.
[87]*C.S.P.*, 1900, no. 174, 7, Scott to McInnes, Feb. 27, 1900.
[88]*Ibid.*, 8, McInnes to the Governor-General in Council, March 27, 1900.

did Martin form a cabinet, and he was the only member who had held a seat in the legislature. Although Scott now urged McInnes to force an immediate session or a dissolution, the latter chose at this juncture to follow scrupulously the advice of his Premier and to delay the election until June when the statutory revision of the Voters' List would be completed. In any case, had not Scott previously informed him that his ministers very properly decided when the legislature should be summoned? Martin's legislative programme clearly substantiated the Lieutenant-Governor's opinion of him, but although it drew reluctant applause from many of his opponents it did not win a majority.[89] The Semlin faction was obliterated. The vast majority of the members-elect recognized no leader and adhered to no policy except self-interest. It was clear, however, that Martin could not remain in office and he resigned. McInnes turned to James Dunsmuir, financial and railway magnate, and the latter called to his cabinet several members of the old Turner administration. A week later McInnes was dismissed by the federal government.[90]

A good case can be made in support of Semlin's dismissal. His projected coalition with the opposition leaders, for whose dismissal he had assumed the responsibility only eighteen months before, was certainly an unprecedented course and one obviously contrary to the wishes of the electorate. Its sole purpose was to keep Martin out and to retain for the other factional leaders some share of the spoils of office. The choice of Martin, disastrous as it was, likewise can be supported: Martin was the strongest political figure in the province, he had led the campaign against Turner, he had secured the defeat of Semlin, and by 1900 he was the only leader who had not tried his hand at cabinet-making. But neither the local legislature nor the federal cabinet looked charitably upon the proceedings.

Commentators have been at a loss to find any reasonable explanation for McInnes' actions. At the time it was fairly generally suspected that he acted in the interests of his son, W. W. B. McInnes, then a young and very ambitious politician.[91] McInnes the younger had been elected to the House of Commons in 1896, but by 1898 he had tired

[89]He had seven certain and six probable supporters in a house of thirty-eight. This was the largest single group.

[90]Some of these events from 1898 to 1900 are treated in greater detail in John T. Saywell, "The McInnes Incident in British Columbia," *British Columbia Historical Quarterly*, XIII (July 1950); and G. F. G. Stanley, "A Constitutional Crisis in British Columbia," *Canadian Journal of Economics and Political Science*, XXI (Aug. 1955). Both surveys are based on the printed correspondence and local newspapers and both are marred by errors of fact and judgment.

[91]The authorities are legion. See the correspondence from Bostock, Bodwell, Templeman, McLagan, Morrison, and others in the Laurier and Sifton Papers.

of his rôle as an impotent back-bencher and contemplated entering
provincial politics. Within six weeks of McInnes' appointment as
Lieutenant-Governor it was charged that he was "pulling with the
present Provincial Government because he wants to get his son in
office out here and cut loose from Ottawa."[92] These charges were
repeated time and time again during the rest of his term. Their
plausibility can hardly be questioned: in July 1898 the Lieutenant-
Governor's private secretary—his eldest son—suggested that Turner
might strengthen his government by bringing W. W. B. McInnes into
it, and the Premier did not lightly disregard "representations from
such a quarter . . .";[93] although he had neither a seat in the legislature
nor a sizeable following, W. W. B. McInnes was approached by
Beaven; and later he and Martin were closely associated. The most
credible explanation that the evidence suggests, however, is not quite
so simple and involves more than personal ambition.

McInnes had strong views regarding the legislative policy needed
in British Columbia, and he genuinely believed that he, more than
anyone else, possessed the ability and qualifications to initiate it. He
first attempted to gain entry into the Laurier cabinet as the representative of British Columbia, and only when this failed did he push his
claims to the office of Lieutenant-Governor. Unquestionably he must
have assumed that as Lieutenant-Governor he could more effectively
fulfil his destiny as the saviour of the province than as a Senator. This
indicates at the outset that he had a very unusual, and mistaken,
impression of the power and influence of a Lieutenant-Governor. It
was later said that he had "a very exalted idea of his powers and
responsibilities" and tended to assume that he had "some sort of a
divine right to take the control of affairs. . . ."[94] His son best explained
his outlook: "he always did what he thought was right—irrespective
whether the acts were conventional or not."[95] The Lieutenant-
Governor then was a man of strong and decided views, a vain man
convinced that some of the responsibility for good and effective government lay in his hands, and a man determined to do what he thought
was "right."

McInnes realized that a vigorous, forward-looking legislative and
administrative programme was essential if the province were to reap
the harvest provided by the material prosperity of the late 1890's. New
conditions demanded new expedients and, perhaps, new leaders. The

[92]Sifton Papers, Bostock to Sifton, Jan. 15, 1898.
[93]C.S.P., 1899, no. 89, 15, Turner to McInnes, Aug. 9, 1898.
[94]Sifton Papers, Bodwell to Sifton, Jan. 20, 1900.
[95]W. W. B. McInnes to the Author, June 5, 1954.

Turner government was obviously incompetent—no one seriously questioned that—and McInnes dismissed it; the Semlin ministry had not the power to move forward—that had been fully demonstrated—and McInnes dismissed it. The association constantly referred to between Martin, the Lieutenant-Governor, and his son was not unnatural, for the three men were generally agreed on what was needed. By the end of 1898 all were in a state of suspended rebellion against the Liberal party to which they nominally belonged. In general it was a reaction against the eastern bias of the Laurier-Sifton national policy and the apparent belief in Ottawa that British Columbia and the Yukon could be ignored with impunity. In a sense it was directed against Sir Clifford Sifton, the western "boss" whose position Martin envied and felt he deserved. These "kickers" in British Columbia openly attacked the repeated disallowance of legislation designed to prevent Oriental immigration and supported by every man in the province; denounced the railway monopoly and the industrial monopoly that it supported, questioned the close association of the federal Liberals with men such as Jaffray and Cox of the Crows Nest Pass Company, and openly encouraged railway promoters in defiance of the federal government; complained of the tariff and the inequity of Dominion-provincial financial relations; and criticized the operation of the federal administrative system in the west. Martin and the Lieutenant-Governor warned Laurier that the party whip was not nearly so effective beyond the Rockies, and Martin illustrated his point successfully by leading an insurrection in Manitoba where Sifton was supposed to be supreme.[96]

In positive terms Martin's policy—for he alone was in a position to put it into effect—far surpassed anything conceived in the province before and did in fact anticipate major legislation for years to come. New regions were to be opened and new industries encouraged by extensive railway building; the increasingly important labour element was to be conciliated by more equitable labour legislation and the restriction of Oriental immigration; the fisheries, agriculture, lumbering, and mining were to be stimulated by active governmental assistance; and, finally, party lines were to be introduced, thus assuring more decisive electoral verdicts and more stable and homogeneous governments. In some ways Martin's policy verged on a provincial rights movement, such as he had led with such effect as a member of the Greenway administration in Manitoba, and he made little secret

[96]See the Martin, T. R. McInnes, and W. W. B. McInnes correspondence in the Laurier Papers.

of his willingness to oppose the federal government in the interests of the province. This was the policy that the Lieutenant-Governor soon regarded as the "right" one, and he was determined to use all his power and influence, whether "conventional or not," to see it put into effect. His own testimony on this point is conclusive: "Doubtless in the eyes of many people it was a 'blunder' for me not to content myself with smoking my pipe and drawing my salary in peace, as other Governors are told to do. But right or wrong, I took a stand for the policy at that time enunciated by the Hon. Joseph Martin. . . . I was ready to stand or fall by that policy then—and I am ready to do so again."[97] Such was the measure of the man.

The familiar charge that McInnes "succeeded in getting the affairs of that province into hopeless confusion" is just a little too much like putting the cart before the horse.[98] The confusion owed nothing to McInnes; it was the inevitable corollary of factional government in a period peculiarly transitional. It was the confusion, on the contrary, that provided McInnes with his opportunity to meddle and intrigue. His attempts to steer a course through it were ill-advised and unsuccessful, although they did stimulate some crystallization of policies and parties. Another three years were to pass, however, before anything resembling stable political conditions was established—and this as a result of the introduction of party lines and by a government that, consciously or otherwise, adopted Martin's policy wholesale.

During these three years McInnes' successor, Sir Henri Joly de Lotbinière, the Liberal who had taken office after Letellier's dismissal of de Boucherville, faced a succession of political crises. The Dunsmuir government, originally supported by all those who opposed Martin, lacked unity and common principles; the cabinet could not contend in the legislature with the self-interest of its supporters.[99] Creeping paralysis and political decay soon sterilized the administration and, paradoxically, before a year had passed only Martin's support enabled Dunsmuir to stay in office. In the autumn of 1901, following the resignation of two ministers and the failure of a replacement to secure re-election, Dunsmuir tendered his resignation. The Lieutenant-Governor refused to accept it:

[97]*Victoria Colonist*, Nov. 27, 1902, McInnes to the Editor.
[98]See for example R. McG. Dawson, "The Independence of the Lieutenant-Governor," *Dalhousie Review*, II (July 1922), 239.
[99]A group of railway financiers from eastern Canada found it an easy matter to create their own party in the assembly, "which left the Government in the position that they had either to give way or fall." (Laurier Papers, 196, Jaffray to Laurier, May 6, 1901.)

... en lui représentant qu'il n'avait pas le droit de résigner un poste auquel il avait été appelé dans un moment de crise, par le voeu unanime de la Province, et dont il avait accepté la responsabilité,—que résigner maintenant serait admettre qu'il n'avait pas mérité la confiance qui lui avait été témoignée par la Province—et qu'il devait rester à son poste jusqu'au moment où le vote des Representants de la Province, s'il lui était hostile, lui donnerait le droit de se retirer—pas avant.[100]

By the end of 1902 Dunsmuir had tired of the game and resigned, recommending that E. G. Prior, a member of his cabinet, be called on to succeed him.

The Prior administration was doomed from its inception. Given an independent support by a small majority of the members, Prior managed to stagger through the first six weeks of the 1903 session. In April, however, a Select Committee was appointed to examine the government's railway policy and it soon revealed that two members of the cabinet had been in collusion with prominent railway interests and had been working at cross-purposes with the rest of the ministry.[101] The Premier, although guilty of no offence, was discredited. Before the committee reported to the assembly Prior announced that he had asked his two colleagues to resign. A third member of the cabinet, W. W. B. McInnes, resigned of his own accord, stating publicly that he did so to facilitate an election on party lines. He informed Laurier, to whom he had been recently reconciled, otherwise:

These disclosures have shattered confidence in all who had anything to do with the transaction. This includes every member of the Government except myself. To protect myself I intended resigning from the Government and would have done so yesterday had not a warm friend of yours in high authority here advised me not to do so until the estimates had passed—as my resignation might imperil their passage. I intend therefore to act as soon as they are passed.[102]

McInnes added that the revelations were clearly of a nature to justify the dismissal of the government.

The collapse of the administration immediately occasioned a non-confidence motion. Prior attempted to counter this by stating that he had been promised a dissolution as soon as supply had been passed; and in answer to Martin's query he assured the assembly that even if

[100]Ibid., 210, Joly to Laurier, Oct. 31, 1901.
[101]British Columbia, Legislative Assembly, Journals, 1903, Appendix, Report of the Select Committee re Columbia and Western Railway Land Subsidy.
[102]Laurier Papers, 265, McInnes to Laurier, May 17, 1903. The "warm friend" was Joly. McInnes did resign before the estimates passed.

defeated "I will still go to His Honour and ask him for a dissolution and I will get it. I expect my right to appeal to the country to be recognized."[103] Nonetheless, the members passed the motion and, to assure complete confusion, recorded a similar want of confidence in Richard McBride, the leading opposition member. Prior's attempts to have supply passed were in vain. Momentarily the ship of state drifted rudderless.

Rather than consider supply the members chose to investigate a government contract that had been secured by the firm of E. G. Prior. The facts were soon made clear: while he had acted as Chief Commissioner of Lands and Works in the absence of the minister, six tenders for a contract had been submitted to the Premier for his information and consideration; no tender was submitted by the firm in which he was a leading member; Prior ordered the government engineer to notify E. G. Prior and Company, of which he was the President, of the terms of the contract and to invite them to submit an estimate; the firm submitted the lowest tender and secured the contract.[104] The Premier saw nothing wrong in his actions. He denied that he had informed his firm of the other bids or had been a party to the final award; and he was no more at fault, he declared, than "a member who is a lawyer, or is Attorney-General, and his partner takes charge of looking after a private bill for anybody and lobbying it through the House."[105] The committee's report was sent at once to the Lieutenant-Governor, who, soon after receiving it, sent the following note to the Premier:

The views which you expressed in explanation and justification of your action, in your answers to the Committee . . . are so incompatible with, and so completely at variance with what I have always understood to be the true principles of Parliamentary Independence of Members and, above all, of Ministers of the Crown, that, while admitting that you must have honestly considered that you were doing no wrong, I am to my sincere regret unable to continue feeling that confidence in your judgement which would justify me in acting any longer on your advice.[106]

Joly's observations were justified, although if his principles had been universally applied there would have been scores of dismissals in the Canadian provinces. The dismissal was extremely gentle and it passed without criticism and with very little comment. Dismissal was old news to British Columbians.

[103]*Victoria Colonist*, May 28, 1903.
[104]British Columbia, Legislative Assembly, *Journals*, 1903, DCCCXXX.
[105]*Ibid.*
[106]Cited in *Canadian Annual Review*, 1903, 214.

One is convinced, however, that Joly welcomed the opportunity when it came. The Prior administration, like its predecessor, had been neither strong nor able, and Prior had been able to keep afloat only by letting the assembly run with the current, the wind, and the tide. More important from Joly's point of view was the fact that Prior stood in the way of government through political parties. Convinced that "avec notre système Parlementaire Anglais il faut absolument la discipline de partis" the Lieutenant-Governor was eager to see party lines established.[107] And by 1903 intelligent men generally had concluded that party lines were essential and leading members of both parties were prepared to gamble their political future for the sake of political stability. An election under Prior would have postponed the transition for an indefinite period and in all probability Joly was extremely pleased not to have to fulfil his earlier promise of a dissolution. After the vote of non-confidence and the contract inquiry Prior should have resigned; the sole alternative, as Joly saw it, was dismissal.

The Lieutenant-Governor called on Richard McBride, Conservative leader in the assembly and perhaps the strongest figure on the opposition benches, persuaded (or forced) him to form a Conservative cabinet, and, after temporary supply had been secured, granted him a dissolution. McBride's margin of victory in the election was narrow and his position was precarious for a few years. The reign of factional anarchy had come to an end, however. The last dismissal at least had been an effective one.

Perhaps the most striking fact about the five dismissals is that they occurred and that they succeeded. In every case but one the Lieutenant-Governor's action was upheld by the electorate or the legislature, the defeat of Joseph Martin, who had assumed the responsibility for the dismissal of Semlin, being the single exception. But it must be remembered that Martin's failure in the June 1900 election was not a repudiation by the electorate of the dismissal; if related to the constitutional question at all it was a disapproval of the selection of Martin as Premier. Moreover, the dismissed government was annihilated; no member of the cabinet was re-elected, and only six supporters were to be found in the next assembly. In any case, the election did not turn on the dismissal of Semlin at all; in fact it was seldom mentioned.

Elections also followed the dismissals of 1878, 1891, and 1903. But British Columbians heard nothing of Prior's dismissal during the election of 1903; no one questioned the dismissal and no party chose to make an issue of it. In 1878 the Quebec Conservatives denounced

107PABC, Lotbinière Papers, Joly to Edmund Joly, May 2, 1902.

the "Grizzly Bear" in Spencer Wood, while the Liberals begged the voters to uphold law, order, and duly constituted authority—usually an effective appeal in Quebec—and with a plea for integrity in public men coupled with an absence of it in the campaign, managed to win a slender majority. A survey of the campaign would reveal, however, that the election was fought on issues much more pragmatic and much more personal than the right of a Lieutenant-Governor to dismiss his ministers. The election of 1892 is perhaps the most significant, for Mercier, embarrassed by the revelations of misrule, attempted to regain power by persuading the people to repudiate the Lieutenant-Governor. Yet he did so not on the grounds that dismissal was an arbitrary power, the exercise of which was incompatible with responsible government, or even that it was unjustified. Rather he argued that the power was exercised arbitrarily; that Angers had acted in the interests not of good government and the province of Quebec, but for the good of the Conservative party and the interests of the Dominion government. He attempted to convince the people of Quebec that Angers' action was a violation of provincial autonomy which, if allowed to go unrepudiated, would in time mean the destruction of the federal agreement and thus the rights of Quebec—racial, religious, linguistic—by the forever hostile government at Ottawa. A similar cry had succeeded in 1886 and 1890. It failed in 1892.

Morally there is no connection between success and right or justice. But in politics the distinction cannot be pushed too far lest one come hard against the unyielding kernel of the democratic principle. Nonetheless to say that the Lieutenant-Governors succeeded is not to say that they were right, that they were justified in using their undoubted power as they did. If only the degree of political motivation—the imponderable X in constitutional history—were known one would be less hesitant to pass judgment.

CHAPTER SIX

THE PREROGATIVE OF DISSOLUTION

WHEN IT WAS rumoured in 1952 that the government of British Columbia planned to dissolve a legislature that had never met, the Lieutenant-Governor's position and powers were warmly discussed. Publicists were not too sure what the conventions of the constitution were: some argued that the Lieutenant-Governor would be bound to refuse the request and, after the inevitable resignation, call on the leader of the opposition; others argued that he had no alternative to accepting the advice tendered to him. "The significant point in this discussion," one close observer noted, was "the unanimity of opinion that the Lieutenant-Governor has no constitutional discretion in the matter."[1]

Among scholars and statesmen it is generally agreed that the Crown has a perfect right to refuse to dissolve. Although some contemplate a fairly frequent use of the reserve power, others find it difficult to imagine the conditions that might justify its exercise. Thumbing through the pages of Anson and Dicey, Lowell and Low, Forsey, Evatt, and Keith, the student finds it difficult to keep his head amid a variety of precedents and arguments. The difficulty is increased by the absence of a modern precedent in the United Kingdom of a refusal to dissolve; yet there is a persistent tradition that the monarch to this day possesses the right. Queen Victoria was no "rubber-stamp" and carefully considered every request for a dissolution. Edward VII denied that he was an automaton "when the question of dissolving Parliament arose in circumstances which admitted of doubt as to the course which should be taken."[2] George V told Bonar Law in 1916 that he would refuse a dissolution if asked, attempted to persuade Lloyd George from dissolving in 1918, and agreed to Ramsay Macdonald's request in 1924 only after the leaders of the other parties had admitted their inability to form an alternative government.[3] Just five years ago Clement Attlee stated that "the monarch has the right to grant or refuse a prime minister's request for a dissolution of Parliament which involves

[1]H. F. Angus, "The British Columbia Election, June 1952," *Canadian Journal of Economics and Political Science*, XVIII (Nov. 1952), 524.
[2]Sir Sidney Lee, *King Edward VII—a Biography* (London, 1925), II, 188.
[3]Sir Harold Nicolson, *King George V—His Life and Reign* (London, 1952), 289, 328, 399.

145

a general election. This is a very real power. It means that there is always someone other than a party leader who is available to take action in critical times."[4]

The question is perhaps of less importance in the United Kingdom than in Canada where the politicians have been much more willing, possibly because of the colonial tradition and the element of irresponsibility in politics that was its legacy, to pay scant regard to constitutional conventions. Lowell's observation that a refusal of dissolution was unlikely in England "because the rules of political fair play are so thoroughly understood among English statesmen that the power is not likely to be misused" should be compared with Goldwin Smith's belief that dissolution had become the plaything of Canadian politicians, who, no less than those in the United States, required "the restraint of written law."[5] Moreover, the present tendency in Canada towards the increasing supremacy of the executive over the legislature suggests the continued validity of Burke's warning:

A House of Commons respected by his ministers is essential to His Majesty's service: it is fit that they should yield to Parliament, and not that Parliament should be new-modelled until it is fitted to their purposes. If our authority is to be held up when we coincide with His Majesty's advisers, but is to be set at nought the moment it differs from them, the House of Commons will shrink into a mere appendage of the administration. . . .[6]

A dissolution, or at least the threat of one, is the best means of keeping the legislature in a state of dutiful obedience. Nor should it be forgotten that "to a very large extent, the notion that the Prime Minister for the time being possesses an absolute and unqualified right to obtain dissolution from the King has derived from the fact that, in England, until comparatively recent times, the three party system, to which we have long been accustomed in some of the Dominions, was almost unknown."[7] With a multi-party or group system such as has often existed in the Canadian provinces the accepted conventions are of limited applicability and may confuse rather than clarify the issue.

[4]*Life*, Feb. 18, 1952, 31.

[5]A. L. Lowell, *The Government of England* (New York, 1920), I, 33; Goldwin Smith, *Canada and the Canadian Question* (London, 1891), 148–9.

[6]Cited in E. A. Forsey, *The Royal Power of Dissolution of Parliament in the British Commonwealth* (Toronto, 1943), 9. As Dr. Forsey observes: "The danger of royal absolutism is past; but the danger of Cabinet absolutism, even of Prime Ministerial absolutism, is present and growing. Against that danger the reserve power of the Crown . . . is in some instances the only constitutional safeguard." (*Ibid.*, 259.)

[7]H. V. Evatt, "The Discretionary Authority of Dominion Governors," *Canadian Bar Review*, XVIII (Jan. 1940), 2.

Moreover the provincial Lieutenant-Governors directly succeeded colonial Governors and followed the precedents and guiding rules established by their predecessors. Officials of the Colonial Office had always been willing to endow the Governor with greater discretion than would have been acceptable in England. The constitutional manual based on the various decisions and precedents was written by the Canadian Alpheus Todd, and remained one of the principal texts well into the present century. Of dissolution Todd was able to write as follows:

The "constitutional discretion" of the governor should be invoked in respect to every case wherein a dissolution may be advised or requested by his ministers; and his judgement ought not to be fettered, or his discretion disputed, by inferences drawn from previous precedent, when he decides that a proposed dissolution is unnecessary or undesirable.
It is the duty of a governor to consider the question of a dissolution of the parliament or legislature solely in reference to the general interests of the people and not from a party standpoint. He is under no obligation to sustain the party in power if he believes that the accession to office of their opponents would be more beneficial to the public interest.

The Governor should weigh carefully the advice of a Premier defeated in the legislature, and "if he believes that a strong and efficient administration could be formed that would command the confidence of the existing assembly, he is free to make trial thereof. . . ."[8] Todd's Lieutenant-Governor would be no rubber-stamp; and his book was in every Government House library.

While Todd was writing his book, Théodore Robitaille, the Lieutenant-Governor of Quebec, provided him with another precedent. The incident was the last in the long chain of events that began with Letellier's dismissal of de Boucherville in 1878 and was followed by Joly's acceptance of office, a narrow Liberal victory at the polls, and a short session of the legislature. By the spring of 1879 Joly had won three by-elections and when the assembly met in June was able to secure a constant majority of three votes. The Legislative Council, being appointed, was almost wholly Conservative and was soon to force the issue. Meanwhile the Conservatives had won the federal election of 1878 and in July 1879 dismissed Letellier. Robitaille, an ardent Conservative, succeeded him at Spencer Wood. Alexander Mackenzie admitted that the end was not clear: "but I fear that

---

[8]Todd was Librarian of Parliament and was often consulted on constitutional matters by such persons as Macdonald, Dufferin, and Lorne. The first edition of his *Parliamentary Government in the British Colonies* was published in 1880. A second edition was published by his son in 1894. Extracts here are from the second edition (London), 799–800.

Robitaille will intrigue with the Upper House to annoy and if possible defeat Joly's government. Robitaille is and will be a mere tool and is appointed for the purpose of being a tool for the future. On the other hand having no originality or head power he will be an awkward tool and may cut the hands of his employers."[9] And Mackenzie was not far wrong. Robitaille's appointment spurred the council to action and when the estimates came before it refused to register its assent

. . . until it shall have pleased His Honor the Lieutenant-Governor to choose advisers disposed to maintain his dignity by the fulfilment of the promises made in his name, to respect the spirit of the constitution and the rights of the Province of Quebec. . . , to uphold the dignity and authority of our institutions by refraining from interference in the application and execution of the law, and who will at the same time be able to enforce their views in the Legislature, and justify the Council in entrusting them with the management of the public funds.[10]

The Lieutenant-Governor received this open demand for dismissal graciously and expressed his hope that the two chambers would find some means of re-establishing harmonious relations.

The Joly government countered with a resolution from the assembly stating that the House of Lords had never in recent years refused to pass supply or use its power to force a change of ministers upon the Crown; that the fate of every government depends upon the elected, not the appointed, members of the legislature; and that the assembly supported the administration and would see with regret "these supplies entrusted to advisers in whom this House would not have expressed its confidence."[11] In a surprise move Joly then adjourned in order to stir up an agitation in the province sufficient to coerce the council. This Canadian version of "Commons versus Lords" cry—"mend them or end them"—failed dismally, and when the legislature assembled two months later Joly discovered that five supporters had been bribed or persuaded to support the opposition. A resolution of non-confidence was passed immediately. Doubtless with faint hope, Joly went to Spencer Wood and asked for a dissolution. The vote in the assembly, he declared, was a direct result "of the unconstitutional position taken up by the Legislative Council" and did not express the opinion of the electorate.[12]

Robitaille's reply was lengthy and emphatic. A dissolution, he said,

[9]*Report of the . . . Public Archives of Nova Scotia*, 1952, 60, Mackenzie to Jones, July 29, 1879.
[10]Quebec, Legislative Council, *Journals*, 1879, 190–1.
[11]*Ibid.*, 337.
[12]*Ibid.*, 358, Joly to Robitaille, Oct. 29, 1879.

must be regarded from two points of view: the cabinet thinks only of the welfare of the party and seeks it in an attempt to increase its own power; but the Lieutenant-Governor must think in terms not of political parties but of the welfare of the community as a whole. ". . . he is strictly bound to enquire whether the more than ordinary exercise of the Royal Prerogatives, with which he is invested, is required for the greater advantage of the Province; for he is responsible towards the Crown for all political troubles and financial damages from which he can save the country, but from which he does not." The government had had a dissolution in the spring of 1878 and, although able to carry on for one session, now found itself in a minority in an assembly elected under its auspices. To appeal to the people on the issue raised by the council was illogical, for both chambers now agreed: "it cannot be alleged that recourse must be had to extraordinary means to terminate a conflict which is in a fair way to be terminated by ordinary means."[13] Faced with this refusal Joly resigned and the Lieutenant-Governor called on J. A. Chapleau, Conservative leader in the assembly, to form a new government. Thus ended *l'affaire Letellier*, a series of events in which it is impossible to separate politics from the constitution.

Four years later, the Lieutenant-Governor of New Brunswick, R. D. Wilmot, previously a member of Macdonald's cabinet and Speaker of the Senate, refused a request for a dissolution. In the absence of party lines it was difficult to ascertain precisely where the balance of political power lay after the election of 1882. Since the majority of the members-elect appeared to be sympathetic to the administration, Premier D. L. Hannington made no attempt to test his strength until the legislature met at its usual time, eight months after the election. The government elected a Speaker on a 21:17 division, but later suffered a 22:18 defeat on a confidence resolution.[14] Before the members of the cabinet had concluded their deliberations, the Lieutenant-Governor, after having read the *Journals*, summoned the Premier. With him Hannington took a hastily prepared cabinet brief in which a dissolution was recommended for the following reasons: the government had won the election, it had won four by-elections since the general election, it had been able to elect a Speaker on the first day of the session, the Legislative Council had unanimously approved the reply to the Address, the defeat had been caused by the defection of three members elected to support the administration, and new issues had arisen that should be submitted to the people. In short, the government had been

---

[13]*Ibid.*, 358–9, Robitaille to Joly, Oct. 29, 1879.
[14]New Brunswick, Legislative Assembly, *Journals*, 1883, *passim*.

defeated unfairly and without warning and in direct opposition to the supposed wishes of the electorate.[15] Wilmot observed in reply that much of this was beyond his official knowledge: "The Lieutenant-Governor cannot enter into the reasons and causes which have influenced individual members in giving their votes; for such action they are responsible to their own constituents." He knew only that the government had lost the support of an assembly that had never before met. "In his judgement, the existing circumstances" were not "of so grave a nature as to require an action, which would involve the Province in turmoil, excitement and expense of a general election."[16]

It is interesting to note that the government did not take this refusal as automatically involving its resignation. For several days, according to the press, Hannington and his colleagues frantically attempted to reconstruct the cabinet, and only when this failed did the Premier resign. As his last act, Hannington recommended that A. G. Blair, the strongest figure on the opposition benches and the man who had engineered his defeat, be asked to succeed him.[17] Blair had no difficulty in forming a government and remained in office until he became a member of Laurier's administration thirteen years later. There was no criticism in New Brunswick of the Lieutenant-Governor's exercise of his prerogative; even the Hannington press, while it asserted the right of the government to dissolve, made no attempt to denounce Wilmot for concluding that the request could not be approved.

A third refusal occurred in Prince Edward Island in roughly similar circumstances. The Conservative government led by N. McLeod had been returned in 1890 with a tender majority (16–14), and had weathered one session with a majority of one. During the fall and winter of 1890–1, however, it lost two by-elections and thus the control of the Legislative Assembly. A few days before the house was to meet in the spring of 1891 the Premier asked for a dissolution "in view of the even strength of both political parties in the Legislature." The truth was, of course, that with a Conservative Speaker the opposition had a majority of one. The Lieutenant-Governor, J. S. Carvell, refused to dissolve and McLeod resigned. A Liberal administration was formed that held three sessions before dissolving in 1893.[18]

Historians have frequently assumed that McInnes refused to dissolve

[15]*Ibid.*, second session, 1883, 21–2, Memorandum of the Executive Council in Committee, Feb. 26, 1883.
[16]*Ibid.*, Memorandum for the Executive Council, Feb. 27, 1883.
[17]LLNB, Lieutenant-Governor's Correspondence, Wilmot to the Secretary of State, March 3, 1883.
[18]Frank Mackinnon, *The Government of Prince Edward Island* (Toronto, 1951), 160–1.

THE PREROGATIVE OF DISSOLUTION 151

on at least two occasions during his three hectic years as Lieutenant-Governor of British Columbia. When he dismissed Turner in August 1898, McInnes observed that he "would not feel justified" in granting another dissolution.[19] It is safe to say that Turner had never contemplated another dissolution. When it looked as if Turner's successor could not command a majority in the legislature the idea of a dissolution appears to have arisen. McInnes asked the Secretary of State if he could "constitutionally grant request for dissolution before new Legislature has formally convened?"[20] Although the Lieutenant-Governor had the "technical" right to grant a dissolution, Scott replied, the exercise of the power would be "extraordinary and unprecedented," and he advised McInnes against it.[21] The legislature was not dissolved. It would be dangerous to interpret this as a refusal of dissolution, for more likely than not the idea originated with the Lieutenant-Governor. Semlin in turn was defeated in the legislature, but chose reconstruction in preference to resignation or dissolution, much to McInnes' dismay.

Over fifty years later this turbulent period was exhumed in a search for precedents when a similar situation recurred in British Columbia. No party won a majority in the provincial election of 1952, and although the Social Credit leader, W. A. C. Bennett, formed a government following the resignation of Byron Johnson, there was some doubt whether he could control the legislature. At one point the harassed Premier asserted his right to dissolve the assembly before it met and thus commenced a long and vigorous public discussion of the Lieutenant-Governor's position and responsibilities. Scott's advice in 1898 was frequently cited in support of the view that the advice to dissolve would have to be refused. In the end Premier Bennett met the assembly; no dissolution appears to have been requested.[22]

The Joly-Prior crisis in British Columbia in 1903 presents a difficult problem. The Premier had been promised a dissolution as soon as the estimates had been passed, but before this was done his government disintegrated and he was defeated in the house. All along Prior insisted that even if defeated he would be granted a dissolution, although it is evident that the vote of non-confidence was expressly designed to force his resignation before the legislature was dissolved. With the estimates

[19]C.S.P., 1899, no. 89, 13, McInnes to Turner, Aug. 8, 1898.
[20]Ibid., 1900, no. 174, 1, McInnes to Scott, Oct. 21, 1898.
[21]Ibid., Scott to McInnes, Oct. 21, 1898.
[22]See Angus, "The British Columbia Election" and E. A. Forsey, "Professor Angus on the British Columbia Election," Canadian Journal of Economics and Political Science, XIX (May 1953), 226–9. Press, July–Aug. 1952.

still not passed the revelations of a Select Committee led the Lieutenant-Governor to dismiss the administration. We cannot say, as does Dr. Forsey, that Prior was refused a dissolution: the original promise was conditional—dissolution would follow supply; this condition had not been fulfilled when he was dismissed; there is no evidence to suggest that the Premier asked for a dissolution between his defeat in the assembly and his dismissal; and if he did not ask he could not be refused.[23]

Only in the three instances mentioned can it be said without fear of error that a dissolution was officially requested and officially refused. In all probability there have been other occasions when a dissolution was refused with equal decisiveness or when the government, realizing that its request would be refused, followed another course. The three cases have much in common: the legislature had been recently elected; the government had admittedly lost the support of the legislature; an alternative government could be formed without difficulty from the existing legislature without a new election; and the refusal to dissolve was supported by the legislature and by the electorate at the next election.

Three relatively recent crises have resulted in a discussion of the power of disolution. It will be recalled that the Saskatchewan election of June 1929 returned no party with a majority.[24] A coalition of Conservatives and Progressives made it apparent that the Liberals would be defeated when the house met, but the government elected to take its chances in the assembly nonetheless. During the debate on a motion of confidence the Attorney General declared that if defeated the government could dissolve. This was an unusual statement in view of the fact that the Conservatives and Progressives, who together had a majority of six, had declared their intention of co-operating in the formation of a new government and had selected a leader. When defeated, however, the government resigned.[25]

The Ontario election of 1943 likewise gave no party a majority: in a house of ninety members the Conservatives had thirty-eight, the C.C.F. thirty-four, the Liberals fifteen, and others three. The Liberal government resigned and Mr. George Drew, leader of the Conservatives, formed a government. Premier Drew survived one short and ineffectual session, but was twice defeated (51:36) in March 1945.[26] The legis-

[23]See chap. v, 144 ff.; Press, May 27–June 1, 1903; Forsey, *Dissolution of Parliament*, 58–9 and sources there cited.
[24]See chap. ii, 44 ff.
[25]Press, Sept. 4–7, 1929; Saskatchewan, Legislative Assembly, *Sessional Papers*, 1929–30, 1–61.   [26]Ontario, Legislative Assembly, *Journals*, March 22, 1945.

lature was immediately dissolved; the Conservative press argued that the Premier would not feel justified in resigning and advising the Lieutenant-Governor to call on the C.C.F. leader to form a government. Dr. Eugene Forsey, who resented both the Premier's assumption that he had the right to advise and the implication that the Lieutenant-Governor possessed no discretion in the matter of dissolution, voiced the criticism of many.

Unless Canada has abandoned the British Constitutional system, therefore, it must be taken as settled that, both in the Dominion and the provinces, a Government defeated in the House has no right to a dissolution on demand; that its duty, in many instances, is simply to resign and make way for another Government in the existing Parliament; and that if it disregards that duty and asks for dissolution when it should not, the Governor-General or Lieutenant-Governor may refuse and call on the Leader of the Opposition to take office.[27]

This argument was accepted by the leader of the opposition in British Columbia eight years later. The Social Credit government, which had never possessed a clear majority in the assembly, was defeated in its first session on a major bill.[28] The Premier declared that he planned to dissolve. Mr. Harold Winch, the official leader of the opposition, declared that it was the Premier's duty to resign, and added that since "the leader of the opposition has the mandatory right to approach the Lieutenant-Governor" he was going to lay before His Honour the "constitutional situation" as he saw it.[29] Members of the cabinet replied that the Premier was completely unfettered in the advice he tendered and clearly indicated that in their mind the Lieutenant-Governor was little more than a cypher. Before accepting the Premier's advice to dissolve, the Lieutenant-Governor consulted Mr. Winch. The C.C.F. leader observed that his party had as many seats as Social Credit, expressed his desire to form an adminstration, and promised that no radical legislation would be undertaken within the existing legislature. The Lieutenant-Governor demanded an assurance from Mr. Winch that he could command a majority in the house. Unable to give this assurance, the latter pointed out that no such assertion was received from Premier Bennett when his government was formed. But since he could not guarantee to control the legislature Mr. Winch was denied permission to form a government and the dissolution requested by the Premier was granted.[30]

[27]E. A. Forsey, "Constitutional Issues in Ontario," *Canadian Forum*, May 1945.
[28]British Columbia, Legislative Assembly, *Journals*, March 24, 1953.
[29]*Victoria Colonist*, March 25, 1953.
[30]*Victoria Times*, March 28, 1953.

Mention is made of these cases not to suggest that any other course should more properly have been followed, but rather as an indication that the impression appears to have become general that the discretionary power of the Crown to refuse a dissolution has lapsed. The Liberal government in Saskatchewan had no right to a dissolution, and had one been asked the Lieutenant-Governor would surely have refused. Unless the Liberals had been prepared to support the C.C.F. leader in Ontario in 1945—an unlikely prospect—there was no alternative government, although the Lieutenant-Governor, perhaps after consultation with the leader of the opposition, should have come to this conclusion. The Lieutenant-Governor of British Columbia showed admirable common sense; if Mr. Winch could not carry on there would have to be a dissolution, and Premier Bennett rather than Mr. Winch was entitled to that dissolution. Premier Bennett's assumption that his only course was to dissolve, however, illustrates the general attitude towards dissolution.

Sir John A. Macdonald occasionally maintained that as a federal officer the Lieutenant-Governor could and should refuse a dissolution whenever the national interest was at stake. A provincial government, in his mind, should not be allowed to dissolve and fight an election on an anti-federal platform. When Tupper feared that the secessionist government of Nova Scotia planned to counter the refusal of the federal and imperial governments to recognize its claims by taking its case to the people of the province, Macdonald advised the Lieutenant-Governor to refuse the request for a dissolution. The legislature, he declared, had not expired, the ministry possessed an overwhelming majority, and, as far as the province was concerned, there were no new issues; for "it must never be forgotten that all questions affecting the Constitution of the Confederation and the Dominion must be settled by the Representatives of the province in the Dominion Parliament and not in the provincial legislatures."[31] Faithful as always to the federal cause, Doyle replied that under no circumstances would he grant a dissolution and, although no dissolution had been requested, he had informed his ministers that he had "no idea of doing so for the very reason you have given me. . . ."[32] The same advice was given Lieutenant-Governor Richey in 1886 when Fielding threatened to dissolve on a similar issue. It was impossible for Macdonald to instruct Richey not to dissolve, for the legal term of the legislature had almost expired. But "as important issues" were "to go before the people"

[31]PAC, Macdonald Papers, 516, Macdonald to Doyle, Sept. 28, 1869.
[32]Ibid., 114, Doyle to Macdonald, Oct. 26, 1869.

he advised the Lieutenant-Governor to "insist that they should not be taken by surprise and that ample time should be given them for consideration." Moreover, declared the Prime Minister, the secessionist issue was beyond the legitimate scope of the provincial government and "you will I have no doubt feel it your duty as a Dominion officer to decline to allow that subject to enter into consideration at all. . . . if necessary you will be supported by the whole weight of the Dominion Government."[33] A year later, when the Premier of Manitoba contemplated an appeal to the electorate against federal disallowance of provincial railway legislation, Macdonald ordered the Lieutenant-Governor to prevent it.[34] The latter replied that Premier Norquay realized that a dissolution would not be granted under the circumstances.[35]

It is possible that a dissolution may have been refused on similar grounds in Manitoba two decades later. When Saskatchewan and Alberta were being established Manitoba sought an extension of its boundaries. Cardinal Sbarretti, the Papal Legate, publicly suggested that if the provincial government gave greater concessions to the Roman Catholics the federal government would undoubtedly regard its aspirations more sympathetically. As was natural the Roblin government assumed that Laurier was responsible for the declaration, and, seeing an admirable opportunity to embarrass the Liberals in the province, decided to seek a mandate from the people to carry the war into Africa. It was stated in the press that the Lieutenant-Governor, D. H. McMillan, a staunch Liberal, refused to dissolve. For several days the cabinet was in almost continuous session and there were daily rumours that various members of the cabinet, including the Premier, were on the verge of resignation. It is significant, perhaps, that the rumours

33*Ibid.*, 526, Macdonald to Richey, May 14, 1886. Richey's reply is of considerable interest. It was too late to object to the date of dissolution, he wrote, "the question having several times been referred to in consultation with the premier who has every reason to expect my acting upon the advise [*sic*] tendered. . . . Of course were I in any way to recognize the resolution which passed the House of Assembly as *legitimately* raising an issue as to whether or not this province should continue as a member of the Confederation, I should have a ground on which to take my stand and should do so, but the subject has never once been alluded to even in the most distant manner in any communication between Mr. Fielding and myself. . . . Mr. Fielding it is true is the leader of my Government and had I felt it to be justifiable and prudent in view of all the circumstances to censure his conduct and declare my want of confidence in his management, I presume this would have been entirely within my prerogative. . . . Such a stretch of power on my part however seemed to be the surest way of fanning to a flame the embers of discontent and I have deemed it the wisest course to ignore what has in no direct way been brought to my notice." (*Ibid.*, 117, May 17, 1886.)
34*Ibid.*, 527, Macdonald to Aikins, Oct. 15, 1887.
35*Ibid.*, 186, Aikins to Macdonald, Nov. 23, 1887. See Chapter VII, 179 ff.

were never denied: the Premier stated that relations with the Lieutenant-General were cordial, while his chief lieutenant, Robert Rogers, openly admitted that he favoured an immediate dissolution. The common opinion was that dissolution had been refused following instructions from Ottawa.[36] That McMillan would have refused to dissolve, if so instructed by his political superiors need not be questioned. On two earlier occasions, when all that could be gained was the political embarrassment of the Tories, he willingly accepted Sifton's suggestion that he refuse to dissolve if asked, and he assured Sifton that he was "ready and quite willing to take any position, and maintain it, which you may think right and Constitutional."[37]

The question of a dissolution was closely related to the Lieutenant-Governor's refusal to accept the resignation of his government on two occasions: in British Columbia in 1901 and in Manitoba in 1922.[38] Joly's refusal to accept Dunsmuir's resignation has been mentioned earlier, and it is necessary only to point out that Laurier and Joly agreed that his resignation would necessitate a dissolution, which, "in the interest of the province, ought to be avoided, if it can at all be avoided."[39] Sir James Aikins, Lieutenant-Governor of Manitoba in 1922, acted on the conviction that there would have to be a dissolution. The election of 1920 had returned twenty-one Liberals, thirteen Farmers, eleven Labour, and nine Conservatives. As he no longer had a majority the Liberal Premier, T. C. Norris, at once discussed with the Lieutenant-Governor the course to be taken, and it was decided that since the Liberals were the largest single group Norris should meet the legislature and let his fate be decided there.[40] During the first session the government received an independent and fluctuating support from both the Farmer and Labour members and was able to remain in office. But Norris was never very far from defeat and Sifton, whose control over J. W. Dafoe's editorial policy was often tighter than has commonly been supposed, instructed his editor not to let the paper "get identified with any such constitutional doctrine as that a Premier

[36]See *Winnipeg Tribune, Manitoba Free Press,* and Toronto *Mail and Empire,* March 30–April 3, 1905.
[37]PAC, Sifton Papers, McMillan to Sifton, Aug. 8, 1901. See also the letters from McMillan of Nov. 23, 1901 and those from Sifton to McMillan on Aug. 4, Aug. 12, and Nov. 25, 1901.
[38]Sir Fenwick Williams refused to accept the resignation of the Blanchard–Hill government following its defeat in 1867 on the grounds that he was soon to be replaced by Doyle and that the task of securing a government should be left to the new Lieutenant-Governor. (See the correspondence in the *Acadian Reporter,* Oct. 4, 1867.)
[39]PAC, Laurier Papers, 210, Laurier to Joly, Oct. 25, 1901.
[40]*Western Municipal News,* Dec. 1923.

is entitled to ask for a dissolution in the first session after he has had a general election."[41] Dafoe replied that he felt that Norris, if defeated, would ask for a dissolution, "but without any very definite belief that this would be accorded him. I have said to Ministers of the Crown with whom I have spoken that they could not expect a dissolution under the circumstances, but that, of course, it was within the power of the Lieutenant-Governor to grant them one if he chose to take the responsibility."[42] Not until the second session, however, did a crisis occur. When the government was defeated on a mild vote of censure Norris immediately tendered his resignation.[43]

The Lieutenant-Governor was not only a brilliant jurist but was also, as former head of the provincial Conservative party (the one who attempted to persuade the Lieutenant-Governor Cameron in 1915 that he was a rubber stamp), a close and astute observer of the political scene. Aikins had anticipated the confusion arising from the multi-party system and during the first session had exerted his influence to secure harmony and moderation between the four groups in the Legislative Assembly. "What might happen in Manitoba is a big question," he had declared, "and I will tell you frankly that I do not know what I would do if any political situation arises." Reporters were assured, however, that his decision would be "in the best interests of the province." Meanwhile: "Cordial co-operation is needed in the legislature and among the people. Fair-play and the interests of all must be considered."[44]

When Norris resigned Aikins asked him whether he believed the legislature would have to be dissolved, or whether an alternative government could be formed. The Premier answered that in his opinion a dissolution was necessary and inevitable, but in view of his defeat in the assembly he did not feel that it was within his right to ask for one. Aikins agreed:

Each group has its own leader and has acted independently of each of the others. Judging from the actions and utterances of their members during the last session and this, it is manifest to me that the political views of these groups are fundamentally divergent and their affiliations quite distinct and, that being so, there will continue to be as in the past no cohesion or continuity of co-operation among them. . . . I am satisfied from the contentions, the disputes and the conflicting views of the several groups or parties in the assembly, that it is not only improbable but prac-

41PAC, Dafoe Papers, M 73, Sifton to Dafoe, Feb. 23, 1921.
42Ibid., Dafoe to Sifton, Feb. 26, 1921.
43Manitoba Free Press, March 21, 1922, Norris to Aikins, March 17, 1922.
44Ibid., March 17, 1921.

tically impossible for them to work together in harmony, or to form an administration strong and durable.[45]

Thus the Lieutenant-Governor refused to accept Norris' resignation. Instead, he asked him to remain in office, pass supply, round out the non-contentious business of the session, and dissolve. The government, so Aikins declared, would be best able to complete the work of the session and clearly had the right to a dissolution, if a dissolution there must be. He emphasized, however, that "where the resignation of the ministry is not accepted, while they continue to possess their official authority and functions, they are not expected, pending an appeal to the electorate, to perform more than routine duties."[46]

Norris concurred in the Lieutenant-Governor's decision, placed the correspondence before the assembly, and asked for non-partisan support in clearing up the session's work. The Farmer leader agreed that Aikins' decision had been a wise one. So too did the Labour leader, F. J. Dixon, although he suggested that the legislature, not the Lieutenant-Governor, could best decide whether an alternative government did exist. Reluctant consent was given by the Conservatives as well. The work went forward with a minimum of delay and of squabbling, the session was soon over, and the legislature dissolved.

There are no known instances of forced dissolutions in Canada, although attempts have been made on several occasions. The Lieutenant-Governor of Prince Edward Island reserved a bill in 1892 against the wishes of his ministers. His expectation was that the government would resign, a new administration would take office, and the legislature would be dissolved. The electorate would thus be called on to consider the measure that the Lieutenant-Governor denounced as unjustifiable, unfair, and unconstitutional. His attempt to force a dissolution in this manner failed, however, for his advisers acquiesced in his decision, reluctant to give up power even momentarily or aware that the electors would side with the Lieutenant-Governor.[47] As has been noted above, Lieutenant-Governor McInnes attempted to force the Semlin government to dissolve in August 1899 but was dissuaded by a rather brusque warning from Ottawa. Doyle was more than prepared to force his government to dissolve on a "loyalty" issue in 1868 after members of his frankly secessionist cabinet had spoken of annexation. His ministers backed down when the issue was placed squarely before them and such extreme action was unnecessary.[48] Schultz con-

45*Manitoba Free Press*, March 21, 1922, Aikins to Norris, March 17, 1922.
46*Ibid.*   47See chap. VIII, 211 ff.
48Macdonald Papers, 114, Doyle to Macdonald, Dec. 7, 1868; chap. VII, 183 ff.

templated forcing Greenway to dissolve before introducing the separate schools legislation, but apparently was not encouraged by Macdonald.[49] In July 1933 the Lieutenant-Governor of British Columbia was preparing an order to dissolve when Premier Tolmie reluctantly and tardily requested him to dissolve a legislature on the eve of its fifth birthday.[50]

One further point remains to be discussed. Macdonald's admonition to Lieutenant-Governor Richey to force Fielding to leave "ample time" between dissolution and the election, regardless of the Prime Minister's political motives, raises an interesting query: can or should the Lieutenant-Governor prevent what might be called "snap" dissolutions designed solely to catch the opposition unawares? In all probability many Lieutenant-Governors have so interpreted their duty, but the fact remains that the officers have been more criticized for permitting hasty dissolutions than they have for refusing or attempting to force a dissolution.

In 1903, for example, Joly was vigorously denounced in the Liberal press for allowing McBride to rush the election. Since the dissolution of the legislature in June the election had been forecast officially for October 31. On the grounds that the electoral machinery had been put into operation much more quickly than he had expected, McBride decided late in September to hold the election on October 3. The affair appears to have been a carefully designed political trick, however, for as early as June 15 a prominent member of the cabinet had suggested that it would be "good tactics not to let the enemy know what is intended until the last possible moment"; in other words, with the election slated for October 31 a proclamation could be gazetted as late as possible announcing an October 3 election and then "we could rush things."[51] Three years later McBride was guilty of the same offence again. In November 1906 Dunsmuir, then Lieutenant-Governor, considered refusing McBride a dissolution because only three years had passed since the last election. Eventually he accepted the Premier's argument that a popular declaration was needed on the government's policy before it could go ahead with new and important measures and agreed to the dissolution, but he insisted at the same time, apparently remembering 1903, that "ample time should be given." Despite this warning, the government delayed proclaiming the dissolution from November 2 to December 24 and then called the election for February

[49]Macdonald Papers, 264, Schultz to Macdonald, Aug. 3, 1889.
[50]Personal information.
[51]PABC, McBride Papers, Carter Cotton to McBride, June 15, 1903; Press, July–Oct. 1903.

12, 1907. The leader of the opposition immediately sent an ineffectual but "most emphatic protest" to the Lieutenant-Governor whose wishes had been so blatantly ignored.[52]

British Columbians were not alone in providing support for Goldwin Smith's observation that dissolution in Canada had "become the plaything of the politicians." The Greenway government in Manitoba formally decided on December 20, 1895, to disobey the remedial order sent by the federal government. On the following day the legislature, which was to have assembled in January 1896, was dissolved and an election set for January 15, 1896. Although the legislature was over three years old and an election was to be expected in 1896 the suddenness of the dissolution took the opposition by complete surprise. The press questioned the fairness of it and in some quarters Lieutenant-Governor Patterson was criticized; one can imagine the reprimand Macdonald would have administered had he been alive.

In Quebec a decade later it was the Conservatives' turn to emphasize the reserve power of the Crown. On November 3, 1904, Laurier swept Quebec and the nation in his second general election. On the following day Premier Parent of Quebec in consultation with some of his colleagues decided that it would be an excellent stroke to capitalize on the spirit of liberalism that had struck the province.[53] Lieutenant-Governor Jetté made no recorded objection when Parent asked him to dissolve the legislature and proclaim November 25 as the date of the election. Having all but ten of the seats the Liberals were well prepared, but the Conservatives had not even time to get candidates in the field. After a futile attempt to persuade Jetté to delay the election, the opposition, with few exceptions, boycotted it by refusing to run candidates. Needless to say the Lieutenant-Governor was roundly denounced.[54]

Four years later in Saskatchewan the relation between the federal and provincial elections was reversed. Laurier wanted to test western sentiment before venturing a federal election, and Premier Scott of Saskatchewan agreed to conduct the experiment. He returned from Ottawa about the middle of July 1908, circularized party leaders to see if an election could be held at once, and on July 20 dissolved the

[52]McBride Papers, McBride to Dunsmuir, Nov. 2, 1906; McBride Papers, Private Collection (Vancouver, B.C.), Dunsmuir to McBride, Nov. 2, 1906; Oliver to Dunsmuir, Dec. 25, 1906.

[53]According to M. Rumilly it had been agreed that Parent was to resign before the next election. Those who had been forcing his retirement were not consulted, and the dissolution had the appearance of a move designed to counter the ambitions of his enemies. Robert Rumilly, *Histoire de la Province de Québec* (Montreal, 1940–55), XI, 164 ff.

[54]Rumilly, *Histoire*, XI, 186 ff.; Press, Nov. 1904.

legislature. The election was announced for August 14, 1908. Conservative spokesmen were scathing in their criticism; the sudden dissolution, they declared, involved an unfair use of the royal prerogative and should not have been permitted even by a Liberal Lieutenant-Governor.[55]

Coming as they did fairly close together, these cases caused considerable comment and criticism throughout the nation. The success of one government encouraged another to attempt the same subterfuge. The reserve power of the Crown seemed to be in permanent eclipse in the Canadian provinces. Premier Whitney of Ontario officially forewarned the electorate and the other parties well in advance of the 1911 election "in order that there may be no suggestion that we desire to hurry the elections."[56] Whitney did what all governments should do. Barring adequate warning it is clearly the responsibility of the Lieutenant-Governor to make certain that the power to dissolve parliament is not merely another weapon in the already over-stocked arsenal of the government in power. An election is supposed to ascertain the will of the people, and this can only be done if every opinion has been laid before them and if every party has had adequate time to prepare its case.

[55]PAS, Scott Papers, Cabinet Circular, July 18, 1908; Press, July–Aug. 1908; *Canadian Annual Review*, 1908, 486 ff.
[56]*Ibid.*, 1911, 453.

CHAPTER SEVEN

A FEDERAL OFFICER

ON THE BASIS of his own definitions Professor K. C. Wheare has argued that Canada is only a quasi-federal state because co-ordinate legislative authority is qualified by the appointment of the provincial Lieutenant-Governor and the supervision of provincial legislation by the central government.[1] This is sufficient to indicate that the Lieutenant-Governor, in theory at least, is an integral part of the scheme which was designed in 1867 to assure the paramountcy of the central government in the federation. One noted Canadian authority observed that the Lieutenant-Governor was to be "a servant of the dominion, a mere instrument of the federal cabinet," and more recently another has called him an "agent and spokesman" of the central government.[2] During the discussions of the Quebec Resolutions opponents of the project in nation-building asserted that the existence of the office represented a threat to provincial autonomy; the Lieutenant-Governors, they said, would "only be tools in the hands of the General Government, who would interfere in the local matters by the continual pressure they would bring to bear upon them. . . ."[3] Could responsible self-government exist in the provinces under such circumstances?

Supporters of the proposed federation, both in Canada and in England, openly admitted that the central government was to be superior to the governments of the provinces and that the Lieutenant-Governor was one agency through which that superiority was to be effected and maintained.[4] Although Macdonald once stated that the Lieutenant-Governor would not be politically dependent upon the authorities in Ottawa, he did emphasize that he would be a federal officer.

As this is to be one united province with the local government and legislature subordinate to the General Government and Legislature, it is obvious that the chief executive officer in each of the provinces must be subordinate as well. The General Government assumes towards the local governments precisely the same position as the Imperial Government holds

[1]In *Federal Government* (London, 1946), 19–21.
[2]W. P. M. Kennedy, *Essays in Constitutional Law* (London, 1934), 42; R. McG. Dawson, *The Government of Canada* (Toronto, 1948), 35.
[3]Canada, *Confederation Debates*, 1865, 860.
[4]See PAC, G 10, 2, Monck to Cardwell, Nov. 7, 1864; United Kingdom, House of Commons, *Debates*, 1867, 185, 1171.

with respect to each of the colonies now; so that as the Lieutenant-Governor of each of the provinces is now appointed directly by the Queen, and is directly responsible to her, so will the executive of local governments be subordinate to the Representative of the Queen, and be responsible and report to him.[5]

When forwarding the Quebec Resolutions Monck pointed out that it was "proposed to maintain the subordination of the local to the general government 1st by retaining in the hands of the General Government the nomination of the local Lieutenant-Governor and his removal for cause." Cardwell replied that Her Majesty's Ministers, who before long were to become strong advocates of provincial rights, heartily endorsed the highly centralist theme of the Quebec Resolutions: "They are glad to observe that, although large powers of legislation are intended to be vested in local bodies, yet the principle of Central Control has been steadily kept in view. The importance of this principle cannot be over-rated. Its maintenance is essential to the practical efficiency of the system, and to its harmonious operation, both in the general adminis-tration, and in the Governments of the several Provinces."[6] And in the House of Commons, Adderley declared that the difficulty lay in making the central power sufficiently strong, but added that "the nomination of the Provincial Governor by the Central Power is in the interest of united government."[7]

Strangely enough the Lieutenant-Governor's position as a federal official was also supported on the grounds that it would protect pro-vincial and minority rights. Thinking perhaps of the English minority in Quebec, George Brown observed that "by vesting the appointment of lieutenant-governors in the General Government, and giving a veto for all local measures, we have secured that no injustice shall be done without appeal in local legislation."[8] Hector Langevin drew the atten-tion of the members from Lower Canada to the fact that the Lieu-tenant-Governor would be responsible to the Dominion, not the im-perial, government. This was of the utmost importance, he declared, for in the federal cabinet would be the members from Quebec "who will be there to cause every encroachment or arbitrary act . . . to be condemned," and in the Canadian Parliament would be "our sixty-five representatives to protest and to vote at need against a government" which "should persist in not recalling any lieutenant-governor who

[5]Canada, *Confederation Debates*, 1865, 42.
[6]PAC, CO 42/643, Monck to Cardwell, Nov. 7, 1864; C 3426, Cardwell to Monck, Dec. 3, 1864.
[7]United Kingdom, *Parliamentary Debates*, 185, 1171.
[8]Canada, *Confederation Debates*, 1865, 108.

should have so failed in his duty to the population which he governed."[9]

However little thought was given to the difficulties that would inevitably arise and limit the Lieutenant-Governor's usefulness as a federal officer, the intentions of the Fathers are clear. The responsibility of the Lieutenant-Governor to the central government was underlined by the statutory provision for his dismissal. He was endowed with the power to exercise some control over provincial legislation and in this at least he was formally subject to instructions from Ottawa. To safeguard his independence as a federal officer he was paid by the central government. Moreover, the office was clearly regarded as the link of federal power and was expressly excluded from the general grant of authority to the provincial governments to amend their own constitutions.[10] With some justice he was officially named "Superintendent" rather than Lieutenant-Governor in one draft of the British North America Act.[11]

The Lieutenant-Governor's position as a federal officer has been overshadowed by his quasi-representation of the Crown and understandably so, for the latter functions are more striking and more important. The Supreme Court of Canada, for example, recently had little difficulty in deciding that the office was "in respect of the Government of the Province" rather than "in respect of the Government of Canada." Counsel for the Department of Justice argued without success that the Lieutenant-Governor's appointment, salary, and tenure, each of which depended upon the central government, must be taken into consideration, and that "the duty of the Lieutenant-Governor to adhere to the instructions of the Governor-General framed by the latter on the advice of his Dominion Ministers is obviously a duty relating to the Government of Canada, not of the province." Counsel for the appellant took the view that regardless of the source of his authority—whether instructions from the federal government, the British North America Act, or his Commission—the Lieutenant-Governor acted solely in his capacity as chief executive officer in the province. Such duality as did exist in the Canadian federal system, they argued, lay with the federal government, not with the Lieutenant-Governor. Territorially his powers were exercisable only in the province and his executive authority was commensurate with the legislative authority of the provincial government.[12]

[9]Ibid., 374.
[10]British North America Act, 1867, section 91, sub-section I.
[11]Sir Joseph Pope, ed., Confederation Documents (Toronto, 1895), 150.
[12]Carroll v. The King, Supreme Court Reports, 1948, 126–35; ibid., 1950,

With this statement of the case both the Supreme Court and the Exchequer Court agreed. Lord Watson's decision in 1892 was frequently cited, although its relevance is not always clear. As far as the Supreme Court was concerned appointment, payment, and tenure were equally irrelevant, while

The additional provisions of the Constitution, namely, that the Lieutenant-Governor receives instructions from the Governor-General, that bills may be reserved for the signification of the Governor-General's pleasure, that an Act that has been sanctioned, may be disallowed by the Governor-General in Council, and finally that the Lieutenant-Governor may be removed from office by the same authority, have I think, no important signification.

The framers of our Constitution have reserved to the Governor-General in Council the necessary authority to interfere in a certain way, in provincial matters, but the exercise of these powers, *contemplated to be for the better government of the province,* does not modify the legal status of the provincial executives, and does not purport to make them act, *on behalf of the federal authority.*[13]

The mysteries of law are indeed great and the layman is well-advised not to look into them. Nonetheless the learned justices can be accused and convicted of hazy and illogical thinking as far as the office of the Lieutenant-Governor is concerned. The Fathers of Confederation, "the framers of our Constitution," were assuredly thinking of the better government of the nation, of which the province was just a part, and both the British North America Act of 1867 and the Lieutenant-Governor's instructions clearly provide that he is to act "on behalf of the federal authority." It would have been equally ridiculous to suggest that before 1926 the Governor-General was not an imperial officer

---

73–80; *Exchequer Court Reports,* 1947, 410–35; *ibid.,* 1949, 169–87. See also *Cases Filed in the Supreme Court of Canada,* 643, 646, in the Library of the Supreme Court, Ottawa. The point at issue was whether a retired judge had to give up his pension as judge upon taking office as Lieutenant-Governor. The relevant section of the Judges Act (*Revised Statutes of Canada,* 1927, c. 105) read: "If any person become entitled to a pension after the first day of July, one thousand nine hundred and twenty, under this Act, and become entitled to any salary in respect of any public office under His Majesty in respect of his Government of Canada, such salary shall be reduced by the amount of such pension." The Supreme Court decided that a Lieutenant-Governor was not acting in respect of the Government of Canada and was therefore entitled to keep his pension. This contradicted all previous practice. When Johnston was appointed in Manitoba in 1873—the appointment was later cancelled—the Order in Council appointing him (no. 867 A, approved July 8, 1873) provided that "the amount of his retiring pension as Judge shall be deducted from his salary as Lieutenant-Governor so long as he holds the latter appointment." This practice was always followed. In 1932 Bennett declared that an ex-judge automatically gives up his pension upon appointment as Lieutenant-Governor. (Canada, House of Commons, *Debates,* 1932, 2941.)

[13]*Supreme Court Reports,* 1948, 131. Italics added.

and was not bound to act on behalf of the imperial authority, but was simply an officer charged with the administration of executive powers in Canada.

This reference to the position of the. Governor-General is neither haphazard nor illogical. As Macdonald pointed out in the Canadian legislature, the central government assumed "towards the local governments precisely the same position as the Imperial Government" had held towards the British North American colonies before Confederation. As in the old imperial system, the central government in Canada was to possess legislative and executive authority over the parts, and the national interest was to be of greater significance than the provincial. The guardian of imperial interests and the link of imperial power was the colonial Governor; the guardian of Dominion interests and the link of Dominion power was the provincial Lieutenant-Governor. Alexander Galt made this perfectly clear in his well-known Sherbrooke speech when he declared that in each province there was to be an officer appointed by the central government

. . . holding to that General Government the same relations as were now held by the heads of the Provincial Governments to the Imperial Government . . . all action beginning with the people and proceeding through the local legislature, would, before it became law, come under the revision of the Lieutenant-Governor, who would be responsible for his action and be obliged to make his report to the superior authority.[14]

Similar pronouncements were made time and time again, leaving no possible doubt as to intention. The most emphatic assertion, as well as the most official, appeared in an Order in Council of 1882: "As the relations between the Governor General and his responsible advisers, as well as his position as an Imperial Officer, are similar to the relations of a Lieutenant Governor with his Ministers and his position as a Dominion Officer, it is only necessary to define the duties and responsibilities of the former in order to ascertain those of a Lieutenant-Governor."[15]

Had it been possible adequately to define the dual duties and responsibilities of the colonial Governor the Fathers of Confederation might have been emboldened to attempt an official definition of the Lieutenant-Governor's position. But as Lord Elgin observed, there was no "class of duties more difficult to define even theoretically than those which devolve upon a Governor under our newly adopted system of constitutional Govt towards the colonists on the one hand, and the

[14]PAC, Macdonald Papers, 52, Pamphlet no. 8.
[15]PAC, Orders in Council, 1882, no. 2284, approved Nov. 29, 1882.

Imperial Govt and Parlt on the other—and what is so difficult to define in theory is not easier to work out in practice."[16] In general, however, whenever imperial policy or interests were affected it was clearly his duty to lead the colony along the road to righteousness (as defined in Westminster), to protect imperial interests, and to act as a shock-absorber between the two governments. As Herman Merivale emphatically stated, "whenever any question is agitated touching the interests of the mother country . . . his functions as an independent officer are called at once into play. He must see that the mother country receives no detriment. In this duty he cannot count on aid from his advisers; they will consult the interests either of the colony or of their own popularity. . . ."[17] To a lesser extent he was to serve as a positive instrument of imperial policy, and at times he was very much a proponent of programmes which emanated from the Colonial Office. The argument that the colonial Governor was not to act on behalf of the imperial authority would have been laughed out of court.

In the instructions given to Archibald before he went to Manitoba in 1870 he was ordered to "guard with independence the general interests of the Dominion and the just authority of the Crown," the first presumably for the better government of the nation and the second, in part, for the better government of the province.[18] On two later ocasions Macdonald used words sufficiently clear to leave no room for doubt as to his conception of the office of Lieutenant-Governor:

> Remember you hold the same position as a Dominion Officer as the GG does under the Imperial Govt.—The GG for the time being always does what he can without infringing on the principle of Self-Governt to urge the carrying out of the Imperial policy—Goest thou and do likewise.[19]

> You are a Dominion officer and as such should act as the GG does in his capacity as an Imperial officer. He takes an active interest in every subject brought before him—expresses his opinions strongly and if in doubt applies for Confidential instructions from the Colonial Minister.[20]

Even Mowat, who pursued a life-long crusade against the federal power, admitted that as Lieutenant-Governor he was "an officer of the Dominion Government" and asked for specific instructions on a matter which in his opinion involved "national considerations."[21]

[16]Sir A. G. Doughty, ed., *The Elgin-Grey Papers 1846–1852* (Ottawa, 1937), II, 577, Elgin to Grey, Jan. 14, 1850.
[17]Herman Merivale, *Lectures on Colonisation and the Colonies* (London, 1861), 649.
[18]*C.S.P.*, 1870, no. 20, 4–6.
[19]Macdonald Papers, 526, Macdonald to Aikins, July 28, 1884.
[20]*Ibid.*, 527, Macdonald to Aikins, Sept. 15, 1887.
[21]PAC, Laurier Papers, 74, Mowat to Laurier, May 2, 1898.

Unquestionably he was prepared—indeed felt himself bound—to act as a federal officer and on behalf of the federal authority.

Although his commission required him "to do and execute all things" pertaining to his office as set out in the commission itself, the British North America Act of 1867, and his instructions, the Lieutenant-Governor was not given any formal instructions for many years after Confederation. Some time in 1867–8, however, Macdonald did toy with general instructions for the officer, and his rough draft repeats almost verbatim various sections of the Governor-General's Commission and Instructions. Two clauses, soon to be removed on Blake's demand from the Governor-General's Instructions, were scored with an X, an indication that Macdonald did not think they were applicable: the first provided that the Executive Council was not to meet unless summoned by the Lieutenant-Governor and that he had the right to enter on the Council record his disapproval of any decision; and the second empowered him to appoint someone to chair the meeting in his absence. The instructions listed the types of provincial bills to be reserved, provided that all statutes and reserved bills, with full comments, were to be sent to Ottawa along with the *Journals* and other records of the legislature, and asked that an annual report on the state of the province—revenue, economy, population, public works, education, and so forth—be submitted to the federal government. This rough draft was never put into final shape, however, and the matter was lost to sight for many years.[22]

When in 1881 Premier Mowat of Ontario threatened to make an issue of the federal power of disallowance by the repeated passage of disallowed acts, Campbell wanted Macdonald to draw up formal instructions for the Lieutenant-Governors that would include an express provision for the compulsory reservation of measures once disallowed.[23] The Minister of Justice's suggestion was not acted on at the time, but when the threat materialized in the following year the federal authorities were stimulated to take action. Campbell drafted general instructions and Macdonald approved them.[24] The instructions were clearly designed to counter the attack on the federal power and provided for the reservation of various types of provincial bills, the dispatch of statutes and proceedings to Ottawa, and the immediate publication of the proclamations of disallowance sent from Ottawa. They were printed and to them were attached relevant extracts from

22Macdonald Papers, 299, 61–9.
23*Ibid.*, 315, Miscellaneous 2/883, section 16, Campbell to Macdonald, Nov. 7, 1881. See also chap. VIII, 203 ff.
24Macdonald Papers, 196, Campbell to Macdonald, Nov. 25, 1882.

the British North America Act and a table of provincial acts disallowed by the federal government. In order that the local government should realize on what authority the Lieutenant-Governor acted he was ordered to communicate his instructions to the cabinet.[25]

For some reason the instructions were never sent to the Lieutenant-Governors. But when Mercier threatened to refuse to publish a proclamation of disallowance in 1887 and thus contest the federal government's right to supervise provincial legislation Campbell's instructions were adopted with minor changes, approved by Order in Council, and, with the Governor-General's Commission and Instructions, the British North America Act, and all relevant Orders in Council, were sent to every Lieutenant-Governor. Every officer was in future to receive the instructions when he took the oath of office, but as this ruling was not adhered to Thompson later ordered that they were to be attached to his commission.[26]

The instructions, which it must be admitted are innocuous, deal largely with reservation and disallowance, subjects that will be considered later. A clause providing that the Lieutenant-Governor shall not leave the province without leave from the federal government has caused some criticism. But despite the complaints the federal authorities have determinedly retained the provision, even though the requests are never refused. As the Undersecretary of State argued: "it is necessary that this Department should be aware at all times of the place where Lieutenant-Governors may be, as urgent communications may be required to be made, and if the Department were not aware of the whereabouts of a Lieutenant Governor of a Province, public business might be hampered."[27] At the same time the Department of State regarded the question of leave as a nuisance and wanted to have it handled by the Governor-General and his staff. This suggestion was unceremoniously vetoed at Rideau Hall: "I feel very strongly that even such an apparently trifling matter as Lieutenant-Governors' leave should only be dealt with by the advice of a responsible Minister," wrote the Governor-General's secretary.[28] The Colonial Secretary observed that the Governors of the Australian states could leave the state for one month during the year with the permission of the Executive Council, but "as your Ministers are aware . . . the Governors of

[25]322, Miscellaneous no. 11, section 14.
[26]PAC, Orders in Council, 1887, no. 1618, approved Oct. 8, 1887; *ibid.*, 1892, no. 1574, approved June 16, 1892.
[27]PAC, Borden Papers, RLB 38, Undersecretary to the Secretary of State, Oct. 12, 1912.
[28]GGO, file 928 A, I, Memorandum for the Undersecretary of State, Nov. 6, 1912.

the States hold their appointments direct from the Crown, and are not subordinate to the Governor-General of the Commonwealth."[29]

The clause was repeatedly "misconstrued, misunderstood, and perhaps disregarded"[30] and with good reason, for the absence of the Lieutenant-Governor, if formally approved, necessitated the appointment of an Administrator. In 1871 Lieutenant-Governor Archibald argued that since Manitoba was so isolated and communications with Ottawa so poor it would be an excellent idea to have a permanent Administrator appointed who could take over if the Lieutenant-Governor were away from the capital, were sick, or died.[31] His suggestion was approved and the practice was applied to British Columbia as well.[32] The same procedure was not followed in the other provinces, however, and was later repealed in Manitoba and British Columbia. The admission of Newfoundland in 1949 brought the matter to the foreground again. The Lieutenant-Governor was accustomed to make frequent trips along the coast, and when subject to instructions from the government of Canada it was found that an Administrator had to be appointed on every occasion. Moreover, it was customary in the province to swear in the cabinet every time an Administrator was appointed. The situation was clearly intolerable and the government of Newfoundland requested the appointment of a permanent Administrator. All the provinces except British Columbia concurred in the proposed change and in 1953 permanent Administrators, usually the Chief Justices of the provinces, were appointed. The Administrator can act only in the event of absence, illness, or other inability, not in the event of death.[33]

The Undersecretary of State's concern that "public business might be hampered" arose from the fact that the Lieutenant-Governor is the only official channel of communication between the central and local governments. Although no statute or Order in Council testifies to its creation, the Department of the Secretary of State for the Provinces was established in 1867, with its head in the cabinet, to handle the communications between the governments. Monck was anxious that "the correspondence between the Govt. here and the Lt. Govs. should be carried on through the Secretary of State for the Provinces and not

[29]Ibid., Harcourt to Connaught, Nov. 30, 1912.
[30]Ibid., Undersecretary of State to the Governor General's Secretary, Oct. 30, 1912.
[31]PAC, Correspondence of the Secretary of State, 1871, file 1155, Archibald to Howe, May 18, 1871; PAM, Archibald Papers, Howe to Archibald, June 12, 1871.
[32]Correspondence of the Secretary of State, 1871, file 1155, Memorandum from Macdonald, Dec. 18, 1871.
[33]Correspondence in the Department of State, Ottawa.

through my office. The Lt. Govs. are officers of the govt of the dominion, and should correspond with the Sec. of State."[34] Macdonald concurred and a circular informed the Lieutenant-Governors that all inter-governmental correspondence was to pass between the Lieutenant-Governor and the Secretary of State for the Provinces. But the desired end was not obtained for many Lieutenant-Governors frequently wrote directly to the Governor-General, and provincial governments and ministers often communicated directly with the federal government. In 1869 another circular was sent to the Lieutenant-Governors. Macdonald believed that uniformity and regularity were essential and that rigid adherence to the practice laid down would enhance the Lieutenant-Governor's strategic position: he would "be able to see all communications passing from his own Government to Ottawa; and he has already, of course, all the communications from here to Quebec."[35]

During the Liberal interregnum, perhaps because of the very close personal relations between the heads of the two governments and perhaps because the Lieutenant-Governor was a Conservative, the government of Ontario asked for a change in the practice. The necessity to pass all communications through the Lieutenant-Governor led to needless circumlocution and delay, it was stated, while direct department to department or minister to minister correspondence would be quicker and more efficient. The Mackenzie administration raised no objection and an Order in Council authorized the change. The Order specifically stated, however, that as the other provinces had made no complaint the new practice would apply only to Ontario.[36] The Macdonald government later rescinded the Order on the grounds that

the Lieut. Governors of the provinces are Federal Officers and stand, therefore, in the same position towards the Dominion Government as does the Governor General towards the Imperial Government, and it is desirable that the same system of correspondence which is practised between the Imperial and Dominion Governments should be followed by the Dominion and Provincial Governments thereby ensuring to the Lieutenant Governors an insight into the business transacted by their respective Governments.[37]

[34]Macdonald Papers, 75, Monck to Macdonald, July 13, 1867. Monck had written to the Colonial Secretary listing the names and offices of the members of the cabinet. Beside "A. G. Archibald, Secretary of State for the Provinces" a Colonial Office official had written "a grand title." (CO 42/663, Monck to Buckingham and Chandos, July 3, 1867).
[35]Macdonald Papers, 516, Macdonald to Cartier, Nov. 24, 1869; ibid., Macdonald to John Sandfield Macdonald, Nov. 24, 1869.
[36]PAC, Orders in Council, 1875, no. 488, approved May 14, 1875.
[37]Ibid., 1880, no. 241, approved Feb. 16, 1880.

At the same time, however, Macdonald and his successors have permitted direct department to department correspondence on a variety of subjects; and as the years passed most of the correspondence between the central and local governments was carried on semi-formally. Thus the Lieutenant-Governor ceased to be the important channel of communication that he once was. Formal communications still pass through his hands however, and since 1887, when Mercier was unable to persuade the Interprovincial Conference to adopt a resolution demanding a new means of official communication, there has been no formal demand for change.[38]

The ruling that provincial Lieutenant-Governors could not communicate with the Colonial Office, except through the Secretary of State and the Governor-General, was generally followed. Galt had made it clear at Sherbrooke that any direct connection between the lowly Canadian provinces and the imperial government was to cease with Confederation. The appointment of the Lieutenant-Governor by the federal government was designed to make such communication impossible: for "inasmuch as the affairs Local Governments had to administer were purely of a local character, not at all Imperial in their nature, it was felt that there was no necessity whatever for their being in communication with the Imperial Government, but that on the contrary very great mischief might arise if they were permitted to hold that communication. . . ."[39] Even Doyle, long accustomed to correspondence with the Colonial Office, adhered to the new regulations and forwarded all his communiques regarding the secessionist movement in Nova Scotia through the Secretary of State. The same course was followed in British Columbia when Trutch attempted to have some Royal Navy vessels kept on the Pacific Coast and later during the dispute over the terms of union. When in 1907 the Lieutenant-Governor of British Columbia merely telegraphed the Colonial Secretary that Premier McBride was on his way to England, Sir Joseph Pope's annoyance knew no bounds. The Lieutenant-Governor had in his opinion "committed a grave breach of constitutional propriety" and "his action, if drawn into a precedent might be attended by much inconvenience to the Dominion Government."[40]

With the exception of reservation and disallowance the federal government obviously placed little stock in the value of formal instruc-

---

[38]*Minutes of the Interprovincial Conference Held at the City of Quebec from the 20th to the 28th October, 1887, inclusively* (Ottawa, 1951), 13.
[39]Macdonald Papers, 52, Pamphlet no. 8.
[40]Correspondence of the Secretary of State, 1907, file 161, Memorandum by Sir Joseph Pope, Undersecretary of State, April 4, 1907.

tions to the Lieutenant-Governor. His position as "agent and spokes-man," as the buffer between local and central authority, depended not on the formal powers granted to him, but on what Elgin described as the "influence of suasion, sympathy, and moderation" backed at times by the constitutional and political power of the central government. It could never be reduced to definition for it depended upon the ability and tact of each Lieutenant-Governor, upon the relations he was able to establish with his advisers, upon the state of Dominion-provincial relations at any given moment, and upon the nature of his contacts and influence in Ottawa. His importance as a federal officer is impossible to assess, for his influence could be constantly exercised in a manner that would never reach the public press or private correspondence.

As an informant the Lieutenant-Governor was not as useful an officer as the colonial Governor. Nothing can be found even approximating the regular and lengthy reports sent by the Governor-General to the Colonial Office; there is no "G Series" or "CO 42" to provide the basis for a study of the office of the Lieutenant-Governor. Some Lieutenant-Governors in the early period, notably those in Manitoba and British Columbia, did keep the federal authorities well informed by a constant stream of dispatches and private letters. But on the whole the officers seemed content to forward legislation—often without any comment, to notify the Secretary of State formally of changes in their government, and to send specific information if asked. What can be found of the official correspondence is unbelievably dull and uninformative. Many Lieutenant-Governors did correspond privately with members of the federal cabinet, particularly with Macdonald, and the nature of their activities can be seen. But as this correspondence occurred largely in periods of acute disagreement between the two authorities it reveals little of the routine work that must always have gone on. Moreover, the practice tended to die after 1896 for Laurier, always willing to delegate political authority in provinces other than Quebec, lacked the widespread political contacts of his Conservative predecessor.

There was really little need for the Lieutenant-Governor to act as observer and informant. During periods of strife he often had inside information and was in an excellent position to act as an intermediary, but on political matters generally there were other, often better informed, sources. In the federal cabinet were representatives from each province, frequently of interests within each province, who knew the province intimately and stood high in the councils of the provincial wing of the party. In the House of Commons and Senate were members who could be depended upon to keep the government well informed on all that was transpiring. Party organization, the press, and increasingly frequent personal contacts all served to lessen the usefulness of the Lieutenant-Governor as a federal officer. As late as 1917 the Colonial Secretary wrote that the Governor-General should be in close touch with the British government since "it was essential that the Secretary of State should receive the fullest information as to all that is going on in Canada, and it has seemed to me that we have not had as much as we might have expected. . . . I know what difficulties there are, but after all, you are entitled to know everything that is going on in Canada. . . ."[41] By this time the Lieutenant-Governor had long since ceased to be of similar importance to his political superiors. Moreover, by this time also the Lieutenant-Governor tended to have only that "superficial acquaintance" with the work of government mentioned above, and although equally entitled to "know everything that is going on" seldom did.

Yet on many occasions the Lieutenant-Governors did perform extremely important services on behalf of the Dominion government. Throughout his term Archibald represented just about all there was of federal authority in Manitoba and was virtually Manitoba's representative in Macdonald's cabinet. In his instructions Archibald was asked to investigate the land problems in the west, as the public lands had been retained in true imperial fashion by the Canadian government; to examine the legal system, the organization of the courts, and the method of policing the area; to establish contact with the Indians (six years before Little Big Horn), determine their number and needs, and suggest the rudiments of a federal Indian policy; to report upon currency and coinage, the state of the Hudson's Bay Company, and immigration.[42] The Lieutenant-Governor faithfully obeyed his instructions and his lengthy and acute reports were often the basis for policy decisions as regards the west. He was also responsible for the defence of Canada from the Great Lakes to the Rockies at a time when "Manifest Destiny" was in full bloom and the Fenians still possessed the capacity to make trouble.[43]

"In consequence of the absence in Manitoba of the necessary

[41]GGO, file 2895 B, I, Long to Devonshire, Sept. 17, 1917. See also PAC, G 3, 26, Secret Circular, March 9, 1892.
[42]Canada House of Commons, *Journals*, 1874, VIII, Appendix 6; Canada, Parliament, *Returns*, "Instructions to Archibald, 1871."
[43]Archibald Papers, Adjutant General to the Commanding Officer, Winnipeg, enc. in Howe to Archibald, Oct. 29, 1870.

machinery for the purpose," Archibald was ordered to superintend the first federal elections: to recommend constituencies, to appoint electoral officers, and to set dates for nomination, polling, and the return of writs.[44] As a combination of federal officer and Liberal Conservative politician he was warned that "the representation in the General Legislature should be particularly attended to," and attend to it he did, fulfilling his promise that he would send at least three of the four members to Ottawa full of good will and determined to uphold the Manitoba settlement.[45] He was asked as well to recommend the two provincial Senators and his suggestions were followed.[46] Because of his close contact with the *métis* leaders, lay and clerical, the Lieutenant-Governor was able to prevent a resurgence of the racial conflict that for a decade lay just beneath the surface. In 1870 he secured Riel's promise that he would seek a seat in neither the local nor central legislature.[47] A year later he played the leading role in the drama that culminated in Riel's temporary exile.[48] In September 1872 he persuaded Riel to withdraw from the Provencher election, thus enabling Cartier to be elected by acclamation—an event that could not have occurred "but for the Governor's close attention and skilful handling of the cards."[49]

Alexander Morris, who succeeded Archibald in 1872, continued to be the chief federal expert on western affairs. Although a Conservative, Morris possessed the confidence of Mackenzie's Liberal administration that came into office in November 1873. The Prime Minister informed Morris that he would write with "all possible frankness on matters affecting your government and bearing upon the general welfare of the country, never doubting your perfect loyalty to those interests," and asked the Lieutenant-Governor to do the same.[50] Morris later remarked that the Liberals had treated him "with entire confidence and thus my duties have been made pleasant."[51] Frugal Scot that he was, Mackenzie was perturbed by the chaotic financial condition of the province and although Morris did not concur in the Prime Minister's suggestion that the provincial government be dis-

[44]*Ibid.*, Howe to Archibald, Jan. 21, 1871.
[45]Macdonald Papers, 517, Macdonald to Archibald, Nov. 1, 1870; *ibid.*, 187, Archibald to Macdonald, Dec. 4, 1870.
[46]*Ibid.*, 518, Macdonald to Archibald, Jan. 25, 1871; *ibid.*, 187, Archibald to Macdonald, March 8, 1871.
[47]Macdonald Papers, 187, Archibald to Macdonald, Dec. 11, 1870.
[48]Canada, House of Commons, *Journals*, 1874, Appendix 6, 55–7.
[49]Macdonald Papers, 252, Morris to Macdonald, Sept. 16, 1872.
[50]PAC, Mackenzie Papers, 4, Mackenzie to Morris, Sept. 22, 1875.
[51]Macdonald Papers, 252, Morris to Macdonald, Nov. 4, 1875.

established, thus enabling the Liberals "to deal with the government of the country *de nove*," he did persuade his ministers to curtail expenditure and, against his better judgment, to abolish the Legislative Council.[52] The Lieutenant-Governor advised the federal government to separate Manitoba and the Territories from an administrative point of view; Blake sought his opinion on the judiciary and judicial appointments in the province; and Mackenzie frequently asked for his views on political appointments. As federal party lines and allegiances penetrated the province and as the federal civil service expanded and became more efficient the need for the Lieutenant-Governor to render such services declined. But for almost a decade they were essential.

In British Columbia Joseph Trutch was of similar value to the Canadian government.[53] Although a local administrative machine existed that he could use, the Lieutenant-Governor was for some time the sole point of federal authority and the Conservatives' only reliable political informant in the province. His advice on the mails, customs and excise services, local taxation, courts and judges, was heavily depended on as the central government worked to integrate the new province into the national system. The administrative burden of the federal elections of 1871 and 1872 was thrown upon his shoulders, as it was upon Archibald's in Manitoba. On such matters as the San Juan Boundary dispute, the pensioning of British forces, naval and military defence, Indian policy, and a variety of lesser subjects Trutch's advice was constantly sought and usually followed. He rightly expected that the federal authorities would consult him on patronage and, like Archibald, in effect nominated the British Columbia Senators.[54] It was the Lieutenant-Governor who secured a seat for Sir Francis Hincks in 1872 and who found the deposit and three shareholders, all "good friends of the Government," for the ill-fated Allan Company that was to build the railway from coast to coast.[55]

In periods of acute disagreement between the provincial and federal governments the Lieutenant-Governor could be of singular importance. On such occasions it was his duty, as a federal officer, to act as a shock-absorber between the two and at all times he was bound, as far as it was within his power, "to make the relations between the

[52]PAM, Morris Papers, Mackenzie to Morris, April 16, 1874.
[53]See generally the Macdonald-Trutch correspondence in the Macdonald Papers, 278 and 518 ff; Walter N. Sage, "The Position of the Lieutenant-Governor in British Columbia in the Years Following Confederation," in Ralph Flenley, ed., *Essays in Canadian History* (Toronto, 1939), 178–203.
[54]Macdonald Papers, 226, Langevin to Macdonald, Aug. 21, Sept. 18, 1871.
[55]*Ibid.*, 278, Trutch to Macdonald, Aug. 28, Sept. 18, 1872; PABC, Helmcken Papers, Nathan to Helmcken, Feb. 24, 1873.

Provincial and Dominion Governments pleasant."[56] During the last two years of his term Trutch found this to be no easy task for the relations between British Columbia and Canada were marred by the non-fulfilment of the terms of union. As soon as the Mackenzie administration openly reneged on Macdonald's promise to build the transcontinental railway a storm of protest burst in British Columbia. While the cabinet laboured to find a settlement that would absolve them of the responsibility for a burden they were unwilling to bear, the Governor-General asked Trutch "to keep the pretensions of his people within reasonable bounds."[57] "It is needless for me to add," wrote Dufferin, "that the Imperial Government would regard with extreme uneasiness and regret anything approaching to a disturbance of the harmonious relations which have been so happily established between Canada and the noble province over which you preside."[58]

At that moment Trutch was on the verge of resignation. He had accepted his appointment with considerable reluctance, he disliked the work—particularly after responsible government had been established, and he found that he was at a "pecuniary disadvantage" in remaining in office. Moreover, as a convinced advocate of the Pacific railway he was completely out of sympathy with the Mackenzie government. But even Macdonald, whose statesmanship often overrode petty political feuds, urged him to stay on in "the interests of B.C. and the Dominion generally."[59] Trutch finally agreed to complete his term although he failed to see how he could "in anyway influence the course of events."[60] Yet hoping for the best he declared that "I shall make it my aim to bring about something approaching to a harmonious understanding in order to secure the commencement as soon as possible of the construction of the Railroad. . . ."[61] Mackenzie later stated that the government received "no assistance" from the Lieutenant-Governor during the long and drawn-out controversy, but J. D. Edgar, who went to British Columbia in the summer of 1874 to negotiate a compromise, reported that Trutch "was always most

[56]Laurier Papers, 498, Laurier to Gibson, Jan. 5, 1909. Even George Brown and Sir Charles Tupper agreed on this point. At Quebec in 1864 Brown declared that he "would have the Lieutenant-Governor appointed by General Government. It would thus bring these bodies into harmony with the General Government." (Pope, *Confederation Documents*, 74.) A year later Tupper informed the Nova Scotia assembly that appointment by the central government was designed "to ensure harmony and co-operation." (Nova Scotia, Legislative Assembly, *Debates*, 1865, 207–8.)
[57]PAC, B 119, PRO 30/6/26, Dufferin to Carnarvon, Feb. 26, 1874.
[58]Mackenzie Papers, 2, Dufferin to Trutch, Feb. 21, 1874.
[59]Macdonald Papers, 278, Trutch to Macdonald, March 10, 1874.
[60]*Ibid.*   [61]*Ibid.*, Trutch to Macdonald, May 25, 1874.

obliging in giving me upon all public questions very full information, which his large experience in the Province rendered of the highest value. He also manifested an earnest wish to see a definite and amicable settlement of the railway question speedily arrived at between the General and Provincial Governments."[62] Actually it was the Prime Minister, not the federal officer, who was at fault:

Mackenzie thinks he has to complain of Trutch in not having rendered him more effectual assistance in his dealings with British Columbia, but my own impression is that Trutch having been appointed by Sir John Macdonald, Mackenzie, who is very narrow and suspicious in such cases, did not confide in him as frankly as a Lieutenant Governor had a right to expect, and that if he M had done so the affair would have been better managed.[63]

Even so Trutch unquestionably did more to make a settlement possible than his Liberal successor, A. N. Richards, appointed by Mackenzie in 1876. Richards foolishly adopted a trenchant Liberal, pro-Ottawa, attitude and destroyed with one blow his position as a mediator, a shock-absorber, a federal officer. He ridiculed the common suggestion that secession was a possible alternative to the fulfilment of the terms of union, and while pleading for moderation took a rather immoderate stand himself, or so it seemed to the irate British Columbians: "It is quite possible that your ideas . . . are sound, but I have no opinion as to the route, trusting to the Dominion Government as representing the whole of the United British North America pursuing such a course as will benefit our great country."[64] The speech on the whole was innocuous, but the inhabitants of British Columbia were in no mood to listen to such Liberal propaganda. The Press immediately abused the Lieutenant-Governor and the Premier completely repudiated him.[65] From that moment Richards ceased to be of any use to the federal government, for he had no influence whatsoever with his ministers. Macdonald's return to office in 1878 and the renewal of the promise to build the line led to improved relations between the two governments, but for many years there were major and minor irritations which Lieutenant-Governor Cornwall did his best to alleviate.

The last fifteen years of the century were marked by increasingly poor relations between the governments of Canada and Manitoba.

[62]William Leggo, *The History of the Administration of the Earl of Dufferin* (Montreal, 1878), 337, Edgar to the Secretary of State, June 17, 1874.
[63]C. W. de Kiewiet and F. H. Underhill, *Dufferin-Carnarvon Correspondence, 1874–1878* (Toronto, 1955), 293, Dufferin to Carnarvon, Oct. 26, 1876.
[64]*Victoria British Colonist*, Oct. 20, 1876.   [65]*Ibid.*, Nov. 9, 1876.

The conflict began early in the 1880's and was essentially the first phase of the western revolt against the eastern bias of National Policy, against domination by the commercial empire of the St. Lawrence. Lord Derby, the Colonial Secretary, anxiously observed the development of a provincial rights movement in Manitoba:

I look with some apprehension at a movement of this kind knowing how advantage will be taken of it by Fenians and Irish Americans, and knowing also how weak are the ties which bind together a newly-made federation, which has no past history of common action to look back upon, and has not become habituated to the restraint which federal union imposes.

This is a little spark as yet, but it may grow into a great fire—advise your advisers not to treat it lightly, as perhaps they may be inclined to do—and let me hear more about it, privately or publicly, or both, as you think best.[66]

These fears were given scant attention in Ottawa where Manitoba was represented by only four members in the House of Commons, and the federal government vigorously and ruthlessly exercised its power of disallowance to protect the monopoly of the Canadian Pacific Railway. The Conservative government led by John Norquay reluctantly and with increasing annoyance submitted to the federal power in the cause of party unity for several years, but by 1886 it was apparent that unless an open break were made with the Conservative administration in Ottawa defeat in Manitoba was inevitable. Macdonald could not have been surprised by the rupture when it did come, for he had been warned from all sides—the Lieutenant-Governor, J. C. Aikins, had warned him time and time again of the political dangers implicit in his policy—that federal policy was intolerable in Manitoba.

When Norquay openly rebelled Macdonald vented much of his wrath on the Lieutenant-Governor. "I don't think you have acted the Lt. Governor over these Ministers of yours," he informed Aikins, in an effort to force him to protect federal interests and support federal policies.[67] Aikins denied that he had been negligent but argued rather that his sharp eye and strong words, both used in the federal cause, had caused considerable ill-feeling within the portals of the government buildings. Nonetheless, he promised to "stay their hand and cry

[66]PAC, Derby Papers, Derby to Lansdowne, March 29, 1884. J. A. Jackson has written an admirable account of much of the conflict ("The Disallowance of Manitoba Railway Legislation in the 1880's," M.A. thesis, University of Manitoba, 1945). See also Alexander Begg, *History of the North-West* (3 vols.; Toronto, 1893–5), 3, 140 ff.
[67]Macdonald Papers, 527, Macdonald to Aikins, Sept. 15, 1887.

halt."[68] When it appeared that Norquay might dissolve and seek a mandate from the people to continue the struggle against the federal government, Macdonald instructed the Lieutenant-Governor to refuse any request for a dissolution and went so far as to suggest that in view of alleged improprieties the Norquay government might be dismissed.[69] By this time, however, the provincial administration was doomed: Aikins refused to let trust funds be used as ordinary revenue, admitted that his confidence in the Premier was gone, and insisted that the legislature be summoned as soon as possible.[70] Realizing that he had the support of the party neither in Manitoba nor in Ottawa and that any Conservative government in the province was doomed, Norquay preferred to resign. His Conservative successor lost a crucial by-election and resigned in turn. The Conservative party in Manitoba was shattered beyond immediate repair, and Macdonald was finally convinced that the railway monopoly and the disallowance of provincial legislation on which it depended could no longer be maintained. The decision to change his policy was probably encouraged by Aikins who went to Ottawa in the spring of 1888 to brief the federal cabinet on the situation in Manitoba.

The constitutional and political conflict did not end there, however, and for seven years Aikins' successor was at the centre of an increasingly inflamed dispute. Until the day of his appointment in 1888 John C. Schultz, an incorrigible partisan, had been actively attempting to oust the Greenway government that had come to power earlier in the year. Before going to Manitoba as Lieutenant-Governor, Schultz had been long closeted with Macdonald. The Prime Minister urged him to establish cordial relations with Thomas Greenway, the Liberal Premier, for "a very slight turn of the rudder sways the course of the ship."[71] In every conceivable way Schultz "acted the Lieutenant-Governor" over his ministers: he insisted on being fully informed of government policy well in advance of legislative or administrative decisions; he constantly badgered Ottawa for instructions and kept the federal government well advised on everything the Greenway administration was doing; he held up Bills, Orders in Council, and routine executive measures until he had received instructions from Macdonald. When the provincial government wanted to summon the legislature in 1888 to secure support in their conflict with the C.P.R., the Lieutenant-Governor, on Macdonald's advice, delayed the meeting of the

[68]*Ibid.*, 186, Aikins to Macdonald, Sept. 25, 1887.
[69]*Ibid.*, 527, Macdonald to Aikins, Oct. 15, 1887.
[70]*Ibid.*, 186, Aikins to Macdonald, Nov. 12, Nov. 30, 1887.
[71]*Ibid.*, 131, Schultz to Macdonald, July 18, 1888.

legislature until the last possible moment. Also on Macdonald's advice he refused to sanction any expenditure on the provincial railway until the courts had decided upon the legality of the contested crossing.[72] Macdonald was enraged beyond measure by this sore spot in the west and informed George Stephen in London that the Manitoba Liberals were "behaving so outrageously that we are 'laying pipe' to upset their Govt. and Lt. Gov Schultz won't stand them long."[73]

The prerogative of dismissal was never exercised (though it may have been contemplated at times), and Greenway refused to be aggravated to the point of resignation. The railway dispute was eventually solved, but no sooner had this been done than the fiery Joseph Martin, Greenway's Attorney General, threw the separate schools question into the ferment of Dominion-provincial relations. The danger and ramifications of the new issue were seen at once, and for a decade the Lieutenant-Governors of Manitoba were to have their hands full. The day after Martin mentioned the abolition of separate schools, which he did without prior consultation with his colleagues, Schultz asked Greenway for a full explanation of the government's policy.[74] This information he passed on to Macdonald whom he advised to stimulate petitions of protest in order to strengthen his hand in dealing with the administration. The Lieutenant-Governor also wanted to reserve the bills abolishing seperate schools and even suggested that he might dismiss Martin from the cabinet.[75] The Prime Minister was probably willing to give Schultz a reasonably free hand, but Thompson advised caution: Martin, he said, would "soon die of his own hand or by the public executioner and I hope the Governor will not rob justice by trying to make him his own victim."[76] Macdonald ordered Schultz to insist upon the fullest information; if the Premier refused to comply he could be dismissed, although such an action should not be taken "except in the last resort and in a matter of very great importance."[77]

While the Manitoba Acts went from court to court the Lieutenant-Governor attempted to restrain the pretensions of his ministers and to persuade them to adopt a more tolerant attitude towards the French-speaking minority. In Ottawa his lengthy reports were appreciated and were frequently read in cabinet. On a number of occasions he was

[72]One of the provincial lines had to cross the main line of the C.P.R. and the latter, with the apparent support of the federal government refused to consent to the crossing.
[73]Macdonald Papers, 528, Macdonald to Stephen, Oct. 22, 1888.
[74]See PAM, Greenway Papers, Schultz-Greenway correspondence.
[75]Macdonald Papers, 264, Schultz to Macdonald, Dec. 9, 1889.
[76]Ibid., 275, Thompson to Macdonald, Dec. 18, 1889.
[77]Ibid., 529, Macdonald to Schultz, Jan. 9, 1890.

asked to press the views of the federal government on his advisers and to see if some compromise could not be accepted.[78] Although the usual five year term expired in 1893 Schultz asked to be retained until "school matters quiet down either by the concessions I am from time to time urging my Premier to make or in some other way."[79] For two more years he stayed in office, but in 1895 political considerations in the federal cabinet made his replacement essential. His term ended on two high notes just as the conflict of authority reached its climax. In April 1895 Schultz obtained John Bourinot's opinion that the provincial government had no alternative to accepting the remedial order.[80] This immediately became public knowledge and caused a violent debate in the House of Commons. Schultz was criticized for being a tool of the federal government; the Bowell cabinet was denounced for leaving him in office after his term had "expired"; and Martin, now in federal politics, assured the house that the Lieutenant-Governor had been a trouble-maker from the day of his appointment.[81] Finally, just a few days before his replacement was sworn in a rumour was current in the eastern press that Schultz planned to dismiss the Greenway administration as a farewell gesture.[82]

Schultz's successor, J. C. Patterson, apparently played an important part in the negotiations that led up to the final settlement. Whereas Schultz was inclined to endorse the federal government's policy and sympathize with its difficulties, Patterson soon saw that there were two sides to the question, even though he had been a member of the federal cabinet. Not only did he seek to convince his political superiors that there were real grievances in Manitoba as far as separate schools were concerned, but also he spoke strongly in favour of Manitoba's demand for better financial terms and a more rational public lands policy.[83] Lord Strathcona reported that Patterson was doing everything within his power to improve relations among the parties to the dispute, although members of the Bowell and Tupper cabinets may have felt that this was done at their expense.[84] Despite his Conservative background, the Lieutenant-Governor was able to convince Laurier and the Liberals that he was a *federal officer*, as well as a Tory politician, and continued to act on behalf of the federal government after the

[78]See PAC, Bowell Papers, Bowell-Schultz correspondence; PAC, Thompson Papers, Thompson-Schultz correspondence.
[79]Thompson Papers, Schultz to Thompson, Aug. 23, 1893.
[80]Greenway Papers, file 7615, Bourinot to Schultz, April 17, 1895.
[81]Canada, House of Commons, *Debates*, 1895, 774–838.
[82]*Saturday Night*, Aug. 10, 1895.
[83]See for example Bowell Papers, file 6408, Patterson to Bowell, Feb. 15, 1896.
[84]PAC, Aberdeen Papers, Strathcona to Aberdeen, April 8, 1896.

Liberal victory of 1896. Convinced that the schools question was "of great moment affecting the welfare of this Province and all Canada" and convinced too that the Lieutenant-Governor was designed "to be a peacemaker, to unite rather than divide," Patterson unquestionably assisted the Liberals in reaching a final settlement.[85] Precisely what he did is not known, but Tarte was later to recommend a healthy grant of patronage to the family on the grounds that "il nous a été utile, vous vous en souvenez, dans l'affaire des écoles."[86]

Perhaps the most active Lieutenant-Governor in the federal cause was Sir Hastings Doyle who reigned in Nova Scotia from 1867 to 1873. Doyle was an ardent supporter of federation and, like other imperial officers in Canada, had been in the vanguard of the movement. Knowing that in Doyle the central government would have an able and willing supporter, Tupper secured his transfer from New Brunswick to Nova Scotia in the autumn of 1867. A strong and sympathetic Lieutenant-Governor was considered essential, for the Nova Scotians were overwhelmingly opposed to Confederation and elected all but two antifederationists in the first provincial election. Under the circumstances there was nothing Doyle could do but permit the formation of a frankly secessionist ministry, but he had no intention of letting his ministers "run wild," as one of his first letters to Macdonald reveals:

We are boiling over here with Anti Confed Bile. The Legislature is to meet on the 29th next, and with such odds as I have against me I cannot see my way to success! . . . odds that would beat the Angel Gabriel if sent here to govern this Province! . . . I have given my advisers to understand that, after enunciating from the N.B. Throne the advantages that would probably flow from Confederation nothing will make me advocate repeal in any speech from the Throne, as I cannot afford to sacrifice either my honour nor [sic] consistency, so that a crisis is likely to arrive here by the end of January. I think the general opinion is that *they* will give way upon this point, *I* most certainly *will not*.[87]

Although "fully aware of the hopelessness of forming another administration (the opposition numbering only two)" Doyle fulfilled his promise, and no mention was made in the Speech from the Throne of the policy on which the government was elected.[88]

Since Doyle attended meetings of the Executive Council he was able to keep the federal government reasonably well informed. In

[85]Laurier Papers, 176, Patterson to Laurier, Oct. 31.
[86]*Ibid.*, 215, Tarte to Laurier, Dec. 6, 1901.
[87]Macdonald Papers, 114, Doyle to Macdonald, Dec. 31, 1867.
[88]G 21, I, file 24 B, Doyle to Monck, Feb. 13, 1868.

August 1868 when Macdonald and others went to Halifax to arrange a settlement, the Lieutenant-Governor was consulted on "every step."[89] He served as the "contact man" during the long negotiations that ended with Howe's entry into the federal cabinet. This done he turned his attention again to the local government, but nothing could be done:

> To go to the Country upon any other matter than that which I threatened the Government, viz: to test the *Loyalty* of the people, would be madness, for we should have nearly the same people back again, *just now*, and probably for some months to come, but I have little doubt that the time *will* come and before we are many months older. Nor do I think that the time has *yet* arrived to form a *coalition* with Tupper and Co. It would, selon moi, be a pity to hurry the movement on, but I think as soon as your Parliament meets and that friend "joe" has the opportunity of speaking out, and that *you* are enabled to tell us how you can financially improve our condition, the coalition might safely take place.[90]

All agreed that if the secessionist movement were to be nipped in the bud, Howe's election had to be secured at any cost. Howe himself was sure of success, but the Lieutenant-Governor warned him that the local government was determined to exercise all its influence against him. Tupper was asked to give Howe all his support and Macdonald was told to bring the power of the federal political machine into play, "for, if he is reelected *they* must give up the Ghost."[91] With Howe's election, said Doyle, "I shall then be able to talk to my 'Locals' pretty *'loud'* as the Yankees say, and force them (My Government) to accept the situation, or *swash them up*, for there is already dissention in their camp."[92]

There was a suggestion that the Lieutenant-Governor might embarrass the provincial government by forcing an early session to consider the Howe-Macdonald agreement. Macdonald himself did not see how Doyle could do this without advice, but told Tupper to go ahead with the plan if there was any chance of success.[93] In the end the project was discarded and another manœuvre began. Soon after the federal authorities had issued the writ for an election in Yarmouth they realized that if the constituency were to be won by a secessionist Howe's election in Hants would be jeopardized. Tupper and Howe pleaded for the recall of the writ, but Macdonald could do nothing. The local

---

[89]Pope, *Memoirs*, II, 34, Macdonald to Monck, Sept. 4, 1868.
[90]Macdonald Papers, 114, Doyle to Macdonald, Dec. 7, 1868.
[91]*Ibid.*, Feb. 3, 1869.
[92]*Ibid.*, Feb. 12, 1869.
[93]*Ibid.*, 516, Macdonald to Howe, Feb. 15, 1869; *ibid.*, Macdonald to Tupper, Feb. 15, 1869.

government, on the other hand, wanted both elections on the same day, since it was believed that if the Hants election could be held earlier than originally expected Howe would be caught unprepared.[94] Consequently the Attorney General informed Doyle that the provincial election laws provided that if two elections were to be held about the same time they were to be held on the same day. Doyle and Tupper put their heads together and sent the Attorney General's opinion to the Sheriff of Yarmouth, hoping that he would return the writ unexecuted; the Attorney General had expected that it would be sent to Hants and thus force an early election there. Doyle's surmise was correct, the writ was returned, and the local government was "very wild about it."[95] Macdonald then issued both writs at the same time, giving Howe sufficient time to organize his campaign, and preventing the provincial government from concentrating exclusively on Howe's defeat. Doyle gleefully reported that the plot "succeeded admirably, but I must not take too much credit for it, as *Tupper* was the originator of the plan!"[96]

Howe's election was a triumphant victory for the federal cause and did much to strengthen the Lieutenant-Governor's hand as a federal officer. Again he forced his ministers to delete any mention of repeal in the Speech from the Throne and even added a few moderate statements of his own. Macdonald informed him that the speeches were "masterpieces in their way, and you now at last, have your Ministry completely at your mercy," while Howe wrote that if the government "could swallow the opening and closing speeches . . . what more could anybody want of them?"[97] With the session of 1869 over Doyle wrote a long interesting letter to Macdonald.

I was doubtful, for a time, how my acts of leniency towards my Govt. might be viewed by your high authorities at Ottawa, surrounded as you were by those who I rather think fancied that I should have taken more energetic measures and over turned my Govt. Quite between ourselves, *Howe* certainly was in favor of my doing so, after he gained his election, and so was Tupper, but the latter, to do him justice, only made it conditional that Vail, my Prov. Sec., and Robertson (the two most moderate of my advisers (?)) would consent to break up the Govt. as it stood, and form one of their own—but this they would not consent to do. I therefore had no constitutional ground whatever for dismissing them, and, had I done so, we should have most undoubtedly been in a *mess*, for, the same

[94]PANS, Lieutenant-Governor's Correspondence, Wilkins to Moody, Feb. 24, 1869.
[95]Macdonald Papers, 114, Doyle to Macdonald, March 15, 1869.
[96]*Ibid.*, March 23, 1869.
[97]*Ibid.*, 516, Macdonald to Doyle, June 16, 1869; PAC, Howe Papers, 9, Howe to Doyle, July 7, 1869.

men, in many instances, would have been returned again, and we should have heard of fresh Delegations; and the state of the Province would have been worse even than before the appeal to the People and as my Govt. has, in point of fact, "accepted the situation" I think it is a proof that my view of our position was the correct one.

I must not, however, take too much credit for there is little doubt, in my mind, that *Howe's victory* has been the great means of my success; for it has enabled me to *speak out* to my Council in a manner I scarcely should have dared to do had he not succeeded in gaining his election. I was then in a position to remind them of their promise made to me, when they felt certain of *beating Howe*, that they would "give in," (asking for "better terms") if he gained his election. I *complimented* them upon the *Patriotic* fight they had made! and asked them what move they now had, except to take Nova Scotia from General Doyle, which they knew they *could* not do, or, to get the Yankees to help them, which they are quite aware meant war with England, and *they* (the Yankees) would not do so.

They said they had no desire for either of my alternatives, so I then put the home question to them, "then, what is left for you, but to accept the situation?" They agreed in thinking they could do nothing else, but they must ask for "better terms" and hoped they might be let down quietly. I told them I wished they might get *even* the terms already granted—and promised they should slide down a very moderate inclined plane![98]

The Lieutenant-Governor's optimism was short-lived. As a last resort the government threatened to dissolve on the issue of repeal, but Doyle assured Macdonald that he would not consider a dissolution.[99] In 1870 and 1871 he again had trouble with the speech, yet succeeded as always in getting his own way. A more serious crisis arose in January 1870 when he refused to sanction an Order in Council providing for an official delegation to Washington.[100] "It was a dangerous step to take," wrote Doyle, "as my Council was unanimous upon the subject . . . and they might have "thrown up the sponge," which at this moment would have been rather inconvenient."[101] When the crucial meeting of council took place, the Lieutenant-Governor "buckled on his armour" and said:

Mr. Troop, there is no one present at this meeting who knows better than you (who are a lawyer), do, that you are asking me to appoint Delegates to Washington, on a mission that concerns the whole Dominion as well as this Province, and I tell you and the other members present, that, *be the consequences what they may* I will not give my approval to that

[98]Macdonald Papers, 114, Doyle to Macdonald, June 25, 1869.
[99]*Ibid.*, Oct. 26, 1869.
[100]The delegation was to seek commercial reciprocity. Trade and commerce had been given to the central government.
[101]Macdonald Papers, 114, Doyle to Macdonald, Jan. 29, 1870.

minute of Council. This staggered them not a little, they looked at each other, and I was in full expectation that they would have risen, made their bows, and requested time to consider what action they should take, but, to my surprise, the Attorney General was the first to speak—he said he quite understood my feeling upon the subject, and that he, for one, would be the last to press me in a false position, and would not press the matter, especially as he thought they could gain their point by sending up a member of the Govt. privately—Others immediately followed the Atty General, breathing peace, and ultimately leaving Mr. Troop in the lurch—so I got upon my Dunghill, and flapped my wings, at having once more beat my Government, by assuming a firm determination not to give way.[102]

Throughout his term Doyle realized that he had an uncertain and varying influence with his ministers and a certain power over them. He realized too that this influence should be exercised on behalf of the federal government whose servant he was. And at the same time he knew that as a federal officer "any rash action" might cause the central government serious embarrassment. As he looked back on his five years as Lieutenant-Governor, he was justly able to conclude that he had fulfilled his "destiny having (notwithstanding the threats that were held out at the commencement of my "reign") lived to see Anti-Confederation a dead issue, and more than that the policy inaugurated by you and your brother Confederates triumphantly sustained in this Province!"[103]

"Anti Confederation" was scotched but not killed in Nova Scotia and it erupted fifteen years later. When the Liberal, and supposedly secessionist, Premier, W. S. Fielding, announced that secession was to be the issue in the 1886 election Macdonald immediately informed the Lieutenant-Governor that it was his duty "as a Dominion Officer to decline to allow that subject to enter into consideration at all."[104] Despite the Prime Minister's promise that the "whole weight" of the federal government would be behind him, the Lieutenant-Governor, M. H. Richey, hesitated to interfere. Fielding had never informed him officially that secession was to be discussed before the electorate, although he had mentioned it in the assembly, and to call him to account for statements reported in the press would in Richey's opinion be "the surest way of fanning to a flame the embers of discontent" and would likely result in a major constitutional crisis.[105]

Following Fielding's decisive victory, the Lieutenant-Governor in-

---

[102]PAC, Correspondence of the Secretary of State for the Provinces, 1870, file 51, Doyle to Young, Jan. 4, 1870.
[103]PAC, Tupper Papers, Doyle to Tupper, Dec. 28, 1872.
[104]Macdonald Papers, 526, Macdonald to Richey, May 14, 1886.
[105]*Ibid.*, 117, Richey to Macdonald, May 17, 1886.

formed Macdonald that "there will be little room left to me for the exercise of moderating powers, and I deem it very important that if any counsel suggests itself to you as desirable to be offered in the present condition of things you would kindly intimate its purport as early as possible and later on it can take the form of instructions if found necessary."[106] Richey believed that Fielding would summon the legislature at once and introduce a secessionist resolution. How could he refuse to adhere to the advice of his ministers in view of the large majority just obtained? And if he did refuse to summon the legislature for such a purpose, "must I not simply and avowedly on the ground of the matter concerning Dominion as well as Provincial interests suspend judgement until I communicate officially with your Government?"[107] With Quebec in flames, Manitoba in semi-revolt, and British Columbia restless, not to mention the repeated legal assaults by Blake and Mowat, Macdonald was probably prepared to sanction any exercise of the prerogative. But on this question he sought the advice of Thompson, one of his more able colleagues and Nova Scotia's representative in the cabinet. The latter strongly urged that the Lieutenant-Governor be instructed to keep clear of the struggle: "I think it would be unfortunate if he should seek advice hereafter as to the course which he should pursue. . . . We should . . . take the line that the question of secession is one that the legislature below has nothing to do with and which is for the Imperial Government to deal with rather than us."[108] If it were known that the Lieutenant-Governor was acting on federal advice, added Thompson, it would unquestionably increase the intensity of the anti-Canadian sentiments, and to advise the Lieutenant-Governor to interfere would be to admit that a conflict existed. Thompson's advice was followed and Richey was doubtless pleased to be spared many unpleasant moments.

In his rôle as peace-maker the Lieutenant-Governor was as often as not to be found on the side of the provincial government. In all probability his influence in Ottawa would be more significant than it was in the province, for many of the nineteenth-century officers had been members of the federal cabinet and confidants of the Prime Minister. Whether their action is any indication of the justice of the provincial claims, the truth remains that many Lieutenant-Governors strongly supported the demand for better financial terms: Archibald, Morris, Aikins, and Patterson in Manitoba; Trutch, Richards, Cornwall, McInnes, and Joly in British Columbia; Wilmot, Tilley, and McClelan

106*Ibid.*, June 16, 1886.
107*Ibid.*   108*Ibid.*, 275, Thompson to Macdonald, July 3, 1886.

in New Brunswick; and Masson and Chapleau in Quebec. Others may also have done so, but their recommendations are not to be found in the public and private correspondence of the period.

Almost without exception the western Lieutenant-Governors were aware that the federal government tended to ignore the genuine grievances in the west. Archibald's work has already been discussed at considerable length. Morris urged the federal government to consider seriously its Indian and half-breed policy, to enlarge Manitoba's boundaries, to improve the judicial system in the province, to change its public land policy—to only a few of the issues that arose during his term. Aikins emphasized the unfairness and danger of the repeated disallowance of provincial legislation. Schultz too, despite his admitted bias, often urged Macdonald to soften his attitude towards Manitoba and meet the provincial government half-way. Patterson was generally more inclined to support provincial views in Ottawa than otherwise, even though he was not a westerner and had had a long career in federal politics, and Bowell somewhat resented his "strong position."

The same was true in British Columbia. As Lieutenant-Governor from 1881 to 1887, Cornwall spent many hours writing long dispatches to Ottawa on the need for a rational policy of salmon conservation, the importance of a consistent Indian policy in the province, on the legitimacy and reality of the opposition to Asiatic immigration on the Pacific Coast, and on the justice of the demands for lower freight rates and improved railway services. McInnes repeatedly warned Laurier that the Liberal variation of National Policy was not popular in the west and did not adequately serve the needs of the province. Even Joly, once a member of the Laurier administration and a close and trusted friend of the Prime Minister, was surprisingly blunt. He informed Laurier "que la tâche de Mr. Dunsmuir serait bien facile, si votre Gouvernement voulait accorder à cette Province la part de l'aide dont elle a plus besoin qu'aucune autre Province, et à laquelle, elle a droit, mais qui lui est refusée. Les résultats de ce refus sont faciles de prévoir."[109] Laurier's annoyance at Joly's tone did not prevent him from asking for more information. His duty being "to cultivate the most amicable relations" between the two governments, Joly told the Prime Minister that nothing would more quickly soothe the Pacific province and restore confidence in the Laurier administration than prompt and sympathetic attention to the provincial claims regarding the fisheries, financial terms, railway development, and Oriental immigration.[110]

[109]Laurier Papers, 210, Joly to Laurier, Oct. 31, 1901.
[110]Ibid., 212, Joly to Laurier, Nov. 18, 1901.

Two years later the Lieutenant-Governor concluded that McBride's claim for better terms was "reasonable and just," while Laurier regarded it as ill-founded and impossible.[111]

Masson had once refused Macdonald's invitation to become Premier of Quebec partly on the grounds that at heart he was a strong supporter of provincial rights and believed that unless federal policy showed a sudden and decisive change a provincial rights movement in Quebec was inevitable—this long before the execution of Riel and the rise of Mercier. As Lieutenant-Governor he attempted to persuade Macdonald to anticipate such an event by better financial terms and grants to the province for railway construction and immigration. When Mercier did gain power in 1887, Masson, feeling that he could no longer be of service as a federal officer, resigned. During the last eight months of office, however, he did his best to prevent an open rupture in Dominion-provincial relations; Mercier was asked to be reasonable and patient and Macdonald to be conciliatory.[112] Chapleau later asked Thompson if he thought "Count Mercier" was still in power and warned him that nothing would more surely cause a resurgence of *le parti national* than an overbearing, selfish attitude on the part of the central government.[113]

Such activities as these were not epoch-making. They indicate, however, that most Lieutenant-Governors took their rôle as peace-maker, as a shock-absorber between the two governments and political authorities, seriously, and within the limits assigned to them did what they could to improve Dominion-provincial relations. The rights and interests of the central government were always uppermost in their mind but they were concerned too with the better government of the province. Relations between the central and local governments have always involved concession and compromise on both sides and the Lieutenant-Governors have advised each in turn according to the needs and circumstances of the moment. Their task was not always easy, for as Dufferin once remarked of the colonial Governor, the Lieutenant-Governor was like a man riding two horses in a circus; he no sooner had one beast under control than the second began acting up. It is significant too that little mention has been made of these activities after the turn of the century. This may in part be the result of a dearth of material, but it is more likely an accurate reflection of the changing nature and decreasing importance of the office of Lieu-

[111]PABC, McBride Papers, Joly to McBride, Aug. 24, 1903.
[112]Macdonald Papers, 109, Masson to Macdonald, Feb. 7, 1885, Aug. 18, 1887.
[113]Thompson Papers, Chapleau to Thompson, Dec. 29, 1893; Correspondence of the Secretary of State, 1896, file 3501, Chapleau to Tupper, May 30, 1896.

tenant-Governor. He is still a federal officer, although he may at times —like some scholars and the public—forget it, but the occasions when his action is required seldom arise. This is not to suggest that Dominion-provincial relations have improved, although they may have become more restrained. As an instrument of federal policy, however, the Lieutenant-Governor has been replaced by the conference, the national political party, the radio, the press, and the telephone.

CHAPTER EIGHT

PROVINCIAL LEGISLATION

WHEN a provincial bill is presented to the Lieutenant-Governor he is authorized by the British North America Act to declare "according to his Discretion, but subject to the Provisions of this Act and to the Governor-General's Instructions either that he assents thereto in the Governor-General's name, or that he withholds the Governor-General's assent, or that he reserves the Bill for the Signification of the Governor-General's pleasure."[1] A bill remains inoperative unless the Governor-General gives his assent within one year of the date of reservation.[2] If the Lieutenant-Governor does assent the Governor-General in Council may disallow the provincial act within one year of receipt.[3] In most studies of Canadian federalism reservation rightly cedes primacy to disallowance, for although both were parts of the design of 1867 and both involve similar review of provincial legislation by the Dominion government, disallowance has been the more important instrument of Dominion supervision. But in this instance the reverse shall be true for the Lieutenant-Governor has only a minor function in the disallowance procedure.

Once again the much-discussed "intentions of the Fathers" are difficult to determine with unimpeachable certainty. The clauses providing for reservation and disallowance were introduced at Quebec by Mowat and reached the British North America Act with their meaning unchanged.[4] Mowat's biographer has written that "this, however, is certainly not the original form of Mr. Mowat's motion,

[1]Sections 55 and 90. See chap. i.

[2]Sections 57 and 90. Only in one instance has a reserved bill been assented to by the Governor-General yet failed to become law because more than one year had passed. That was in Prince Edward Island in 1878. (W. E. Hodgins, comp., *Correspondence . . . upon the Subject of Dominion and Provincial Legislation 1867–1895* (Ottawa, 1896), 1201 ff; Alpheus Todd, *Parliamentary Government in the British Colonies* (2d rev. ed.; London, 1894), 443.)

[3]Sections 56 and 90.

[4]There is little indication that the Quebec draftsmen gave much thought to the question of executive supervision of legislation. Bills and acts passed by the Canadian Parliament would be reserved and disallowed "in the usual manner" and provincial legislation would be dealt with "in like manner." (Sir Joseph Pope, ed., *Confederation Documents* (Toronto, 1895), 48–9.) The British North America Act merely set out the procedure to be followed with regard to Dominion legislation and provided that a substitution of terms would make the same sections applicable to provincial legislation.

which is stated to have been adopted after debate. I have his own authority for saying that he desired the Provincial Legislatures to be made co-ordinate with, and not subordinate to, the General Legislature, and the power of veto over provincial, as well as federal legislation, to remain vested, as it had theretofore been, in the Imperial authorities."[5] Since Biggar's assertion has been accepted in the latest (and semi-official) study of reservation and disallowance some comment is perhaps necessary.[6] In the first place although Mowat's resolutions were debated, the records of the Quebec Conference strongly suggest that they were accepted as read.[7] And secondly it should be remembered that Mowat simply introduced the official Canadian resolution. Now it is true that Mowat later repeatedly and emphatically declared his preference for a form of federalism different than that designed in 1864, and before the century had run its course had seen the achievement of much of his aim. But even in his own story Mowat did not suggest that he introduced a clause different from that passed.

Although personally he had failed to appreciate the argument, Mowat recalled that a widespread assumption had existed in 1864 that the colonial relationship required the power of control to reside somewhere; and "the question that presented itself to the Confederation Conference was, Where should this power be?" The imperial government had rarely interfered with Canadian legislation, yet, said Mowat, "the notion was that the Dominion Government would exercise that power of veto less frequently than the Imperial Government would exercise it. Nobody then had the idea that it would be more freely exercised . . . , that it would be used as a curb upon the Provincial Legislatures."[8] Unfortunately Mowat's novel testimony clashes with other evidence; and as he was speaking in the Ontario legislature on the resolutions passed at the Quebec Conference of 1887 the credibility of his statement is not increased by the occasion that brought it forth.

Unquestionably the colonial relationship did necessitate the continued existence of the veto in one form or another. Logically, since the link betwen the provinces and the British government was to be completely severed by the creation of an intermediary, the power could be entrusted to the new entity. But more important was the undeniable fact that in the federation as in the empire the parts were to be subject

[5]C. R. W. Biggar, *Sir Oliver Mowat* (Toronto, 1905), I, 132.
[6]G. V. La Forest, *Disallowance and Reservation of Provincial Legislation* (Ottawa, 1955), 5.
[7]Pope, *Confederation Documents*, 31, 88.
[8]Toronto *Globe*, March 1, 1888; *ibid.*, July 4, 1887.

in the last analysis to the whole.[9] It is well known that the participants in the Canadian confederation debates regarded the appointment of the Lieutenant-Governor and the power over provincial legislation as essential principles of the centralized design.[10] It was natural that the centralists would soft-pedal the implications and possible incidence of Dominion power given the opposition from the decentralist bloc. Their general temerity and ambiguity permitted Dunkin to observe that "the power of disallowing local bills, and also that of reserving them for the sanction of the General Government, are on the one hand represented as realities—powers that will really be exercised by the General Government to restrain improper local legislation—to make everything safe for those who want a Legislative rather than a Federal union; but on the other hand, to those who do not want a legislative union, it is represented that they mean nothing at all, and will never be exercised."[11] Nonetheless friend and foe alike admitted that reservation and disallowance were part of the core of Dominion power. Yet at the same time it was quite apparent that no one knew exactly how the powers would be used.

Late in the spring of 1868 with the first session of the first Dominion Parliament over and legislation arriving from the provinces, Macdonald turned his attention to the supervision of provincial legislation. As Minister of Justice he prepared a memorandum on disallowance in which he suggested that a provincial statute should be disallowed if it were illegal or unconstitutional in whole or in part, if it clashed with Dominion legislation in fields that were shared by the two authorities, or if it appeared to be detrimental to the national interest.[12]

---

[9]It is interesting to note that at the Federal Convention of 1787 Alexander Hamilton proposed that state laws contrary to the law or constitution of the central government be void: "the better to prevent such laws being passed, the Governor or president of each state shall be appointed by the General Government and shall have a negative upon the laws to be passed in the State. . . ." There was no question here of the colonial relationship. (C. C. Tansill, ed., *Documents Illustrative of the Formation of the Union of the American States* (Washington, 1927), 980.)

[10]See Canada, *Confederation Debates*, 1865; La Forest, *Disallowance and Reservation*, 5–12; Chap. vii above.

[11]Canada, *Confederation Debates*, 1865, 490.

[12]Hodgins, *Dominion and Provincial Legislation*, 61–2, Report of the Minister of Justice, June 8, 1868. David Mills, later to become an eminent Liberal legal authority, noted in his diary: "Sent a memorandum today to Sir John A. taking exception to the doctrine he lays down as to when it is proper to veto the acts of the Local Legislature. He lays down two grounds. The first when they are clearly against public policy. The second when they are *ultra vires*. To this last ground I take exception, as it is a judicial determination and should be left to the courts exclusively." (University of Western Ontario Library, Mills Papers, Diary entry dated May 4, 1868.) During the debates on the Quebec Resolutions Cartier had declared that the power of disallowance would be used "in case of unjust or unwise legislation." (Canada, *Confederation Debates*, 1865, 502.) Macdonald too later

Unfortunately Macdonald left no such clear and straightforward statement of his views on the power of reservation. In 1868 and forever thereafter there was considerable doubt as to the proper exercise of the Lieutenant-Governor's authority to reserve provincial bills.

About the same time, however, Macdonald did wrestle with a draft of general instructions for the Lieutenant-Governors. The section on reservation closely followed the relevant sections in the Governor-General's instructions:

And for the execution of so much of the powers vested in you by virtue of the B.N.A. Act, 1867, as relates to the declaring either that you assent in my name to Bills passed by the Legislature of the said Province, or that you withhold my assent therefrom, or that you reserve such Bills for the signification of my pleasure thereon, you are hereby instructed that when any Bill is presented to you for my assent of either of the classes hereinafter specified you shall (unless you shall think proper to withhold my assent from the same) reserve the same for the signification of my pleasure thereon; subject nevertheless to your discretion in case you should be of opinion that an urgent necessity exists requiring that such Bill be brought into immediate operation; in which case you are authorized to assent to such Bill in my name, transmitting to me by the earliest opportunity, the Bill so assented to, together with your reasons for assenting thereto. . . .[13]

Five classes of subjects followed: measures involving a grant of money to the Lieutenant-Governor; measures inconsistent with treaty obligations; measures interfering with the military forces; measures of an unusual nature conceivably prejudicing the rights of the Crown or its subjects outside the province; and measures similar to those once disallowed by the Governor-General. What is omitted is of more significance than what is included: bills affecting divorce, coinage and currency, and differential duties. There was only one logical reason why these subjects should have been excluded. They were clearly within the legislative competency of the federal government. In other words, Macdonald appears to have been thinking at this stage of reservation as still being in great part an instrument of imperial policy, although now placed in the hands of Dominion officials. Such a conclusion is supported by Langevin's assertion "that reservation will take place only in respect of such measures as are now reserved for Her Majesty's sanction."[14]

Confirmation of this belief may be found in a private report on

---

wrote that the power of disallowance need not be used against *ultra vires* acts, unless it was "likely to cause mischief by being allowed to remain on the Statute Book." (PAC, Macdonald Papers, 534, Macdonald to Meredith, 14 Jan., 1883.)

[13]Macdonald Papers, 299, Miscellaneous, 61–9.

[14]Canada, *Confederation Debates*, 1865, 377.

reservation drawn up by Macdonald for the Governor-General. The report was written, wrote Sir John Young, "without consultation with his Colleagues, in his capacity as the framer and main promoter of the British North America Act, and therefor as a person extremely anxious to secure its well-working."[15] The Prime Minister observed that within their respective spheres the Lieutenant-Governor and the Governor-General possessed the same power to reserve bills. Although the powers of the provincial legislatures had been substantially reduced by Confederation, he continued, "they have jurisdiction in very many cases to which the Royal Instructions would seem to apply." Thus Macdonald urged Young to secure advice from the Colonial Office as to his course when provincial legislation encroached on the subjects mentioned in the seventh paragraph of his Instructions.[16] Lord Granville's reply to this query was emphatic: "The prohibitions . . . rest on grounds of imperial policy, and therefore the Governor-General of the Dominion is not at liberty, even on the advice of his ministers, to sanction or assent to any provincial law in violation of them. He would indeed be bound to instruct the Lieutenant-Governor of the province not to give such assent."[17] Granville's observations were approved by the Canadian government in an Order in Council that was sent to the Lieutenant-Governors "for their information and guidance."[18] This then was the first declared principle regarding reservation, and it was for some time the only positive one. When Blake succeeded in having the seventh paragraph deleted from the revised instructions of 1878 the Order in Council automatically lapsed. No bill was reserved under its authority.[19]

Reservation was not mentioned in the instructions given to Archibald in 1870. But from the second new province, where Trutch was embarrassed by his ignorance of constitutional procedure under res-

[15]PAC, G 21, 60, Young to Granville, March 11, 1869.
[16]Macdonald Papers, 515, Macdonald to Young, Jan. 16, 1869.
[17]Hodgins, Dominion and Provincial Legislation, 63, Granville to Young, May 8, 1869.
[18]PAC, Orders in Council, approved July 17, 1869.
[19]A British Columbia bill respecting the qualifications of voters was reserved in 1872 on the advice of the Attorney General partly on the grounds that it conflicted with the instructions furnished to the colonial governors. Macdonald reported that the provincial Lieutenant-Governors were not bound by such instructions, but only by instructions from the Governor-General in Council "or through any member of the Council." Moreover, he added, there was nothing preventing such legislation in the Instructions issued to the Governor-General since 1867. Since the bill was otherwise within the powers of the provincial legislature Macdonald advised the Governor-General to give his assent. (Hodgins, Dominion and Provincial Legislation, 1011, Report of the Minister of Justice, Sept. 18, 1872.)

ponsible government, came a request for advice. The Lieutenant-Governor, Macdonald answered, must either assent to provincial bills or reserve them for the consideration of the Governor-General. Trutch was to be guided in all cases by the advice of his ministers unless he received "positive instructions from the Governor-General, through the Secretary of State for the Provinces, to the contrary."[20] The Lieutenant-Governor followed this advice to the letter, and in the first two sessions reserved five bills on the recommendation of the Attorney General.[21] As Minister of Justice, Macdonald made no objection to this procedure in British Columbia, yet, at the same time, he declared unconstitutional a similar practice in Ontario.[22]

Two measures for the incorporation of the Orange Order were passed by the Ontario legislature in 1873. The bills were introduced by a private member, treated as an open question by the Liberal cabinet—a majority of which opposed the bills—and passed with large majorities. When called upon in the normal course of events to advise the Lieutenant-Governor, Mowat, the Premier and Attorney General, recommended that the bills be reserved.[23] The Macdonald government was placed in an extremely difficult position, so subtly embarrassing in fact that Macdonald at once suspected trickery. The Conservatives secured considerable support from the Orange Order in Ontario. Yet the Orangemen were the declared enemies of Roman Catholicism, and the measures had been strenuously opposed by Ontario Roman Catholics—in the country, in the legislature, and in the cabinet.[24] To advise assent to the measures would have been foolhardy, as Macdonald well knew, for Roman Catholics throughout Canada would have been up in arms. Not to advise assent would certainly alienate the Orangemen.[25] It was a neat attempt to trap

[20]Macdonald Papers, 519, Macdonald to Trutch, Oct. 27, 1871.
[21]PABC, Attorney General's Letterbook, *passim*.
[22]In Manitoba, Archibald, still his own premier, reserved several bills during the first two sessions. Macdonald wrote: ". . . it is fortunate that your Cabinet allows you to reserve them without remonstrance. Such being the case the Governor General must deal with them as being reserved by you with the advice of your Council. . . ." (Macdonald Papers, 521, Macdonald to Archibald, Sept. 24, 1872.)
[23]*Ontario Sessional Papers*, 1874, no. 19.
[24]See, for example, the petition from the four Roman Catholic bishops in Ontario, PAC, Correspondence of the Secretary of State for the Provinces, 1873, no. 122.
[25]Had he wished to advise assent Macdonald might not have been able to carry his colleagues with him. A British Columbia bill to legitimatize children born out of wedlock was reserved in 1872 and Macdonald later informed Trutch: "the Act [*sic*] . . . has not yet been reported on. This question is a ticklish one as it affects the Lower Canadians. By law their children born out of wedlock are legitimatized by subsequent marriage. There is no doubt the Act is beyond the

him, Macdonld dryly commented a decade later, but he was "too old a bird to be caught with such chaff."[26]

With the deck so clearly stacked against him the Prime Minister simply refused to play. His apology was made in the form of a somewhat ambiguous constitutional document.[27] The power of reservation, he declared, was originally an instrument of imperial policy and was exercised by the Governor-General solely in his capacity as an imperial officer. Similarly, "the Lieutenant-Governor should reserve a Bill in his capacity as an officer of the Dominion, and under instructions from the Governor-General." The Lieutenant-Governor must adhere to the advice of his ministers unless a bill conflicted with "his instructions or his duty" as a federal officer. And provincial ministers, he hastened to add, were bound to advise the Lieutenant-Governor to assent to all measures passed by the legislature. In the case in question, the Attorney General of Ontario, who had voted for the bills in the assembly, should have advised assent. The bills were clearly within the competence of the provincial government and no instructions had been issued to reserve them.

Truly "too old a bird to be caught with such chaff," Macdonald refused to take any action on the reserved bills. In so doing he established a precedent for reserved measures really within the competence of the provincial government. The federal government would make no report on the bill, thus allowing it to lapse and leaving the whole matter to be dealt with *de novo* by the government of the province. "If the Acts [*sic*] should again be passed," Macdonald's report concluded, "the Lieutenant-Governor should consider himself bound to deal with them at once, and not ask Your Excellency to intervene in matters of provincial concern, and solely and entirely within the jurisdiction and competence of the legislature of the province." The report to the Governor-General finished, Macdonald sent a hurried note to the Lieutenant-Governor of Ontario, a close friend and ex-colleague.

I have at last had time to draw my report to the Governor-General on the Orange Bills of your last Session. I have been obliged to hit your Ministry over your shoulders, and report that you ought not to have reserved those Bills for the Governor-General's assent.

Bills are only reserved when, in the opinion of the Executive, they are

competence of the Provincial Legislature, but my Quebec colleagues do not care about being parties to a formal Order in Council against the law." (Macdonald Papers, 522, Macdonald to Trutch, Dec. 20, 1872.) The bill was allowed to lapse without comment. An even more difficult situation was created by the Orange Order bills.   [26]Canada, House of Commons, *Debates*, 1882, 920.

[27]Hodgins, *Dominion and Provincial Legislation*, 104–5, Report of the Minister of Justice, Aug. 25, 1873; PAC, Orders in Council, approved Aug. 29, 1873.

beyond the competence or jurisdiction of the Legislature, or contrary to instructions.

The Governor-General is not called upon to take the advice of his Canadian Ministers on the reservation of a Bill. All that he has to do is look at his Royal Instructions. In the same way every Bill passed by a Provincial Legislature should be assented to unless the Lieutenant-Governor is satisfied that it is beyond the jurisdiction of the Local Legislature or if it be contrary to the instructions received from the Governor-General.[28]

The private letter to Howland was much clearer than the official report. The Prime Minister admitted that the provincial ministers were not bound to advise assent to every measure, but could, if the bill seemed to be beyond the competence of the provincial legislature or contrary to the Lieutenant-Governor's instructions, recommend that it be reserved.[29]

Although Macdonald observed that the Governor-General was "not called upon to take the advice of his Canadian Ministers on the reservation of a Bill," he might have added that such advice could be given. A recommendation that the Oaths bill be reserved had been considered in 1873, but for political reasons the idea had been discarded. A year later the Liberal administration advised Dufferin to reserve a measure "in deference to the language of the Royal Instructions. . . ."[30] After the Instructions were revised in 1876–7 and the provisions for compulsory reservation omitted, Lord Lorne found himself at odds with a member of Macdonald's cabinet over the precise status and nature of the power of reservation. Lorne noted:

In an interview between the Governor-General, Sir John Macdonald, Sir Leonard Tilley, and Sir Charles Tupper on the 25th November, 1879, the Governor-General said that it seemed to him that the language used by Sir A. Campbell and affirmed by his Colleagues might be held as expressing the opinion that Ministers could not advise the Governor-General to reserve Bills passed by the Houses, and that if this was intended it was an unfortunate docking of their own powers.

Sir John emphatically repudiated this conclusion and agreed that the power to advise the Governor-General to reserve Bills still rested with the Ministry.[31]

[28]Macdonald Papers, 523, Macdonald to Howland, Aug. 26, 1873.
[29]This could, of course, make possible a recurrence of the dilemma Macdonald then faced. And it raised as well the problem of cabinet-legislature relations. But it was (and is) possible that after the measure has passed the cabinet would realize that the bill was *ultra vires* or contrary to instructions. The Attorney General's duty in that case would be to inform the Lieutenant-Governor of this fact. As Macdonald pointed out, however, this advice need not be binding on the Lieutenant-Governor; he would have to exercise his personal discretion and be "satisfied" that the advice was justified.
[30]PAC, Orders in Council, approved June 4, 1874.
[31]PAC, G 18, 70, Memorandum on a Point raised with reference to the Governor General's Prerogative, Nov. 27, 1879.

A decade later, with reference to a Canadian act respecting appeals in criminal cases, the Colonial Secretary inferred "from the fact that you were not advised to reserve the Bill for the signification of Her Majesty's pleasure, that your ministers were of opinion that it leaves the prerogative right to entertain appeals untouched. . . ."[32]

Regarding the Ontario bills, Mowat did not take Macdonald's censure without return. In the absence of instructions to the Lieutenant-Governor, he declared, current practice would be governed by pre-Confederation usage and precedents. Colonial Governors had been forbidden to assent to measures similar to those once rejected by the British government; and among such measures, Mowat proudly observed, was a Prince Edward Island bill to incorporate the Orange Order.[33] The Ontario Premier made no attempt to deny that he had supported the bills in the assembly, that his cabinet had split, and that the subject was politically treacherous. But he did maintain that his attention had not been drawn to the questionable constitutionality of the bills until they had been passed by the assembly.

The question being then raised and discussed, and the undersigned having given to it his best attention, it seemed to him that to concur in advising the Lieutenant-Governor to reserve the bills . . . , was the fitting course in view of the constitutional consideration . . . , as well as in deference, not only to the opinions of his colleagues, who had voted against the bills when before the Assembly, but in deference also to the advisers of His Excellency the Governor-General, and to the convenience of the parties whom the bills were designed to incorporate.[34]

If, as Macdonald said, the measures were within the competence of the provincial legislature, why not assent to them? Mowat knew why, of course, but he could not help chiding the Conservative leader who, "being a prominent member of the order," was "not to be supposed adverse to the bills, or solicitous to find reasons to prevent their becoming law." Macdonald had resigned, however, before Mowat's lengthy dispatch was completed. Later in the Ontario legislature the Conservatives followed Macdonald's lead and charged Mowat with lack of respect for the elementary rules of responsible government and the position of the assembly. Mowat replied that reservation was

[32]G 3, 22, Knutsford to Lansdowne, May 1, 1888.
[33]Macdonald had denied that the provincial Lieutenant-Governors were bound by pre-1867 practices. (See fn. 19 above.) Mowat was apparently unaware of the Order in Council of July 17, 1869. This made it clear beyond question that the Lieutenant-Governor was bound to reserve measures similar to those once disallowed or reserved and not assented to.
[34]*Ontario Sessional Papers*, 1874, no. 19, 4, Memorandum on the Report of the Minister of Justice dated Aug. 25, 1873, by the Attorney General of Ontario, Dec. 16, 1873.

better for all concerned than disallowance, and went on to say that Macdonald's refusal to act on the bills could find no precedent "in the history of Colonial Government."[35] The *Globe* could not resist the temptation to lash out at Macdonald as well: "Sir John A. Macdonald shirked his duty, and, unwilling to offend his Catholic supporters simply sent the Bill back without instructions one way or the other."[36]

The subject did not arise again until 1882 when the indefatigable Mowat once more stirred up contentious issues in the ill-defined sphere of Dominion-provincial relations. The disallowance and repeated passage of the Ontario Streams acts resulted in an airing of the whole question of federal control of provincial legislation in the House of Commons where three men of no mean legal ability spoke at length. D'Alton McCarthy ridiculed the suggestion that there was any real difference between reservation and disallowance. The Lieutenant-Governor, he admitted, was a Dominion officer charged with the protection of federal interests and in duty bound not to assent to any measure that interfered with the rights of the national government. But since the Lieutenant-Governors had not been given any instructions,

they are left without directions what course to take in any given measure, and consequently, the result is that they give *pro forma* their assent to a measure, which thereby becomes law, subject to being disallowed. It is, in fact, an *ad interim* allowance and becomes an *ad interim* law. . . . the matter is one of shadow more than substance. Suppose the Lieutenant-Governor reserved this Bill to-day, would there be any practical difference from his having reserved it? What earthly difference would it make?[37]

There was much truth in McCarthy's argument, for in the absence of instructions the Lieutenant-Governor's assent did not indicate that the statute was free from objection. Of course, even if instructions had been issued and a bill reserved in compliance with them the measure would still have to be considered by the Department of Justice. Yet the instructions would not only limit the field of provincial legislative activity, but also would provide some guide to the probable end of a measure that seemed to be incompatible with them.

Since reservation and disallowance both involved review by the federal government, Blake was inclined to believe that the former might well be abolished. As Minister of Justice in the Mackenzie administration, Blake had succeeded in having removed from the

[35]Toronto *Globe*, Jan. 10, 1874.
[36]*Ibid.*, Jan. 12, 1874.
[37]Canada, House of Commons, *Debates*, 1882, 894.

Governor-General's instructions the list of measures to be compulsorily reserved, and was doubtless not in favour of such a list being inserted in future instructions to the Lieutenant-Governor.[38] In the absence of any instructions, declared Blake, the exercise of the power of reservation was of doubtful constitutionality.

> I say that he has no constitutional right as a rule to reserve Bills. . . . If a Governor disapproves of a Bill it is his duty to settle that matter with his Ministers while the Bill is yet before the Assembly. . . . If he chooses to take the responsibility of making a quarrel between himself and his Ministers on that subject he has a right to do so; but when he permits the measure to pass through the local Legislature and it comes before him for his assent, he has no right to refuse assent. He has no right to turn what would be a conflict between himself and his Ministers into a much more serious thing, a quarrel between himself and the Assembly. . . .[39]

Ministers similarly have no right to turn a disagreement between themselves and the assembly into one between the Lieutenant-Governor and the legislature, and thus must advise assent to all measures passed by the assembly. This argument was in essence not very different from Macdonald's in 1873. Much of its force was removed, however, when Blake admitted that there were exceptional cases, not yet defined, where this reasoning would not hold.

Macdonald generally agreed with the opposition leader, although he denied that reservation was unconstitutional merely because no permanent formal instructions had been issued to the Lieutenant-Governors. He emphatically supported the argument that reservation on the advice of the provincial government was irregular. At the same time every act of the Crown must be covered by ministerial responsibility; and as far as reservation was concerned the responsibility for the Lieutenant-Governor's action lay with the Dominion ministers. As usual he compared the position of the Governor-General and the Lieutenant-Governor:

> The Governor-General has a two-fold position, first as representative of the Sovereign with a responsible body of advisers, and secondly as an Imperial officer, and if he gets instructions to reserve a Bill he is obliged to do so and the Ministers in England are responsible to the British Parliament for the proper use of the Royal Prerogative.[40]

In the same way the Lieutenant-Governor had no right to reserve a

[38]*C.S.P.*, 1877, no. 13, Blake to Carnarvon, *circa* July 1, 1876.
[39]Canada, House of Commons, *Debates*, 1882, 909–10. It will be remembered that Letellier had charged his ministers with placing him in conflict with the assembly because they had not informed him in advance of the legislation proposed. Blake appears to have overlooked this latter possibility.
[40]Canada, House of Commons, *Debates*, 1882, 920.

bill unless instructed to do so, and the federal ministers would be responsible to the Canadian Parliament for his actions. Power and responsibility must lie with the same authority. Macdonald agreed that there was little difference between reservation and disallowance; both were an affront to the provincial government, a limitation on its power whether by a federal official or a department of the central government.

This debate and the bitter controversy over the Ontario legislation forced the cabinet to turn its attention to the principles and procedures to be followed in the supervision and control of provincial legislation. Macdonald drew up a report on reservation while Campbell, as we have seen, drafted general instructions. The Prime Minister's report was little more than a repetition of his comments in 1873. In England the cabinet could not advise the Queen to veto a bill; it must advise assent or it must resign. The British North America Act did not give the Governor-General the power of reservation in order to increase the powers of his Canadian ministers, but granted it to him "as an Imperial officer and for the protection of Imperial interests. It arises from our position as a dependency of the Empire, and to prevent legislation which in the opinion of the Imperial Government is opposed to the welfare of the Empire and its policy." For the exercise of that power, "with or without instructions," the Governor-General was responsible to the British government alone.

As the relations between the Governor-General and his responsible advisers, as well as his position as an Imperial officer, are similar to the relations of a Lieutenant-Governor with his Ministers and his position as a Dominion officer. . . . the same principles and reasons apply, *mutatis mutandis*, to the Provincial Governments and Legislatures.

The Lieutenant-Governor is not warranted in reserving any measures for the assent of the Governor-General on the advice of his Ministers.

He should do so in his capacity as a Dominion officer only and on instructions from the Governor-General. It is only in a case of extreme necessity that a Lieutenant-Governor should without such instructions exercise his discretion as a Dominion officer in reserving a Bill. In fact, with the facility of communication between the Dominion and Provincial Governments such a necessity can seldom if ever arise.[41]

The minute was approved and sent to the Lieutenant-Governors.

Campbell's draft instructions ordered the Lieutenant-Governor to reserve three types of measures: bills similar to those previously disallowed, bills similar to those once reserved and to which assent was not given, and bills that affected the electoral divisions within the

[41]Hodgins, *Dominion and Provincial Legislation*, 77–8. Report of the Minister of Justice, approved Nov. 29, 1882.

province unless a majority of the members representing those divisions agreed to the redistribution.[42] Attached to the draft was a printed circular containing all the relevant sections of the British North America Act and a table of disallowed acts. These instructions were never sent to the Lieutenant-Governors, however, and when finally issued in 1887 the Lieutenant-Governors' instructions stated only that all bills, assented to or reserved, were to be forwarded to Ottawa at once. Thus the Order in Council of November 1882 remained the only authoritative pronouncement on the subject of reservation, since the 1869 dispatch, which was formulated as an Order, may be said to have lapsed a decade later when the list of subjects to be reserved was omitted in the revised instructions to the Governor-General.

Macdonald's ruling was not universally accepted. Sir John Thompson, for one, openly disagreed with him. In 1889 the Mercier government introduced a bill identical to one disallowed the year before, and Thompson, the Conservative Minister of Justice, urged Macdonald to instruct the Lieutenant-Governor of Quebec to reserve it.[43] Accepting this advice the Prime Minister informed Angers that "as has been the practice in similar cases, where an act once disallowed has been re-enacted, you should reserve this Bill for the Governor-General's assent."[44] Reluctant to provoke a crisis with Mercier, the Lieutenant-Governor demurred, arguing that such a step "*on his own discretion*" would seriously weaken his "influence on his Ministers and the House." Angers pointed out that the practice of reserving such bills did not seem to have been adopted anywhere, and noted in particular that the Ontario Streams act had been passed and disallowed in three successive years. Moreover, he added, it had been repeatedly stated that a Lieutenant-Governor should reserve a bill only on specific instructions. Therefore if the federal authorities wanted the measure reserved let them send him specific instructions in an Order in Council that he could lay before his ministers.[45]

Thompson vigorously dissented from Lieutenant-Governor Angers' views regarding the reservation of previously disallowed measures.

I think that that must stand like any other point on which the Lieutenant Governor has to consider whether the enactments of his Legislature are at variance with the policy of the General Government, and that if

---

[42]Macdonald Papers, 322, Miscellaneous no. 11, section 14; *ibid.*, 196, Campbell to Macdonald, Nov. 25, 1882. There was to be no *quid pro quo* for the Redistribution Act of 1882.
[43]Macdonald Papers, 274, Thompson to Macdonald, Jan. 11, 1889.
[44]*Ibid.*, 528, Macdonald to Angers, Jan. 25, 1889.
[45]*Ibid.*, 186, Angers to Macdonald, Jan. 28, 1889.

they are at variance with the policy of the General Government, whether that policy may have been indicated to him through enactments of the Parliament of Canada on similar subjects, by Orders in Council, or by the disallowance of previous statutes in any of the Provinces, the better course would be for him to insist that the proposed enactments be reserved for the assent of the Governor General.[46]

The Ontario acts should have been reserved, added Thompson, and if they had been "the Province of Ontario would not have lost any of its rights, while a good deal of ill feeling would have been spared."[47]

Read carefully, Thompson's statement indicates that he held very different views from Macdonald and that in his mind the power of reservation was a much more significant part of the federal system than it had been. It was in fact in line with the use of the power by such able and active Lieutenant-Governors as Archibald, Morris, and Tilley. The Minister of Justice realized that he was implicitly criticizing Macdonald's *dicta*, but he suggested that his chief could only have been speaking of measures "about which there could be no dispute as to the competency of the Legislature" and that did not "conflict with Dominion policy or Imperial policy. . . ." He pointed out how difficult, if not impossible, it would be for the federal government to issue specific instructions to the Lieutenant-Governor on every bill that might conceivably be reserved, for the measures normally did not reach Ottawa until they had been passed by the legislature of the province and presented to the Lieutenant-Governor. As a rule there was insufficient time between the date of third reading and prorogation for the bills to be sent to Ottawa, considered by the Minister of Justice, and made the subject of an Order in Council. To order the Lieutenant-Governor to reserve a bill on the basis of its contents at first reading would be haphazard for it might be changed substantially in passage. Thus in Thompson's view the Lieutenant-Governor was not merely a cypher acting only on instructions, but was rather an active overseer endowed with general authority to guard the rights and interests of the central government.

Macdonald's ruling of 1882 remained the only official one. It was confirmed in 1895 by Sir Charles Hibbert Tupper, then Minister of Justice, as setting out "the constitutional principles which should

[46]*Ibid.*, Thompson to Macdonald, Feb. 2, 1889.
[47]In 1881 Campbell had urged Macdonald to have the Streams Bill reserved by instructing the Lieutenant-Governors to reserve any measure once disallowed. If such instructions were sent "Mowat *wd.* not venture probably to introduce it." (*Ibid.*, 315, Campbell to Macdonald, Nov. 7, 1881; *ibid.*, 195, Campbell to Macdonald, Nov. 10, 1881.) Blake held the same view: "The former Act for the same purpose having been disallowed it was proper that the Lieutenant-Governor should reserve this Bill. . . ." (Hodgins, *Dominion and Provincial Legislation*, 1183.)

govern the action of a Lieutenant-Governor in the exercise of his authority. . . ."[48] In the last recorded comment of a Minister of Justice on the subject, nearly half a century after Macdonald had delivered his opinion, the 1882 report was still cited as the governing document.[49] Whether Macdonald's interpretation was right or wise is not in our province to decide; it was at least in keeping with his character. Canada's "elder statesman" consistently refused to commit himself, and general dogmatic instructions would have been a very definite and permanent commitment. Likewise, "the old chieftain" had no faith greater than that in himself. Essentially—and always—the politician, *he* would decide whether it was desirable (or possible), from a political standpoint, to deal harshly with provincial legislation. The greatest threat to the dominance of his party and the maintenance of his government, the threat that in the end materialized and destroyed both, was the growth of political movements advocating provincial rights. Acutely aware of this, Macdonald had no desire to have issues forced upon him at any moment and on any ground by over-zealous Lieutenant-Governors or designing provincial politicians. In addition he saw full well that the power of reservation in the Canadian federal system was unusual and awkward. Unless the responsibility of the federal government was clearly laid down some confusion would inevitably arise as to whether the Lieutenant-Governor acted as the provincial chief executive or as a federal officer; and if he were to accept responsibility, Macdonald wanted to have complete control over the decisions reached.

Since few agreed on the precise nature of the power of reservation and since no instructions were issued by the Dominion government it is not surprising to see a great variety of practices being followed in the provinces.[50] Macdonald was particularly opposed after 1873 to reservation on the advice of provincial ministers, and both his memoranda had been designed to combat this practice. Of the forty-five bills reserved between 1867 and 1882, when the officers were officially informed of his opinion, at least ten were reserved as a result of such advice. With the possible exception of the two bills to incorporate the

[48]*Ibid.*, 763–4, Report of the Minister of Justice, March 14, 1895.
[49]Canada, House of Commons, Unpublished Sessional Papers, 1924, no. 276, Report of a Committee of the Privy Council, May 5, 1924.
[50]The evidence for the following comments is scattered and lengthy, and unless it seems essential citations have been avoided. The official reports and correspondence are not complete. Additional information has been found in private correspondence, in the incomplete files of the Lieutenant-Governors' correspondence in the provincial archives, and in the files of the Department of the Secretary of State in the PAC. A list of reserved bills is given in Appendix B.

Orange Order in Ontario in 1873 and one with similar intent in Prince
Edward Island in 1878 there does not appear to have been any attempt
to escape political responsibility by advising or encouraging reservation.[51] Since the Order in Council of 1882 only two bills have been
reserved on advice. Macdonald's ruling was respected on this issue
at least.

But many Lieutenant-Governors (and their advisers) gave a broad
interpretation to discretion and duty, and tended to disregard Macdonald's statement that bills should, as a rule, only be reserved on
instructions from Ottawa. Specific instructions were issued only once
between 1867 and 1882.[52] Of the remaining forty-four bills, twenty-
two were reserved because they seemed to be either beyond the legislative competency of the provincial government or contrary to Dominion policy and the national interest. Eight were similar to bills
previously reserved and not assented to or to acts disallowed.[53] Seven
were reserved because the Lieutenant-Governor disapproved, five in
Manitoba while the Lieutenant-Governor acted as his own Premier
and the other the railway bill that was closely bound up with the
dismissal of the de Boucherville administration in 1878. Two were
reserved because they affected the prerogative rights of the Crown,
one because it dealt in an unusual manner with private property, and
one to secure a ruling on the Lieutenant-Governor's power. No reason
can be determined for the reservation of New Brunswick bills in 1868
and 1872 and a Prince Edward Island bill in 1881.

[51]The P.E.I. bill was reserved technically because similar measures had not been
approved by the British government before Confederation. In all probability the
cabinet encouraged the Lieutenant-Governor to reserve. It was introduced by a
private member and passed both houses, despite the Attorney General's assertion
in the assembly that it was of questionable validity, "every Protestant Member
present in both . . . voting for, and every Catholic member . . . against it." (PAC,
Correspondence of the Secretary of State, 1878, file 803, Hodgson to the Secretary
of State, July 11, 1878.) Two bills reserved in British Columbia in 1872 had been
unsuccessfully opposed by the government. Since party lines and party discipline
did not exist the administration took such a defeat very lightly and certainly never
thought of resigning. Both bills were clearly *ultra vires* and the Attorney General
advised Trutch to reserve them. This was not, however, an attempt to evade political responsibility. (British Columbia, Legislative Assembly, *Journals*, 1872, 13–18,
70; PABC, Attorney General's Letterbook, McCreight to Trutch, April 8, 11, 30,
1872.)
[52]Proposed New Brunswick legislation had been petitioned against by residents
of the United States and the federal authorities ordered the Lieutenant-Governor
to reserve the bill, even though they were not sure of its content. (*C.S.P.*, 1877,
no. 89, 67, Undersecretary of State to Tilley, March 16, 1874.)
[53]In 1882 Cauchon reserved a bill to incorporate the Orange Order. Although no
record remains of his reasons it is likely that the knowledge that similar measures
had not been given the Governor-General's assent reinforced his own inclinations
and the undoubted Roman Catholic pressure. On the other hand, however, the
Lieutenant-Governors of Ontario and P.E.I. had been censured by the Minister
of Justice for reserving bills within the legislative jurisdiction of the province.

Macdonald's 1882 strictures appear to have had little effect on the whole. Of the twenty-four bills reserved since his report only two have been reserved after specific instructions from the federal government and one after a private letter from Macdonald himself. The Laurier cabinet knew that a bill was to be reserved in British Columbia in 1907 and approved in advance the decision of the Lieutenant-Governor. Five bills were reserved in Quebec because they trenched on federal legislative power, and three in British Columbia because they conflicted with Dominion immigration policy. Two measures were reserved in Alberta and three in Manitoba that were similar to acts previously disallowed, although in each case the real reason was probably personal disapproval.[54] In two instances discussed below reservation resulted from a serious disagreement between the Lieutenant-Governor and his ministers on policy and law. No record remains of five bills reserved since 1882.

Lieutenant-Governors assumed a much broader discretion than Macdonald had been willing to grant them, and exercised their power in a manner much more akin to Thompson's views. Had it been Thompson who, in the early years, had been called on to outline the principles and practices that were to be followed, the history of reservation might have been different indeed. It is significant that there is no one consistent reason—even in any province or with any officer —for reservation: many bills obviously *ultra vires* were reserved, but many others were not; many similar to measures disallowed were reserved when re-enacted, but many others were not. This was to be expected of course, since the federal government refused to lay down positive principles that were to be followed. The alternative was to adhere rigidly to Macdonald's statement that bills were to be reserved only on instructions. But some Lieutenant-Governors preferred a more active and independent rôle.

Unless assented to by the Governor-General (on the advice of his ministers) a reserved bill remains inoperative. Only thirteen of the sixty-nine reserved bills have received this assent. (Eight of the thirteen occurred between 1873 and 1878.) In all but two of these instances the Lieutenant-Governor, while expressing doubt as to the validity of the measure, recommended that if his fears were unfounded assent should be given. Never has the Minister of Justice advised assent against the wishes of the Lieutenant-Governor who reserved the bill,

[54]Macdonald regarded two of the reservations by Schultz in Manitoba as "unconstitutional" although they were similar to bills previously disallowed. Still he added that he was not sorry to see them reserved. (Macdonald Papers, 529, Macdonald to Schultz, April 5, 1890.)

even though he frequently failed to understand what objections there were to it or why it had been reserved.

Macdonald established the precedent in 1873 that bills within the legislative competency of the provincial government and reserved without instructions would be allowed to lapse without comment. Mowat took strong exception to this decision:

The refusal to advise the allowance of bills, because their reservation was unnecessary, was a course which had no precedent that the undersigned can discover; nor is the reason for the refusal very intelligible. If, from a Dominion point of view, the bills were deemed so free from objection that they need not have been reserved, the strongest possible reason was afforded by that circumstance, for their instant allowance by the Governor-General, under the advice of his Council.[55]

Despite Macdonald's political motivation in the specific instance when the decision was reached, the precedent is eminently understandable and has been upheld by later Ministers of Justice.[56] Blake declared that he had refused to advise any action on reserved bills within the competence of the provincial governments, for "we do not want Local Governments or Local Governors, or persons in any of the provinces, to shuffle their responsibilities on the shoulders of the Government here."[57] James Macdonald confirmed the ruling in 1879[58] and in 1893 Thompson cited the 1873 statement as dealing "fully and exhaustively with the matter."[59] Before 1873 eight bills had been assented to although within the legislative jurisdiction of the provinces. But since then only five of a like nature have received similar assent and in each case there were exceptional circumstances that justified such action.[60]

Perhaps the most significant feature of this study of reservation is the decline in the exercise of the power. Forty-two bills were reserved

[55]Ontario, Legislative Assembly, *Sessional Papers*, 1874, no. 19, 5, Memorandum by Mowat, Dec. 16, 1873.
[56]In 1874 Carnarvon refused to recommend action on the reserved Canadian bill to regulate the construction of marine telegraphs on the grounds that the Canadian government had the power to deal with the subject. (C 1171, Carnarvon to Dufferin, Oct. 29, 1874.)
[57]Canada, House of Commons, *Debates*, 1882, 911.
[58]Hodgins, *Dominion and Provincial Legislation*, 1200.
[59]*Ibid.*, 1225.
[60]Two Prince Edward Island measures had been reserved because previous ones dealing with the land question had been refused assent. Blake recognized the legitimacy of the reservation but recommended that assent be given since amendments satisfactorily removed the previous objections. A New Brunswick bill had been reserved in 1874 on instructions, but closer examination revealed that it was unobjectionable. A Nova Scotia bill was suspected to be *ultra vires*, but between the date of reservation and consideration by the federal government the courts indicated that it was not. Assent was given to a Prince Edward Island bill for reasons of convenience.

between 1867 and 1878, while only twenty-seven have been reserved since; six have been reserved since 1914 and none since 1937. The frequent use of the power in the early years, particularly in the first decade after Confederation, may be attributed in part to the shadowy and ill-defined boundary between the legislative authority of the central and local governments. More important, perhaps, is the fact that over half of these bills were reserved in Manitoba and British Columbia, where political experience and constitutional and legal knowledge were noticeably absent and where obeisance to federal authority was very pronounced in the period immediately following their establishment. Nor should it be forgotten that most of the early Lieutenant-Governors were men who had taken a prominent part in the federal movement and who had the interests of the national government at heart; their successors were less able and inclined often towards provincial, rather than Dominion, rights and interests. When all is said, however—and many other factors could be mentioned—the truth remains that the federal government was largely instrumental in negativing the use of the power by its officers and thus causing its decline. Introduced in imitation of the imperial power, the authority to reserve provincial legislation was never really made a working cog in the federal system. During his long political career Macdonald set many precedents for good and evil, and it was his policy to discourage the use of reservation. Rather than instruct Lieutenant-Governors to reserve bills he frequently advised them not to.[61] In his unwillingness to

[61]Record remains of several other cases. Doyle was advised not to reserve the militia bill in 1868 but did so anyway. (Macdonald Papers, 514, Macdonald to Doyle, Sept. 21, 1868.) Richey was advised not to reserve two bills in 1888 after he had suggested that the bills be reserved. (PAC, Campbell Papers, Richey to Campbell, March 17, 1888; PAC, Thompson Papers, Richey to Thompson, April 16, 1888.) In 1873 Trutch was ordered not to reserve two bills; one was reserved on the advice of his ministers and the other was later disallowed. (Macdonald Papers, 522, Macdonald to Trutch, Jan. 17, March 3, 1873.) Cornwall was instructed not to reserve two bills in 1883, one of which was later disallowed, while the other escaped a like fate only because the provincial government agreed to amend it. (PAC, Correspondence of the Department of the Secretary of State, 1883, file 2457; Macdonald Papers, 525, Macdonald to Cornwall, June 11, 1883; PABC, Lieutenant-Governor's Correspondence, Cornwall to the Secretary of State, May 15, 1883.)

The crisis over the Manitoba separate schools legislation provides the most interesting example and also reveals more of Schultz's activity. In Ottawa Macdonald gave Schultz, the Lieutenant-Governor, the impression that the legislation contemplated by the Greenway government would be unconstitutional and should be reserved. (Macdonald Papers, 264, Schultz to Macdonald, April 9, 1890.) When the bills were introduced Schultz wired their content to Ottawa and asked for instructions. Thompson recommended that the Lieutenant-Governor be advised to give his assent, and Macdonald informed his proconsul that he should in all prabability assent to the bills. (Ibid., 274, Thompson to Macdonald, Dec. 18, 1889; ibid., 529, Macdonald to Schultz, Jan. 8, 1890.) Schultz remained of the opinion

make any extensive use of the power Macdonald was not alone. Blake and Sir Charles Hibbert Tupper also deprecated its use and expressed the view that it was better to let the questionable measure pass and disallow it if necessary. Disallowance was unquestionably a more rational instrument of federal control, while in time the judiciary largely ousted them both.

Macdonald probably realized that reservation although a part of the federal scheme could readily become a disguise for what was essentially prerogative action executed by the Lieutenant-Governor as the chief executive officer in the province. That is to say, a Lieutenant-Governor could easily reserve a measure of which he disapproved on the grounds that it affected Dominion interests, and in this way he could avoid the inevitable constitutional repercussions that would inevitably follow an outright veto. In many instances reservation might properly be termed veto, particularly when no instructions were issued by the central government and when federal interests were not clearly at stake. (Letellier's reservation in 1878 could be placed in this category.) The federal government would thus be responsible in part for an action that it did not initiate and perhaps did not approve. On other occasions, even when the reservation could be justified, provincial politicians were inclined to take a critical attitude; and Macdonald was never one to encourage criticism if there were no balancing gains. Several of these cases might profitably be considered.

In 1892 the Lieutenant-Governor of Prince Edward Island, J. S. Carvell, reserved a bill that abolished the Legislative Council, substantially changed the electorate, and allegedly contained a gerrymander. The bill, he felt, was unjustified, unfair, and unconstitutional; although of major importance it had never been before the people; amendments sent down from the Legislative Council were treated by

---

that the bills should be reserved, particularly after he saw them, and he was supported in his opinion by the Chief Justice, who appeared to be his legal adviser. (*Ibid.*, 264, Schultz to Macdonald, March 24, 1890.) All the while the Lieutenant-Governor was under fire from the French-Canadian and Roman Catholic community in the province. Taché begged him to reserve the bills and doubtless greatly influenced Schultz, who realized the Archbishop's political influence and who saw that the Conservative party might gain from his action. Until the very last moment Taché believed that the bills would be reserved. Schultz almost insisted that he be permitted to reserve the bills; both he and Taché believed that the bills would be reserved; and both were annoyed when Macdonald ordered him to give his assent. Schultz had in fact refused to prorogue the assembly until he received Macdonald's last word in the vain hope that he would be permitted to reserve the bills. (PAM, Greenway Papers, no. 2852, Schultz to Greenway, March 28, 1890; Thompson Papers, Taché to Ouimet, March 14, 1894; Dom Benoit, *Vie de Mgr-Taché, Archevêque de St. Boniface* (2 vols.; Montreal, 1904), II, 568; PAM, Lieutenant-Governors' Papers, 1890, *passim*.)

the Assembly as "suggestions," despite the Speaker's ruling to the contrary; and the debates on the bill were carried on behind closed doors. The Lieutenant-Governor feared that an election would be held as soon as the bill was assented to, and if it were later declared unconstitutional in whole or in part the confusion would be immense. The Premier refused to promise Carvell that an election would not be held until the validity of the legislation was assured, but coyly "contended that circumstances might arise to justify" an appeal to the people. Under these conditions the Lieutenant-Governor reserved the bill.[62]

The reservation did not surprise the provincial government. Even before the Lieutenant-Governor had seen the measure the Premier had asked what he intended to do; no recommendation regarding the bill was forwarded by the Attorney General and no advice was given by the Premier; and for some time after the bill was reserved the ministry did nothing but contact Prince Edward Island Liberals in Ottawa in order to have the issue raised in the House of Commons.[63] Later the Executive Council asked the Lieutenant-Governor to secure the return of the bill from Ottawa and assent to it, but this Carvell refused to consider.[64] It was generally known that the cabinet was "at daggers drawn with the Lieutenant-Governor" and the opinion was frequently expressed that the government should resign. Carvell realized that his action was just cause for resignation and was willing to force an appeal to the electorate, or so he told Thompson.

Under all these circumstances I was quite prepared to have the people express themselves regarding this matter. My Government it appeared was not, and assumed the responsibility of the reservation; and, I may add, have since expressly acquiesced in my decision not to solicit a return of this bill. . . .

With every disposition to allow my advisers all the constitutional free play they are entitled to, I cannot, in the interests of the people of this Province—in the interests of good government, remain silent with regard to the peculiarities of this bill and the unusual methods employed to secure its passage.[65]

Thompson was extremely annoyed, for the issue caused him serious embarrassment in Ottawa. Carvell had acted on his own discretion and with regard to a matter that was of no immediate concern to the fed-

[62]Correspondence of the Secretary of State, 1892, no. 2310, Carvell to Thompson, May 25, 1892.

[63]Thompson Papers, Carvell to Thompson, May 9, 1892; Canada, House of Commons, *Debates*, 1892, 2238 ff.

[64]Hodgins, *Dominion and Provincial Legislation*, 1222–5.

[65]Correspondence of the Secretary of State, 1892, no. 2310, Carvell to Thompson, May 25, 1892.

eral government. Quite clearly the bill was not beyond the legislative power of the provincial government and should not have been reserved. Thus no action was taken.[66] During the next session of the island legislature a new bill with some of the teeth removed was passed and Carvell gave his assent. The refusal of the government to resign strongly suggests that the original bill was as unusual and as unjust as the Lieutenant-Governor maintained, and, despite Thompson's censure Carvell probably concluded that he had acted wisely.

In British Columbia, on the other hand, Joly backed down when Prior threatened to resign if a bill were reserved. In 1903 the Lieutenant-Governor was presented with a bill to which he hesitated to assent for a number of reasons: the measure had had a long and chequered history; railway administration within the province, with which the bill dealt, was notoriously corrupt; at the time of its passage the subject with which the bill was concerned was before the courts, and it was admittedly designed to prevent the province's case being lost on what the Premier termed "a legal technicality." Prior informed Joly that the matter was exclusively a provincial one, that no national interests were in any way involved, that instructions to reserve had not been received by the Lieutenant-Governor, and that reservation or veto without instructions would be taken as a sign of lack of confidence.[67] Eventually Joly reluctantly assented to the measure, but until the whole matter was legitimately cleared up he refused to permit any subsequent action to be taken.[68]

Four years later Joly's successor as Lieutenant-Governor of British Columbia, James Dunsmuir, reserved a bill prohibiting Asiatic immigration on the grounds that similar measures had been repeatedly disallowed and that its passage would "seriously interfere with our international relations and Federal Interests."[69] This was undeniable and the reservation passed with little comment. Several months later, however, it was learned that the Premier had known beforehand that the bill was to be reserved and had so informed the Laurier government. The opposition immediately attempted to embarrass the administration: the bill (introduced by a private member—but a leading Conservative) should have been opposed, rather than supported by

[66]Hodgins, *Dominion and Provincial Legislation*, 1225: "The reasons given by his Honour are not sufficient to warrant your Excellency in accepting any responsibility with regard to the measure."

[67]Correspondence of the Department of the Secretary of State, 1903, no. 1195, Memorandum for the Lieutenant-Governor, April 28, 1903; PABC, Premiers' Papers, Prior to Joly, April 30, 1903.

[68]PABC, McBride Papers, McBride to Grace, July 4, 1903.

[69]British Columbia, Legislative Assembly, *Sessional Papers*, 1907–8, no. 99, Dunsmuir to the Secretary of State, April 29, 1907.

the government in the legislature; or when it passed (with government support) the Premier was bound to advise assent. If the Lieutenant-Governor was not prepared to accept that advice it was the government's duty to resign. It was apparent that most people were not quite sure what had transpired, but it looked very much as if they had been deceived.

The course of events is reasonably clear. The McBride cabinet had no desire to oppose such a popular measure in the legislature, yet the Premier knew that the bill would never be sanctioned by the federal government. The Lieutenant-Governor too was fully aware of the past history of the Oriental immigration issue in British Columbia for, as one of the major employers of cheap labour, he had been personally concerned. Dunsmuir and McBride obviously discussed the situation and the decision was reached to reserve the bill. The Attorney General did not even bother to prepare a report.[70] When in Ottawa before the provincial legislature had been prorogued, McBride had been asked about the bill and had informed the Secretary of State that Dunsmuir was going to reserve it. Scott at once asked the Lieutenant-Governor if he could "rely on this assurance" and was informed immediately that he could.[71]

Long before this, however, the Laurier cabinet had considered its probable action. The Japanese Consul had been pressing the federal government and the members of the cabinet were agreed that assent should be withheld. But Laurier was in London attending the Colonial Conference and his colleagues hesitated to act without his consent. Scott informed the Prime Minister of the cabinet's decision and asked for permission to instruct Dunsmuir to reserve the bill.[72] Laurier thought the idea a "good one" for "we are bound to have the Treaty respected."[73] Before Laurier's letter reached Ottawa the bill had been reserved.

An interesting footnote might be added here. Evidence revealed before a Royal Commission then sitting indicated that Dunsmuir was at that very moment negotiating for a large shipment of Japanese labourers. Here, said the local politicians, was the reason for his action. Because of the immediate furor in British Columbia leading Liberals urged Laurier to ask Dunsmuir to resign.[74] In the assembly a private

[70]See the press reports of the legislative debates on Jan. 20–1, 1908.
[71]British Columbia, Legislative Assembly, *Sessional Papers*, 1907–8, no. 99.
[72]PAC, Laurier Papers, 460, Scott to Laurier, April 15, 1907.
[73]*Ibid.*, Laurier to Scott, April 26, 1907.
[74]*Ibid.*, 493, W. W. B. McInnes to Laurier, Dec. 4, 1907; *ibid.*, 510, Templeman to Laurier, March 17, 1908.

member attempted to impeach the Lieutenant-Governor on four counts: the bill had been reserved without instructions, the whole proceeding was unconstitutional, his action had destroyed the people's confidence in him, and there were grounds to believe that he had acted in his own personal interests.[75] The leader of the opposition declared that "the confidence of the people of this Province in His Honour the Lieutenant-Governor is greatly impaired, if not wholly destroyed," and demanded Dunsmuir's dismissal.[76] Both resolutions were supported by one-third of the Legislative Assembly.

The most often discussed reservations were and are those in Alberta in 1937. The Social Credit party under William Aberhart had come into power in 1935 pledged to radical social, economic, and political cures for the depression. After a lull of eighteen months, when the cabinet semed anxious to escape its commitments, an insurgent movement forced the government to act. In the summer session of 1937 a number of drastic measures were pushed through the legislature, the most important of which was the Credit of Alberta Regulation Act that would have enabled the provincial government to control the operation of banks within the province.[77] The storm of protest was unprecedented; "it is questionable whether any single piece of legislation had commanded such universal attention."[78] Leading constitutional lawyers across the nation declared that the Alberta legislation was *ultra vires* and the Attorney General admitted as much in the provincial legislature. The latter's assertion caused the government some concern, and the Attorney General, Mr. John W. Hugill, was asked by the caucus to assure "us that he feels in a position on every count to recommend that the Lieutenant-Governor gives his assent to every Social Credit measure."[79] The Attorney General refused to give this assurance and later when asked by the Lieutenant-Governor

[75]British Columbia, Legislative Assembly, *Journals*, 1908, 7; Press, Jan. 2–22, 1908. One would like to know how often a Lieutenant-Governor has used his position in his own interests. F. S. Barnard refused to assent to prohibition in British Columbia unless the government promised to appoint a commission to determine damages to be paid to the liquor interests and continued to put pressure on successive Premiers for three years. Barnard had married the daughter of a wealthy brewer. (PABC, Premiers' Papers, Barnard to Oliver, March 27, 1919.) Even the extremely respectable Mortimer Clark asked Whitney not to overlook the Metropolitan Bank, of which he was a director, when depositing the federal subsidies. (PAC, Whitney Papers, Clark to Whitney, Jan. 4, 1908.)
[76]British Columbia, Legislative Assembly, *Journals*, 1908, 7.
[77]On the whole subject of Alberta legislation see E. A. Forsey "Canada and Alberta: the Revival of Dominion Control over the Provinces," *Politica*, IV (June 1939), 95–123; C. B. Macpherson, *Democracy in Alberta* (Toronto, 1953); J. R. Mallory, *Social Credit and the Federal Power in Canada* (Toronto, 1954).
[78]Cited in Mallory, *Social Credit*, 73.
[79]*Ibid.*, 74.

for his opinion as to the competence of the provincial government to enact such measures bluntly declared that the bills were *ultra vires*. Under the circumstances the assent of the Lieutenant-Governor, Mr. J. C. Bowen, was not taken for granted. As one commentator wrote: "Validity of the Bills having been questioned and denied inside the house and in many other quarters during the week, tension was at a high pitch within the chamber up to the minute the whole list was read and the lieutenant-governor signified royal assent to them all. . . . There had been doubts in many quarters that he would assent to the acts after their constitutionality had been questioned."[80]

Within ten days the questionable acts had been unceremoniously disallowed by Mackenzie King's Liberal administration. "Momentarily stunned into silence" the Aberhart administration decided to call another session in September to consider "a fresh crop of provocative and controversial bills."[81] There was no question but that the federal government and the federal power were to be openly defied. In the interval the provincial government attempted to reach its goal by means of a number of Orders in Council, all of which were grossly illegal and were later so declared by the courts.[82] Meanwhile, measures were secretly drawn up in cabinet, discussed and approved in the Social Credit caucus, and were then sprung on the legislature as soon as it assembled. The Premier declared that the session would be a short one—without debate or division—and the bills were obviously to be railroaded through. It was a highly inflamed session. One member moved that the Royal Canadian Mounted Police, the federal government's standing army, be expelled from the province; and one of the ministry's leading advisers was arrested for "counselling to murder." At the end of the session the Lieutenant-Governor reserved the three major pieces of legislation: one was little more than a reenactment of an act disallowed several weeks before; another was designed to enable the province to tax the banks out of existence and was clearly not within the legislative competency of the provincial government; and the third, the Accurate News and Information Bill, gave the government almost unlimited power to control the provincial press. The outcry against the last measure was by far the greatest. *The Times* termed it the last desperate resort of a desperate government, the *Halifax Herald* declared that it would mean the end of a free press in Alberta, and the *Toronto Globe and Mail* stated that there was "nothing in the way of press control, outside the Fascist and Com-

[80]*Edmonton Journal*, Aug. 6, 1937.
[81]Mallory, *Social Credit*, 77.   [82]*Edmonton Journal*, Sept. 23, 1937.

munist countries, that is comparable with it in the suppression of freedom of personal liberty."[83]

Why did the Lieutenant-Governor reserve these bills? He did not act on instructions from Ottawa as has been sometimes assumed, but acted on his own discretion.[84] Unquestionably the rapidity with which the Dominion government disallowed the acts of the previous session and the strong language used encouraged him to take the initiative; and the sense of outrage that prevailed throughout the nation must also have stimulated him. It is likely that Mr. Hugill, who had been forced to resign after his calculated indiscretion of the previous session, had something to do with it as well. Events had shown that he had been legally correct and his opinions could therefore be given some weight. And before the Calgary Club in September Mr. Hugill declared:

Anything that is fundamentally bad in law should not even appear as law. The lieutenant-governor has the power to withhold his consent to such legislation, and should use it more frequently, particularly when there is mass demagoguery, railroad tactics, and other things. . . .

The lieutenant-governor has a more important part to play in government than is generally realized. He is there to sense the will of the people, and has the power to call an election. He is much more than a mere figurehead. . . . he is a safeguard when there is a tendency to rush legislation through as the will of the people when it is not the will of the people and probably never was.[85]

However exaggerated it was, such a statement must have affected the Lieutenant-Governor, new to his office and not particularly learned in such things.

After the August session, while the storm raged around him, the Lieutenant-Governor studied, as far as he was able, the nature of the office that he held, the relations of the central and local governments, and the status of the power of reservation. When the bills appeared in the assembly he studied them carefully, and then, his mind apparently made up, he prepared a case for reservation. To be doubly sure he presented his brief to the Chief Justice, who assured him that his argument was sound on every point. A few minutes before prorogation, without any previous intimation to the Premier (for the latter had never consulted him), the Lieutenant-Governor informed Aberhart that he would reserve the bills for consideration of the Governor-

[83]Cited in *Edmonton Journal*, Oct. 4, 1937.
[84]Canada, House of Commons, *Debates*, 1938, 1067. Mr. Lapointe stated, "Mr. Speaker, there were no instructions sent to the lieutenant-governor of Alberta." This has been verified by information from the Lieutenant-Governor's family.
[85]*Edmonton Journal*, Sept. 23, 1937.

General in Council.[86] His action was applauded everywhere except in the ranks of the Social Credit party and perhaps in the East Block on Parliament Hill. All the bills were later declared *ultra vires* by the Supreme Court of Canada.

The Alberta government had no intention of letting the issue go uncontested. It was at once stated that federal control of provincial legislation could no longer be considered as legal, legitimate, or practicable. The power of reservation, so it was said, was dead; it had died through *non user*. Only three bills had been reserved since 1914 and none of these had received any publicity, even in British Columbia where the reservations occurred. The last case had been in 1920. All that need be said of this argument is that although authorities might well differ on the length of time needed for a precedent to become obsolete, few would contend that an interval of seventeen years is at all sufficient. This is particularly true when the power is clearly set out in a still very vital statute.

The more common argument was that the Lieutenant-Governor's power to reserve provincial bills was inextricably related to the Governor-General's power to reserve Dominion bills. It was strongly suggested that the latter's power had lapsed through *non user* after 1878 when the list of subjects had been omitted from the revised instructions then given to Lord Lorne, and that the Imperial Conference of 1926 had simply recognized that the power was no longer exercisable. If the one had lapsed, so ran the argument, so too had the other. It is true that reservation in the federal system was modelled on reservation in the imperial system, but the accuracy of the argument ends there. There was no inextricable relationship between the two; nor had the Governor-General's right to reserve lapsed by 1926.

Blake succeeded in having the list of measures to be reserved excluded from the revised instructions, but even in these instructions the existence of the power was explicitly recognized. Campbell mistakenly termed reservation an "obsolete prerogative" and was immediately taken to task by the Governor-General. The alteration in the instructions, stated Lorne, "in no way interferes with the power of reservation, and of disallowance, these powers being fully set forth in the British North America Act." Leading members of the cabinet agreed with Lorne that the right remained, no longer obligatory but permissive.[87]

---

[86]Information from the family of the Lieutenant-Governor and from Mr. R. A. Andison, Clerk of the Executive Council; *Edmonton Journal*, Oct. 7, 1937, quoting Aberhart.

[87]G 18, 70, Memorandum on a Point raised with reference to the Governor General's Prerogative, Nov. 27, 1879.

In 1886 Lansdowne reserved a Canadian bill on the grounds that it would embarrass "pending negotiations" between Great Britain and the United States. "I quite understand that the reservation of the Bill is on my responsibility," he informed Macdonald following a lengthy discussion, but "Lord Granville's telegram leaves no other course open, altho' his words . . . do not suggest reservation eo nomine."[88] This was the last time a Dominion bill was reserved, but the power was not regarded as obsolete merely because it was not being exercised. In 1897, for example, when the Laurier administration toyed with an upward revision of the tariff much to Joseph Chamberlain's annoyance, Lord Aberdeen suggested that it might be necessary, in the interests of the empire, for him to reserve the contemplated tariff bill. "As to the position of the Governor General in a matter of this kind," he noted, "I am of course aware that notwithstanding the alteration of 1878 the present instructions require the Governor General to reserve legislation for the decision of the Imperial Government, if he sees reason for such a proceeding."[89]

Aberdeen was not alone. In 1906 the Colonial Office circulated a dispatch ordering all the Dominion Governors to reserve any bill affecting the immigration of Asiatics, but the dispatch was withdrawn because of immediate opposition from Australia and New Zealand.[90] A decade later the Canadian Governor-General was officially advised by the Colonial Office that, although specific instructions had been omitted after 1878, section 55 of the British North America Act was still in full force and he could therefore constitutionally exercise his discretion and was "at liberty to defer assenting to or reserving a Bill pending the receipt of instructions from the Secretary of State."[91] Actually the 1926 declaration was less a recognition that the power had lapsed than it was a recognition of the incompatibility between its exercise and the new status attained by the dominions. There has been no development of "Dominion Status" within the federal system however. Some scholars and many politicians may claim a new status for the provinces, but their arguments lack either legal or constitutional validity. Lord Watson's decision in 1892, so often cited, neither explicitly nor implicitly questioned the statutory provisions for the Dominion control of provincial legislation. The provinces have indeed moved a long way from the lowly place assigned to them in 1867;

[88]Macdonald Papers, 86, Lansdowne to Macdonald, June 2, 1886.
[89]G 12, 92, Aberdeen to Chamberlain, May 4, 1897.
[90]Correspondence of the Secretary of State, 1906, no. 2460, Elgin to Grey, May 9, 1906.
[91]GGO, file 1120 C.

their legislative, financial, and political power has reached an extent then undreamed of. This changing balance of power, in theory if not in practice, has not affected the statutory right of the Lieutenant-Governor to reserve provincial bills.

The federal government was quite willing to have the arguments submitted to the Supreme Court in a test reference. The Court was asked:

Is the power of reservation . . . vested in the Lieutenant-Governor by section 90 . . . still a subsisting power?
If the answer . . . be in the affirmative, is the exercise of the said power . . . subject to any limitations or restrictions, and if so, what are the nature and effect of such limitations or restrictions?

The Supreme Court unanimously decided that the power still existed and that it was subject only to the limitation that the Lieutenant-Governor's discretion "shall be exercised subject to any relevant provision in his Instructions from the Governor General."

Counsel for the government of Alberta argued that Watson had legally repudiated the doctrine of inferior status on which reservation and disallowance had been implicitly based. The Chief Justice denied this interpretation, pointing to the appointment, payment, and dismissal, of Lieutenant-Governors by the federal government as adequate confirmation of the view that the relationship between the provinces and the Dominion, as far as the office of Lieutenant-Governor was concerned, existed as set out in the British North America Act. Mr. Justice Kerwin declared that the development of Dominion status did not affect the Canadian federal system and observed that the Statute of Westminster expressly repudiated such a suggestion. The Court refused to support the contention that the power had lapsed:

We are not concerned with CONSTITUTIONAL USAGE. WE ARE CONCERNED WITH QUESTIONS OF LAW WHICH, WE REPEAT, MUST BE DETERMINED BY REFERENCE TO THE ENACTMENTS OF THE BRITISH NORTH AMERICA ACTS OF 1867 to 1930, the Statute of Westminster, and, it might be, to relevant statutes of the Parliament of Canada, if there were any.

And nowhere could the Justices find any support for the doctrine of lapse. Reservation of provincial bills was still a power to be exercised by the Lieutenant-Governor, "according to his Discretion," but "subject to any relevant provisions in his Instructions." It still is.[92]

[92]Re Reservation and Disallowance, *Supreme Court Reports*, 1938, 71–99. At the 1950 Constitutional Conference the Premiers of Quebec, Manitoba, Saskatchewan, and Alberta went publicly on record as favouring the amendment of the British North America Act so as to abolish the power of reservation, and it is likely the other provincial Premiers agreed. Premier Duplessis stated he favoured

The British North America Act also authorizes the Lieutenant-Governor, "according to his Discretion," but subject to the statute and his instructions, to withhold his assent to provincial bills.[93] This provision was immediately repudiated. "There are, as you know, only two courses open to you," assent or reservation, Macdonald informed Trutch in 1871.[94] In his 1882 report Macdonald declared emphatically that the power of veto "is now admitted to be obsolete and practically non-existent. The expression *"Le Roi"* or *"La Reine s'avisera"* has not been heard in the British Parliament since 1707, in the reign of Queen Anne, and will in all probability never be heard again."[95] This statement was upheld forty-two years later when the federal government was forced to comment on the veto of a bill by the Lieutenant-Governor of Prince Edward Island. The action was termed "regrettable." Although the British North America Act granted the power to the officer, ran the official report, it was to be used only in his capacity as a federal officer and thus on instructions from Ottawa. But in this instance the Lieutenant-Governor had no instructions "either general or specific to justify the exercise of this extraordinary power."[96]

Regardless of these pronouncements, twenty-eight provincial bills have been vetoed since 1867.[97] In every case but one assent appears to have been withheld on the advice or with the concurrence of the provincial cabinet. In no instance was the Lieutenant-Governor instructed by the federal government to withhold assent. Several Lieutenant-Governors apparently preferred to veto bills rather than to reserve them, thus saving the federal government the trouble of examining them. This appears to have been the case in New Brunswick, where nine bills were vetoed between 1870 and 1882, and in Nova Scotia, where Archibald withheld assent from six bills between 1875

this "since, in our opinion, it is advisable to proclaim the sovereignty, in their respective spheres, of the Federal Parliament and of the Provincial Legislature. . . ." See: Canada, *Proceedings of the Constitutional Conference of Federal and Provincial Governments (Second Session, Quebec, September 25–28, 1950)* (Ottawa, 1950).

[93]Sections 55 and 90.

[94]Macdonald Papers, 519, Macdonald to Trutch, Oct. 27, 1871.

[95]Hodgins, *Dominion and Provincial Legislation*, 77–8. When an assembly was established in the North-West Territories in 1888 the Lieutenant-Governor was not given the power of veto, but could reserve bills.

[96]Canada, House of Commons, Unpublished Sessional Papers, 1924, no. 276.

[97]There might have been many more if the British Columbia constitution did not empower the Lieutenant-Governor to refer bills back to the assembly after third reading. Trutch referred many back, apparently on his own authority, but in later years the provision was probably of value to the ministry who could in this way correct revealed flaws in the legislation. Dr. E. A. Forsey has informed me that down to 1944 eighty-eight bills had been sent back to the assembly.

and 1883. The usually well-informed Alpheus Todd wrote that he was told (probably by Archibald himself), that the six Nova Scotia bills had been vetoed on advice, "in an anxious desire to keep within the bounds assigned to the provincial legislature . . . and to refrain from enacting any measure to which exception could be justly taken. . . ."[98] Recent investigations have borne this out.[99] Although the Nova Scotia bills, judging by their titles, appear to veer more towards federal powers than those in New Brunswick, Todd suggested that the bills in the latter province were vetoed under similar circumstances and for the same reason. In one sense then, the Lieutenant-Governors were acting as federal officers, despite the reluctance of the central government to endorse and approve their actions.

Five of the eight bills vetoed in Ontario resulted from the negligence of the cabinet and the Legislative Assembly. In each case two bills with the same object had been introduced and passed; and the Lieutenant-Governor simply withheld assent from one of them at the end of the session. Three other measures were vetoed when it was discovered, after passage, that they had effects not contemplated when they were drafted and discussed. The veto was expressly stated to be on the advice of the Executive Council and on the understanding that the Legislative Assembly desired it.[100]

The Prince Edward Island examples differ markedly from those in the other provinces. On each of the four occasions a political motive can be seen.[101] Three of the bills were vetoed on advice, or at least with the willing concurrence of the cabinet. In 1945, however, the Lieutenant-Governor withheld assent from a measure designed to liberalize the existing prohibition law. His ministers were not informed of the course he planned to take "until he surprised the legislature with his refusal."[102] The Lieutenant-Governor gave no reason for his action, but since he addressed the Temperance Federation the day before and expressed deep concern about the bill the reason is not difficult to ascertain.[103]

Although the withholding of assent, in view of the unanimity of the statements concerning it, is clearly irregular, it is not illegal: "the

[98]Todd, *Parliamentary Government in the British Colonies* (2nd rev. ed.), 395–6.
[99]J. M. Beck, *The Government of Nova Scotia* (Toronto, 1957), 181 ff.
[100]Ontario, Legislative Assembly, *Journals*, 1885, 1888, 1894, 1898, 1906, 1908, 1909.
[101]See Frank Mackinnon, "The Royal Assent in Prince Edward Island. . . ," *Canadian Journal of Economics and Political Science*, XV (May 1949), 217; and Mackinnon, *The Government of Prince Edward Island* (Toronto, 1951), 154–5.
[102]Mackinnon, "The Royal Assent in Prince Edward Island," 217.
[103]Mackinnon, *The Government of Prince Edward Island*, 155.

refusal of a Lieutenant-Governor to give the royal assent to a bill when he should not have refused does not make the bill an Act in law—nor does it subject the Lieutenant-Governor to the supervision of the Courts."[104] Once vetoed, a bill must be passed again by the legislature before it can be presented to the Lieutenant-Governor for his assent. This decision was reached as a consequence of the Prince Edward Island veto in 1945. A few months after he had withheld his assent the Lieutenant-Governor left office and his successor, on the advice of his ministers, issued a proclamation which stated that he had given the royal assent to the measure. In due time the validity of the bill was questioned before the provincial Supreme Court. The Chief Justice declared: "The precision with which the BNA Act set forth the procedure for later consideration of Bills assented to or reserved seems to me to indicate an intention to cover the whole field of Royal Assent, and to exclude the possibility of a withheld assent being later conferred by a method similar to (or, a fortiori, less precise than) the methods prescribed for later proceedings on assents granted or reserved."[105] The royal assent was never given legally and the bill, once vetoed, remained inoperative unless re-enacted by the legislature and assented to in the usual manner by the Lieutenant-Governor.

The Lieutenant-Governor has also a minor, but essential, duty when the federal government disallows a provincial statute. By the terms of the British North America Act the disallowance takes effect from the date that it is made public by the provincial Lieutenant-Governor either by message to the legislature or by proclamation.[106] When Macdonald and his colleagues were forced to turn their attention to the principles and practices governing federal control of provincial legislation in 1882 it was discovered that in many cases the disallowances had not been so signified. Although every disallowed act was legally in force, in practice they had been universally regarded as inoperative. Nonetheless, the Minister of Justice immediately ordered all the Lieutenant-Governors to proclaim every disallowance in the province since 1867.[107] Macdonald also advised Campbell to send a confidential note to each Lieutenant-Governor emphasizing the importance of immediate action; "otherwise the local Ministers may refuse to issue Proclamations and make a row."[108] The Prime Minister obviously feared that Mowat would "make a row," for the disallow-

---

[104]*Orpen* v. *A.G. Ont.* (1924), 56 O.L.R. 337–8.
[105]*Gallant* v. *Rex*, [1949] 2 D.L.R. 428–30.
[106]Sections 56 and 90.
[107]PAC, Orders in Council, approved Dec. 12, 1883.
[108]Campbell Papers, M 24, Macdonald to Campbell, Dec. 7, 1882.

ance of the Ontario Streams act had not then been proclaimed. The order passed without comment however. The permanent instructions issued to the Lieutenant-Governor order him to signify disallowance by proclamation "forthwith."

Although Mowat failed to live up to expectations in 1882, Mercier threatened to "make a row" in 1888. Early in September 1888 a Quebec act that clearly trenched on the federal power to appoint judges was disallowed.[109] Two weeks later, noting that no proclamation had been issued by Lieutenant-Governor Angers, Macdonald wrote to him.

Now as by the BNA Act the disallowance of a Dominion Act is to be proclaimed by the Governor General—so the disallowance of a Provincial Act is to be proclaimed by the Lieutenant-Governor. In the one case as an Imperial officer and in the other as a Federal officer. This duty cannot be obstructed or delayed by the Dominion or Provincial Ministrys. I have no doubt you fully understand all this, but I write you on the subject as I am informed that Mercier has declared his determination not to issue a proclamation of the disallowance.[110]

At the same moment Angers was composing a long letter to Macdonald. He observed that it was essential that the disallowance take effect at once. The legislature was not in session, however, and the signification would have to be made by proclamation. But since the official *Gazette* was under the control of the Provincial Secretary the publication of the proclamation would have to be approved by the cabinet, and Angers had good reason to believe that Mercier would be obstructive. "Is this not a proclamation that can be issued by the Lieutenant-Governor individually? as a federal officer?" he asked.[111]

Macdonald consulted the Minister of Justice and his senior political colleague from Quebec, Sir Hector Langevin, before replying. All were agreed that the Lieutenant-Governor had to issue the proclamation and if the provincial government would not approve publication, the Lieutenant-Governor must issue it on his own authority. "The true course is to order the Minister controlling the Gazette to publish the Proclamation in it," wrote the exasperated and harassed Macdonald, "and on refusal to appoint another in his stand. If Mr. Mercier upholds his colleague in this disobedience he must bring on a crisis and the responsibility will be his."[112] Faced with such a crisis Mercier gave in. But he did so neither willingly nor quietly: "Il convoqua une grande

109See Robert Rumilly, *Histoire de la Province de Québec* (Montreal, 1940–55), VI, 41–3; Thompson Papers, Chapleau to Thompson, March 5, 1888.
110Macdonald Papers, 528, Macdonald to Angers, Sept. 18, 1888.
111*Ibid.*, 186, Angers to Macdonald, Sept. 19, 1888.
112*Ibid.*, 528, Macdonald to Angers, Sept. 22, 1888.

assemblée de protestation au marché Saint-Jacques de Montréal. Laurier vint à cette assemblée, dénonça 'la politique néfaste de centralisation de Sir John' et rappela la lutte triomphante du Manitoba contre un désaveu fédéral."[113] Mercier took Laurier's words to heart and re-enacted the bill. Thompson, the Minister of Justice, refused to tolerate this open defiance and after he had vainly sought to have Angers reserve it, advised that the act be disallowed at once. It was "the imperative duty of the Lieutenant-Governor to proclaim it as soon as it comes to his knowledge. From that duty it is not in my power, or even in the power of His Excellency to relieve him. The personal responsibility of a Federal officer charged with such duty, admits of no relief, unless the Imperial Parliament which laid the duty upon him think it proper to absolve him from it."[114] Mercier had passed the measure again only to fan the flame of provincial resentment, however, and he made no attempt to prevent the publication of the proclamation.

Premier Aberhart refused to permit the publication of the proclamations of disallowance in 1937. As far as one can tell neither the Lieutenant-Governor nor the federal government made any attempt to force the issue. The proclamations were published not in the *Alberta Gazette* but in the *Canadian Gazette* over the signature of the Lieutenant-Governor.[115] This solution was of course open to Macdonald and Thompson, but unlike their successors in Ottawa they were apparently determined to uphold the rights of the federal government and, in this instance at least, the powers and duties of the Lieutenant-Governor.

Like most historical writing the discussion in this chapter has centred on the unusual rather than the normal. More important, if less apparent, are the routine duties in connection with provincial legislation with which the Lieutenant-Governor is charged as a federal officer. It is his responsibility to see that all acts passed by the provincial government are sent to Ottawa "with such explanatory observations as the nature of the law may require."[116] This duty of

[113]Rumilly, *Histoire*, VI, 243.
[114]Macdonald Papers, 274, Thompson to Desjardins, July 10, 1889.
[115]Private information from officials of the Department of State; *Canadian Annual Review*, 1937, 111; J. E. Mallory, "Disallowance and the National Interest: the Alberta Social Credit Legislation of 1937," *Canadian Journal of Economics and Political Science*, XIV (Aug., 1948), 350.
[116]British North America Act, 1867, sections 56 and 90. See also G 17 A, Memorandum for the Secretary of State for the Provinces from Monck, Jan. 11, 1868. Until 1952 the Lieutenant-Governor was bound by his instructions to send the acts within ten days of his assent. The Department of State found this inconvenient, however, and new instructions order him to send the acts within ten days of prorogation.

course is fundamental, and although the statutes are now as a rule sent automatically by the provincial government such has not always been the case and in the last analysis the Lieutenant-Governor is completely responsible.[117] In the past many officers have been censured for not making certain that fair and certified copies of provincial acts were sent to Ottawa without delay.

Far exceeding the number of occasions when reservation or disallowance was necessary were instances when the Lieutenant-Governor was able to prevent the need for such action. Often advised in advance of government legislation, he was able to warn his ministers that the measure proposed would be inacceptable to the federal government or that it was beyond the legislative powers conferred on the province by the British North America Act. Reservation in one sense was an admission of failure; sometimes he had not seen the bills beforehand, while on occasion his Premier refused to accept his advice. Unless a provincial statute was completely *ultra vires*, or the provincial government in general conflict with the federal authority, the Minister of Justice would, as a rule, suggest amendments rather than recommend that the act be disallowed. These suggestions were sent to the Lieutenant-Governor for the information of his government, and it was his duty to present, as strongly as possible, a brief for the federal government. In persuading his ministers that the proposed changes were just, the Lieutenant-Governor doubtless benefited from the sanctions possessed by the federal authorities, but a good deal depended as well on his own ability and energy. Nor should it be forgotten that until 1914 most Lieutenant-Governors were men of considerable ability and experience, usually well-versed in constitutional law and practice. As a result the opinions they expressed carried weight now impossible.

On the other hand the Lieutenant-Governors frequently pleaded the provincial case before the federal cabinet. Seemingly irregular or unconstitutional legislation was supported on the grounds of political expediency or public necessity. In fields where the provinces could not legislate the Lieutenant-Governor was occasionally able to persuade the central government to legislate in its stead and in a manner desired by the provincial administration. His advice was not taken lightly in Ottawa, for, if he had not been a member of the cabinet before his appointment, he had at least been high in the party councils and in close association with members of the federal cabinet.

Such activities as these, constant but undramatic, should not be

[117]The author has been informed on excellent authority that Aberhart refused to send the disputed Alberta bills and that the Lieutenant-Governor was ultimately responsible for their dispatch.

overlooked just because they caused no comment and left few records. To do so is to belittle the importance of the officer, particularly in the first half-century after Confederation when all the kinks were being ironed out. The reservations themselves were of some importance. That only sixty-nine bills were reserved and one hundred and twelve acts disallowed does not necessarily indicate that the Lieutenant-Governor played an insignificant rôle in the federal supervision of provincial legislation. The evidence strongly suggests that on many occasions he was able to reconcile the aspirations of his government with the federal division of powers and the interests of the central government and thus make reservation or disallowance unnecessary.

CHAPTER NINE

TENURE OF OFFICE

THE DECLARATION in section 59 of the British North America Act, 1867, that a Lieutenant-Governor cannot be removed within five years of his appointment, except for cause assigned, has given rise to the belief that five years constitute the legal term of office. Contrary to this common assumption there is no fixed term. The same section of the Act states that "he shall hold office during the pleasure of the Governor-General," while the Lieutenant-Governor's Commission appoints him "during the will and pleasure of Our Governor General of Canada." At the same time it is quite clear that the Fathers of Confederation contemplated a normal term of five years. Observing at Quebec in 1864 that the colonial Governor's term was six years, Macdonald pointed out that he had fixed the Lieutenant-Governor's at five, "that being the duration of our Parliaments."[1] Few officers have been replaced the moment their five years ended. Unless there was an urgent need for the patronage the federal government often added many months to the normal term: the personal wishes of the incumbent or of his successor as to the date of change were taken into consideration; frequently, disturbed political conditions in the province made a change in the executive inadvisable; and in some instances political rivalries within the party regarding the new appointment led to lengthy delays. These minor extensions, running from a few months to a year, caused little comment at the time, although there was usually some criticism from anxious aspirants for the office.

There have not been many prolonged extensions. In the last decade of Conservative supremacy, as a result perhaps of internal disintegration and the absence of real leadership after Macdonald's death, there were three lengthy extensions, and the Liberals were quick to bring the subject up in the House of Commons. They were on safe ground in censuring the Conservatives, for the Mackenzie administration had hardly been in power long enough to grant any extensions to its supporters, and on the only occasion when he had been faced with a request Mackenzie declared than "on consulting the law" he found

[1]Sir Joseph Pope, ed., *Confederation Documents* (Toronto, 1895), 78.

that he "could not make a temporary arrangement."[2] In the House
of Commons David Mills, legal and constitutional expert on the
opposition benches, charged that the government was pursuing an
irregular and unconstitutional practice in permitting Tilley, formerly
a member of the cabinet, to remain in office long after his five year
term had expired. Thompson brusquely replied that although Tilley
had been Lieutenant-Governor of New Brunswick for six years the
government had given no thought to a replacement.[3]

Thompson was better prepared when the Liberals returned to the
same question during the next session. The provisions of the British
North America Act were not being violated, he said, for the statute
provided only that a Lieutenant-Governor could not be removed
within five years of his appointment except for cause assigned. Liberal
spokesmen suggested that tenure beyond five years compromised the
independence of the Lieutenant-Governor: "after the first period of
five years have [sic] expired, then he holds office simply as a tenant
at will. . . . that position is altogether out of harmony with the constitutional principle which is intended to make the Governor independent of the control or interference of the Government here."[4]
Cartwright displayed his usual bluntness: "The Constitution . . . never
contemplated that Lieutenant-Governors should be allowed to hold
office simply at caprice and pleasure, on the understanding that if
they pleased their friends at Ottawa they may keep a comfortable
situation, and that if they do not please their masters they shall be
bundled out without any formality. . . ."[5] Laurier agreed that extended
terms were incompatible with the desired independence of the Lieutenant-Governor.[6]

This was the old provincial rights argument in a new form, and as
it was the only political antidote to Conservative centralism the
Liberals refused to leave it alone. This particular phase had probably
been stimulated by Mercier's agitation in Quebec, following his dismissal by Angers, and represented a means of criticizing the supposed
partiality of the Lieutenant-Governors without coming to cases. In
1895, however, the Liberals were presented with a perfectly tailored
situation in Manitoba where Lieutenant-Governor Schultz, seven years
after his appointment, was doing all in his power to assist the federal

2PAC, Mackenzie Papers, 6, Mackenzie to Morris, Dec. 28, 1877.
3Canada, House of Commons, *Debates*, 1892, 4732 ff.
4*Ibid.*, 1893, 82.
5*Ibid.*, 89.
6*Ibid.*, 84.

government in the separate schools dispute. Apparently convinced that the situation was fraught with grave danger and determined to make their own position clear the Liberals moved

That, in the opinion of the House, section 59 of the British North America Act of 1867, which prevents the removal of a Lieutenant-Governor of a province for five years from the date of his appointment, except for cause assigned . . . was intended to prevent the undue influence of Federal Ministers in provincial affairs; and the practice which has become prevalent, of permitting Lieutenant-Governors to continue in office for a long period of time after the expiry of their commissions, by which they become removable at any time, without assignment of cause, is an abuse of authority calculated to impair responsible government in the provinces of the Dominion.[7]

It was indeed a neat and subtle statement; the first half was unquestionably true, but the second begged several important questions and was clearly not proven. The government was nonetheless placed on the defensive and decided to treat the motion as tantamount to a vote of censure on Schultz and federal policy in Manitoba. Before calling forth the battalions, however, Sir Charles Hibbert Tupper and Foster did attempt to show that the extensions were exceptional, free from any ulterior motives, and had occasioned no evil consequences.

The assertion that the practice of extending terms for a "long period" had become "prevalent" was wide of the mark. Only the extensions of Robinson (Ontario, 1880–7), Tilley (New Brunswick, 1885–93), and Schultz (Manitoba, 1888–95) could be so regarded. Robinson remained in Ontario because he desired to do so and had protested vigorously when Macdonald informed him in 1885 that he was to be replaced. Since there was no pressing need for the patronage, the Prime Minister reluctantly allowed him to remain in office, knowing perhaps that the position would be an ideal retreat for Sir Alexander Campbell who would soon have to be forced out of the cabinet. Mowat later recommended Robinson for imperial honours, sufficient proof that provincial independence had not been compromised.[8] Tilley too had every desire to stay in office as long as possible. He had devoted his life and his fortune to the Conservative party and was tired, ill, and impoverished. Although he had remained the party chieftain in New Brunswick during his first term (1873–8), the indications are that after his return in 1885 he abstained from partisan activity. He was replaced in 1893, in all probability as a result of the Liberal criticism.

[7]*Ibid.*, 1895, 4256 ff.
[8]PAC, G 3, 21, Holland to Lansdowne, Sept. 14, 1887, enc. Mowat to Holland, Aug. 18, 1887.

Superficially it would appear that Schultz could not be so easily dismissed. As we have seen his term of office coincided with the open conflict between the Greenway and Macdonald administrations over disallowance, freight rates, and separate schools. Although the Lieutenant-Governor played an extremely active and important rôle in the attempts to work out a settlement and although he was a trusted partisan, his extension did not result from any desire on the part of the federal government to hold him captive and urge strong measures upon him. Schultz himself asked to be retained in office "until some political exigency arose" requiring his removal.[9] Thompson replied that the government appreciated "very highly what you have done to make matters run smoothly in Manitoba. . . , but I do not feel able to assure you that my colleagues will be disposed to allow any appointment which they consider available to remain long in abeyance, as the pressure for patronage of this kind is so strong."[10] But it was precisely because the pressure for patronage was so strong that Schultz remained in office for two more years.[11] The end came in March 1895 when political exigencies forced the removal of J. C. Patterson from the federal cabinet: Bowell informed Schultz that Patterson was to replace him, expressed his regret that Schultz would have to retire, thanked him for all that he had done, and promised him a K.C.M.G.[12] There had been no attempt to take political advantage of Schultz's desire to stay in office or of his vulnerability; on the contrary throughout his term the federal government had to restrain its over-zealous officer.

In this as in so many other ways, Laurier forsook his old principles for those of his opponents as soon as he reached the political summit, and made a deliberate policy of not replacing Lieutenant-Governors the moment their five years had expired.[13] In the Senate an old Conservative taunted the Liberals, and Scott could only reply that Lieutenant-Governors would be replaced whenever "public interest requires it. . . . At present we are under the unfortunate influence of the example set by our predecessors."[14] Mowat remembered the old party cry, however, and insisted that Laurier give him a new Commission or pass an Order

[9]PAC, Thompson Papers, Schultz to Thompson, Aug. 23, 1893: "I confess that I would like to hold the position till school matters quiet down either by the concessions I am from time to time urging my Premier to make or in some other way. . . ."
[10]*Ibid.*, Thompson to Schultz, Sept. 8, 1893.
[11]Three factions within the Manitoba wing of the party had candidates and rather than offend any two of them the appointment was postponed.
[12]PAC, Bowell Papers, 124, Bowell to Schultz, March 21, 1895.
[13]PAC, Laurier Papers, 368, Laurier to Joly, June 8, 1905.
[14]Canada, Senate, *Debates*, 1903, 141.

in Council appointing him for a second term. Otherwise he had no desire to stay in office, for "it was obviously the intention that he should have as much independence during his term as would be practicable."[15] Borden too had memories of the old controversy and when Prime Minister asked the Minister of Justice for an official ruling. A Lieutenant-Governor, he was told, held office during pleasure and no official action was necessary to permit him to stay in office for more than five years.[16] During the Second World War the King government asked all the Lieutenant-Governors to stay in office for the duration. No new Commissions were granted, for "both under the statute and the commission the appointment continues after the expiration of the five-year period until a new appointment is made."[17] The legal and constitutional question may thus be said to have been settled, and since the question of "independence" has not been raised for half a century it too may be taken as a matter of "history."

The only criticism of second terms, signified by the renewal of the Lieutenant-Governor's Commission, has come from disappointed candidates for the office. Since 1867 eleven incumbents have been given a second consecutive term.[18] If the federal government had responded to the pressure placed upon it at least half the officers before 1914 would have been given two terms. This pressure, even if supported by a friendly provincial government, was stoutly resisted in Ottawa. Macdonald always refused applications for a second term as a matter of course, and by 1887 considered blunt refusal to be the "declared policy of the Government."[19] His reason was political not constitutional: "If I re-appointed one Lieutenant-Governor the others who are all political friends would feel slighted if the same favour was not granted them."[20] Moreover, he might have added, the patronage was too important to cut in half. In opposition Laurier declared that he had no objection to second terms and when in power he re-appointed three Lieutenant-Governors. He did not relish the practice, however, and did so only when "the office could not be filled otherwise without

15Laurier Papers, 241, Mowat to Laurier, Oct. 10, 1902.
16PAC, Borden Papers, OC A 144, Doherty to Borden, Aug. 6, 1913.
17Montreal Gazette, Jan. 20, 1945; King to Duplessis, Dec. 31, 1944.
18Archibald (1873–83) and Grant (1916–25) in Nova Scotia; Jetté (1898–1908) and Fiset (1940–50) in Quebec; Pugsley (1917–28) and MacLaren (1945-   ) in New Brunswick; McMillan (1900–11) and Aikins (1916–26) in Manitoba; Bulyea (1905–15) and Brett (1915–25) in Alberta; and Newlands (1921–30) in Saskatchewan.
19PAC, Macdonald Papers, 527, Macdonald to Robinson, Feb. 28, 1887. Macdonald did give Archibald a second term, but he did so only because Mackenzie had promised it to him (supposedly to keep him out of politics in Nova Scotia during the 1878 election).
20Ibid., 526, Macdonald to Robinson, Oct. 12, 1885.

extreme difficulties."[21] Since 1911 the Conservatives have granted two second terms and the Liberals five. It is likely that as the office becomes increasingly difficult to fill in most of the provinces those who desire or are willing to stay on will readily be given two terms—or as many as they want. The fact that the appointments were prolonged not only during but also after the war indicates that the pressure for patronage has fallen off. Prime Minister St. Laurent's testimony is conclusive in any case.[22]

On two occasions the federal government has invoked the power of dismissal authorized by section 59 of the British North America Act:

A Lieutenant-Governor shall hold Office during the Pleasure of the Governor General; but any Lieutenant-Governor appointed after the Commencement of the First Session of the Parliament of Canada shall not be removable within Five Years from his Appointment, except for Cause assigned, which shall be communicated to him in writing within One Month after the Order for his Removal is made, and shall be communicated by Message to the Senate and to the House of Commons within One Week thereafter if the Parliament is then sitting, and if not then within One Week after the Commencement of the next Session of the Parliament.[23]

The clause was debated at considerable length at Quebec, but as usual we have little record of the discussion. Macdonald, who introduced it, did leave some clue as to his intentions. Tenure, he declared, must be "during pleasure," for "the person may break down, misbehave, etc." The Lieutenant-Governor would be a very important official and consequently "he should be independent of the Federal Government, except as to removal for cause, and it is necessary that he should not be removable by any new political party. It would destroy his independence. He should only be removable upon an address from the Legislature."[24] Could Macdonald have possibly meant the provincial legislature? If so—and if his plan had been followed—there would have been a score of dismissals within the following half century; tenure would have in effect been placed in the hands of the provincial governments and the Lieutenant-Governor would thus have ceased to be of any use as a federal officer. Clearly he meant the federal parliament, but one could hardly agree that the Lieutenant-Governor was then to be absolutely independent of the party in power.

[21]Laurier Papers, 385, Laurier to Mickle, Nov. 6, 1905.
[22]See chap. II, 21.
[23]This excluded the temporary appointments made at first in all the provinces. Belleau was re-appointed in Quebec.
[24]Pope, Confederation Documents, 78.

In an attempt to persuade his countrymen that there was no danger in the proposed federal union, Langevin argued that the power of dismissal was really a guarantee of provincial and minority rights. The Lieutenant-Governor, he declared, would be responsible to the central government for all his actions:

And in that Government we shall have more than one vote; we shall be represented in it by our ministers, who will be there to cause every encroachment or arbitrary act which the lieutenant-governor may allow himself to commit, to be condemned. If the Central Government should refuse to do us this justice, and should persist in not recalling any lieutenant-governor who should have so failed in his duty to the population which he governed, we should have our sixty-five representatives to protest and to vote at need against a government which should dare to act in such a way.[25]

It is possible that the distinction between appointment, which was by the Governor-General in Council, and tenure, which was during the pleasure of the Governor-General, was designed to reconcile those fearful of provincial and minority rights. It was to be argued later that this distinction was meaningless, a slip of the pen and nothing more. Yet it would appear to have been a deliberate distinction first made in the fourth draft of the British North America Act.[26]

No one pretends to know precisely what was intended. Legitimate "Cause" was never in any way defined, and Macdonald's "break down, misbehave, etc." is of little help. Mackenzie seemed to feel that "mental and physical inability would be a sufficient cause,"[27] while one Lieutenant-Governor feared that he would be dismissed for allowing a corrupt ministry to stay in office.[28] Nor was it clear whether the Governor-General was to exercise any more than his ordinary discretion in the matter of dismissal. Both of these questions were to be answered for all practical purposes when in 1878–9 the Macdonald government decided to exercise the power of dismissal.

Within six weeks of Letellier's dismissal of the de Boucherville cabinet Macdonald, then in opposition, introduced a motion of censure in the House of Commons: "*Resolved* that the recent dismissal by the Lieutenant-Governor of Quebec of his Ministers was, under the circumstances, unwise and subversive of the position accorded to the

[25]Canada, *Confederation Debates*, 1865, 374.
[26]Pope, *Confederation Documents*, 64, 150, 196.
[27]Mackenzie Papers, 2, Mackenzie to Thibideau, Oct. 21, 1876.
[28]Macdonald Papers, 226, Ouimet to Macdonald, Oct. 12, 1880. Ouimet stated that in 1873–4, when his government had been proven corrupt, Lieutenant-Governor Caron "manifested the fear that he might be dismissed from his office, if he persisted in retaining the Ouimet administration."

advisers of the Crown since the concession of the principle of Responsible Government to the British North American colonies."[29] In his lengthy address Macdonald dwelt on three major points: the right and duty of the federal government to supervise the behaviour of its appointees; the grave precedent that would be established by the dismissal of a Lieutenant-Governor; and the lack of wisdom shown by Letellier in dismissing the government just before the crucial federal election of 1878. The first point, he argued, could be supported by the analogy with the colonial Governor whose actions were closely watched by the imperial government. However grave the precedent, he suggested that the dismissal of a government with large majorities in both chambers was a cause sufficiently serious to justify Letellier's dismissal. And finally, the time of the dismissal suggested purely political motives, a fact of which the Lieutenant-Governor must have been aware. Masson, selected because of his unblemished reputation and strongly ultramontane principles, delivered the major oration from the Quebec wing of the Conservative party. His argument was similar to Macdonald's although he did emphasize that Letellier's views of his office were fundamentally incompatible with the recognized conventions governing the relations between a Lieutenant-Governor and his advisers.

The Liberals were caught in a dilemma from which there proved to be no escape. J. D. Edgar advised Mackenzie to "shunt the discussion of Letellier's action out of both Senate and Commons by some means, so that you may be able to keep clear of any subsequent responsibility."[30] But this the government was unable to do, and the best had to be made of an uncomfortable situation. Although some Liberal Quebec back-benchers came nobly to Letellier's defence and attempted to justify his action, the members of the cabinet refused to do so for the simple reason that they felt unable to support the Lieutenant-Governor. Mackenzie termed the dismissal of de Boucherville "a most dangerous step" and was sorry that Letellier "did not assign better reasons for it."[31] "My own feelings are so strong against any exercise of arbitrary power," he wrote, "that I doubt the wisdom or justice of the dismissal, but I give no opinion to anyone."[32] Laurier immediately

[29]Canada, House of Commons, *Debates*, 1878, 1878 ff.
[30]PAO, Edgar Papers, Edgar to Mackenzie, March 27, 1878.
[31]Mackenzie Papers, 6, Mackenzie to Richards, May 12, 1878. Originally believing that de Boucherville had resigned, Mackenzie said, "it would be very embarrassing for a liberal Ministry to come in making themselves responsible for a bold refusal to sanction a Bill adopted by both Houses. We have always as Liberals fought against this. . . ." (*Ibid.*, Mackenzie to Pelletier, March 4, 1878.)
[32]Edgar Papers, Mackenzie to Edgar, March 26, 1878.

concluded that what Letellier had done was "clearly unconstitutional" and decided to take no part in the controversy.[33] Consequently, when Macdonald introduced his motion of censure the Liberals refused to consider the dismissal, but tried rather to raise the issue of provincial rights and escape responsibility. "Whether it was wise or unwise is a matter of opinion, and who is that to be decided by?" asked Mackenzie. "Are we to constitute ourselves as a court of Justice to sit upon Lieutenant-Governors?" To Macdonald's affirmative nod, the Prime Minister replied: "Well I deny it, I deny utterly that assumption. We, no doubt, may exercise a judicious policy in criticizing such actions, and I do not deny that cases may arise wherein it might be the duty of the authorities at Ottawa to interfere; but where it is simply the case of the removal of one Ministry and the appointment of another. . . ." To condemn the Lieutenant-Governor of Quebec would be to condemn the government and people of Quebec. The whole question was in the hands of those in Quebec and "nothing could be more fatal to the provincial autonomy which exists under the Confederation Act than such an unwise and unwarranted interference. . . ."

If the people sustain the Administration which has assumed the responsibility of this Act, it is not within the power of this House to condemn or set aside the Constitution these people sustain. If, on the other hand, that Ministry . . . should not be able to sustain itself, then we should have entered upon another phase of the constitutional question, coming up in regular order, and subject to natural laws, which flow from our written constitution and responsible system of government.[34]

Laurier plucked the same strings: the federal system resulted from the existence of Quebec as a racial, religious, and linguistic minority, and the adoption of Macdonald's resolution would be "a direct invasion of the federal system under which we live."[35] Despite the taunts and jibes of the opposition, the Minister of Justice, Rodolphe Laflamme, refused to speak, and Blake refused both to speak and to vote for the government. The resolution was eventually defeated on a straight party vote in the House of Commons, although Blake and other Ontario Liberals were deliberately absent. But in the Senate, where the Conservatives had a majority, it was agreed that Letellier's action was "at variance with the constitutional principles upon which Responsible Government should be conducted."[36]

[33]Lucien Pacaud, *Sir Wilfrid Laurier: Lettres à Mon Père et à Ma Mère* (Arthabaska, 1935), 9, Laurier to Pacaud, March 5, 1878.
[34]Canada, House of Commons, *Debates*, 1878, 1902 ff.
[35]*Ibid.*, 1918.
[36]Canada, Senate, *Debates*, 1878, 595.

Mackenzie in a sense apologized to Letellier for not rushing to his defence, and in so doing explained the course the Liberals had decided to follow.

I can quite understand the reasoning of the people who did not understand my speech or who were disappointed with my line of argument. They no doubt expected me simply to defend you. They did not see that if I felt at liberty to defend you I also admitted by that course the right of the opposition to attack.

I considered it to be the right course to take the ground that we had no business to interfere and that any interference by us would be a great constitutional wrong on the Province of Quebec: that if we undertook to supervise your actions we might, and should, control the action of all the Provinces when a ministerial crisis occurred. Such a course would be fatal to responsible government in the Provinces and would reduce the local governments to the condition of irresponsible municipal corporations. . . .

It would be useless to deny that the dismissal of a Ministry holding such a Ministerial vote in the legislature was looked upon by many of your friends as a very grave step, which no temporary party advantage would justify, unless it could be supported by the strongest reasons even though constitutional in itself. Liberals are always necessarily jealous of the arbitrary exercise of power. What a friendly Governor does today may be done by an unfriendly Governor tomorrow. Besides all Gubernatorial actions must be assumed to be done from a sense of duty and in the public interest. A few members reasoning in this line expressed doubt as to the advisability of the act while admitting the soundness of my line of argument.

Had you failed to find a Minister to assume the complete responsibility of your course the matter would of course (have) assumed a different phase. It was gratifying that every member of the liberal party then in the House voted down Sir John's motion.

The motion went too far, or not far enough. If there was a right to interfere at all then the motion should have condemned your course and demanded your recall. It should have declared your action unconstitutional. Instead of this it only said the action was "unwise". What right have we to declare the action of a local governor or Parliament unwise (?)[37]

Macdonald's motion was delicately and deliberately worded. He wished only to censure and establish the principle of federal responsibility and then pass the poisoned chalice to the government.

Meanwhile following Joly's defeat in the assembly the Quebec house was dissolved and an election was under way. In his prorogation speech the Lieutenant-Governor had charged the electorate much as a judge might charge a jury; the voters were to renounce political allegiances

[37]Mackenzie Papers, 6, Mackenzie to Letellier, April 22, 1878.

to consider carefully and impartially the constitutional question, for if Letellier were the judge he was also the accused and by their votes his fate would be determined. But the election was contested on many issues other than the dismissal, and it was really the general dissatisfaction after a decade of Conservative rule, plus the feuds within the party itself, more than the dismissal, that caused the Conservative majority to fall from twenty-five to three. Largely through the personal intervention of the Lieutenant-Governor—or so it was stated and never denied—two Conservatives changed sides when the assembly met, one even having the audacity to accept the nomination as Speaker and to vote himself into office, and Joly banked on a majority of one—the Speaker. Nonetheless, the opposition was able to pass a motion censuring the government for having "persisted in remaining in power without having been supported by the majority of the Legislative Assembly, upon their taking office and without yet being supported by such majority."[38] Paradoxically this resolution was followed by another promising the government the support of the assembly! Supply was soon passed, no contentious measures were introduced, and the government, saved from defeat on several occasions by the casting vote of the Speaker, prorogued as soon as possible. It was a drawn battle: if the Conservatives had lost the election Joly had hardly won it, and if the Premier could do very little with the assembly the Conservatives in turn could not pass a want of confidence motion.

According to every report Letellier had seldom left his office in the legislative buildings during the session and had played a valiant part in directing Liberal strategy, liberally entertaining wavering Conservative members, and generally keeping the party united. The Conservative determination to secure revenge, if it had ever languished, became an obsession. Chapleau's rage knew no bounds:

I have never been discouraged by reverse of fortune, and the unexpected and disastrous result of [the] last elections has not lessened my vigour. I must admit that stupidity, prejudice, and treachery have given a horrible blow to my long cherished hope of revenge against the unscrupulous act of our new *ruler* in the Province of Quebec. A fine team Joly has received at the hands of Letellier to drive him in the roads of honours and power! A brainless speechless and faithless Englishman, properly matched with an hereditary traitor conceived in 1844 by the renegade French Solicitor General of Sir Charles Metcalfe!

Still dragged as it is by two dearly bought and too well paid brutes, the car of State is going on, protected by the mob and gang of bullies revelling every day in the "First Commoner's" rooms.

[38]Quebec, Legislative Assembly, *Journals*, 1878, second session, 9.

No solution was in sight, lamented the new Conservative leader in Quebec, unless the "flowing fountain" could offer some suggestions. Up to this time

I have thought that a dignified tone in the discussion, a system of delicate persuasion, rather than absolute command, would better keep within my lead the dozen of new members on my side of the House; and so far I cannot complain of the result. But I must say I am at my "wit's ends."

What are the next steps to take? I am afraid that our friends and supporters have so much of conservative instincts as to believe that "respectful submission to constituted authority," be that authority an illegitimate and imposed one, is the true and patriotic course to follow.[39]

Unable to dislodge Joly in Quebec City, the Conservatives did succeed in removing Mackenzie in Ottawa. Federal Conservatives had campaigned in Quebec on the understanding that if the party were victorious Letellier would be removed, and with Macdonald's new government resting on a firm base of forty-five Quebec seats the Lieutenant-Governor's execution was only a matter of time. Even before the final returns were in Chapleau reminded Macdonald of his promise to remove "the Grizly Bear which Mackenzie has sent to adorn the park of Spencer Wood. . . ."[40] Within a week of the election, long before Macdonald had taken office, rumours circulated regarding Letellier's successor. Many months were to pass, however, before Letellier was ejected from Government House, and in the meantime reverberations from Quebec were to disturb Rideau Hall, the Colonial Office, and even Balmoral Castle.

Macdonald had no sooner formed his government than a concerted drive began for Letellier's dismissal. The opening salvo was fired by three of the dismissed ministers—Chapleau, Angers, and Church—who formally petitioned that the Lieutenant-Governor "should be dealt with under the authority granted the Honorable the Privy Council by the 59th Section of the British North America Act, 1867."[41] From Quebec came scores of letters and petitions all urging immediate dismissal. The most impressive was a petition signed by over fifty leading Quebec Conservatives, a "Great Charter signed by the Barons of the Province" as Chapleau described it, which stated that Macdonald's resolution had pledged the party to dismissal, that Conservative candidates had promised dismissal during the federal election, and that if the party were to remain united and survive, the promise would have to be ful-

[39]Macdonald Papers, 204, Chapleau to Macdonald, June 16, 1878.
[40]Ibid., 39, Chapleau to Macdonald, Sept. 19, 1878.
[41]C.S.P., 1879, no. 19, 29, dated Nov. 7, 1878.

filled.[42] J. A. Mousseau, soon to become a member of Macdonald's cabinet and later Premier of Quebec, stated the case bluntly:

I understand some of your colleagues are indifferent to Letellier's removal. . . . The mere rumour of that sentiment prevailing in head-quarters threw discouragement here. The feeling in our province is intense on the subject.

Conservatives do very well know what legitimate political warfare is; they understand equally well that Letellier, in his *Coup d'Etat* and in all the attending circumstances, degraded his high position and introduced into our midst political *banditism*, which, if not resisted and *visited* with condign punishment, will kill our party and disgrace our Province. . . .

You see, sir, I am dealing with the political aspect only of Letellier's *Coup d'Etat* and removal. I leave to you the constitutional aspect and considerations: that is within your province. But I cannot help saying what everybody says: "If Letellier did not do enough to deserve being *kicked out*, what more must he do?"[43]

By the end of November 1878 it was quite clear to Macdonald that he must dismiss Letellier or face a serious defection of Quebec members. The Prime Minister may have questioned the widom of the dismissal and may well have lamented "that it was impossible to make Frenchmen understand constitutional government," but he had very little practical freedom.[44]

Fully aware that it was treacherous ground on which the Liberals had chosen to fight, Macdonald stepped warily. Joly was still in office, thus making the autonomy cry even more effective, while the Lieutenant-Governor had adopted the party line.

It is my duty to spare no effort to defeat the present attempt to violate in my person the established constitutional principle that the Representative of the Sovereign is irresponsible for acts performed within the legitimate sphere of the duties imposed upon him by the "British North America Act", which was clearly introduced to confer local self-government on the Provinces, and to make . . . the Lieutenant-Governor practically independent during the fixed term of his incumbency.[45]

The Liberal press laboured the same point, while Sir Francis Hincks favoured it with his supposedly impartial support.[46] Unable to avoid fighting on this ground, the Conservatives found the most successful antidote in the argument that it was really Letellier's action that constituted the threat to provincial autonomy. If a federal appointee could

[42]Macdonald Papers, 95, Chapleau to Macdonald, Dec. 2, 1878.
[43]*Ibid.*, Mousseau to Macdonald, Nov. 15, 1878.
[44]St. Aldwyn Papers, PCC 61, Lorne to Hicks Beach, Dec. 26, 1878. (Notes from the MSS kindly made available by D. G. Creighton.)
[45]C 2445, 115, Letellier to the Secretary of State, April 18, 1879.
[46]*Journal of Commerce*, Nov. 22, 1878.

oppose the wishes of the legislature, overthrow a government chosen by the people simply because he disagreed with its policy, and thus interfere to thwart the wishes of the electorate, without fear of censure or recall, then no province would be free from the depredations of irresponsible officials sent out from Ottawa. The Conservative argument, although not without merit, was the weaker of the two in this instance, if only because the indefatigable Joly was still clinging to office.

Macdonald's position was precarious; "the small, local, utterly gratuitous disturbances of the Letellier affair aroused nearly as much anxiety as a first-class tempest in national politics."[47] Although convinced that the federal government had the power to dismiss and always prepared to exercise federal power, he had no desire to raise the bogey of provincial rights;[48] yet politically the support of the strong Quebec contingent was dependent upon the dismissal of Letellier, and with the new tariff still to be accepted by Parliament not a vote could be wasted. Late in 1878 a subtle plan appears to have taken shape in his mind: Letellier was to be dismissed for the sake of the party and National Policy, but his dismissal was to be effected more by Parliament than by the cabinet; a resolution of censure would be introduced by a private member, theoretically treated as an open question (although the Whips would assure passage), and the government would then act on the resolution of the Commons.[49] The plan was not long a secret, for early in December Mackenzie wrote that "Letellier's dismissal is resolved upon after first getting some independent Member to make a condemnatory motion in Parliament."[50]

All went according to plan. Mousseau introduced a resolution identical to Macdonald's in the previous session and the same arguments, only longer and more violent, were heard again. For a long time no member of the cabinet spoke—this was clearly not to be a government-inspired vote of censure—until frequent Liberal jibes forced Langevin to say a few words. Debate was cut short at 4 A.M., March 13, 1879, when the Quebec members rushed from the house to check the authenticity of a rumour that Letellier had given Joly another dissolution.[51]

[47]D. G. Creighton, *John A. Macdonald: The Old Chieftain* (Toronto, 1955), 260.
[48]His fears were justified. Four years later Mills could still declare that "the Letellier case can be made to do duty against the Ministry." (PAO, Blake Papers, Mills to Blake, Jan. 2, 1882.)
[49]See Macdonald Papers, 95, Mousseau to Macdonald, Nov. 21, 1878.
[50]Mackenzie Papers, 7, Mackenzie to Huntington, Dec. 7, 1878.
[51]Macdonald Papers, Misc. Folio, Precis of the debate of March 13 for the Governor-General.

The vote was a party one, 137 to 52, although many Ontario Liberals were again absent.

The first stage had been successfully reached and passed, but another obstacle remained to be overcome or circumvented. Macdonald had long known that the Governor-General was strongly opposed to the dismissal of Letellier. Lord Lorne had come to Canada with his mind already made up, and he had no sooner stepped ashore at Halifax in November 1878 than he gave Macdonald notice of his opinions.[52] Lorne had secured his views ready-made from Lord Dufferin who had promised Mackenzie "to inform Lord Lorne of the real position of the case."[53] According to the Liberal Prime Minister, Dufferin thought Letellier's course "was a very high handed one but after our first interview he always admitted that you was [sic] within your right."[54] In his conversation with Lorne, Dufferin must have emphasized the provincial rights argument—though on frequent previous occasions he had shown himself to be a centralist—for the new Governor-General maintained throughout the crisis that "there is such a manifest danger to Provincial Autonomy if the Provincial Assemblies be not regarded as giving the measure of public approval or disapproval of an act for which a Provincial Minister has declared himself to be responsible that I do not see how the dismissal of the Lieutenant-Governor can be justified, except on the party grounds of an incensed and local minority."[55] Mackenzie, after long experience, had faith in Lord Dufferin's powers of persuasion, as well as in Lorne's "constitutional knowledge" and believed from the outset that the Governor-General would "not agree to the outrage demanded by the rank and file of the Tories."[56]

Lorne was young and inexperienced and above all he was the son-in-law of the Queen. The situation was clearly one that required kid gloves. Macdonald made himself the buffer and gave Lorne the impression that he held a moderate position (which was probably true), that the English-speaking members of the cabinet shared his views, but that they were being driven by the French-speaking wing of the party, represented in the cabinet by Langevin, Masson, and Baby, the first two of whom, so Lorne reported, were "violent partisans, and completely under the influence of the Priests."[57] From the beginning the

[52]Argyll Papers, Letterbook I, Lorne to Hicks Beach, Dec. 3, 1878. (Notes from the MSS kindly made available by D. G. Creighton.) See also W. S. MacNutt, Days of Lorne (Fredericton, 1955), 20 ff; Creighton, Macdonald, 260, ff.
[53]Mackenzie Papers, 7, Mackenzie to Letellier, Jan. 31, 1879.
[54]Ibid.
[55]St. Aldwyn Papers, PCC 61, Lorne to Hicks Beach, April 3, 1879.
[56]Mackenzie Papers, 7, Mackenzie to Letellier, Jan. 31, 1879.
[57]St. Aldwyn Papers, PCC 61, Lorne to Hicks Beach, April 3, 1879. Baby was

Prime Minister sought Lorne's assistance, or perhaps pretended to seek it, in keeping the French within bounds. The Governor-General first attempted to quiet Masson, an intimate friend of the dismissed de Boucherville, and then prepared a memorandum embodying his views of the case.[58] In this memorandum Lorne observed that the Lieutenant-Governor of Quebec would always be French-speaking and a native of the province and would thus always be to some extent a partisan. His independence would best be secured by guaranteeing his tenure of office. Moreover, there was no need to bring the matter up again since Joly had been sustained and the House of Commons had once rejected a motion of censure.[59] Both Macdonald and Lorne realized that the memorandum would have no effect, and the Governor-General prepared for the clash that was bound to arise.

Sir Michael Hicks Beach, the Colonial Secretary in Disraeli's cabinet, agreed with Dufferin and Lorne that the dismissal of Letellier would be a grave and perhaps disastrous exercise of federal power, but he advised Lorne to accept the decision of his ministers

> . . . recording and stating that you take that course solely in consequence of your ministers' representations. The "cause assigned" should be signed by the Premier who should take the responsibility if either House objects. . . . At the same time I think you should as far as possible resist the proposal: e.g., your reply to the first minute advising it might state your objections and conclude by asking them to reconsider the question on that account; if they still adhere to their advice, and intimated that your consent was necessary to their continuance in office, you should give way.[60]

When Macdonald informed Lorne that the cabinet had decided upon dismissal following the vote of censure, the Governor-General replied that he could not agree with the policy recommended on the grounds that it would set "a dangerous precedent" and asked the Prime Minister to state his reasons for the advice in writing.[61] Macdonald must have been aware that Lorne would not push his opposition to the point

---

more moderate than his colleagues and somewhat cynically realistic. "If the Letellier affair cannot be settled to the satisfaction of the Quebec Conservatives I trust there will be sufficient *sens politique* to prevent a split in the ranks and thereby reduce the Province to a state of helplessness. A practical view of the position should be taken, and the most be made of it. My Canadian Pacific Railway Policy should be urged: the acceptance of this policy by Sir John—failing the dismissal of Letellier—would reconcile the Province to the bitter disappointment, and would save the prestige of the Quebec Conservatives, now at stake." (PAC, Caron Papers, Baby to Caron, March 10, 1879.)

[58]Argyll Papers, Lorne to Hicks Beach, Dec. 3, 1878; PAC, G 12, 77, Lorne to Hicks Beach, Jan. 7, 1879.

[59]Macdonald Papers, 95, dated Dec. 30, 1878.

[60]Argyll Papers, Hicks Beach to Lorne, Feb. 11, 1879.

[61]C 2446, 104, Lorne to Hicks Beach, April 9, 1879.

244   THE OFFICE OF LIEUTENANT-GOVERNOR

of forcing the government's resignation, but rather than make an issue
of the disagreement he saw in it a way to circumvent the political and
constitutional dilemma. As a crisis should be avoided at any cost and
because the dismissal involved a new exercise of federal power, the
legality of which should be settled by an impartial authority, the whole
matter should be referred to the Colonial Office. This would take many
weeks, perhaps even months, and passions might in the meantime cool.
In any case the desk would be cleared for other, more important, matters of state. "Old Tomorrow" was living up to his name. Needless to
say both the Colonial Secretary and the Quebec Conservatives were
furious, but "home" the question went nevertheless.

Bared to its essentials the controversy centred around two questions:
what was legitimate cause and where did the power of dismissal reside?
Despite the desire of both parties in Quebec to argue the case for and
against Letellier's action the Colonial Secretary refused to enter into
any discussion on that score. To London hastened Langevin and John
Abbott to argue the case for the central government (and the Conservatives) and Premier Joly to forward the argument of the Quebec
provincial government (and the Liberals).

The government of Quebec continued to stress the danger to
the federation implicit in the projected dismissal of the Lieutenant-
Governor. A report of the Executive Council stated the case clearly:

> That if a Lieutenant-Governor could be dismissed by a vote of censure
> of the Senate and House of Commons, the result would be that the duty
> of a Lieutenant-Governor would be so to govern as to obtain the approval
> not of the local but of the federal legislature.
> That the adoption of such a principle would entirely destroy the au-
> tonomy and the independence guaranteed to the province by the British
> North America Act of 1867.
> That the maintenance of the said local and provincial autonomy and
> independence imperiously demand that questions of purely local and pro-
> vincial interest should not be subjected to the control and influence of the
> Federal Legislature and the Federal Government.[62]

Officially neither the government of Quebec nor the Liberal party went
on record as to what might constitute cause for dismissal. Of only one
thing were they sure; it was in this case a matter for the province, not
the Dominion, to decide.

In a lengthy memorandum for the Governor-General and the
Colonial Office Macdonald took precisely the opposite view. The
British North America Act clearly established the British practice of
tenure during pleasure, although, because of the more intimate poli-

[62]C 2445, 124, April 24, 1879.

tical and personal relations within Canada, the five year clause was introduced "to operate as a check upon the caprice and arbitrary exercise of the power of dismissal. . . ." Convinced that a Lieutenant-Governor could be removed whenever the "public interest" required it, the Prime Minister did agree that the power should not be exercised without extreme care; "but it is not necessary that he should be tried, convicted, or even charged with gross moral or personal wrong." On the contrary:

If, as in the case of Imperial Officers of like position, it becomes neces-sary or expedient for the advantage, good government, or contentment of the people governed that he should be removed, it is the duty of the Dominion Government to discard him. His usefulness may have been destroyed by accident or misfortune as well as by fault, but still the use-fulness once gone the officer should also go. . . . In Mr. Letellier's case it is not in the opinion of His Excellency's advisers at all necessary in order to justify their advice to go behind the vote of Parliament, it is sufficient for them that Parliament has passed a censure of his official conduct. After such a vote it must be obvious that he cannot either with profit or advantage be maintained in his position.[63]

Macdonald too had refused to give his interpretation of cause, but neatly side-stepped the real issue. His argument, however, was accepted by the Colonial Secretary who curtly told Joly that the federal govern-ment could dismiss a Lieutenant-Governor "if he wears a black cravat, when they wish him to wear a blue one."[64]

The second question was little more than a shadow. It will be re-membered that the British North America Act distinguished between the power of appointment and dismissal, the former by the Governor-General in Council and the latter by the Governor-General. Lorne referred to this distinction and asked for an authoritative ruling as to its significance. Joly too reminded Hicks Beach of the difference and suggested that "it was for the sake of allowing Lieutenant Governors to discharge their duty to the province independent of the changes of Party Government at Ottawa. . . ."[65] Macdonald declared that no such interpretation could be made. Action by the Governor-General alone was contrary to "the *lex non scripta* of the constitution" and was im-possible, for the Lieutenant-Governor was dismissable for cause and someone had to be "responsible to Parliament for the reasonableness of such cause, and must defend it there, and be liable to censure should

[63]C 2445, 106–110, Memorandum dated April 14, 1879.
[64]A. Joly de Lotbinière, "Mr. Joly's Mission to London in the Case of Lieu-tenant-Governor Letellier de Saint-Just," *Canadian Historical Review*, XXXI (Dec. 1950), 403.
[65]*Ibid.*

the cause be deemed insufficient."[66] Langevin suggested that the word-ing might have been "accidental," and effectively observed that the statute also appeared to place the appointment of Senators and judges in the hands of the Governor-General, yet no one doubted that this was done on advice.[67] The Law Officers of the Crown, to whom the matter was referred, sharply disagreed with the Canadian minister, stating that it was "impossible to suppose that the Legislature had not a definite intention where the language is so carefully guarded." More-over, they added in an unsolicited *obiter dictum*, "we think the nature of the subject matter dealt with furnishes an argument why the Legis-lature should have reserved for the decision of Her Majesty's repre-sentative, without reference to the political parties which might for the moment be in the ascendant, such a question as the dismissal of a Lieutenant-Governor. In no other way could the independence of the Provincial Assemblies be preserved." On both grounds the Law Officers concluded that it was "a matter in which the Governor General must act upon his own individual discretion."[68]

As so often happened the Colonial Office was caught midway be-tween the Canadian demand for complete autonomy in internal affairs and the legalistic and doctrinaire attitude of its sister departments.[69] "As a statement of law" Sir Robert Herbert, Permanent Undersecre-tary in the Colonial Office, had no doubt that the Law Officers' con-clusion was "unquestionable."[70] But he knew at the same time that it would not be acceptable in Canada, even by the bulk of the Liberals, for it was Blake and the Liberals who had argued so strongly against a similar interpretation of another clause several years before.[71] Con-sequently Herbert sought a compromise: Lorne would be told to act on the advice of his ministers, yet it would be officially suggested that the Governor-General possessed "a personal responsibility which he cannot discharge by simply stating that he acts ministerially. . . ."[72] In effect, however, Macdonald's view of the case was accepted.

Although Sir John Rose informed Macdonald on May 9, 1879, that Hicks Beach would instruct Lorne to act on advice it was almost two months before the dispatch was sent to Canada.[73] The delay may

---

[66]C 2445, 109, Macdonald's Memorandum, April 14, 1879.
[67]Macdonald Papers, 95, Extracts from Langevin's diary on his interview with Hicks Beach, May 5, 1879.
[68]PAC, CO 42/759, Report of the Law Officers, n.d.
[69]See: D. L. M. Farr, *The Colonial Office and Canada, 1867–1887* (Toronto, 1955).
[70]PAC, CO 42/759, Memorandum on the report of the Law Officers, June 14, 1879.   [71]Farr, *The Colonial Office and Canada*, 107–27.
[72]CO 42/759, Memorandum on the report of the Law Officers, June 14, 1879.
[73]Macdonald Papers, 95, Rose to Macdonald, May 9, 1879.

have been due in part to the extreme caution displayed by the Disraeli administration, for Lorne after all was the son-in-law of Queen Victoria. She had been kept informed at all times and the final dispatch was several times before the cabinet and once before the Queen before its final approval.[74] More likely, however, it was due to Macdonald's request that a decision be delayed as long as possible in the hope that tempers might cool and a difficult session run to its close before anything had to be done. The Governor-General warned Hicks Beach that Langevin was not in Macdonald's confidence on this point, and the Colonial Secretary must have been amused by the impatient underling urging haste while his chieftain advised delay.[75]

Hicks Beach realized that all he could do in the last resort was "to preach a constitutional homily for the benefit of the Dominion, and tell Lord Lorne that he must follow the advice of his Ministers if, after my homily, they persist in their views. . . ."[76] To the very end there had been no consideration of Letellier's action. A Lieutenant-Governor, wrote Hicks Beach, had "an unquestionable constitutional right to dismiss his provincial ministers if, from any cause, he feels it incumbent upon him to do so," yet he should always "maintain the impartiality towards rival political parties which is essential to the proper performance of the duties of his office." For any action he might take the Lieutenant-Governor was directly responsible to the central government, whose officer he was, and although the Governor-General's views would be entitled to "peculiar weight" he should, in this as in other matters affecting only the internal affairs of Canada, follow the advice of his ministers. In view of changing political conditions in Canada and Quebec the cabinet might be well advised to reconsider their original advice, for it must

. . . be clearly borne in mind that it was the spirit and intention of the "British North America Act, 1867", that the tenure of the high office of Lieutenant-Governor should, as a rule, endure for the term of years specifically mentioned, and that not only should the power of removal never be exercised except for grave cause, but that the fact that the political opinions of a Lieutenant-Governor had not been, during his former career, in accordance with those held by any Dominion Ministry who might happen to succeed to power during his term of office, would afford no reason for its exercise.[77]

In Quebec meanwhile the Joly government had strengthened its

[74]*Ibid.*, 226, Langevin to Macdonald, June 21, 1879; Lady Victoria Hicks Beach, *The Life of Sir Michael Hicks Beach* (London, 1932), I, 65.
[75]St. Aldwyn Papers, PCC 61, Lorne to Hicks Beach, April 9, 1879.
[76]Lady Victoria Hicks Beach, *Life of Sir Michael Hicks Beach*, I, 65.
[77]C 2445, 127–8, Hicks Beach to Lorne, July 3, 1879.

hold on office by winning three crucial and hard-fought by-elections. Assured now of control of the Legislative Assembly, Joly summoned the legislature and persuaded the lower house to pass a resolution insisting that the Letellier affair was exclusively a provincial matter and thanking the Governor-General "for his firmness and wisdom in arresting the encroachment attempted by the Federal Parliament and Government on the rights of this Province. . . ."[78] These events and the cautionary dispatch from the Colonial Secretary strengthened Lorne's hand and he asked the cabinet to consider both carefully before advising dismissal again. Still under the impression that the Quebec members of the cabinet alone desired dismissal, the Governor-General insisted that the cabinet be unanimous and demanded that the members then absent in England be included in the decision.[79] Within a week the same advice was returned and Lorne had no alternative but to acquiesce, but he agreed only on the condition that the Order in Council "be so drawn as to make clear the sole responsibility of Cabinet for action taken."[80] The Lieutenant-Governor of Quebec was dismissed by Order in Council on the grounds "that after the vote of the House of Commons during last Session, and that of the Senate during the previous Session Mr. Letellier's usefulness as Lieutenant-Governor was gone."[81] Macdonald felt that the precedent would serve as a warning to future Lieutenant-Governors; but Letellier replied that "si c'était à refaire, je ferais exactement ce que j'ai fait. Je renverrais même le gouvernement de Boucherville plus vite."[82]

For good or evil a precedent had been established. The Dominion government had clearly illustrated that it had the power to dismiss a Lieutenant-Governor "if he wears a black cravat, when they wish him to wear a blue one." The Liberals formally introduced a motion of censure in the House of Commons during the session of 1880; the "cause assigned" was inadequate and virtually meaningless for it begged the basic question; and in any case the matter was exclusively one of provincial concern.[83] The succeeding two decades saw frequent mention of the independence of the Lieutenant-Governor by the Liberals. The argument was always the same: interference with the Lieutenant-Governor represented a threat to provincial autonomy. Laurier had

[78]Quebec, Legislative Assembly, *Journals*, 1879, 64.
[79]*C.S.P.*, 1880, no. 18 A, 5, Memorandum to the Privy Council, July 14, 1879.
[80]*Ibid.*, 6, Lorne to Macdonald, July 23, 1879.
[81]*Ibid.*, no. 18, 1–2, Report of a Committee of the Privy Council, approved July 25, 1879.
[82]Robert Rumilly, *Histoire de la Province de Québec* (Montreal, 1940–55), II, 197.
[83]Canada, House of Commons, *Debates*, 1880, 1779–87.

not been long in power when he was given an opportunity to disavow the Letellier precedent, if he desired, and to commit Liberal principles to the stern test of action.

The dismissal of Lieutenant-Governor McInnes by the Laurier administration in 1900 offers few points of comparison with that of Letellier. There was no large and effective pressure group from British Columbia forcing the government to dismiss as there had been in 1878–9, for the handful of provincial members possessed neither weight nor influence in Ottawa. McInnes was a Liberal (of sorts) and the question of his dismissal was in great part free from the party machinations that had characterized the Letellier dispute. Finally, his prerogative acts if not more irregular were at least more frequent, and his "usefulness" more obviously destroyed. In this as in all else, however, politics and the constitution are inseparable, and both aspects must be considered and given due weight.

Unquestionably McInnes paved the way for his dismissal by his close association with Joseph Martin. One of *les enfants terribles* of Canadian politics, Martin was both hated and feared in Ottawa, not only by Sifton with whom he still struggled for the political control of the west, but also by Mills, Cartwright, and Scott—not to mention the French-speaking members of the cabinet who could not help but remember the origin of the Manitoba schools question. Although a Liberal, Martin was in many ways critical of the Laurier administration and his policy was based on a determined revolt against federal policy in western Canada. He had remained true as it were to the western Liberalism of the 1880's and 1890's, a form of liberalism that had been bred in opposition to National Policy and nourished on the alliance of the strong central government, the Canadian Pacific, and high finance on which it rested. A democrat as well as a demagogue, Martin had long been opposed to railway monopoly, federal control of railway policy, and the general exploitation of the nation's economy by a small group in eastern Canada. Although his claims could not be lightly passed over, his membership in the Laurier cabinet was impossible; and at the bidding of the directors of the Crows Nest Pass Coal Company the Canadian Pacific Railway gave him a lucrative post in Vancouver to keep him out of the way and, it was futilely hoped, out of politics.

From the late summer of 1899 when Martin left the Semlin cabinet every effort was made by Sifton, Mills, Scott, and Cartwright to prevent his assumption of power in British Columbia. Late in the same year two enterprising railway financiers and coal magnates,

Messrs. Jaffray and Cox, both of whom were also directors of the Toronto *Globe,* warned McInnes that Martin must be kept out of office at any cost.[84] The Lieutenant-Governor later assumed that he had been dismissed because he had called on Martin in February 1900, for he was made well aware that "the great corporations, whose influence is apparently all powerful at Ottawa, would do their utmost to have me politically assasinated if I should dare call on Mr. Martin." But neither the "threats of the corporations" nor "the chink of their coin" could influence him away from what he considered to be his "line of duty"; it was the interests of "the people of British Columbia rather than Sir Wilfrid Laurier and the Crows Nest Pass coal magnates" that he was bound to consider.[85] Had Martin been triumphant at the polls little could have been done, but he was not. And it is significant that the first communication Laurier received after the election of June 9, 1900, was a wire from Jaffray: "Strong representations from BC by leading friends urging your immediate action as to Lieutenant-Governor's course and position advising immediate dismissal as necessary and popular. Have consulted friends here [Toronto] who agree with this."[86] It would be dangerous to exaggerate the importance of this pressure, yet the evidence does suggest that it was the selection of Martin more than the dismissal of Turner and Semlin that resulted in the dismissal.

Apart from the political background there were good constitutional reasons for McInnes' dismissal. For three years the federal government watched with ever mounting concern as the Lieutenant-Governor became involved in one crisis after another. The dismissal of Turner was looked upon in Ottawa as "a little more drastic than that usually adopted under similar conditions" and McInnes was warned not to repeat "so dashing a method" of changing his advisers.[87] A year later when McInnes was attempting to force a dissolution or a meeting of the legislature, Scott observed that the Lieutenant-Governor had "very crude notions of constitutional government" and decided that since he was a federal officer the Dominion government was obligated to prevent any further "gross errors of judgement." McInnes "cannot afford to dismiss a second cabinet without cause," he wrote, and "if he does we may be pressed to recall him."[88] The Lieutenant-Governor

---

[84]*Vancouver Province,* Jan. 17, 1926, article by his son who was in 1899 his private secretary. The accuracy of the story need not be questioned. No study of Martin has yet been written.

[85]*Vancouver Daily World,* June 26, 1900.

[86]Laurier Papers, 143, Jaffray to Laurier, wire, June 11, 1900.

[87]*C.S.P.,* 1900, no. 174, 1, Scott to McInnes, Aug. 30, 1899.

[88]Laurier Papers, 123, Scott to Laurier, Aug. 30, 1899.

did dismiss another ministry and, worse still, permitted Martin to come into office. Agitation for dismissal began almost at once.

Taking the first opportunity to define his own position, Laurier informed a staunch political friend from British Columbia that "there is nothing to be done by us in this matter. McInnes seems to be acting in a very strange way, but the remedy is in the hands of the people of British Columbia. . . ."[89] When the matter was raised in the House of Commons the Prime Minister echoed his sentiments of 1878:

The question which exists in British Columbia today is certainly a very serious one, but . . . it is not an unconstitutional one. It is today in the hands of the people of British Columbia. The Lieutenant-Governor has acted within the precincts of his power. Whether he has acted wisely or not is a question which is submitted not to this government, not to this parliament, but to the people of British Columbia.[90]

Dismissal of a government was indeed a dangerous step, added Laurier, but McInnes had in both cases found new advisers who had assumed the responsibility for his action. His duty now was to dissolve the legislature and appeal to the people "on the question which he had himself, by his conduct, placed before them. If they approve of the action of the Lieutenant-Governor, in my judgement, that is the end of the question. If they disapprove of it by returning to the House of Assembly a majority opposed to the present government, it is obvious that the Lieutenant-Governor will be found to have taken a very serious step."

The McInnes affair was frequently discussed in cabinet and the Lieutenant-Governor was ordered to keep Ottawa informed on all that was transpiring in British Columbia. By the first of April, when McInnes had neither dissolved the legislature nor forced Martin to face the assembly, strong words were used by some members of the Laurier administration. Cartwright noted tersely: ". . . I am strongly in favour of requiring him to hold the local elections within the shortest time the law permits and if he refuses or neglects to do so of dismissing him instantly. . . . In fact I would be willing to take the responsibility of dismissing Mr. McInnes without even giving him the alternative."[91] The Minister of Trade and Commerce added that the selection of Martin and his retention of office after the vote in the assembly was "absolutely without excuse and deserved the severest punishment we can inflict. . . ." At a cabinet meeting early in April there appears to

[89]*Ibid.*, 142, Laurier to Morrison, March 1, 1900.
[90]Canada, House of Commons, *Debates*, 1900, 1386 ff.
[91]Laurier Papers, 150, Cartwright to Laurier, April 7, 1900.

have been complete concurrence in a highly critical résumé prepared by the Minister of Justice. The dismissals of Turner and Semlin were unwarranted, so his report read, but while McInnes was protected in the first case by Semlin's assumption of responsibility, he was not in the second for Martin was in no way the leader of a responsible government. Under the circumstances the duty of the federal government seemed clear.

The action of the Lieutenant Governor, being so at variance with the usage and principles of parliamentary government, it seems to me that the Advisers of His Excellency, while they should be careful not to interfere with the constitutional rights and privileges of a provincial ministry, and legislature, must take care that the representative of the Crown who has been appointed upon their advice, keeps within the limits of constitutional usage; and if this is done, there is but one of two lines of action open to the Lieutenant Governor—to immediately call the Legislature together, and to give it an opportunity of tendering advice in respect to the new administration, or to dissolve the Legislature and go at once to the country. It would be a gross breach of the Lieutenant Governor's constitutional authority, to allow the Executive Government to be carried on by men every one of whom is without seats in the Provincial Legislature. The course here suggested rests entirely upon the obvious and well settled principles of responsible government, and it is the most moderate line of action which the circumstances permit.

It seems to me our duty in the matter is not a question of policy, but of settled law and usage, and I do not see how it is possible to avoid interference consistent with our duty, as guardians of the constitutional law of the province, so far as it depends upon any unwarranted action of the Lieutenant-Governor.[92]

McInnes was instructed to convene the legislature or dissolve it. He obeyed the command, selected the latter course, and called an election for June 9, 1900. When the lengthy delay was questioned he was able to cite the provisions of the Election Act, which called for a revision of the Voters' List, and there was little the federal ministers could do but grumble.[93]

Martin denounced the repeated interference from Ottawa as "entirely opposed to sound Liberal principles," thus keeping his argument too on the hallowed theme of provincial rights.[94] McInnes complained

[92]Ibid., 151, Memorandum for the Prime Minister, April 10, 1900. It might be noted that Mills, the Minister of Justice, was one of Martin's enemies in the cabinet. See in the University of Western Ontario Library, David Mills' Letterbook, Mills to Henderson, Nov. 3, 1899, and other letters.

[93]The correspondence on this point is printed in C.S.P., 1900, no. 174. Martin had always planned to dissolve, but if the dissolution could be postponed until May 7 a revision of the lists would be statutorily necessary. The revision would not only enhance his chances but would also allow him time for organization.

[94]Laurier Papers, 151, Martin to Laurier, April 13, 1900.

that on two previous occasions he had been advised to follow scrupulously the advice of his ministers, but now he was urged to dispense with that advice. Scott lost all restraint and bluntly informed the Lieutenant-Governor that the circumstances were very different: "In the one there was a responsible government, whose members had been endorsed by the people; in the latter case not a single member of the existing government had then, or even has up to the present time, rceived the approval of the people." The situation in British Columbia, he concluded, was "without parallel in the history of constitutional government. . . ."[95] Laurier refused to interfere at all in the local election. His instructions to McInnes "were for the purpose of recalling him to the important, aye fundamental duty of appealing and appealing without delay to the people of British Columbia" and he told Martin that the latter was "remiss in not having the House dissolved as Joly did in 1878."[96] British Columbia Liberals opposing Martin sought in vain to secure a declaration from the Prime Minister against him, for, although he was fully aware of the nature of Martin's campaign and the trouble that was in store for the federal government if he were elected, Laurier was determined to remain neutral. This was not simply because Martin was an old friend and associate, for whose ability Laurier still had the highest regard, but also because "the Lieutenant-Governor has taken an action which may possibly, as he is an officer of the Dominion, have to be reviewed by us. It would be most unseeming that we should take part in the question which is now submitted to the electors of this province."[97]

The election of June 9, 1900, gave Martin seven certain and six probable supporters in an assembly of thirty-eight members. But if the electorate had not endorsed him it had decisively repudiated the Semlin administration. Only one member of the Semlin cabinet had chosen to run—and he barely saved his deposit—while only six supporters were returned. No leader could claim a personal following as large as Martin's, but it was apparent that a coalition of groups would be formed against him. Martin and McInnes had previously argued that the latter's future was bound up with Semlin's success rather than with Martin's failure; only if Semlin were returned, they argued, would the Lieutenant-Governor's action have been openly repudiated by the electorate. Given the atomization of local politics the argument was in many ways a logical one, but Laurier and his colleagues seemed unable

[95]C.S.P., 1900, no. 174, 26, Scott to McInnes, June 2, 1900.
[96]Laurier Papers, 151, Laurier to Martin, April 20, 1900.
[97]Ibid., 144, Laurier to McLagan, April 14, 1900.

to think in any but two-party terms and it was given no consideration.

As soon as no doubt existed concerning Martin's inability to form a government from the new legislature, Laurier informed McInnes of the cabinet's decision "that the result of the appeal to the people of British Columbia makes it impossible for you to remain Lieutenant-Governor of British Columbia and that you should telegraph your resignation today."[98] McInnes refused to let Laurier avoid the responsibility for an outright dismissal, however, on the grounds that his resignation would be construed as an admission of error and would relieve the Prime Minister of the obviously unwelcome task of justifying the dismissal.[99] Laurier's reply was prompt, and on June 21, 1900, the Governor-General approved the following Order in Council:

> On a memorandum . . . stating that the action of the Lieutenant-Governor of British Columbia in dismissing his Ministers has not been approved by the people of the province, and further, that in view of recent events . . . it is evident that the Government of that province cannot be successfully carried on in the manner contemplated by the constitution, under the administration of the present Lieutenant-Governor, His Honour Thomas R. McInnes, whose official conduct has been subversive of the principles of responsible government.
>
> The Right Honourable the Premier submits that therefore Mr. McInnes' usefulness as Lieutenant-Governor of British Columbia is gone, and he recommends that Mr. McInnes be removed from the said office. . . .[100]

Only in British Columbia, where a few of Martin's supporters took a defiant stand, was there any criticism of the dismissal.

In a carefully prepared statement the Minister of Justice reviewed the crises and justified the government's action. He described the dismissal of Turner as "an extraordinary course," the choice of Beaven as "reflection upon his own political sagacity," the dismissal of Semlin as "a most improper proceeding," and the selection and retention of Martin as the act upon which the future of the Lieutenant-Governor depended. The whole sequence of events led to the ineluctable conclusion "that from first to last, he never rightly grasped either the spirit or the principles of our system of government, so far as it related to the functions of the representative of the sovereign in a province of this Dominion." Lieutenant-Governor McInnes, he added, "mistook constitutional history for constitutional law, and he assumed that he could follow the practices of George III as readily as those of Her Majesty. . . ."[101]

98*Ibid.*, 159, Laurier to McInnes, June 19, 1900.
99*Vancouver Daily World*, June 26, 1900.
100*C.S.P.*, 1900, no. 174, 26.   101Canada, Senate, *Debates*, 1900, 1033 ff.

In a memorandum drawn up at the Governor-General's request, the Secretary of State declared that "public opinion condemning the Lieutenant-Governor's conduct as expressed by a large majority of the members of the present Legislature, by the preceding Legislature, by Boards of Trade in the Province, and by the public press throughout the Dominion, made it evident that the late Lieutenant-Governor had ceased to command the respect of the people of the Province and that his removal could no longer be deferred."[102] Lord Minto approved of the action and made no attempt to interfere, for "there was no room for constitutional doubts" since the "Letellier case clearly established the constitutional position of the Federal Government towards its Lieutenant-Governors as well as the powers of the Governor General."[103] The last word was written by a permanent official in the Colonial Office who concluded that the Canadian government had acted "not only legally but wisely," and with his conclusion one must agree.[104]

These two cases of dismissal stand alone and as far as one can tell the federal government never again considered dismissing a Lieutenant-Governor. They proved beyond all doubt that the central government possessed the unrestricted power to dismiss, but like most types of federal power it was only exercised in the face of strong opposition from the advocates of decentralization and provincial rights. Only those who knew what "cause assigned" was supposed to mean could conclude with any finality whether the dismissals were legally justified. There can be little doubt, however, that both dismissals were broadly justifiable. Obviously there could never be peace in Quebec as long as Letellier was Lieutenant-Governor. Nor could peace be maintained in the Conservative party unless Letellier was dismissed, and in a sense the dismissal can be described as "an act of party vengeance."[105] Macdonald would have rebuffed this description with the argument that consideration of the national interest—the tariff, the railway, and the depression—demanded a strong and united party in Parliament, and if Letellier's dismissal was necessary to secure that end then his dismissal was in the national interest as well. At the same time there was a good deal of truth in Lorne's observation that Macdonald succumbed more readily to the pressure from his Quebec followers "because he has always been against making the Lieutenant-Governors over the Provincial Governments in any sense the office

102CO 42/876, Memorandum for Lord Minto, July 16, 1900. (Copy from the Public Records Office.)
103G 12, Minto to Chamberlain, July 19, 1900.
104CO 42/876, Memorandum on Minto to Chamberlain, July 19, 1900.
105Goldwin Smith, *Canada and the Canadian Question* (London, 1891), 150.

bearers in Sovereign States, and thinks the 'Home Rule' given should be only in the nature of wide municipal powers."[106] In other words, Macdonald regarded the dismissal as another clear-cut illustration of the overriding power of the central government.

The dismissal of McInnes was essential too although in a different way. As the Order in Council stated it was evident that the government of the province could not be carried on "in the manner contemplated by the constitution" with McInnes in office. There could not be that mutual confidence between the Lieutenant-Governor and his advisers so necessary for the harmonious working of cabinet government. Unquestionably the close relations between McInnes and Martin had prejudiced many members of the federal cabinet against the Lieutenant-Governor and dismissal was clearly popular in other circles where Laurier looked for political support. That Laurier found the principle of dismissal distasteful is undoubted, and only when McInnes left him no alternative did he exercise the power lawfully possessed by the federal government. In 1878 and 1879 Laurier had argued that dismissal was virtually a delegated power, held in trust by the federal government and to be exercised only upon request, and in 1900 he exercised that power only when he became convinced that the province of British Columbia overwhelmingly demanded it.

[106]St. Aldwyn Papers, PCC 61, Lorne to Hicks Beach, April 22, 1879.

CHAPTER TEN

EPILOGUE

NEARLY a century has passed since the leading statesmen in British
North America met at Quebec to draft a constitution for a federal
union of the colonies they represented. Two fundamental decisions
were reached with little difficulty and even less discussion: cabinet
government was to be retained in each of the new provinces and the
Lieutenant-Governor was to be the chief executive officer; the parts of
the union were to be subordinate to the whole and the Lieutenant-
Governor was to be one of the instruments through which that subordination could be secured. These decisions were neither startling nor
new, for always before them the architects had the model of the old
colonial system under which they had lived and practised their political
craft. The problem of federation was of the utmost difficulty yet they
worked surely and skilfully. Perhaps their intimate knowledge gave
them a deceptive feeling of confidence for the prototype was hardly
as applicable as they imagined. Little thought appears to have been
given to the inevitable differences between the quasi-federalism of the
Third Empire and the new federalism of the Canadian nation. The
legal and constitutional forms were in many ways similar it is true,
but the forces operative within these forms were different beyond
comparison; and intense political forces seldom respect arbitrary bar-
riers that seek to channel and restrain their flow.

Escaping from the statutory boundaries, with the aid of Lords
Watson and Haldane, political forces have radically altered the nature
of Canadian federalism. What Professor K. C. Wheare has theoretically termed a quasi-federal system became in time what he defines as a
true federal system; that is, co-ordinate legislative and administrative
authority has replaced the intended subordination of the provinces to the
Dominion. The Lieutenant-Governor is no longer in practice "a mere instrument of the federal cabinet" nor is he even an "agent and spokesman"
for the central government. Reservation was from the beginning a
cracked if not broken reed; disallowance was a more satisfactory and
acceptable instrument of federal control; but in time judicial review
largely ousted them both. A resurgence of federal power will not depend
on the resurrection of these instruments of control, but must result

257

from a changed public opinion and a more flexible interpretation of the constitution by the Supreme Court of Canada. Nor is a renascence of federal power likely to have any effect on the office of Lieutenant-Governor.

Only in a limited sense is it true that the changing balance of power between the central and local governments has caused the diminution of the Lieutenant-Governor's rôle as a federal officer. Constitutionally it has had little effect for the Lieutenant-Governor's position was not basically dependent upon any statute and could hardly be undermined by judicial interpretation. His statutory power to reserve provincial bills was never affected by legal decisions and as late as 1937 was declared to be completely unimpaired. But the power of reservation was never of fundamental importance or usefulness. It had been important in the colonial system, for serious evils might have followed the operation of an illegal or inacceptable statute for several months. If speed were essential, however, a provincial act could be disallowed in Canada within a matter of days. Moreover, since reservation and disallowance involved similar review by the Department of Justice (and the cabinet) there was much to be said for following the latter course whenever possible.

Politically the changing balance of power within the federation did have important effects on the office. Both as an imperial officer and as the representative of the Crown the colonial Governor, as well as his superiors in the Colonial Office, was politically untouchable. The central government in Canada, however, was not politically immune and any unpopular action by the Lieutenant-Governor, if acting in the Dominion interest or on instructions from Ottawa, would be paid for at the polls. There were thus political limitations to his usefulness as a federal officer; in one sense he could only be as influential in the provinces as the federal government was strong. Doyle realized this when he observed how much his hand would be strengthened by Howe's election, for the election of the anti-Confederation leader as a supporter of the Macdonald administration would vastly increase the power and prestige of the Conservative party and the central government in Nova Scotia. Thompson realized it when he warned Macdonald against encouraging Richey to withstand Fielding and the provincial rights movement in any way.

Through the Governor alone could the Colonial Office remain informed as to events in the colonies, and well into the present century the Governor-General was expected to be *au courant* of Canadian affairs and favour the Colonial Secretary with periodic, informative dispatches. The government of Canada had little need for this type of service. Joseph Chamberlain might send fervent imperialists to Ottawa to act as missionaries in the great cause; Macdonald and Laurier could lay their policy before the electorate. In time of crisis the colonial Governor of necessity stood between the government of the colony and the Colonial Office; seldom did a delegate from the colonial cabinet go to Whitehall and deal directly with the Colonial Secretary. The Lieutenant-Governor also acted as an intermediary and as a shock-absorber between the two governments, but personal communications, direct contacts of infinite variety, and Dominion-provincial conferences in time lessened his usefulness in this connection.

Given cabinet government in the provinces the Lieutenant-Governor's position as representative of the Crown could never be completely separated from his position as a federal officer. By 1867 the power of the Sovereign in Great Britain was negative rather than positive but monarchical influence was ever present and could not be ignored. In the colonies the Governor was much more powerful positively and much more influential. It is hardly correct to say that the Governor lagged behind the Sovereign in his adaptation to responsible government, for this system is empirical not statutory and it evolves in different ways and at varying speeds according to the institutional and political structure. Owing to the nature of politics in British North America it developed more slowly than in England, and for the same reason more slowly in New Brunswick than in the province of Canada. It need only be added that, after 1867 as before, the power and influence of the Governor was inversely proportionate to the stage of constitutional development reached in each of the colonies or provinces.

As time passed the Lieutenant-Governor like his greater prototype became less and less actively engaged in the work of government. "The image, in little, of a constitutional king" became increasingly hazy until it seemed to be almost a mirage. In the United Kingdom where this constitutional development proceeded naturally "from precedent to precedent" the monarch was seldom regarded as an obstacle to the democratization of the constitution during the nineteenth century. But in Canada, where self-government was limited by the powers vested in the Governor-General, constitutional developments often took the form of continued and determined attacks upon his powers. This steady progression towards Dominion autonomy, which so obsessed historians a generation ago, is supposedly the kernel of the Liberal tradition, from Baldwin and Lafontaine, through

Blake and Laurier, to King and Lapointe. It is true that Canadian Liberalism was in great part founded on opposition to irresponsible government, yet by 1867 most Conservatives had adopted the principle as well. Certainly few Canadians would choose to criticize this estimable tradition, but it should be suggested that no clear distinction was made by the autonomists between the Governor-General as the representative of the Colonial Office and the Governor-General as the representative of the Crown. At first sight at least the consequences seem sufficiently clear. Full responsible government was rightly equated with complete self-government and the latter was in turn, wrongly it would appear, equated with an impotent Governor-General. And it has always been impossible to separate the evolution of the offices of Governor-General and Lieutenant-Governor.

For reasons too obvious to mention even the most sanguine could never pretend that any appointed official could even closely approximate the position of the Sovereign. The decline in the influence of the Lieutenant-Governor, however, need not have been so rapid and so complete if one elementary maxim had been learned and scrupulously followed: the monarch may be politically biased but must be politically neutral. The elevation of Canadian politicians to the office of Lieutenant-Governor did not place them above "the dirt and confusion of local factions," it simply changed the field, scope, and nature of their political activities. Important as provincial, sectional, or factional leaders before their appointment, the Lieutenant-Governors continued to work for the party to which they still belonged even if only on matters of patronage. This was true even in Ontario, politically and constitutionally the most mature of the Canadian provinces, and from Howland to Hendrie no Lieutenant-Governor disassociated himself from his party. Appointment to the office was not only a reward, it was also a favour; as Macdonald informed Campbell, "you have now arrived at the summit of political position through the party and must now come to the rescue."[1] To confide in the Lieutenant-Governor was too often like giving secrets to the enemy.

The extent to which the Lieutenant-Governor's reserve and discretionary power was exercised on political grounds is difficult to determine. The important fact is that he was never beyond suspicion. It is significant perhaps that no Lieutenant-Governor wittingly took any discretionary action that would be to the disadvantage of his party. Moreover, circumstantial evidence of political partiality is often strong if not conclusive. The Liberal Letellier dismissed a Conservative

[1]PAO, Campbell Papers, Macdonald to Campbell, Oct. 5, 1887.

government at a very crucial moment for both parties and even Mackenzie doubted his motives; Robitaille worked hand in glove with the Quebec Conservatives and made possible their return to office by refusing a Liberal request for a dissolution; the Conservatives hailed Angers as the saviour when he rid the province of Mercier, the feared and hated Liberal; Cameron forced the Conservative administration led by Roblin to undergo a fatal examination and was generally believed to be "in collusion with the Grits"; and Lake momentarily threatened to employ the same tactics in Saskatchewan. Even in British Columbia, where party labels were deceptive if not meaningless, it was often charged that McInnes acted in the Liberal interest. By 1901 politicians in British Columbia had come to regard the Lieutenant-Governor as little more than a party tool and Laurier found it difficult to convince them that Joly could not readily dismiss Dunsmuir and call on a Liberal to form a new government.

Many Lieutenant-Governors, whose names have not appeared in this study, gratuitously offered their services "politically or otherwise" if the need arose. The return of some to active politics after leaving office was not suggestive of even a semblance of neutrality. Most of them indeed had no conception of the meaning of political neutrality. Langelier, for example, assured Laurier that he would maintain "complete neutrality" between the parties, but in the same breath promised to use his position to reconcile the warring factions within the Liberal party.[2] The Conservatives could hardly be expected to regard this useful enterprise as evidence of political neutrality. In short, while normal constitutional development reduced the Lieutenant-Governor's power political partiality destroyed his influence.

As long ago as 1891 Goldwin Smith dogmatically asserted that the office of Lieutenant-Governor could only be defended on the grounds that it provided "a decent retirement for those who have spent their energies in public life but on whom the public refuse to bestow pensions."[3] Smith was harsh and premature: only thirteen years earlier one commentator had suggested that the Lieutenant-Governors be made *ex officio* members of the Senate in order that the nation would not be deprived of their knowledge, experience, and ability;[4] as Smith wrote, Schultz was performing useful services in Manitoba; and as the book appeared Angers was watching the escapades of the Mercier government with increasing anxiety. Were Smith alive today he would

2PAC, Laurier Papers, 679, Langelier to Laurier, May 2, 1911.
3Goldwin Smith, *Canada and the Canadian Question* (London, 1891), 157.
4William Leggo, *The History of the Administration of the Earl of Dufferin* (Montreal, 1878), 613.

unquestionably qualify his assertion, for in many provinces the office has ceased to be a reward for the industrious but impoverished politician and can only be considered a luxury to be enjoyed by the few who can bear the expense. With his sole *raison d'être* not generally applicable Smith would doubtless favour abolition, and many Canadians would probably agree with him.

Although there has never been any movement for reform of the office there have been frequent suggestions that it be abolished. The ultra-democratic Progressive groups in western Canada have repeatedly urged that course. During the 1920's, when the Progressive movement was in full bloom, the office offended their democratic principles; during the 1930's, with the prairie provinces facing bankruptcy and hundreds of thousands on relief, it offended their sense of justice. In more recent years members of the C.C.F. and Social Credit parties have spoken strongly in favour of abolition. M. F. Hepburn, Liberal Premier of Ontario, openly attempted to force the abolition of the office for reasons partly financial and partly political and constitutional. No sooner were the results of the 1934 provincial election known—the election that brought Hepburn to power—than he publicly asked the Chief Justice to swear him in. In a press report of the same day he observed that the Lieutenant-Governor could be "starved out"; "there might be technicalities to overcome in getting rid of the King's representative in Toronto but it is still possible to get around them," he declared.[5] The process of attrition did not succeed, however, and although Government House was closed and the Lieutenant-Governor's allowances sharply reduced the office remained untouched. A year later at the Dominion-Provincial Conference Hepburn formally suggested the abolition of the office, but his proposal received no support.[6] In the House of Commons, J. F. Pouliot, long a Liberal M.P. for Témiscouata, has periodically urged the federal government to abolish the post but neither the government nor the members have shown any interest.

There is little to be said in favour of abolition. The most common argument is that the office is expensive. Yet it costs every Canadian just over two cents a year to maintain it. Moreover, every province can pay what it wishes and there is nothing to compel the provincial government to pay anything. Other arguments, for example that the office is anti-democratic or useless, are patently ridiculous and need not be seriously considered. Even if these arguments were true,

[5]*Winnipeg Free Press*, June 26, 1934.
[6]Toronto *Globe*, Dec. 13, 1935.

however, there is much to be said for a formal chief of state who is little more than a ceremonial figure. Americans frequently complain that the time of the President or the state Governor is too often consumed by toasts and scissors. This complaint need never be heard in Canada for the Governor-General and the Lieutenant-Governors are admirably outfitted to lend colour and dignity to any occasion. In addition the Lieutenant-Governor as the representative of the Crown does fulfil traditional and symbolic functions and does, in a minor way, bring to every province in the nation some of the majesty of the mother of parliaments and does thus represent the continuity of political and constitutional development.

Perhaps the only convincing argument against abolition, however, is one the abolitionists themselves admit: as long as the present system of government is retained in the provinces the Lieutenant-Governor's *functions* cannot be abolished. To have the provincial Chief Justice act permanently as the chief executive officer would serve no useful purpose. He has not the time to perform any ceremonial duties, and the saving to the province would be meagre. Whether the executive and judicial branches of the government could be so combined presents an interesting legal problem as well. Prime Minister King declared it was "open to question whether, under the legislation relating to judges and the organization of the courts, it would be competent for the federal government to impose permanently on the Chief Justice of a province additional duties not directly associated with his office."[7] In many ways the Chief Justice would make an excellent Lieutenant-Governor in functions if not in name. Presumably he is well informed on matters of constitutional law and practice and even constitutional history; and he has been detached from politics for many years, if he were ever an active politician, thus making it more possible for him to profess and perhaps maintain the strictest impartiality. If the Chief Justice took his duties seriously those persons and governments who regard the Lieutenant-Governor as a rubber-stamp might well regret the change.

It has been suggested that the Lieutenant-Governor's duties should be reduced to the automatic signing of papers, and if this were done it would matter little who held the office. R. MacGregor Dawson, one of Canada's leading political scientists, once stated that "there is little or no real benefit to be derived from having a Lieutenant-Governor who has power to act against the advice of his ministers, and so long

[7]Prime Minister King—Premier Douglas correspondence, 1944. (Courtesy of Premier T. C. Douglas.)

as the provinces of the Dominion are content with this remnant of the days before responsible government, they must expect to be ranked as colonies rather than as self-governing states."[8] "The independence of the Lieutenant-Governor as it exists today," he added, "is a menace rather than an aid to responsible government; and it is only by a severe limitation of functions, combined if possible with a greater care in selecting men, that this office can be brought into accord with the other parts of the Constitution." Professor Dawson was writing during the golden years of the autonomy movement, and at this late date it is difficult to see precisely why the power and influence of the Crown must be considered as an infringement of responsible government. Moreover there are many Canadians who, for one reason or another, would regret any formal limitation of the Lieutenant-Governor's reserve power. As Lapointe said, "he represents law; he represents order; he represents authority";[9] and occasions may arise in the future as they have in the past when, in the best interests of the province, the reserve power should be invoked. In any case the personal responsibility of selecting a Premier in unusual circumstances can never be abolished or defined.

There is unquestionably much to be said against the office as it exists today; but the proposed cures often seem worse than the disease. Those who regard with regret the waning influence of the Crown in the Canadian provinces might sympathize with several suggestions. In the first place, as Laurier said, when the federal government considers an appointment "two characteristics ought to be look for . . . some knowledge of constitutional law, and a fair mind."[10] To this should be added the greatest degree of political impartiality possibly available, even if appointments from outside the province are necessary. Finally, tenure could be in practice, as well as in law, during pleasure. Longer terms might make the office more attractive to those without independent incomes and would also provide some continuity in the frequently turbulent political scene in the province. A Lieutenant-Governor, carefully selected, scrupulously impartial, with fifteen years' experience under a number of governments, might often be a force for good. In the non-constitutional sphere there is everything to be said for this course, as the career of the Hon. R. F. McWilliams, Lieutenant-Governor of Manitoba from 1940 to 1953, sufficiently demonstrates.

[8]R. MacG. Dawson, "The Independence of the Lieutenant-Governor," *Dalhousie Review*, II (July 1922), 245.
[9]Canada, House of Commons, *Debates*, 1932, 2989. See E. A. Forsey, "The Crown and the Constitution," *Dalhousie Review*, XXXIII (Spring 1953), 31–49.
[10]Laurier Papers, 579, Laurier to Oliver, June 28, 1909.

In the political arena no harm could come from a Lieutenant-Governor who *reins* but does not govern.

But in all probability the office of Lieutenant-Governor will continue to evolve—if that word may be used—as it has in the past. Occasionally some political or constitutional crisis will necessitate some discretionary action. Those favoured by the Lieutenant-Governor's action will be staunch upholders of the prerogative; those disappointed will denounce him as a partisan and term his power an antiquated relic of a bygone age, an atavism in the body politic. And the public momentarily awakened will ask where the Lieutenant-Governor comes from and where he goes.

APPENDIXES

LIEUTENANT-GOVERNORS SINCE CONFEDERATION*

Ontario

Major-General H. W. Stisted	July 1, 1867
W. P. Howland	July 14, 1868
John W. Crawford	Nov. 5, 1873
D. A. Macdonald	May 18, 1875
John B. Robinson	June 30, 1880
Sir Alexander Campbell	Feb. 8, 1887
Sir George A. Kirkpatrick	May 28, 1892
Sir Oliver Mowat	Nov. 18, 1897
Sir William M. Clark	April 20, 1903
Sir John M. Gibson	Sept. 22, 1908
Lt.-Col. Sir John S. Hendrie	Sept. 26, 1914
L. H. Clarke	Nov. 27, 1919
Col. Henry Cockshutt	Sept. 10, 1921
W. D. Ross	Dec. 20, 1926
Col. Herbert A. Bruce	Oct. 25, 1932
Albert Matthews	Nov. 23, 1937
Ray Lawson	Dec. 26, 1946
L. O. Breithaupt	Jan. 29, 1952

Quebec

Sir Narcisse F. Belleau	July 1, 1867
R. E. Caron	Feb. 11, 1873
Luc Letellier de St. Just	Dec. 15, 1876
Théodore Robitaille	July 26, 1879
L. F. R. Masson	Oct. 4, 1884
A. R. Angers	Oct. 24, 1887
Sir Joseph A. Chapleau	Dec. 5, 1892
Sir Louis A. Jetté	Jan. 20, 1898
Sir Charles A. Pelletier	Sept. 15, 1908
Sir François Langelier	May 5, 1911
Sir Pierre E. Leblanc	Feb. 9, 1915
Sir Charles Fitzpatrick	Oct. 21, 1918
Louis P. Brodeur	Jan. 8, 1923
Narcisse Pérodeau	Jan. 8, 1924
Sir Lomer Gouin	Dec. 31, 1928
H. G. Carroll	April 2, 1929
E. L. Patenaude	April 29, 1934
Sir Eugene M. Fiset	Dec. 30, 1939
Gaspard Fauteux	Aug. 25, 1950

Nova Scotia

Lieut.-Gen. Sir W. F. Williams	July 1, 1867
Major-Gen. Sir C. Hastings Doyle	Oct. 18, 1867
Joseph Howe	May 1, 1873
Sir Adams G. Archibald	July 4, 1873
M. H. Richey	July 9, 1883
A. W. McLelan	July 9, 1888
Sir Malachy Bowes Daly	July 11, 1890
A. G. Jones	July 26, 1900
D. C. Fraser	March 27, 1906
J. D. McGregor	Oct. 18, 1910
David MacKeen	Oct. 19, 1915
MacCallum Grant	Nov. 29, 1916
J. R. Douglas	Jan. 12, 1925
J. C. Tory	Sept. 14, 1925
Frank Stanfield	Nov. 19, 1930
W. H. Covert	Oct. 5, 1931
Robert Irwin	April 7, 1937
Frederick Mathers	May 31, 1940
Lieut.-Col. Henry E. Kendall	Nov. 17, 1942
J. A. D. McCurdy	Aug. 12, 1947
Alistair Fraser	Oct. 1, 1952

*Dates of Commission are those found in the official records of the Department of State.

APPENDIX A (*continued*)

New Brunswick

Major-Gen. Sir C. Hastings Doyle	July 1, 1867
Col. F. P. Harding	Oct. 18, 1867
L. A. Wilmot	July 14, 1868
Sir Samuel L. Tilley	Nov. 5, 1873
E. B. Chandler	July 16, 1878
R. D. Wilmot	Feb. 11, 1880
Sir Samuel L. Tilley	Oct. 31, 1885
John Boyd	Sept. 21, 1893
J. A. Fraser	Dec. 20, 1893
A. R. McClelan	Dec. 9, 1896
J. B. Snowball	Jan. 30, 1902
L. J. Tweedie	March 2, 1907
Josiah Wood	March 6, 1912
G. W. Ganong	June 29, 1917
William Pugsley	Nov. 6, 1917
W. F. Todd	Feb. 24, 1923
Major-Gen. H. H. McLean	Dec. 11, 1928
Col. Murray MacLaren	Feb. 5, 1935
W. G. Clark	March 5, 1940
D. L. MacLaren	Nov. 1, 1945

Manitoba

Sir Adams Archibald[1]	May 20, 1870
Alexander Morris	Dec. 2, 1872
J. E. Cauchon	Oct. 8, 1877
J. C. Aikins	Sept. 29, 1882
Sir John C. Schultz	July 1, 1888
J. C. Patterson	Sept. 2, 1895
Sir D. H. McMillan	Oct. 10, 1900
Sir D. C. Cameron	Aug. 1, 1911
Sir James A. M. Aikins	Aug. 3, 1916
Lt.-Col. T. A. Burrows	Oct. 9, 1926
J. D. McGregor	Jan. 25, 1929
W. J. Tupper	Dec. 1, 1934
R. F. McWilliams	Nov. 1, 1940
J. S. McDiarmid	Aug. 1, 1953

British Columbia

Sir Joseph W. Trutch	July 5, 1871
A. N. Richards	June 27, 1876
C. F. Cornwall	June 21, 1881
Hugh Nelson	Feb. 8, 1887
Edgar Dewdney	Nov. 17, 1892
T. R. McInnes	Nov. 18, 1897
Sir Henri Joly de Lotbinière	June 21, 1900
James Dunsmuir	May 11, 1906
T. W. Paterson	Dec. 3, 1909
Sir Frank Barnard	Dec. 5, 1914
Col. E. G. Prior	Dec. 9, 1919
W. C. Nichol	Dec. 24, 1920
R. R. Bruce	Jan. 21, 1926
J. W. F. Johnson	July 18, 1931
E. W. Hamber	April 29, 1936
W. C. Woodward	Aug. 29, 1941
C. A. Banks	Oct. 1, 1946
Clarence Wallace	Oct. 1, 1950
Frank M. Ross	Oct. 3, 1955

[1]Archibald's resignation was accepted on April 9, 1872, and an Order in Council was passed appointing F. G. Johnson as temporary Lieutenant-Governor. Johnson did not assume office and his appointment was cancelled by on Order of June 3. (PAC, Orders in Council, 1872, nos. 337 and 578.)

APPENDIX A (continued)

Prince Edward Island	
William Robinson	June 10, 1873
Sir Robert Hodgson	July 4, 1874
T. H. Haviland	July 10, 1879
A. A. Macdonald	July 18, 1884
J. S. Carvell	Sept. 2, 1889
G. W. Howlan	Feb. 21, 1894
P. A. MacIntyre	May 23, 1899
D. A. Mackinnon	Oct. 3, 1904
Benjamin Rogers	June 1, 1910
A. C. Macdonald	June 3, 1915
Murdock MacKinnon	Sept. 2, 1919
F. R. Heartz	Sept. 8, 1924
Charles Dalton	Nov. 19, 1930
G. D. DeBlois	Dec. 28, 1933
B. W. LePage	Sept. 11, 1939
J. A. Bernard	May 18, 1945
T. W. L. Prowse	Aug. 25, 1950
Saskatchewan	
A. E. Forget	Aug. 24, 1905
G. W. Brown	Oct. 5, 1910

Sir Richard S. Lake	Oct. 6, 1915
William Newlands	Feb. 17, 1921
Lt.-Col. H. E. Munroe	March 31, 1931
A. P. McNab	Sept. 10, 1936
Thomas Miller	Feb. 27, 1945
R. J. M. Parker	June 22, 1945
J. M. Uhrich	March 23, 1948
W. J. Patterson	June 25, 1951
Alberta	
G. H. V. Bulyea	Aug. 24, 1905
R. G. Brett	Oct. 6, 1915
William Egbert	Oct. 20, 1925
W. L. Walsh	April 24, 1931
Lt.-Col. P. C. H. Primrose	Sept. 10, 1936
J. C. Bowen	March 20, 1937
J. J. Bowlen	Feb. 1, 1950
Newfoundland	
Sir Albert J. Walsh	April 1, 1949
Sir Leonard C. Outerbridge	Aug. 17, 1949

APPENDIX B

RESERVED BILLS*

Bill	Reason for reservation	Action taken
N.B. 1867–8: Re presentation to Parishes	Not known.	Bill having been petitioned against by clergy and laity of Church of England was allowed to lapse.
N.S. 1868: To amend the Militia Acts of 1865[1]	Lt.-Gov. believed it to be beyond power of provincial govt. Macdonald advised him to accept advice of cabinet. Attorney General advised him to do as he pleased, although in his opinion the bill was *intra vires*.	Bill was *ultra vires* and had it been passed it would have been disallowed. Assent not given.
P.Q. 1868: To incorporate St. Louis Hydraulic Co.	Reserved on advice as it appeared to fall within Dominion power.	Apart from question of constitutionality, the bill would harm navigation and decrease property values. Assent not given.
N.B. 1869: Re appointment of Justices of the Peace[2]	Bill called for in consequence of question having been raised as to the Lt.-Gov.'s power to appoint by Commission as before 1867. Lt.-Gov. apparently desired ruling.	Assent given as the bill was within the jurisdiction of the province.
N.B. 1869: Re marriage licenses[2]	Prepared at Lt.-Gov.'s request to secure ruling on provincial power.	Assent given as the bill was within jurisdiction.
N.B. 1869: In amendment of statutes on harbours[2]	Lt.-Gov. approved of the bill but felt it might fall within Dominion powers.	Assent not given. Bill *ultra vires*.

*References are given to sources other than Hodgins, *Dominion and Provincial Legislation*, Gisborne and Fraser, *Provincial Legislation* (see Bibliography), and the official government documents.

[1]PANS, Lieutenant-Governors' Correspondence, 1868; PAC, Macdonald Papers, 514, Macdonald to Doyle, Sept. 21, 1868; *ibid*, 114, Doyle to Macdonald, Oct. 30, Nov. 30, 1868.

[2]LLNB, Lieutenant-Governors' Correspondence, Wilmot to Macdonald, May 8, 1869.

APPENDIX B (*continued*)

Bill	Action taken	Reason for reservation
N.B. 1871: Re Synod of the Church of England	Reserved on advice as affecting the rights of the Crown.	Doubts unfounded. Assent given.
Man. 1871: To authorize the construction of railways	Beyond legislative authority of the province.	*Ultra vires.* Assent not given. without compensation. Assent not given.
Man. 1871: To authorize the construction of a telegraph line	Beyond legislative authority of the province.	*Ultra vires.* Assent not given.
Man. 1871: To incorporate Western Railway Co.	Beyond legislative authority of the province.	*Ultra vires.* Might interfere with the Pacific railway. Assent not given.
Man. 1871: To incorporate Red River Bridge Co.	Proposed bridge would interfere with river navigation.	Construction of such bridge inexpedient over a river navigable for 400 miles. Assent not given.
Man. 1872: To incorporate Manitoba Central Railway Co.	Beyond legislative authority of the province. "Wretchedly drawn."	While within the competence of the provincial legislature, a portion of the line would run through region through which Pacific railway must pass. It would "seem wise" to postpone the incorporation of a Co. that may "rival, prejudice, or obstruct the more important line." Assent not given.
Man. 1872: To incorporate the Assiniboine and Red River Navigation Co.	Beyond legislative authority of the province.	Bill is within the competence of the provincial legislature, but in making shareholders in the company partners in the same it is contrary to the "first principles which govern the corporation of companies." Assent not given.
Man. 1872: To incorporate the Law Society of Manitoba[3]	"Premature and objectionable" for a number of reasons.	Lieutenant-Governor's argument is strong. Assent not given.

[3]Macdonald Papers, 187, Archibald to Macdonald, Feb. 24, 1872.

APPENDIX B (continued)

Bill	Reason for reservation	Action taken
Man. 1872: Re Land Surveyors	"Objectionable" for a number of reasons.	Lieutenant-Governor's argument is strong. Assent not given.
B.C. 1872: To amend the Qualification of Voters Act, 1871[4]	Attorney General advised that it was beyond legislative authority of the province. Also conflicted with instructions issued to colonial Governors.	Within provincial competence. Provincial Lieutenant-Governors are not bound by such instructions.
B.C. 1872: To amend the Military and Naval Settlers' Act, 1863[5]	Attorney General advised reservation on the grounds that it might be in conflict with the Terms of Union with Canada.	Agreed. Assent not given.
B.C. 1872: To impose a Wild Land Tax[6]	Attorney General advised reservation on the grounds that it might be in conflict with the Terms of Union with Canada.	Agreed. Assent not given.
B.C. 1872: To render legitimate children born out of wedlock[7]	Attorney General advised reservation as beyond provincial jurisdiction. Repugnant to English law. "It seems to hold out an inducement to persons living in a state of concubinage to continue therein. . . ."	Bill deliberately allowed to lapse without comment.
N.B. 1872: To amend Act to regulate sale of liquor	Not known.	Bill does not appear to have been sent to Ottawa.
B.C. 1872–73: To render legitimate children born out of wedlock[8]	Identical bill reserved and not assented to in 1872.	No action.

4PABC, Attorney General's Letterbook, McCreight to Trutch, April 8, 11, 1872.   5Ibid., April 6, 1872.
6Ibid., April 11, 30, 1872. The bill was introduced by a private member. The government first refused to bring it in on the grounds that due to a shortage of type it could not be printed. Later attempts to amend it failed. (Victoria British Colonist, April 5, 1872.)
7PABC, Attorney General's Letterbook, McCreight to Trutch, April 8, May 8, 1872. Chap. VIII.
8Ibid., Walkem to Trutch, Feb. 21, 1873; Macdonald Papers, 278, Trutch to Macdonald, January 31, 1872.

APPENDIX B (*continued*)

Bill	Reason for reservation	Action taken
Ont. 1873: To incorporate Orange Order[9]	Attorney General advised reservation because similar bills had previously been disallowed or reserved and not assented to.	No action. Bill within provincial powers and should not have been reserved.
Ont. 1873: Same[9]	Same.	Same.
Man. 1873: Re the study and practice of law	Lieutenant-Governor objects to the content of the bill.	No action.
Man. 1873: To impose a Wild Land Tax	Although Lieutenant-Governor approved of the bill he reserved it because a similar bill had been reserved and not assented to in B.C.	Different than the B.C. bill. Assent given.
Man. 1873: Re Aliens	Beyond legislative authority of the province.	Assent given. Within provincial powers.
Man. 1873: Half-Breed Land Grant Protection	Lieutenant-Governor felt that legitimate objection could be made to the bill on principle, although the intention was good.	Assent given. General effect would be beneficial. Flaws could be removed later if necessary.
Man. 1873: To amend the Act for the prevention of Prairie Fires	Likely to prove injurious to the interests of the Dominion. Contrary to sound principles of legislation.	Assent not given. Unfair. Interfere with survey of public lands.
Man. 1873: To incorporate the Eastern Railway Co. of Manitoba	Possible interference with the Pacific Railway. Objectionable also in that shareholders are partners.	Assent given. Considered unobjectionable.
N.S. 1874: To Facilitate arrangements between Railway Companies and their Creditors	May encroach upon Dominion power.	Assent given. Bill within competence of the provincial legislature.
N.B. 1874: To amend Meduxnikik Boom Co. Act[10]	Reserved following instructions from Ottawa. Alleged that it would deprive Americans of their rights under Webster-Ashburton Treaty.	Assent given. Bill found free from objection as a result of several changes.

[9] Chap. VIII, 197 ff.

[10] *C.S.P.*, 1877, no. 89, 67, Undersecretary of State to Tilley, March 16, 1874.

APPENDIX B (continued)

Bill	Reason for reservation	Action taken
P.E.I. 1874: Land Purchase Act[11]	Unusual and perhaps unjust interference with private rights and property.	Agreed. Assent not given.
P.E.I. 1875: Land Purchase Act[12]	Never stated. Although bill designed to remove objections made to the 1874 bill, it is likely that Lieutenant-Governor was governed by the same considerations. Previous bill not assented to.	Previous faults removed. Assent given.
Man. 1875: Re Land Surveyors and Survey of Lands	In general is injurious to Dominion interests and creates conflict of authority. Also illiberal and unjust.	Agreed. Assent not given.
P.E.I. 1876: To amend Land Purchase Act, 1875	Not known. In all probability because of the troubled history of the subject. Bill seemed unjust on surface and assent had been refused to No. 32 above.	Assent not given. Bill dealt with rights of parties in litigation under the Act it proposes to amend.
P.E.I. 1876: Re Govt. House Farm	Not known. Previous Act on the same subject had been disallowed by the British government.	Assent given. Although the bill properly reserved no injury will follow passage of the act. Lieutenant-Governor is not opposed.
Man. 1876: To incorporate Manitoba Investment Association Ltd.	Beyond legislative authority of the province.	Assent not given. Bill would result in inconvenience but since other provinces have passed similar legislation it should not have been disallowed.
B.C. 1877: To amend the Gold Mining Amendment Act, 1872	Reserved on the advice of the Attorney General who felt that it might be beyond provincial powers.	Assent not given. Bill should have been dealt with by the local authorities themselves.

[11]Prince Edward Island, Legislative Assembly, *Journals*, 1875, Appendix E; Canada House of Commons, *Debates*, 1882, 903. C1351; PAC, B119, PRO 30/6/27, Dufferin to Carnarvon, Nov. 26, 1874.
[12]PAC, Correspondence of the Secretary of State, 1875, file 755.

APPENDIX B (continued)

Bill	Reason for reservation	Action taken
Que. 1878: Re the Quebec, Montreal, Ottawa and Occidental Railway[13]	Lieutenant-Governor objected to the principle of the bill.	No action taken. No record of report to Ottawa.
P.E.I. 1878: Re the Church of England in the province[14]	Interfered with the prerogative of the Sovereign as head of the Church.	Assent given. Bill within legislative jurisdiction of the province and no Dominion or imperial interest affected.
P.E.I. 1878: To incorporate Grand Orange Lodge[15]	Identical in principle with an Act disallowed in 1863. Impolitic as designed to stir up religious differences.	Assent not given. Bill within provincial competence and should not have been reserved.
N.S. 1878: To incorporate the Independent Order of Oddfellows	Beyond the legislative authority of the province as it attempts to deal with crimes.	Assent not given. Beyond provincial competence.
Man. 1879: Re Public Printing[16]	Affects privileges guaranteed to the French minority in the Manitoba Act. Beyond provincial power.	No action taken. No record of report to Ottawa.
P.E.I. 1881: Re Factories in Incorporated Cities	Not known.	No action taken. No record of report to Ottawa.
Man. 1882: To incorporate the Loyal Orange Lodge[17]	Not known. Undoubted pressure from Roman Catholics was probably reinforced by knowledge that the bill would not be assented to.	No action taken. No record of report to Ottawa.
N.B. 1889: To prevent the advertising of Foreign Lotteries	No record.	No action taken. No record of report to Ottawa.

[13]Chap. v, 113 ff.
[14]This bill failed to become law as more than one year had passed. Chap. ix, n. 2.
[15]Correspondence of the Secretary of State, 1878, file 803, Hodgson to Scott, July 11, 1878; Chap. viii, n. 51.
[16]PAM, Lieutenant-Governor's Letterbook, Cauchon to Lorne, Sept. 20, 1879.
[17]See A. G. Morice, *Dictionnaire historique des Canadiens et des Métis français de l'Ouest* (2d ed.; Quebec, 1912), 60.

APPENDIX B (*continued*)

Bill	Reason for reservation	Action taken
Que. 1890: To render a marriage civilly valid	Beyond legislative authority of the province.	No action taken. Lieutenant-Governor reported the reservation and asked for a decision.
Que. 1890: To legalize a marriage	Same.	Same.
Man. 1890: Re Sales of Lands for Taxes[18]	Similar to Act disallowed in 1889. Re-enacted "in a spirit of defiance." Might cause confusion if it became law even temporarily.	Assent not given. Bills might have been assented to and disallowed. Lieutenant-Governor informed privately that the Dominion government was not sorry the bills were reserved, but that reservation without instructions was unconstitutional.
Man. 1890: Re arrears of Taxes in Winnipeg[18]	Same.	Same.
Man. 1891: To authorize companies . . . incorporated out of the province to transact business therein[19]	Similar to Act disallowed in 1890. Would have affected immigration between passage and disallowance. Reserved on instructions from Ottawa.	No action taken.
P.E.I. 1892: Re the Legislature of P.E.I.[20]	Lieutenant-Governor considered the bill unjustified, unfair, unconstitutional, and passed under unusual circumstances.	Assent not given. Bill within provincial competence and should not have been reserved.
Que. 1892: To legalize a marriage	Same as bill reserved in 1890. Beyond provincial power. It is also *ex post facto* and unjust.	Should the bill be passed as a statute consideration would be given the questions involved. Assent not given.

[18]Macdonald Papers, 264, Schultz to Macdonald, March 31, April 9, 1890; *ibid.*, 529, Macdonald to Schultz, April 5, 1890; PAM, Schultz' Letterbook, Lieutenant-Governor's Secretary to the Provincial Secretary, April 1, 1890.
[19]Macdonald Papers, 264, Schultz to Macdonald, April 11, 1891; *ibid.*, Macdonald to Schultz, April 17, 1891.
[20]Chap. VIII, 211 ff.

APPENDIX B (continued)

Bill	Reason for reservation	Action taken
Que. 1892: To incorporate La Banque Hypothécaire Canadienne	Beyond legislative authority of the province.	Should the bill be passed as a statute consideration would be given the questions involved. Assent not given.
N.B. 1892: To declare rights of the Crown as represented by the Govt. of the Province in certain lands and property[21]	Bill deals with Government House and there is thus some question as to whether it is not a matter to be dealt with by the Dominion government. Reserved on advice.	Rights of the Dominion in the property must be determined by the federal, rather than the provincial, government. Assent not given.
N.B. 1894: To amend an Act respecting the use of Tobacco by Minors	Reserved on the advice of the Attorney General who felt that the bill might be beyond the competence of the provincial legislature and that a ruling should be secured.	Question of jurisdiction cannot be answered with finality. Doubtful if it falls within provincial authority. But it would not have been disallowed if passed. Assent not given.
P.E.I. 1894: To amend an Act re peddlars	Not known.	No action taken. No record of report to Ottawa.
B.C. 1897: Re employment of Chinese and Japanese[22]	Beyond legislative authority of the province. Might interfere with Dominion interests and international relations. In all probability the Dominion government advised or encouraged reservation. Provincial cabinet opposed bill in the legislature. Similar Acts disallowed.	Agreed. Assent not given.
N.B. 1899: Re licensing of non-residents engaged in employment of labour	Not known.	No action taken. No record of report to Ottawa.
Que. 1904: To amend Code of Civil Procedure	Doubtful validity as beyond the legislative authority of the province.	Agreed. Assent not given.

[21] Correspondence of the Secretary of State, 1892, file 2561, Blain to Sedgwick, Jan. 16, 1893.
[22] PAC, Laurier Papers, 48, W. W. B. McInnes to Laurier, May 31, 1897; *ibid.,* 65, Mowat to Laurier, Dewdney to Mowat, Feb. 16, 1898.

APPENDIX B (*continued*)

Bill	Reason for reservation	Action taken
B.C. 1904: To amend the Municipal Elections Act	Not known. Possibly on advice of Premier.	No action taken. No record of report to Ottawa.
P.E.I. 1904: Re North River Road and Victoria Park[23]	Injuriously affect Government House farm.	No action taken.
B.C. 1907: To regulate Immigration into B.C.[24]	Interfere with Dominion and imperial policy. Previous measures on the same subject disallowed.	Bill as drafted could have no effect. Assent not given.
B.C. 1915: To amend the Poolrooms Act	Concerns aliens and might interfere with "our International relations and Federal interests."	"Whatever effect these provisions may have as aliens or international relations" the Minister of Justice would not recommend that assent be given.
B.C. 1919: To amend the Vancouver Island Settlers' Rights Act, 1904	Reserved on instructions from Ottawa. Previous Act on the same subject disallowed as being unjust invasion of property rights and undue interference with the policy of the Dominion.	Assent not given. Simply a re-enactment of disallowed act.
B.C. 1920: Same	Reserved on instructions from Ottawa for the same reasons.	Assent not given.
Alta. 1937: Re the Taxation of Banks[25]	No reason officially given. Probably beyond legislative authority of the province. Similar measure disallowed.	No action taken.
Alta. 1937: To consolidate the Credit of Alberta Regulation Act[25]	Same.	No action taken.
Alta. 1937: To ensure the Publication of Accurate News and Information[25]	No reason officially given. Probably because of its extremely unusual content.	No action taken.

[23]Correspondence of the Secretary of State, 1904, file 1334, McIntyre to Scott, May 12, 1904. Reported to Ottawa, but no mention in Gisborne and Fraser, *Provincial Legislation.*

[24]British Columbia, Legislative Assembly, *Sessional Papers,* 1907–8, no. 99; Chap. VIII, 213 ff.

[25]Chap. VIII, 215 ff.

APPENDIX C

Commission

KNOW YOU that We, reposing special trust and confidence in the prudence, courage, loyalty, integrity and ability of you the said...............
....have by and with the advice of Our Privy Council for Canada, thought fit to constitute and appoint, and We do hereby constitute and appoint you the said
....to be the Lieutenant Governor in and over the Province of......................................
....one of the Provinces of Canada, during the will and pleasure of Our Governor General of Canada.

AND WE DO HEREBY authorize and empower and command you the said...in due manner to do and execute all things that shall belong to your said command, and the trust We have reposed in you, according to the several powers, provisions and directions granted or appointed you by virtue of the Act of the Parliament of the United Kingdom of Great Britain and Ireland, passed in the Thirtieth year of Her late Majesty's Reign, called and known as "The British North America Act, 1867", and of all other Statutes in that behalf and of this Our present Commission, according to such instructions as are herewith given to you and hereunto annexed or which may from time to time be given to you, in respect of the said Province ot...under the sign manual of Our Governor General of Canada, or by order of Our Privy Council for Canada and according to such Laws as are or may be in force within the said Province of...

AND WE DO HEREBY further appoint that so soon as you shall have taken the prescribed oaths and entered upon the duties of your office, this Our present Commission shall supersede Our Commission under the Great Seal of Canada, bearing date the..day of
....one thousand nine hundred and
....appointing ....
....to be the Lieutenant Governor of the said Province of...

IN TESTIMONY WHEREOF We have caused these Our Letters to be made Patent and the Great Seal of Canada to be hereunto affixed.

WITNESS...

AT OUR GOVERNMENT HOUSE, in Our City of Ottawa, this........
....day of..
in the year of Our Lord One thousand nine hundred and........................
....and in the..
....year of Our Reign.

Instructions to the Lieutenant Governor or other Chief Executive Officer or Administrator for the time being, carrying on the Government of the Province of ....

WHEREAS it is enacted in and by "The British North America Act, 1867", that for each Province there shall be an Officer, styled the Lieutenant-Governor, appointed by the Governor General in Council by instrument under the Great Seal of Canada; and whereas, by and with the advice of the Queen's Privy Council for Canada, I have, by Commission under the Great Seal of Canada, constituted and appointed ....to be Lieutenant-Governor in and over the said Province of................................ ...., one of the Provinces of Canada, and thereby authorized and empowered and commanded him in due manner, to do and execute all things belonging to his said command and trust according to the several powers, provisions and directions granted or appointed to him by virtue of the said Act, and of all other Statutes in that behalf, and of the said Commission, according to such instructions as were with the said Commission given unto him, or which might, from time to time, be given to him in respect to the said Province of............... ...., under my Sign Manual or by order of the Queen's Privy Council for Canada, and according to such laws as are or may be in force within the said Province of ....

I. Now, therefore, I do by these my Instructions under my Sign Manual, by and with the advice of the Queen's Privy Council for Canada, declare my pleasure to be that the Lieutenant-Governor of the Province of..,for the time being, shall, with all due solemnity, cause the said Commission under the Great Seal of Canada, appointing him Lieutenant-Governor, to be read and published in the presence of the Chief Justice for the time being or other Judge of the Supreme Court (or, as the case may be) of the said Province and of the members of the Executive Council in the said Province.

II. And I do further declare my pleasure to be that the Lieutenant-Governor and every other officer appointed to administer the Government of the said Province, shall take the oath of allegiance in the form provided by the said Act, and likewise that he or they shall take the usual oaths for the due execution of the office of Lieutenant-Governor, which oaths the said Chief Justice for the time being of the said Province (or Court, as the case may be) or in his absence, or in the event of his being otherwise incapacitated, any Judge of the Supreme Court (or other court, as the case may be) of the said Province, or in the case of emergency any one duly commissioned by me, shall and is hereby required to tender or administer unto him or them.

III. And I do authorize and require the Lieutenant-Governor, from time to time, to administer to all and every person or persons, to whom he is by the said Act directed to administer the same, the said oath of allegiance and generally to administer such other oath or oaths as he lawfully may, and as may from time to time be prescribed by any Laws or Statutes in that behalf provided.

IV. The Lieutenant-Governor is to take care that all Laws assented to by him in my name, or reserved for signification of my pleasure thereon, shall, when transmitted by him, be fairly abstracted in the margin, and be accompanied in such cases as may seem to him necessary, with such explanatory observations as may be required to exhibit the reasons and occasions for proposing such Laws.

V. The Lieutenant-Governor shall, within ten days after the prorogation of the Legislature or after adjournment of the Legislature for a period of more than ten days or for an indefinite period, send an authentic copy of each Act to which he has assented during the session of the Legislature or during the session of the Legislature prior to the commencement of the adjournment, as the case may be, to the Secretary of State of Canada.

VI. The Lieutenant-Governor, on receipt of a copy of an Order in Council disallowing an Act with my certificate of the date on which the Act was received by me, shall forthwith make proclamation in the said Province of such certificate, and of the disallowance of the said Act.

VII. The Lieutenant-Governor shall not quit the Province without having first obtained leave from me for so doing, under my Sign Manual, or through the Secretary of State of Canada.

AUGUST, 1952.

BIBLIOGRAPHY

A NOTE ON SOURCES

THIS STUDY was undertaken to fill a gap in Canadian constitutional history. No one had previously attempted a comprehensive survey of the office of Lieutenant-Governor. Stimulated by Dr. Eugene Forsey, a number of scholars have examined the problems of reservation and disallowance; Dr. Walter N. Sage has investigated the Trutch period in British Columbia; and F. A. Milligan surveyed the early history of the office in Manitoba. The studies of provincial governments in the Canadian Government Series promised in time to provide a reservoir of information from which an analysis of the office might be made, but there appeared to be no prospect of this series' being completed in the near future. At this date only the studies of Prince Edward Island by Frank Mackinnon and Nova Scotia by J. M. Beck have been completed. The author felt more seriously the absence of first-class political histories of the provinces. The value of Robert Rumilly's *Histoire de la Province de Québec* served to accentuate the appalling shortcomings of other provincial histories. The author was thus forced not only to examine the constitutional crises and the development of the office of Lieutenant-Governor, but also to construct, usually from manuscript sources, a rough political framework on which he could work.

The publication of some correspondence considerably eased the burden. The two volumes on provincial legislation were particularly valuable. Correspondence in the *Canadian Sessional Papers*, several United Kingdom Parliamentary Papers, and the Journals of the House of Commons and the provincial assemblies was often helpful. The earlier practice of the Public Archives of Canada to print source material has apparently ended for all time. The Nova Scotia Archives has recently printed some useful correspondence, and it is hoped that the Champlain Society's venture into modern Canadian history with *The Dufferin-Carnarvon Correspondence 1874–1878* will prove to be successful.

It was originally hoped that the records of the Department of the Secretary of State (before 1873 the Secretary of State for the Provinces) would be a central source for this study, but the official correspondence proved to be incomplete and unbelievably dull and uninformative. The scattered collections of Lieutenant-Governors' correspondence in the provinces were also of limited value. The Governor-General's official correspondence, the much-examined G series, was often of considerable importance.

As the references in the text suggest, the study was largely based on a wide variety of private papers. From 1867 to 1891 the Macdonald Papers were the major source, while those of his colleagues—Bowell, Caron, Tupper, and Thompson—provided additional information and bridged the gap between Macdonald's death and the accession of Laurier five years later. The Liberal interregnum (1873–8) could only be sketchily covered with the Mackenzie Papers, all outgoing, and the odd item in the Blake Papers. The Lieutenant-Governors' correspondence and the Riel and Greenway Papers made possible a fairly complete picture of events in Manitoba. But in the other provinces there was very little to supplement the private papers of the federal leaders.

From 1896 to 1911 the manuscript coverage is less satisfactory. The voluminous Laurier Papers are comparable to those of Macdonald in extent but not in content. Macdonald's Conservative party was a federation and the central figures appeared to retain a firm hand over the provincial and sectional groups, while Laurier's Liberal party was a looser confederation wherein political authority was more often than not delegated. The Sifton Papers is the only major collection that supplements the Laurier Papers, although the Tarte, Willison, and Lemieux collections were useful on certain points. The Scott Papers were extremely valuable, not only for Saskatchewan and Alberta in 1905 and for Saskatchewan history before 1905, but also for the crisis of 1910 in Alberta. The McBride and Joly Papers make British Columbia's politics intelligible from 1900 to 1915. The Borden Papers were of some use for the period after 1911, but generally speaking the manuscript coverage ends with the fall of Laurier.

For obvious reasons the author was often forced to rely heavily on the newspapers. It was impossible to do a complete survey of provincial newspapers, but they were examined whenever there was any possibility of significant political or constitutional developments. Between 1901 and 1938 the *Canadian Annual Review* is an admirable index to provincial politics and indicates when the newspapers could most profitably be consulted. Since most Canadian newspapers were the very partial organs of political parties or groups the author tended to avoid accepting press reports as evidence unless their testimony could be in some way corroborated by other materials; and in no case was it accepted if there appeared to be the least contradiction with more reliable sources.

In the following list of materials the extent and inclusive (examined) dates of the major collections are given whenever possible. As much of the material was found in filing cases, letterbooks, folios, and cardboard boxes this was often impossible. The PAC measures its collections in shelf feet.

BIBLIOGRAPHY

PRIMARY SOURCES

Manuscript: Personal
Alberta: University of Alberta Library (UAL)
  Alex Rutherford: 4 vols. (1905).

British Columbia: Public Archives (PABC)
  H. P. P. Crease: 100 vols.
  Henri Joly de Lotbinière: Microfilm 1 reel (1900–6).
  Richard McBride: 125 vols. (1903–15).
  John Robson: 2 vols. and misc. letters.
  William Smythe: 1 vol.

Canada: Public Archives (PAC)
  J. J. C. Abbott: 1 ft. (1891–2).
  Lord Aberdeen: 8 ft. (1893–8).
  A. R. Angers: Misc.
  R. L. Borden: 125 ft. (1911–21).
  Mackenzie Bowell: 18 ft. (1869–96).
  A. P. Caron: 44 ft. (1880–96).
  J. A. Chapleau: 1 vol. (1885).
  J. W. Dafoe: Microfilm 9 reels (1896–1944).
  Dufferin-Carnarvon Correspondence: B 119 PRO 30/6: Microfilm 2 reels (1874–8).
  Joseph Howe: 74 vols. (1867–73).
  A. B. Hudson: 2 vols. (1915–26).
  P. Landry: Misc.
  Wilfrid Laurier: 195 ft. (1854–1918).
  Rodolphe Lemieux: 4.5 ft. (1895–8). Collection closed. Two volumes examined with permission.
  J. A. Macdonald: 119 ft. (1864–91).
  Alexander Mackenzie: 1.5 ft. (1873–8).
  Clifford Sifton: 105 ft. (1896–1905).
  Israel Tarte: 3 ft. (1880–98).
  J. W. Taylor: Microfilm 9 reels (1870–7).
  J. S. P. Thompson: 51 ft. (1876–94).
  Charles Tupper: 6 ft. (1864–1913).

C. H. Tupper: Microfilm 17 reels (1896–1921).
J. S. Willison: 20.5 ft. (1890–1927).

Manitoba: Public Archives (PAM)
    A. G. Archibald: Misc. (1870–2).
    Thomas Greenway: 2 vols: 12,000 letters (1888–98).
    Alexander Morris: Misc. (1872–7).
    Louis Riel: Misc. (1860–85).
    Rodmond Roblin: 2 vols. (1915).

Ontario: Department of Public Records and Archives (PAO)
    Edward Blake: 150 vols. (1867–87).
    Alexander Campbell: 18 vols. (1867–92).
    C. C. Clarke: 4 vols. (1870–94).
    J. D. Edgar: 4 vols. (1872–99).
    W. H. Hearst: 9 vols. (1914–19).
    Alexander Morris: 7 vols. (1870–7).
    J. P. Whitney: 46 vols. (1905–14).

———— University of Western Ontario Library
David Mills: 13 vols. and misc.

Saskatchewan: Public Archives (PAS)
    William Martin: 44 vols. (1916–22).
    Walter Scott: 30,000 letters. (1905–16).

Manuscript: Official

British Columbia: Public Archives
    Attorney Generals' Letterbook (1871–5).
    Lieutenant-Governors' Correspondence: Misc. (1871–98).
    Provincial Secretaries' Correspondence: Misc. (1870–90).
    Premiers' Papers: 70 vols. (1898–1919).
    Records of the Executive Council: Misc. (1871–98).
    Records of the Senior Naval Commander, Esquimalt: Misc. (1866–98).

Canada: Public Archives
    CO 42/ : Microfilm 247 reels (1867–94).
    Correspondence of the Department of the Secretary of State: 51 ft. (1873–1911).
    Correspondence of the Department of the Secretary of State for the Provinces: 13 ft. (1867–73).
    Orders in Council: 147 ft. (1867–99).
    Records of the Governor-General's Office (*circa* 1864–1900):

G	1:	84 ft.	G	12:	17 ft.
G	2:	6 ft.	G	17:	13 ft.
G	3:	6 ft.	G	18:	18 ft.
G	8:	33.5 ft.	G	20:	63 ft.
G	10:	6 ft.	G	21:	180 ft.

———— Governor-General's Office (GGO)
Miscellaneous files relating to the office of Lieutenant-Governor examined by permission. Files closed.

Manitoba: Public Archives
Lieutenant-Governors' Correspondence: Misc. (1870–1911).
Minutes of the Executive Council: Misc. (1867–1880). Examined by permission in the office of the Deputy Provincial Secretary.

New Brunswick: Legislative Library (LLNB)
Lieutenant-Governors' Correspondence: Misc. (1867–90).
Minutes of the Executive Council: Misc. (1867–1914). Minutes from 1880 to 1914 examined by permission in the office of the Clerk of the Council.

Nova Scotia: Public Archives (PANS)
Lieutenant-Governors' Correspondence: Misc. (1867–1908).
Minutes of the Executive Council (1867–76). Examined by permission in the office of the Deputy Provincial Secretary.

Printed Collections

"Alexander Mackenzie—A. G. Jones Correspondence," *Report of the Board of Trustees of the Public Archives of Nova Scotia for the year 1952* (Halifax, 1952), 15–66.

Buckle, G. E., ed., *The Letters of Queen Victoria* (2d series; 3 vols.; London, 1928).

Chisholm, J. A., ed., *The Speeches and Public Letters of Joseph Howe* (2 vols.; Halifax, 1909).

de Kiewiet, C. W. and Underhill, F. H., *The Dufferin-Carnarvon Correspondence 1874–1878* (Toronto, 1955).

Doughty, Sir A. G., ed., "The Durham Papers," *Report of the Public Archives of Canada 1923* (Ottawa, 1924), 19–410.

—— *The Elgin-Grey Papers 1846–1852* (4 vols.; Ottawa, 1937).

Gisborne, F. H. and Fraser, A. A., comps., *Correspondence, Reports of the Ministers of Justice, and Orders in Council upon the Subject of Provincial Legislation 1896–1920* (Ottawa, 1922).

Hodgins, W. E., comp., *Correspondence, Reports of the Ministers of Justice, and Orders in Council upon the Subject of Dominion and Provincial Legislation 1867–1895* (Ottawa, 1896).

Kennedy, W. P. M., ed., *Statutes, Treaties and Documents of the Canadian Constitution 1713–1929* (2nd ed., London, 1930).

Pacaud, Lucien, *Sir Wilfrid Laurier: Lettres à Mon Père et à Ma Mère* (Arthabaska, 1935).

Pope, Sir Joseph, ed., *Confederation: Being a Series of hitherto Unpublished Documents on the British North America Act* (Toronto, 1885).

Tansill, C. C., ed., *Documents illustrative of the Formation of the Union of the American States* (Washington, 1927).

Walrond, Theodore, ed., *Letters and Journals of James, Eighth Earl of Elgin* (London, 1872).

Government Records
Alberta
Legislative Assembly, *Journals.*

British Columbia
  Legislative Assembly, *Journals.*
  —————*Sessional Papers.*
  Legislative Council, *Debates on Confederation, 1870.*

Canada
  *Dominion Provincial and Interprovincial Conferences from 1887 to
    1926* (Ottawa, 1951).
  *Proceedings of the Constitutional Conference of Federal and Provincial
    Governments 1950* (3 vols.; Ottawa, 1950).
  Department of Justice, *Memorandum on Office of Lieutenant-Gover-
    nor: Its Constitutional Character and Functions* (Ottawa, 1938; new
    ed., 1955).
  —————*Memorandum on Dominion Power of Disallowance of Pro-
    vincial Legislation* (Ottawa, 1938).
  House of Commons, *Debates.*
  —————*Journals.*
  Legislative Assembly, *Parliamentary Debates on the Subject of the
    Confederation of the British North American Provinces* (Quebec,
    1865).
  Parliament, *Sessional Papers.*
  House of Commons, *Debates.*
  —————*Journals.*
  Senate, *Debates.*
  —————*Journals.*

Manitoba
  Legislative Assembly, *Journals.*
  —————*Sessional Papers.*

New Brunswick
  Legislative Assembly, *Journals.*
  —————*Synoptic Report of Debates.*

Newfoundland
  Legislative Assembly, *Journals.*

Nova Scotia
  Legislative Assembly, *Journals.*

Ontario
  Legislative Assembly, *Journals.*
  —————*Sessional Papers.*

Prince Edward Island
  Legislative Assembly, *Journals.*
  Legislative Council, *Journals.*

Quebec
  Legislative Assembly, *Journals.*
  Legislative Council, *Journals.*
  Legislature, *Sessional Papers.*

—— Royal Commission: *Inquiry into the Baie des Chaleurs Railway Matter, Proceedings of the Commission and Deposition of Witnesses, 1891.*

—— *Royal Commission . . . to Make Enquiry into Different Matters and Things concerning the Good Government of this Province, 1892.*

Saskatchewan
Legislative Assembly, *Journals.*
—— *Sessional Papers.*

United Kingdom
Parliamentary Debates.
Parliamentary Papers.

Newspapers

Calgary Albertan	*Regina Morning Leader*
Edmonton Bulletin	*St. John Daily Telegraph*
Edmonton Journal	Toronto *Globe*
Halifax Morning Chronicle	Toronto *Mail and Empire*
Halifax Morning Herald	Toronto, *Saturday Night*
Montreal Gazette	*Vancouver Province*
Montreal Herald	*Vancouver World*
Montreal, *La Presse*	*Victoria British Colonist*
Ottawa Citizen	*Victoria Daily Standard*
Ottawa Free Press	*Victoria Daily Times*
Ottawa Journal	*Winnipeg Free Press*
Quebec, *Le Canadien*	(*Manitoba Free Press*)
Quebec, *L'Evènement*	Winnipeg, *Le Métis*
Regina Daily Star	Winnipeg, *The Manitoban*
Regina Leader-Post	Winnipeg *Tribune*

SELECTED SECONDARY SOURCES

Books

Beck, J. M., *The Government of Nova Scotia* (Toronto, 1957).

Begg, Alexander, *History of the North-West* (3 vols.; Toronto, 1893–5).

Benoit, Dom, *Vie de Mgr-Taché, Archevêque de St. Boniface* (2 vols.; Montreal, 1904).

Blake, Edward, *Edward Blake and Liberal Principles; Anti-monopoly and Provincial Rights* (Toronto, 1882). PAC Pamphlets, II, 444.

Borden, Henry, ed., *Robert Laird Borden: His Memoirs* (2 vols.; Toronto, 1938).

Buchan, John, *Lord Minto: A Memoir* (London, 1924).

Buckingham, William and Ross, G. W., *The Hon. Alexander Mackenzie: His Life and Times* (5th ed., Toronto, 1892).

Casgrain, P. B., *Letellier de Saint-Just et Son Temps* (Quebec, 1885).

Cauchon, Joseph, *The Union of the Provinces of British North America* (Quebec, 1865).

Choquette, P. A., *Un Demi-Siècle de Vie Politique* (Montreal, 1936).

Clement, W. H. P., *The Law of the Canadian Constitution* (3d ed.; Toronto, 1916).

Clokie, H. McD., *Canadian Government and Politics* (2d ed.; Toronto, 1945).

Collins, J. E., *Canada under the Administration of Lord Lorne* (Toronto, 1884).

Colquhoun, A. H. U., *Press, Politics and People: The Life and Letters of Sir John Willison, Journalist and Correspondent of The Times* (Toronto, 1935).

Creighton, D. G., *John A. Macdonald: The Old Chieftain* (Toronto, 1955).

Dawson, R. MacG., *The Government of Canada* (Toronto, 1948).

——— *The Principle of Official Independence* (London, 1922).

Evatt, H. V., *The King and His Dominion Governors: A Study of the Reserve Power of the Crown in Great Britain and the Dominions* (London, 1936).

Farr, D. M., *The Colonial Office and Canada, 1867–1887* (Toronto, 1955).

Forsey, E. A., *The Royal Power of Dissolution of Parliament in the British Commonwealth* (Toronto, 1943).

Hannay, James, *Lemuel Allan Wilmot* (Toronto, 1928).

——— *Sir Leonard Tilley* (Toronto, 1928).

Harkin, W. A., ed., *The Political Reminiscences of the Right Hon. Sir Charles Tupper, Bart* (London, 1914).

Hendry, J. McL., *Memorandum on the Office of Lieutenant-Governor of a Province: Its Constitutional Character and Functions* (Ottawa, 1955).

Hicks Beach, Lady Victoria, *Life of Sir Michael Hicks Beach, Earl of St. Aldwyn* (2 vols.; London, 1932).

Hopkins, J. C., ed., *The Canadian Annual Review of Public Affairs* (Toronto, 1901–38).

Howard, J. K., *Strange Empire: A Narrative of the Northwest* (New York, 1952).

Irwin, L. B., *Pacific Railways and Nationalism in the Canadian-American Northwest, 1845–1873* (Philadelphia, 1939).

Jamieson, A. B., *Chartered Banking in Canada* (Toronto, 1953).

Keith, A. B., *Imperial Unity and the Dominions* (Oxford, 1916).

—— *The King and the Imperial Crown: The Powers and Duties of His Majesty* (London, 1936).

—— *Responsible Government in the Dominions* (2d. ed.; 2 vols.; Oxford, 1928).

Kennedy, W. P. M., *Essays in Constitutional Law* (London, 1934).

Kerr, D. G. G., *Sir Edmund Head: A Scholarly Governor* (Toronto, 1954).

La Forest, G. V., *Disallowance and Reservation of Provincial Legislation* (Ottawa, 1955).

Langelier, Charles, *Souvenirs Politiques* (2 vols.; Quebec, 1909–12).

Lefrey, A. J. F., *The Law of Legislative Power in Canada* (Toronto, 1897–8).

Leggo, William, *The History of the Administration of the Earl of Dufferin* (Montreal, 1878).

Le Lieutenant-Gouverneur de Québec et les Prérogatives Royales (Montreal, 1878). PAC, Pamphlets, II, 61.

Lingard, C. C., *Territorial Government in Canada: The Autonomy Question in the Old North-West Territories* (Toronto, 1946).

Loranger, T. J. J., *Letters upon the Interpretation of the Federal Constitution known as the British North America Act 1867, First Letter* (Quebec, 1884). PAC, Pamphlets, II, 584.

Lowell, A. L., *The Government of England* (2 vols.; New York, 1920).

Mackinnon, Frank, *The Government of Prince Edward Island* (Toronto, 1951).

MacNutt, W. S., *Impressions of a Governor General: Days of Lorne* (Fredericton, 1955).

Macpherson, C. B., *Democracy in Alberta: The Theory and Practice of a Quasi-Party System* (Toronto, 1953).

Mallory, J. R., *Social Credit and the Federal Power in Canada* (Toronto, 1954).

Merivale, Herman, *Lectures on Colonisation and the Colonies* (New ed.; London, 1861).

Nicolson, Sir Harold, *King George V—His Life and Reign* (London, 1952).

Pope, Sir Joseph, *Memoirs of the Right Honourable Sir John Alexander Macdonald, G.C.B., First Prime Minister of the Dominion of Canada* (Rev. ed.; Toronto, 1930).

Ross, H. R., *Thirty-five Years in the Limelight: Sir Rodmond P. Roblin and His Times* (Winnipeg, 1936).

Rumilly, Robert, *Histoire de la Province de Québec* (26 vols.; Montreal, 1940–55).

Saunders, E. M., ed., *The Life and Letters of the Right Hon. Sir Charles Tupper, Bart., K.C.M.G.* (2 vols.; London, 1916).

Skelton, O. D., *Life and Letters of Sir Wilfrid Laurier* (2 vols.; Toronto, 1921).

Smith, Goldwin, *Canada and the Canadian Question* (London, 1891).

Stanley, G. F. G., *The Birth of Western Canada: A History of the Riel Rebellions* (London, 1936).

Tarte, J. I., *1892: Procès Mercier: les Causes qui l'ont provoqué— Quelques Faites pour l'Histoire* (Montreal, 1892). PAC, Pamphlets, II, 1767.

Todd, Alpheus, *On the Position of a Constitutional Governor under Responsible Government* (Ottawa, 1878). PAC, Pamphlets, II, 30.
——— *Parliamentary Government in the British Colonies* (Boston, 1880).

Todd, Alpheus, ed., *Parliamentary Government in the British Colonies* (2d. rev. ed.; London, 1894).

Tremblay, Ernest, *La Question du Jour* (Montreal, 1878). PAC, Pamphlets, II, 70.

Turcotte, L. P., *L'Honorable R. E. Caron, Lieutenant-Gouverneur de la Province de Québec* (Quebec, 1873).

Ward, Norman, *The Canadian House of Commons: Representation* (Toronto, 1950).

Wheare, K. C., *Federal Government* (London, 1946).

Whitelaw, W. M., *The Maritimes and Canada before Confederation* (Toronto, 1934).

Articles

Angus, H. F., "The British Columbia Election, June 1952," *Canadian Journal of Economics and Political Science*, XVIII (Nov. 1952), 518–25.

Burpee, L. J., "Joseph Howe and the Anti-Confederation League," *Transactions of the Royal Society of Canada*, Third Series, X (May 1916), 409–73.

Campbell, R. H., "The Repeal Agitation in Nova Scotia 1867–69," *Collections of the Nova Scotia Historical Society*, XXV (1942), 96–129.

Dawson, R. MacG., "The Independence of the Lieutenant-Governor," *Dalhousie Review*, II (July 1922), 230–45.

Doughty, Sir A. G., ed., "Notes on the Quebec Conference, 1864," *Canadian Historical Review*, I (March 1920), 26–47.

Ebbs-Canavan, Frances, "Manitoba's First Premier and Attorney-General, Henry Joseph Clarke, Q.C., 1871–1874," *Manitoba History*, I (March 1949), 1–12.

Evatt, H. V., "The Discretionary Authority of Dominion Governors," *Canadian Bar Review*, XVIII (Jan. 1940), 1–9.

Ex-Governor, "His Excellency the Governor," *National Review*, XV (1890), 614–24.

Forsey, E. A., "Are Provinces to have Dominion Status?" *Saturday Night*, Feb. 28, 1948.

—— "Canada and Alberta: The Revival of Dominion Control over the Provinces," *Politics*, IV (June 1939), 95–123.

—— "Constitutional *Annus Mirablis*," *Public Affairs*, XIV (autumn 1951), 43–46.

—— "Constitutional Issues in Ontario," *Canadian Forum*, XXV (May 1945), 35–37.

—— "Disallowance of Provincial Acts, Reservation of Provincial Bills, and Refusal of Assent by Lieutenant-Governors since 1867," *Canadian Journal of Economics and Political Science*, IV (Feb. 1938), 47–59.

—— "Lieutenant-Governors are not Ambassadors," *Saturday Night*, March 20, 1948.

—— "Mr. King and Parliamentary Government," *Canadian Journal of Economics and Political Science*, XVII (Nov. 1951), 451–67.

Gosnell, R. E., "Prime Ministers of British Columbia," *Vancouver Daily Province*, Feb. 5 to Aug. 27, 1921.

Groulx, Abbe L., "Correspondence Langevin-Audet," *Revue d'Histoire de l'Amérique française*, I (1947), 271–7.

Heighington, Wilfrid, "Parliamentary Status and Provincial Legislatures," *Canadian Bar Review*, XI (May 1933), 295–307.

Ireland, W. E., ed., "Helmcken's Diary of the Confederation Negotiations, 1870," *British Columbia Historical Quarterly*, IV (April 1940), 111–28.

Johnson, R. P., "The Fenian Invasion of 1871," *Papers read before the Historical and Scientific Society of Manitoba*, Third Series, VII (1952), 30–9.

Keith, A. B., "Ministerial Responsibility in the Dominions," *Journal of Comparative Legislation*, XVII (1917), 227–32.

Longley, R. S., "Sir Francis Hincks, Finance Minister of Canada, 1869–1873," *Annual Report of the Canadian Historical Association*, 1939, 112–21.

MacFarlane, R. O., "Manitoba Politics and Parties after Confederation," *Annual Report of the Canadian Historical Association*, 1940, 45–55.

Mackenzie, N. A. M., "Constitutional Questions in Nova Scotia," *Journal of Comparative Legislation*, XI (1929), 87–95.

Mackinnon, Frank, "The Royal Assent in Prince Edward Island: Disallowance of Provincial Acts, Reservation of Provincial Bills, and the Giving and Withholding of Assent by Lieutenant-Governors," *Canadian Journal of Economics and Political Science*, XV (May 1949), 216–20.

Mallory, J. R., "Disallowance and the National Interest: The Alberta Social Credit Legislation of 1937," *Canadian Journal of Economics and Political Science*, XIV (Aug. 1948), 342–57.

—— "The Lieutenant-Governor as a Dominion Officer: The Reservation of the Three Alberta Bills in 1937," *ibid.* (Nov. 1948), 502–7.

Milligan, F. H., "Reservation of Manitoba Bills and Refusal of Assent by Lieutenant-Governor Cauchon, 1877–1882," *Canadian Journal of Economics and Political Science*, XIV (May 1948), 247–8.

—— "The Establishment of Manitoba's First Provincial Government," *Papers read before the Historical and Scientific Society of Manitoba*, Third Series, V (1950), 5–18.

Parker, Elizabeth, "Manitoba's First Lieutenant-Governor," *Dalhousie Review*, X (Jan. 1931), 519–24.

Pritchett, J. P., "The Origin of the so-called Fenian Raid on Manitoba in 1871," *Canadian Historical Review*, X (March 1929), 23–42.

Sage, W. N., "Amor de Cosmos, Journalist and Politician," *British Columbia Historical Quarterly*, VIII (July 1944), 189–212.

—— "From Colony to Province: The Introduction of Responsible Government in British Columbia," *ibid.*, III (Jan. 1939), 1–14.

—— "John Foster McCreight, the First Premier of British Columbia," *Transactions of the Royal Society of Canada*, Section II (1940), 173–85.

—— "The Position of the Lieutenant-Governor in British Columbia in the Years following Confederation," in Ralph Flenley, ed., *Essays in History Presented to George Mackinnon Wrong* (Toronto, 1939), 178–203.

Scott, F. R., "Centralization and Decentralization in Canadian Federalism," *Canadian Bar Review*, XXIX (Dec. 1951), 1095–1125.

—— "Political Nationalism and Confederation," *Canadian Journal of Economics and Political Science*, VIII (Aug. 1942), 386–415.

—— "The Special Nature of Canadian Federalism," *ibid.*, XIII (Feb. 1947), 13–26.

Stanley, G. F. G., "A 'Constitutional Crisis' in British Columbia," *Canadian Journal of Economics and Political Science*, XXI (Aug. 1955), 281–92.

Staples, Lila, "The Honourable Alexander Morris: The Man, His Work," *Annual Report of the Canadian Historical Association*, 1928, 91–101.

Thomas, L. G., "The Liberal Party in Alberta, 1905–1921," *Canadian Historical Review*, XXVIII (Dec. 1947), 411–27.

Trémaudan, A. H., "Louis Riel and the Fenian Raid of 1871," *Canadian Historical Review*, IV (June 1923), 132–43.

Underhill, F. H., "National Political Parties in Canada," *Canadian Historical Review*, XVI (Dec. 1935), 367–88.

Waites, K. A., "Responsible Government and Confederation: The Popular Movement for Popular Government," *British Columbia Historical Quarterly*, VI (April 1942), 97–123.

Whalen, Hugh, "Social Credit Measures in Alberta," *Canadian Journal of Economics and Political Science*, XVIII (Nov. 1952), 500–17.

Whitelaw, W. M., "Reconstructing the Quebec Conference," *Canadian Historical Review*, XIX (June 1938), 123–37.

———— "Responsible Government and the Irresponsible Governor," *ibid.*, XIII (Dec. 1932), 364–87.

Wilson, G. E., "New Brunswick's Entrance into Confederation," *Canadian Historical Review*, IX (March 1928), 4–24.

Unpublished Monographs

Clague, R. E., "The Political Aspects of the Manitoba School Question, 1890–1896," M.A. thesis, University of Manitoba, 1939.

Holmes, J. L., "Factors Affecting Politics in Manitoba: A Study of the Provincial Elections 1870–1899," M.A. thesis, University of Manitoba, 1936.

Hunt, P. R., "The Political Career of Sir Richard McBride," M.A. thesis, University of British Columbia, 1953.

Jackson, J. A., "The Disallowance of Manitoba Railway Legislation in the 1880's: Railway Policy as a Factor in the Relations of Manitoba with the Dominion," M.A. thesis, University of Manitoba, 1945.

Milligan, F. A., "The Lieutenant-Governorship in Manitoba 1870–1882," M.A. thesis, University of Manitoba, 1948.

Morrison, J. C., "Oliver Mowat and the Development of Provincial Rights in Ontario: A Study in Dominion-Provincial Relations 1867–1896," M.A. thesis, University of Toronto, 1947.

INDEX

www.ingramcontent.com/pod-product-compliance
Lightning Source LLC
Chambersburg PA
CBHW032101040426
42336CB00040B/636